EATING AND ITS DISORDERS

Research Publications
Association for Research in Nervous and Mental Disease
Volume 62

Eating and Its Disorders

Research Publications:
Association for Research in Nervous and
Mental Disease
Volume 62

Editors

Albert J. Stunkard, M.D.

Department of Psychiatry
University of Pennsylvania
Philadelphia, Pennsylvania

Eliot Stellar, Ph.D.

Department of Anatomy
University of Pennsylvania
Philadelphia, Pennsylvania

Raven Press ■ New York

Raven Press, 1140 Avenue of the Americas, New York, New York 10036

Library of Congress Cataloging in Publication Data
Main entry under title:

Eating and its disorders.

(Research publications / Association for Research in
Nervous and Mental Disease; v. 62)
    Includes bibliographies and index.
    1. Appetite disorders—Addresses, essays, lectures.
2. Body weight—Regulation—Addresses, essays, lectures.
3. Obesity—Treatment—Addresses, essays, lectures.
I. Stunkard, Albert J., 1922–   . II. Stellar,
Eliot, 1919–   . III. Series: Research publications
(Association for Research in Nervous and Mental Disease);
v. 62. [DNLM: 1. Appetite disorders—Physiopathology.
2. Body weight.   3. Feeding behavior—Physiology.
4. Obesity—Therapy.   5. Anorexia nervosa—Therapy.
6. Neuroregulators—Physiology.   7. Appetite disorders—
Therapy.   WM 175 El4]
RC552.A72E18   1984   616.3′9   83-17691
ISBN 0-89004-891-6

Made in the United States of America

Second Printing, November 1984
Third Printing, September 1985

ASSOCIATION FOR RESEARCH IN NERVOUS AND MENTAL DISEASE

RESEARCH PUBLICATIONS: ASSOCIATION FOR RESEARCH IN NERVOUS AND MENTAL DISEASE

Titles marked with an asterisk (*) are out of print in the original edition. Some out-of-print volumes are available in reprint editions from Hafner Publishing Company, 866 Third Avenue, New York, N.Y. 10022.

Preface

Each year the Association for Research in Nervous and Mental Disease selects for review a field in which recent advances have been of particular interest to neuroscientists and clinicians. This year's topic—Eating and Its Disorders—is notable for the extent of these advances in both neuroscience and clinical medicine. The authors of the 19 chapters comprising the present volume were carefully chosen to describe the state of the art in the research areas in which they are leaders. The result is an up-to-the-minute account of the latest findings in this exciting and rapidly developing area.

A notable aspect of this field is not only the extent of the new research findings but also the degree to which they are being integrated into theoretical models that are having an increasing impact on research and practice. Both investigators and clinicians will be gratified to learn how basic research in the neurosciences is beginning to bear directly on the care of patients. The volume reviews the current status of three areas:

1. *The Brain and Its Signals* describes brain mechanisms that underlie food intake and states of hunger and satiety, as well as the signals of the brain that activate these mechanisms. A striking aspect of this first section of the book is the resurrection of Stellar's 1954 dual central control model of hunger and satiety. For a long time after the inadequacy of the old "centers" concept was revealed, this model was largely disregarded. Now investigators are returning to it, in an updated and vastly more complex form. Two outstanding examples of signals from the periphery to the brain—cholecystokinin and plasma amino acid ratios—are described by the investigators who have discovered them.

2. *The Regulation of Body Weight* makes it clear why this topic has captured the imagination of lay persons as well as professionals. The increasing evidence that body weight is regulated in humans as well as animals is lucidly described as are the several redundant mechanisms that contribute to the stability of this regulation. The role of adipose tissue in the establishment of a body weight (or body fat) set point is clearly elucidated, as is the complementary role played by lean body mass in the restoration of body weight after a reducing diet. New evidence is presented on the part played by physical activity in the regulation of body weight, and an ingenious "boundary model for the regulation of eating" helps us to understand circumstances in which human beings override this regulation.

3. *Treatment* describes new developments in the management of obesity, anorexia nervosa, and bulimia. The most promising such developments in the field of obesity are new surgical measures for the control of severe obesity and new behavioral treatments for young adolescents. A note of caution in the treatment of obesity is introduced by a consideration of whether the generally modest ben-

efits of successful treatment of many obese persons are not outweighed by the negative effects of unsuccessful treatment and, even more, by the contribution to society's unfortunate obsession with body weight. This obsession must surely play a role in the recent increase in anorexia nervosa and bulimia, which are the subject of four chapters. Two chapters deal at some length with anorexia nervosa and with the apparent benefits of behavior therapy and family therapy. The final two chapters of the book describe two apparently successful and complementary treatment approaches to bulimia—the behavioral and the pharmacological.

Appearing as it does during a period of heightened interest in eating disorders and concern for treatment, this volume should provide encouragement over the rate of progress of research. For the clinician, it provides specific therapeutic suggestions.

The Editors

Contents

Contributors

W. Stewart Agras
Department of Psychiatry and
  Behavioral Sciences
Stanford University School of Medicine
Stanford, California 94305

John E. Blundell
Department of Psychology
University of Leeds
Leeds, LS2 0JT, United Kingdom

Kelly D. Brownell
Department of Psychiatry
University of Pennsylvania
133 South 36th Street
Philadelphia, Pennsylvania 19104

Stephen W. Corbett
University of Wisconsin
Madison, Wisconsin 53706

A. H. Crisp
St. George's Hospital Medical School
  and Department of Psychiatry
Jenner Wing, Cranmer Terre
Tooting London SW17
England

Christopher G. Fairburn
Department of Psychiatry
University of Oxford
Warneford Hospital
Oxford, England

Irving M. Faust
The Rockefeller University
1230 York Avenue
New York, New York 10021

Sebastian P. Grossman
The University of Chicago
Chicago, Illinois 60637

C. Peter Herman
University of Toronto
Department of Psychology
Toronto, Canada M5S 1A1

Jules Hirsch
Rockefeller University
1230 York Avenue
New York, New York 10021

Bartley G. Hoebel
Department of Psychology
Princeton University
Princeton, New Jersey 08544

James I. Hudson
Mailman Research Center
McLean Hospital
Belmont, Massachusetts 02178 and
Department of Psychiatry
Harvard Medical School
Boston, Massachusetts 02115

Jeffrey M. Jonas
Mailman Research Center
McLean Hospital
Belmont, Massachusetts 02178 and
Department of Psychiatry
Harvard Medical School
Boston, Massachusetts 02115

Richard E. Keesey
University of Wisconsin
Madison, Wisonsin 53706

Helena C. Kraemer
Department of Psychiatry and
  Behavioral Sciences
Stanford University School of Medicine
Stanford, California 94305

Rudolph L. Leibel
Rockefeller University
1230 York Avenue
New York, New York 10021

Janet Polivy
University of Toronto
Toronto, Canada

Harrison G. Pope, Jr.
Mailman Research Center
McLean Hospital

Belmont, Massachusetts 02178 *and*
Department of Psychiatry
Harvard Medical School
Boston, Massachusetts 02115

Gerard P. Smith
Department of Psychiatry
Cornell University Medical College and
Edward W. Bourne Behavioral Research
  Laboratory
New York Hospital—Cornell Medical
  Center
New York, New York 10028

Eliot Stellar
Department of Anatomy
University of Pennsylvania
Philadelphia, Pennsylvania 19104

Judith S. Stern
Department of Nutrition and
The Food Intake Laboratory
University of California
Davis, California 95616

Albert J. Stunkard
Department of Psychiatry
University of Pennsylvania
Philadelphia, Pennsylvania 19104

Theodore B. Van Itallie
St. Luke's Hospital and
Columbia University
421 W. 113th Street
New York, New York 10025

Orland W. Wooley
Psychiatry Department
University of Cincinnati Medical Center
Cincinnati, Ohio 45267

Susan C. Wooley
Psychiatry Department
University of Cincinnati Medical Center
Cincinnati, Ohio 45267

Judith J. Wurtman
Laboratory of Neuroendocrine
  Regulation
Massachusetts Institute of Technology
Cambridge, Massachusetts 02139

Richard J. Wurtman
Department of Neuroendocrine
  Regulation
Massachusetts Institute of Technology
Cambridge, Massachusetts 02139

Introduction

Albert J. Stunkard

Eating and obesity have been in the forefront of research on brain and behavior for more than 30 years, ever since obesity was first produced experimentally by hypothalamic damage. They still occupy this position of preeminence, as the flood of new research described in this volume makes clear. Furthermore, this research has contributed far more than just a vast number of new facts. Our understanding of eating and obesity is increasingly informed by new theoretical models. Separate models are developing to account for brain function, for the signals from the periphery to the brain, and for the events in the periphery that generate these signals. Furthermore, these models are quite compatible with each other and quite capable of being assembled into larger and more complex structures. Indeed, the extent of this compatability is a source of wonder, as is the fact that investigators starting from such widely differing premises and working towards such widely differing goals could develop such remarkably complementary systems. The present volume provides the outlines of the developing schema that link adipose tissue, hormonal and neural messages from it to the brain, and the vastly complex brain mechanisms that integrate these messages to produce behavior. It must be a measure of the success of this schema that the idea of set points and the regulation of body weight has so quickly seized the popular imagination. It appears that we are arriving at that happy day when basic research in the neurosciences can bear directly on the care of patients. The present volume attests to the linkage between brain mechanisms and eating disorders to a degree that I have not seen elsewhere.

The volume begins with a consideration of the brain and the signals to it that lead to eating behavior. There follows an account of the regulation of body weight, particularly of adipose tissue. It ends with a description of the latest thinking about obesity, anorexia nervosa, and bulimia.

THE BRAIN AND ITS SIGNALS

The first chapter of the book is heavy with reminiscence and laden with implications for the future. For it was in 1954 that its author, Eliot Stellar, first proposed the model that is so resoundingly resurrected in the chapters that follow. It is fitting that Stellar introduce this volume, and include the figure from his seminal 1954 paper, for his "dual central neural control" model laid out the basic pattern of excitatory mechanisms in the lateral hypothalamus that subserve hunger and inhibitory mechanisms in the ventromedial hypothalamus that subserve satiety and it indicated how their response to sensory and humoral signals provided the biological basis for motivation and reward.

In the years that followed, as we learned more about the brain, and as the inadequacy of the old "centers" concept of hunger and satiety was revealed, it became fashionable to disregard this model. But, as Grossman points out in Chapter 2, as we learned *still* more about the brain, the soundness of this basic concept became clear. It was just that things were far more complicated than anyone had realized. One interesting implication drawn from this model is Grossman's own "hedonic disinhibition hypothesis" of hypothalamic function, which accords the ventromedial hypothalamus an influence far greater than that of a simple sensory area for the recording of nutrient availability. As he points out, animals with ventromedial lesions do a lot more than just overeat. They are, for example, hyperresponsive to sensory inputs of all types, and it is the consequent exaggeration of affective reactions that leads to their overeating, which, it should be noted, is confined to palatable substances. Grossman proposes that the concept of satiety be broadened to include hedonic as well as nutritive matters. He proposes that such a broadened view of satiety explains much of the behavior of hypothalamically damaged animals and he argues that the fact that the same brain mechanisms that subsume nutritive functions also subsume hedonic ones should enhance our trust in the concept of satiety.

As Grossman provides general evidence in support of the original Stellar model, Hoebel provides a wealth of detailed, new information about the ever more complex mechanisms that support this structure. In addition to the original feeding and satiety pathways, Hoebel describes the associated "antifeeding" and "antisatiety" pathways to which Leibowitz and he have made such extensive contributions. And he continues his two-decade-long love affair with self-stimulation, now immeasurably enriched by the growing understanding of the neurotransmitters that effect reinforcement and aversion. Nowhere has research in brain and behavior made more impressive strides in recent years than in elucidating the brain pathways whereby peripheral signals are transformed into eating behavior, and nowhere have these pathways and their messages been more clearly presented than in Hoebel's masterful account.

Blundell, too, returns to Stellar's dual control system as he describes the way in which drugs can be used as "pharmacological scalpels" to dissect the components of systems governing food intake. Drugs, as he points out, avoid many of the problems associated with lesions and stimulation. But they, too, are not the simple, straightforward agents they had seemed to be in the good old days, for their actions are powerfully influenced by factors intrinsic to the organism such as body weight and the state of arousal as well as by extrinsic factors such as palatability and nutrient content of the diet. Effective study of the pharmacology of ingestive behavior appears more and more to require a field approach. This kind of approach certainly complicates matters, but it may well force us to come closer to the way things actually work.

What signals to the brain set in motion the complex events that lead to eating and, as important, satiety? The days are long past when one signal, such as Mayer's "available glucose," could be invoked as the sole messenger from the periphery to the brain. As the remarkable stability of body weight has become apparent, along with the complexity and redundancy of the regulations that support this stability, it has seemed more and more likely that several messengers are required. Two of the most intriguing represent very different kinds of signals—cholecystokinin and the plasma composition of amino acids. Ten years of pioneering research on cholecystokinin are synthesized by Smith into his imaginative "gut hormone hypothesis of postprandial satiety." This hypothesis views the luminal surface of the gut not, as it had traditionally been seen, simply as a mechanism for the absorption of nutrients. Instead it becomes "a great sensory sheet extending from the mouth to the end of the small intestine," exquisitely sensitive to the chemical and physical stimuli of food and responding to them with hormonal and neural messages to the brain. Painstaking work has established that cholecystokinin acts on gastric vagal afferents which end in the nucleus of the solitary tract, inhibiting food intake and, in the process, perhaps contributing to the regulation of body weight that seems, in part at least, to be localized in this area. Smith points out that the fact that cholecystokinin inhibits the central nervous system makes it a particularly useful analytic probe, since inhibition is critical to the central integration of behavior. For the first time, in this volume as well as for one of the first times in research in the neurosciences, one of the findings has direct therapeutic implications: Cholecystokinin has been shown to reduce food intake in humans, opening up fascinating possibilities for the treatment of clinical conditions that may represent failures of postprandial satiety.

An entirely different type of satiety signal is proposed in Wurtman's already popular theory of the control of food intake by ingested nutrients. In contrast to tightly controlled nutrients such as calcium and glucose, the amino acids contain none of the necessary feedback loops. As a result, their concentrations vary widely and herein lies their attraction as messengers. The one which has been the focus of much of Wurtman's recent interest has been tryptophan, the precursor of serotonin, which is increasingly recognized as essential to satiety and to the control of food intake. Because it comprises such a small percentage of protein, and because it behaves differently from other large neutral amino acids in response to insulin, the effects of tryptophan cannot be predicted independently of these other agents. Accordingly, Wurtman places major emphasis on the ratio of these amino acids, which determines, in effect, the "available" tryptophan, in the language of Mayer's glucostatic theory. It is this availability of tryptophan that regulates its conversion to serotonin.

Serotonin has been recognized for some time as vital to the control of food intake through the mechanism of satiety. But Wurtman points out that, in addition to overall satiety, serotonin helps to control the far more specific satiety that defines the ratio of protein to carbohydrate within a meal. Hoebel has shown how specific neural systems may be specialized to carry information about carbohydrate and protein. Blundell has shown how the serotonin-reuptake-blocker fenfluramine causes animals to select away from carbohydrate and towards protein. Now, Wurtman shows how this selection is mediated by ingested nutrients. A carbohydrate meal, for example, by increasing the delivery of tryptophan to the brain, increases the production of serotonin to cause a selection away from carbohydrate (and towards protein) at the next meal. Here is a mechanism that not only controls food intake, but even the relative stability of the protein/carbohydrate ratio within a meal and between meals. Again this basic research has clinical implications. If carbohydrate craving plays a major part in the development of an obese or bulimic syndrome, this mechanism may be invoked therapeutically. Wurtman and Wurtman report that doses of fenfluramine small enough not to decrease overall food intake will selectively suppress craving for carbohydrates.

REGULATION OF BODY WEIGHT

When we turn from the brain mechanisms subserving the regulation of body weight and the signals which activate them to the tissues from which some of these signals emanate, we enter another region of great complexity. Paths through this region have been cleared, however, by the increasingly popular view that body weight is regulated and that a set point determines the level at which this regulation occurs. In the forefront of those who have advanced this view is Keesey, whose chapter with Corbett provides further data and, surprisingly, further theory in support of the idea of a body weight set point. The theory is the ingenious invocation of "Kleiber's rule," that the energy needs of a wide variety of animals are proportional to the ¾ power of their body weight. As Keesey points out, this rule applies only when the body weight of the animal is at that particular level which it normally maintains and defends. And this level is what is generally meant by a set point. Thus, by referring the question to a general biological property, Keesey shows how, theoretically, one can define the nature of a set point other than by the trial and error of determining the body weight that any particular animal will defend. It is, according to this theory, the body weight at which its daily energy needs can be predicted from its metabolic size.

This theory is useful in understanding the metabolic processes that defend body weight, a subject to which Keesey has contributed so much. They include the thermogenesis of overfed rats and the hypometabolism of underfed ones. The theory also makes it clear how lateral hypothalamic lesions act to reduce body weight: They prevent the fall in metabolic rate that would otherwise accompany reduced food intake. Under normal circumstances, this fall in metabolic rate would adjust caloric expenditure to caloric intake and maintain body weight at its previous level. Deprived of this metabolic contribution to regulation, the organism responds to the decrease in food intake with a decrease in body weight. A similar mechanism appears to permit rats made obese by high-fat diets to elevate a body weight set point and then to defend it at this new level.

This form of experimental obesity produced by the long-term effects of a high-fat diet is the topic of the chapter by Faust. In it he demonstrates how, for a period of time, the increased body fat is contained within the normal complement of fat cells. Then, apparently under the pressure of hypertrophy of these fat cells, the number of fat cells increases and the animal is able to maintain an increased level of body fat with fat cells of normal size. Unlike rats in which the immediate effects of enlargement of fat cells leads to hyperinsulinemia, these rats maintain their increased body weight with normal insulin levels, and defend this weight just as effectively as they had defended their earlier, lower weight. Faust has apparently produced a new model of experimental obesity and one with strong clinical implications. If fat cell hypertrophy can give rise to fat cell hyperplasia, then perhaps the treatment of human obesity may not be as futile as it had seemed when sustained weight loss was the only goal. Perhaps merely preventing weight gain has prophylactic value.

Van Itallie contributes a colorful expression for the effect described by Faust. He proposes the term "ratchet effect" to illustrate how, once formed, fat cells become a permanent part of the body's fat cell population and how repeated cycles of overeating leading to fat cell enlargement can produce permanent fat cell hyperplasia. Such a sequence is clearly more likely in organisms with a genetic propensity towards obesity, and Van Itallie notes how, once their increased fat cell population has been established, Zucker obese rats are programmed to divert fuel from the circulation into adipose tissue. The human parallels are striking. Van Itallie notes that this sequence may occur in obese persons when they try to lose weight, and he describes the loss of as much as 22% of lean body mass in a patient on a reducing diet.

Our preoccupation with adipose tissue has perhaps led us away from appropriate concern with the complementary issue of lean body mass in the loss of weight and the maintenance of this loss. Van Itallie does a service by suggesting that the drive to overeat and regain weight following a reducing diet may derive less from the proverbial empty fat cells crying to be fed than from the biologically far more plausible need to replenish depleted stores of body protein.

Still another approach to the regulation of body weight is provided by Hirsch's theoretical essay on a sufficient psychobiological explanation for obesity. With customary elegance, he derives support for the regulation of body weight from a statistical consideration of the distribution and variability of body weights in the population, and he links these speculations to data on fat cell size and number such as those presented in Faust's chapter. According to this view, the "channel" of body weight characteristic of each person (comparable to tolerance about a set point) is determined by fat cell number, whereas one's position within the channel is determined by fat cell size. Throughout his essay, Hirsch stresses the importance of regulation in determining the levels of body weight and body fat and notes that the complexity of these regulatory processes make it unlikely that we will ever stumble on *the* cause of obesity. As a result, any putative factor implicated in the cause of obesity must be subjected to rigorous evaluation within the confines of a complete regulatory system.

Two chapters provide an easy transition from the concern with the regulation of body weight to the chapters on treatment which follow. For each of them deals in its own way with an aspect of this regulation. The first of these chapters, by Stern, asks whether obesity is a disease of inactivity, the second describes Herman and Polivy's "boundary model" for the control of eating.

Stern points out that people are eating less and weighing more than at the turn of the century and that a decrease in physical activity provides a plausible reason for this paradox. Yet, it has proved singularly difficult to move beyond this simple notion to a more precise understanding of the role of physical activity in the regulation of body weight. To what extent does physical activity influence body weight, if at all? In today's skeptical climate regarding the long-term effects of weight-reduction programs, this question assumes unusual importance. For physical activity is increasingly touted as a panacea, as the only readily available means for lowering a body weight set point. But the supporting evidence is disappointingly meager.

Animal investigation provides few clear guidelines. In some genetically obese species, such as the Zucker rat and the *ob/ob* mouse, increasing physical activity has little effect on the development of the obesity, whereas in others, such as the yellow obese mouse, simply providing access to a running wheel can essentially prevent its occurrence. Under these circumstances, the few studies of humans assume great importance. Stern describes three methods whereby physical activity can influence human obesity. First, it causes caloric expenditure, even though of only limited amount. Second, and perhaps more importantly, it appears to increase metabolic rate for some time following the exercise. Third, and of great practical and theoretical importance, physical activity may counteract the effects of a low-calorie diet in lowering metabolic rate. Stern describes a new study with precisely such an outcome. This new finding, interpreted in the light of Keesey's analysis of the metabolic defense of body weight set point, provides the first good evidence that exercise may indeed lower such a set point in humans.

The regulation of body weight is also a concern of Herman and Polivy, for their "boundary model" is designed to explain phenomena that are not readily accommodated by notions of physiological regulation. Prominent among these phenomena is the curious "counter-regulation" of food intake among dieters that they discovered some years ago. In contrast to the "normal" effects of a preload in suppressing subsequent food intake, dieters, also called "restrained eaters," responded to a preload by eating more. To explain this paradox, Herman and Polivy invoke a "range of biological indifference" between physiologically determined hunger and satiety in which social and cognitive influences play the predominant role in food intake. It is within this range that dieters may respond to violation of their cognitively prescribed limits by eating more rather than less. Although their boundary and the idea of "counter-regulation" would appear of particular value in the understanding of bulimia and anorexia nervosa, Herman and Polivy modestly eschew this effort and confine their speculations to "normal" dieters. According to their view, bulimics and anorectics differ from "normal" dieters qualitatively as well as quantitatively, for the former regularly enter the aversive zones of satiety and/or hunger that lie outside the boundaries that constrain the activities of the "normal" dieters.

TREATMENT

The section on treatment begins with Stunkard's chapter on obesity, which notes that for the first time such a discussion contains a theory of obesity with therapeutic relevance and a classification of obesity with therapeutic consequences. The theory is that of the regulation of body weight about a set point. The classification divides obesity into three types—severe (more than 100% overweight), moderate (41–100% overweight) and mild (40% or less overweight). For severe obesity with its grave health consequences, should therapy be required, surgery, particularly gastric restriction procedures, is the treatment of choice. Not only is surgery the only treatment which produces enduring weight losses, but gastric restriction procedures may be associated with such benign consequences as to suggest that they act by lowering a body weight set point.

For both moderate and mild obesity, behavior modification is the treatment of choice, and clearly superior to the use of appetite-suppressant medication. This negative impression of medication results from the rebound in body weight which predictably follows weight loss achieved by these agents. Again, the regulation of body weight provides a useful explanation: Appetite-suppressant medication acts by a temporary lowering of a body weight set point that promptly returns to its former level as soon as the medication is stopped. Two further aspects of behavior modification are of interest. Mild obesity is treated as effectively—and far more economically—by the many lay groups as by physicians. Moderate obesity, on the other hand, which requires weight losses far greater than those produced by lay groups, is best managed by combining diet with behavior modification under medical auspices.

Brownell's chapter on the treatment of obesity in children describes the many psychological and social burdens that obesity inflicts on children, and it makes a plea for early intervention. This course has become considerably more feasible in recent years, thanks in large part to the second generation of behavioral treatments of children to which Brownell has contributed so significantly. One of these contributions was a study described in some detail, in which the judicious use of parental support produced clinically significant weight losses which were maintained for at least 1 year. Furthermore, treatment of obesity in the schools has provided a significant, low-cost addition to clinical programs. After years of pessimism, it now appears that the treatment of obese children is at least as promising as the treatment of adults. Brownell's chapter should encourage further efforts to explore this promise.

This tale of progress in the treatment of obesity should not blind us to the very real problems that still exist. In their chapter, Wooley and Wooley ask whether obesity should be treated at all, and not solely because of the limited efficacy of treatment. They remind us, in addition, of the old medical admonition *primum non nocere*. And they ask whether the generally modest benefits of successful treatment outweigh the negative effects of unsuccessful treatment and the contribution to society's obsession with weight. They note that the ill effects of obesity may have been exaggerated, particularly among the mildly obese, who constitute the great majority of obese persons and, as a result, the benefits of successful treatment may also have been exaggerated. Second, as we know, treatment is very often not successful, and Wooley and Wooley point to the regulation of body weight about an elevated set point as an explanation for this sad fact. But the major harm that may come from treatment of obesity is neither in the modesty of the benefits of successful treatment nor in the disappointments of unsuccessful treatment. The harm may be done rather by the support that is implicitly given to the massive prejudice against obese people that pervades every aspect of our society. Wooley and Wooley maintain with good reason that this prejudice and the cultural obsession with weight is in large part responsible for the development of the eating disorders. Vomiting, for example, may be a quite reasonable response to the social demand to maintain a body weight which ensures hunger, and Wooley and Wooley note that it should not surprise us that intelligent, young women seize upon it.

The chapter by Agras is the first of four to deal with the eating disorders that may have been accentuated by these cultural pressures. Although the number of patients suffering from anorexia nervosa is a tiny fraction of the obese population, the treatment of anorexia nervosa has increasingly engaged the attention of psychiatrists. Whether this attention has resulted in improvement in treatment and whether certain treatments are better than others is the question addressed by Agras and Kraemer. These are difficult questions to answer. Despite the great attention now paid to this disorder, anorexia nervosa still occurs infrequently. Only one controlled study has had sufficient subjects to make it even theoretically capable of demonstrating significant differences between treatments, and it was too limited in duration to do so. Under the circumstances, special research strategies are called for and this excellent chapter proposes some. One is the development of a data base from the literature, such as Agras and Kraemer have assembled, to provide a historical control for newly developed treatments. As they note, in the absence of a clearly superior treatment, there is no point in large clinical trials. Instead, they recommend small-scale research, especially single case studies, to follow up the suggestions that have emerged from clinical studies. There is little converging evidence from these studies that current pharmacological agents help but good evidence that behavior modification does. Accordingly, Agras and Kraemer propose a research agenda for anorexia nervosa: dissection of current treatment programs (which have merit) to identify which of their components are effective and which are not.

The chapter by Crisp almost belies the view that anorexia nervosa is an infrequent disease; he reports on the treatment of 329 patients! In the course of 20 years of research, he has become the leader of anorexia researchers, and this chapter provides a broad and comprehensive account of his views on the disorder, its manifold determinants, and its treatment. The chapter presents clearly Crisp's belief that the basic mechanism underlying anorexia nervosa is a weight phobia, the fear of mature body weight and the need to avoid it at all costs. As in any phobia, the behavior is maintained by the relief of anxiety. As to why anorexia nervosa has increased in frequency in recent years, Crisp proposes that it provides one solution to the problem of adolescent expression, and its limitation, in a society which is becoming largely bereft of limits. This lack of social structure, according to him, has led to such extreme forms of self discipline. "Anorexia nervosa is a biological solution to an existential problem in modern society," and as such "it is the ultimate illustration of social need completely overriding the normal biological set point mechanisms of mature body weight."

Crisp's extensive experience with treatment renders his opinions of interest, particularly in the light of Agras's recommendation that future research follow-up the suggestions that have emerged from clinical studies. Like Agras, Crisp has found that drugs did not affect the outcome of treatment. And supplementing Agras's report, he reports that family therapy did have a favorable effect.

The last two chapters of the book deal with bulimia, the eating disorder that has quite recently attracted great attention, both for the rapidity with which its prevalence seems to have increased and for the therapeutic impotence that is has aroused in physicians suddenly called on to treat it. Propitiously, these chapters describe two apparently successful and complementary treatment approaches, the behavioral and the pharmacological.

Fairburn's scholarly discussion deals first with current popular views which speak of bulimia as a "killer disease" that is reaching "epidemic" proportions. His own epidemiological investigations show clearly that it is neither. Much more rigorous epidemiological studies will be required before we have firm estimates as to its prevalence, in part because this prevalence is relatively low. In his chapter, Fairburn describes a form of cognitive behavior therapy which appears to have been the first to achieve a measure of success in this condition. It is carried out over a period of 6 months on an outpatient basis in a manner described in sufficient detail that the experienced clinician should have little difficulty putting it into practice. The need for effective treatment of this disorder is so great and the interest so high that there is every reason to believe that Fairburn's treatment measures will be widely explored in the very new future.

The final chapter, by Hudson, Pope, and Jonas, ends the volume on a happy note. They begin with three lines of evidence, much of it newly acquired, which suggest that bulimia is closely related to major affective disorder. This evidence is the high prevalence (80%) of major affective disorder in (their) bulimic patients, the response to laboratory tests indicative of affective disorder and a family study that revealed that the morbid risk for major affective disorder among first-degree relatives of bulimics is as great as that among the relatives of persons suffering from bipolar disease itself and considerably greater than that of a well-matched control group. This background makes it reasonable that antidepressant medication should be helpful in the treatment of bulimia and a small number of uncontrolled studies have found this to be the case. The present chapter is notable for the first report of a controlled trial, and it, too, showed a highly significant effect: Imipramine decreased binge-eating 70% in comparison with a placebo. In addition, this response was correlated with improvement in depressive mood, further supporting the relationship of bulimia to affective disorder and opening up new avenues of understanding of this baffling disorder.

The time has come for the reader to turn to the rich fare of this volume. There is much here for persons of many callings—for neuroscientists, for physiologists, for nutritionists and, perhaps most of all, for clinicians who are trying to help persons suffering from eating disorders. May all their efforts contribute to the relief of this suffering.

Eating and Its Disorders, edited by A. J. Stunkard and E. Stellar. Raven Press, New York © 1984.

Neural Basis: Introduction

Eliot Stellar

Department of Anatomy, University of Pennsylvania, Philadelphia, Pennsylvania 19123

It is a great pleasure to introduce this first session of the Association for Research in Nervous and Mental Disease's symposium on the *Psychobiology of eating and its disorders*. And it is quite fitting that the first session is concerned with "neural bases," for understanding behavior and treating its disorders depends on understanding how the brain and the rest of the nervous system function. Eating behavior is an excellent model, as well as an important behavior in its own right. In behavioral and physiological terms, eating is concerned with the regulation of caloric intake and with food preferences and aversions, and therefore, food choices. Conceptually, we speak of the motivation for food and the reward value of foods. Subjectively, we refer to hunger and satiation and to the affect of hedonic experience associated with eating.

In 1940, when I first began to study eating behavior, we had no idea of what mechanisms in the brain were responsible for the management of eating. Within a decade, however, we had penetrated the brain. By 1954, I was able to write a review paper on the physiology of motivation which proposed excitatory and inhibitory mechanisms in the ventromedial and lateral hypothalamus that were sensitive to peripheral sensory and humoral input and that provided the biological basis of hunger and satiation. For that paper, I adapted a figure showing a schematic drawing of the hypothalamus and its connections from Ingram's chapter in the 1940 Association for Research in Nervous and Mental Disease's publication on the *Hypothalamus*. My modification of it is shown in Fig. 1.

For many years, research focused on these mechanisms in the hypothalamus, but as knowledge grew, we became aware that extensive ascending monoamine pathways originating in the brainstem were coursing through the hypothalamus and making monosynaptic connections with it as well as the forebrain. We also learned that major peripheral input was coming from adipose tissue, from gut hormones, and from receptors in the GI tract and that much of it was reaching the brain over the vagus nerve. In addition, we have learned that there are windows in the blood-brain barrier. These are the circumventricular organs that allow the internal environment extensive influence on the hypothalamus and other structures lining the ventricles. Finally, we learned that a major component of the brain mechanism of eating behavior lies in the caudal medulla, posterior to the hypothalamus, but connected to it.

So the story of an extensive brain mechanism with rich interactions with the periphery is still unfolding. Today, we will hear from those people most respon-

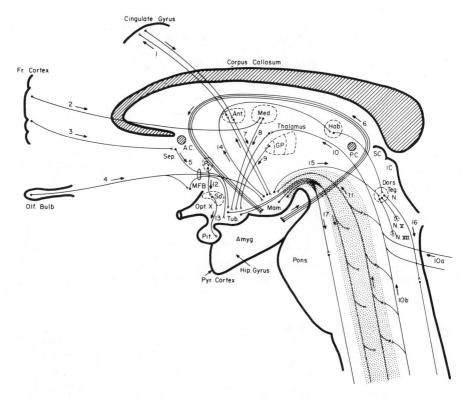

FIG. 1. Mid-saggital schematic drawing of the brain, showing the extensive afferent and efferent connections with the hypothalamus as they were known in 1954.

Abbreviations

A.C.: Anterior commissure
Amyg.: Amygdala
Ant.: Anterior thalamic nuclei
Cingulate gyrus: Cortex of cingulate gyrus
Dors. Teg. N.: Dorsal tegmental nucleus
Fr. cortex: Cortex of frontal lobe
GP: Globus pallidus
Hab.: Habenular nucleus of thalamus
Hip. gyrus: Hippocampal gyrus
IC: Inferior colliculus
Mam.: Mammillary nuclei
Med.: Dorsal medial thalamic nucleus
MFB: Medial forebrain bundle

N.V.: Motor nucleus, Vth nerve
N.VII: Motor nucleus, VIIth nerve
Olf. bulb: Olfactory bulb
Opt. X: Optic chiasm
P.C.: Posterior commissure
Pit.: Pituitary gland
Pv.: Paraventricular nucleus
Pyr. cortex: Pyriform cortex
Ret.: Reticular formation
SC: Superior colliculus
Sep.: Septal nuclei
So.: Supraoptic nucleus
Tub.: Tuber cinereum.

Afferents to hypothalamus: 1. Corticothalamic fibers; 2. Frontothalamic fibers; 3. Frontoseptal fibers; 4. Olfacto-hypothalamic tract; 5. Septo-hypothalamic fibers; 6. Fornix; 7. Mammillothalamic tract; 8. Thalarmo-hypothalamic fibers; 9. Pallido-hypothalamic fibers; 10. Sensory systems ascending to thalamus, 10a. cranial afferents, 10b. somatic and visceral afferents; 11. Sensory collaterals to hypothalamus; 12. Paraventriculo-supraoptic fibers, *Efferents from Hypothalamus:* 13. Supraoptic hypophyseal tract; 14. Mammillohabenular tract; 15. Mammillotegmental tract: 16. Dorsal longitudinal fasciculus; 17. Descending efferents relaying in brain stem and medulla.

sible for extending our knowledge and enriching our conceptual schemes about the psychobiology of eating behavior.

REFERENCES

1. Ingram, W. R. (1940): Nuclear organization and chief connections of the primate hypothalamus. *Ann. Nerv. Ment. Dis.,* 20:195–244.
2. Stellar, E. (1954): The physiology of motivation. *Psycholog. Rev.* 61:5–22.

Eating and Its Disorders, edited by A. J.
Stunkard and E. Stellar. Raven Press,
New York © 1984.

Contemporary Problems Concerning Our Understanding of Brain Mechanisms that Regulate Food Intake and Body Weight

Sebastian P. Grossman

University of Chicago, Chicago, Illinois 60637

It has become fashionable to consider the psychology of hunger and its disorders mainly in terms of metabolic processes. To some extent, this is a healthy concern with mechanisms that had been neglected for too long. I do believe, however, that recent reviews have gone too far in disregarding or even denying the essential role the brain plays in integrating hunger-related information which, of course, includes but clearly is not limited to, metabolic signals. I would like to open this chapter with a few remarks that will, I hope, help to reestablish a more balanced view.

In our field, new information and insights come in very small packages, which tend to question existing theoretical concepts but do not offer superior alternatives. One is as baffled by the inadequacy of the old as by our inability to do better. Nothing could illustrate this point more eloquently than contemporary discussions of the hypothalamic theory of hunger and satiety that Brobeck, Stellar, Teitelbaum, and their colleagues at the University of Pennsylvania formulated in the 40s and 50s. This seminal theory has generated a staggering amount of empirical research and conceptual stimulation. The first few thousand related research papers generally supported the theory enthusiastically—more recent ones have increasingly questioned it on various grounds. Because of the resulting confusion, it has become fashionable in many quarters to disregard the theory entirely and to dismiss the problem of central regulation as essentially unsolvable at the present time.

My own reading of the contemporary literature leads me to the less pessimistic view that the basic conceptual structure is sound but in need of gradual evolution and change, based on the insight that essential psychological processes such as hunger and satiety may be far more complexly determined than most of us imagined. [I might add here that Stellar's 1954 version of the hypothalamic theory (55) envisioned plenty of complexity.] The central theme of this chapter, then, is that our notions of hunger and satiety, rather than the basic notion of hypothalamic integration, need to be refined in the light of recent experimental observations.

5

THE VENTROMEDIAL "SATIETY CENTER"

The notion of a ventromedial hypothalamic satiety mechanism originally arose from the observation that mammals, including man, overeat and become obese when this area is damaged. Nothing has happened in the past 40 years to change that fact. We have, however, asked increasingly sophisticated questions about the basic phenomenon and now know that the influence of the ventromedial hypothalamus (VMH) on hunger or satiety is far more complex than the original notion that implied a sensory area that records nutrient availability or utilization.

The first serious question that was raised quite a few years ago concerns the issue of hedonic evaluation. The classic syndrome of hypothalamic "rage" suggested many decades ago that lesions in the VMH release affective reactions. More recent research has unequivocally shown that animals with VMH lesions are, in fact, hyperreactive to sensory inputs of all modalities. When one adds to this the well-documented observation that animals with VMH lesions overeat only when their food is palatable but become anorexic when its taste or other sensory properties are even mildly aversive, it is easy to reach the conclusion that their excessive food intake may reflect an inability to resist the temptation of haute cuisine rather than a basic disorder of neural mechanisms designed to regulate food intake by metering the availability or rate of utilization of nutrients.

The "hedonic disinhibition hypothesis," as I have called it a number of years ago (19), receives support from numerous observations including the fact that (a) the exaggerated response to hedonic factors also influences the VMH animal's water intake; (b) that it can be overcome by starvation or dehydration (when other signals of preempting negative hedonic tone presumably predominate); (c) that animals with VMH lesions also do not work well for food rewards when their efforts are only infrequently rewarded (so that the negative effects of frequent frustration cancel the occasional gratification of appetite); and (d) that the finickiness as well as the apparently reduced motivation to work for food or water can be overcome by prelesion experience (which presumably reduces the negative affective response to aversive tastes or the frustration of nonreward).

The extensive experimental literature on this subject has been reviewed repeatedly in recent years by myself (20,22) as well as others (29,49), and there is little doubt that an exaggeration of affective reactions influences the ingestive behavior of the animal with VMH lesions. But does this invalidate the notion of a hypothalamic satiety mechanism? I believe, quite the contrary, that it strengthens the idea by broadening the concept of satiety in a way that most of us find intuitively appealing. Not being able to say "no" to a delicious dessert even at the end of a big meal does not prove that satiety mechanisms do not exist but indicates that satiety is a relative rather than absolute phenomenon which takes hedonic as well as nutritive considerations into account. The fact that the same brain mechanism that is believed to do the latter also seems to be equipped to do the former should enhance rather than diminish our trust in the concept.

A second issue that has recently come to dominate our journals is the potential contribution of endocrine and metabolic disturbances to the VMH lesion syndrome. Ventromedial hypothalamic lesions do produce metabolic disturbances that result in the increased removal of essential fuels from the circulation. There is no doubt that this in turn decreases satiety or, to look at the other side of the same coin, increases hunger. Unfortunately, some investigators have concluded that this accounts for the VMH syndrome. In my opinion, that is just another example of our proclivity to oversimplify.

Animals with VMH lesions have elevated plasma insulin levels (25) as well as exaggerated pre- and postabsorptive insulin responses to food (34,35,53). This is undoubtedly a factor in the abnormal fat deposition seen in animals with VMH lesions even during pair-feeding. However, its role in the etiology of the overall VMH syndrome has, in my opinion, been exaggerated, mainly on the basis of experiments that have demonstrated a reversal of VMH obesity after vagotomy.

Vagotomy itself makes eating and the process of digestion difficult and at least initially quite unpleasant. Swallowing may be difficult because of esophageal flaccidity; the ingestion of solid food leads to gastric distention because of dehydration and chronic constriction of the pylorus (12,27,30,32), whereas the consumption of liquid diets produces a highly aversive "dumping syndrome" at least in part due to the influx of fluid into the intestinal lumen (26,48,52). Given the VMH animal's well-documented hyperreactivity to noxious stimuli, it is not at all surprising that it ceases to overeat and begins to lose weight after vagotomy. It is important to note here that other forms of obesity (such as dietary, genetic, or ovariectomy-induced obesity) that are not accompanied by affective hyperactivity and are not reversed by vagotomy.

A more sensitive test of the influence of vagally mediated metabolic disturbances can be obtained when one reverses the order of the surgical interventions because it has been shown repeatedly that rats with VMH lesions do not display excessive reactions to noxious stimuli when given preoperative experience. We (8,30) as well as others (31) have performed that experiment several times and have also blocked vagally mediated insulin release more selectively by pharmacological means (9). We have consistently found that prelesion vagotomy decreases but does not abolish VMH overeating and obesity. King et al. (31) have, in fact, reported entirely normal effects of VMH lesions made 150 days after vagotomy. Their behaviorally effective VMH lesions did not increase basal insulin levels, confirming earlier reports that the increase in basal insulin commonly seen after VMH lesions is vagally mediated.

These results suggest that basal hyperinsulinemia is not an essential condition for overeating and obesity after VMH lesions. This conclusion is in excellent agreement with recent reports by Sclafani and associates (4,50) that obesity-producing parasagittal hypothalamic knife cuts did not elevate basal insulin levels until the animals were allowed to overeat.

These results are particularly interesting in view of an earlier report by Bernardis and Frohman (2) which indicated that only lesions *inside* the ventromedial nucleus consistently produce hyperinsulinemia. The hyperphagia/obesity syndrome, on the other hand, is known to be due entirely to the destruction of tissue ventrolateral to that nucleus (5,28). It seems likely that the typical, large lesion that destroys both the ventromedial nucleus and surrounding tissue may, in fact, produce several independent but potentially interacting symptoms, including not only hyperreactivity to taste but also hyperphagia and hyperinsulinemia.

A related issue is the current controversy concerning the role of the hypothalamus in "gluco-regulatory" functions. Mayer suggested (38) that the hypothalamus might contain special receptors sensitive to the rate of glucose utilization. Much subsequent research has shown that intrahypothalamic injections of glucose or 2-deoxy-D-glucose which blocks the metabolic pathways for glucose do not significantly modify food intake and that goldthioglucose-induced hypothalamic lesions probably reflect vascular dysfunctions rather than direct effects of hypothalamic neurons. [See Epstein et al. (13) for review.] Should one conclude therefore that the hypothalamus does not influence glucose homeostasis? Once again the answer is, in my opinion, clearly "no."

There is extensive electrophysiological evidence for gluco-sensitive cells in the diencephalon that modulate their activity in response to changes in the glucose concentration of their immediate environment or in the general circulation (7,45,46). These cells may not influence hunger or satiety as directly as we have initially believed but exert at least part of their regulatory function by modulating the rate of nutrient utilization itself. Two examples from the recent literature may help to illustrate this important point:

Steffens and his colleagues (11,54) have shown that norepinephrine injections into the lateral hypothalamus (LH) elicit insulin secretion and greatly enhance insulin release during a meal. Similar injections (11,54) into the VMH elicit glucagon release as well as a concurrent increase in plasma glucose. When this hypothalamic influence on pancreatic secretory activity is blocked, an exaggerated insulin and glucose response occurs during and after a meal which causes an abnormally rapid removal of nutrients into storage and this in turn increases hunger. The hypothalamic influence of hunger in this case is rather indirect but nonetheless quite real.

Shimazu (51) has reported complementary results of electrical or chemical stimulation of the LH and VMH on liver metabolism which indicate that activation of the LH promotes the absorption of glucose into glycogen whereas stimulation of the VMH conversely increases the conversion of glycogen into glucose.

Clearly, the hypothalamus receives information about the state of the organism's energy supplies and influences their disposition. To do so efficiently, it must also be able to assure adequate resupply of energy by exercising control over feeding behavior.

It might be useful to mention, at this point in our discussion, that central glucoreceptors have, in fact, been demonstrated although their exact location is still in doubt. Intrahypothalamic injections of 2-deoxy-D-glucose produce only disappointingly small effects on food intake (1,18), although effects on gastric secretion have been reported that are fully as large as those seen after insulin-induced hypoglycemia (10). Moreover, intracerebroventricular injections of 2-DG (42) elicit significant feeding as well as an increase in blood sugar and decrease in body temperature (14,43). Nicolaidis (43) observation that long-term infusions of insulin into the hypothalamus decrease food intake and body weight and my own preliminary finding that shorter, meal-related infusions *increase* food intake may or may not be related to these putative glucoreceptor mechanisms.

THE LATERAL HYPOTHALAMUS

Much of the controversy that has surrounded the hypothalamic theory of hunger in recent years is, in my opinion, due to our proclivity to build oversimplified models and look for unitary explanations of the effects of extremely crude interventions in the functions of major areas of the brain. Recent assertion that the effects of LH lesions are entirely due to an interference with sensory-motor or arousal functions rather than mechanisms concerned with energy metabolism and hunger seem a prime example.

That notion is based primarily on the debilitating effects of intracerebroventricular injections of the neurotoxin 6-hydroxy-dopamine (6-OHDA) which deplete catecholamines from all areas of the brain. When administered in conjunction with a variety of other drugs, its action can be restricted, to some extent, to dopamine-containing cells. One of the major dopamine systems in the brain, the nigrostriatal pathway, has been implicated in behavioral arousal by the observation that electrolytic as well as neurochemical lesions of its origin result in a persisting comatose condition that is complicated by severe motor dysfunctions (59).

When intraventricular 6-OHDA treatments succeed in depleting 95% or more of striatal (and other brain) dopamine, a similar syndrome of general unresponsiveness to the environment and severe motor disturbances is observed (58). After a period of days or weeks, there is some recovery which includes a return of voluntary ingestive behavior. It is important to note, however, that the sensory-motor capabilities of these animals do not return to pretreatment levels and it should not come as a surprise that their feeding response to such stimuli as exogenous insulin also continues to be impaired (57).

Lateral hypothalamic lesions often produce similar, though typically less severe and persistent sensory-motor dysfunctions which have been studied in great detail by Teitelbaum and his colleagues (33,36,37). The results of these studies as well as related work by others on the trigeminal system (66) and on the behavior of 6-OHDA-treated animals (58,59) have made major contributions to our understanding of the LH syndrome in drawing attention to specific as well as nonspecific sensory-motor and arousal dysfunctions that undoubtedly influence the behavior of rats with LH lesions, especially during the initial postoperative period. I do not, however, subscribe to the view that the LH syndrome is no more than an incidental aspect of a general sensory-motor dysfunction. This is not the forum for an elaboration of the many reasons I can muster in support of this position but a few, which I consider particularly salient, may illustrate the issues:

(1) Lateral hypothalamic lesions that have persisting and severe effects on food intake regulation and related endocrine and metabolic functions typically reduce striatal dopamine by only 40 to 60% (16,44). Indeed, we have observed major

changes in food intake regulation in animals that sustained only 20 to 25% depletions. Yet, intraventricular 6-OHDA injections have little or no effect on food intake unless they deplete striatal (as well as other brain) dopamine by 95% or more (58).

(2) Surgical knife cuts, rostral, lateral, dorsal, or caudal to the LH produce a broad spectrum of behavioral and neurochemical deficits that range all the way from the "pet-rock" syndrome seen after nearly complete central dopamine depletions to animals that display some deficits in food-intake regulation (presumably because relevant connections with the lower brainstem have been interrupted) but no detectable sensory-motor or arousal dysfunctions.

We have accumulated behavioral and biochemical data from several hundred such animals and subjected them to standard statistical correlational analyses. After months of exhaustive study, we obtained no consistent evidence for significant relationships between the lesion effects on striatal dopamine on the one hand and behavioral indices of disturbances in food intake regulation on the other, once the animals had recovered from the initial period of aphagia and adipsia (21).

(3) More recently, we (23), as well as others (56,64) have shown that microinjections of the neurotoxin kainic acid (KA) into the LH produce transient aphagia and adipsia (some of our animals were still not eating after 10 days) as well as the classic, persisting components of the LH lesion syndrome, including impaired responding to insulin, 2-deoxy-D-glucose, hypertonic saline, etc. These injections do not destroy all LH cells, and their effects are less severe than those of electrolytic lesions in the area. They nonetheless deserve attention because: (a) the pattern of deficits mimics the LH syndrome perfectly without inducing the somnolence and akinesia that have complicated the interpretation of the effects of electrolytic lesions; and (b) intrahypothalamic KA injections do not interrupt fibers of passage and do not deplete the striatum (or other brain regions) of dopamine (23,47).

The interpretation of these KA studies are complicated by two problems: (a) The animals tend to be hyperexcitable and this could, possibly, interfere with their food intake and/or reaction to various experimental treatments; and (b) the KA-induced cellular loss is not restricted to the LH but involves adjacent areas such as the ventral thalamus, preoptic region, and zona incerta where electrolytic lesions (and, in the case of the zona incerta, local KA injections) have been shown to affect ingestive behavior (3,6,39–41,60–53).

In a recent series of experiments (24), we have provided some answers to both of these problems by means of iontophoretic applications of KA to the LH. This procedure can be adjusted so that a significant proportion of the neurons of the LH are destroyed without incidental involvement of cells of the zona incerta, ventral thalamus, or preoptic region. We have found that such injections do produce transient aphagia and adipsia and impaired responses to glucoprivic challenges even though only 20 to 40% of the cells in the region of the LH that is typically destroyed by electrolytic lesions were lost. In these animals, there was no evidence at all of sensory-motor or arousal dysfunction, either of the depressive nature commonly seen after electrolytic lesions or the hyperexcitability often encountered after mechanical injections of KA into the LH.

I would like to conclude from this and related evidence that hunger and associated metabolic events are integrated by the hypothalamus. You may object on the grounds that Grill and his associates (15) have recently demonstrated that decerebrate rats swallow more nutrients after deprivation or exogenous insulin. This is an important finding but does not, in my opinion, detract from the concept of hypothalamic regulation. In a parallel case, we have known for nearly a century that decerebrate animals display components of affective reactions but cannot integrate them into appropriate complex behaviors until hypothalamic influences are available (17,65). It is, in fact reassuring that a similar pattern of organization may characterize another behavior that is essential for survival.

REFERENCES

1. Balagura, S., and Kanner, M. (1971): Hypothalamic sensitivity to 2-deoxy-D-glucose: effects on feeding behavior. *Physiol. Behav.,* 7:977–980.
2. Bernardis, L. L., and Frohman, L. A. (1971): Effects of hypothalamic lesions at different loci on development of hyperinsulinemia and obesity in the weanling rat. *J. Comp. Neurol.,* 141:107–116.
3. Blass, E. M., and Kraly, F. S. (1974): Medial forebrain bundle lesions: Specific loss of feeding to decreased glucose utilisation in rats. *J. Comp. Physiol. Psychol.,* 86:679–692.
4. Bray, G. A., Sclafani, A., and Novin, D. (1982): Obesity-inducing hypothalamic knife cuts: Effects on lipolysis and blood insulin levels. *Am. J. Phsiol.,* 243:R445–R449.
5. Brobeck, J. R., Tepperman, J., and Long, C. N. H. (1943): Experimental hypothalamic hyperphagia in the albino rat. *Yale J. Biol. Med.,* 15:831–833.
6. Brown, B., and Grossman, S. P. (1980): Evidence that nerve cell bodies in the zona incerta influence ingestive behavior. *Brain Res. Bull.,* 5:593–597.
7. Brown, K. A., and Melzack, R. (1969): Effects of glucose on multi-unit activity in the hypothalamus. *Exp. Neurol.,* 24:363–373.
8. Carpenter, R. G., King, B. M., Stamoutsos, B. A., and Grossman, S. P. (1978): VMH lesions in vagotomized rats: A note of caution. *Physiol. Behav.,* 21:1031–1035.
9. Carpenter, R. G., Stamoutsos, B. A., Dalton, L. D., Frohman, L. A., and Grossman, S. P. (1979): VMH obesity reduced but not reversed by scopolamine methyl nitrate. *Physiol. Behav.,* 23:955–959.
10. Colin-Jones, D. G., and Himsworth, R. L. (1970): The location of the chemoreceptor controlling gastric acid secretion during hypoglycemia. *J. Physiol. (Lond.),* 206:397–409.
11. De Jong, A., Strubbe, J. H., and Steffens, A. B. (1977): Hypothalamic influence on insulin and glucagon release in the rat. *Am. J. Physiol.,* 233:E380–E388.
12. Ellis, H., and Pryse-Davies, J. (1967): Vagotomy in the rat: A study of its effects on stomach and small intestine. *Brit. J. Exp. Pathol.,* 48:135–141.
13. Epstein, A. N., Nicolaidis, S., and Miselis, R. (1975): The glucoprivic control of food intake and the glucostatic theory of feeding behavior. In: *Neural Integration of Physiological Mechanisms and Behavior,* edited by G. F. Mogenson and F. R. Calaresu, pp. 148–168. University of Toronto Press, Toronto.
14. Fiorentini, A., and Mueller, E. E. (1972): Sensitivity of central chemoreceptors controlling blood glucose and body temperature during glucose deprivation. *J. Physiol. (Lond.),* 248:247–271.
15. Flynn, F. W., and Grill, H. J. (1982): Insulin elicits ingestion in chronic decerebrate rats. *Neurosci. Abstr.,* 75:13.
16. Glick, S. D., Greenstein, S., and Waters, D. H. (1974): Lateral hypothalamic lesions and striatal dopamine levels. *Life Sci.,* 14:747–750.

17. Goltz, F. (1982): Der Hund ohne Grosshirn. *Pflugers Arch.*, 51:570–614.
18. Gonzalez, M. F., and Novin, D. (1974): Feeding induced by intracranial and intravenously administered 2-deoxy-D-glucose. *Physiol. Psychol.*, 2:326–330.
19. Grossman, S. P. (1966): The VMH: a center for affective reaction, satiety, or both. *Physiol. Behav.*, 1:1–10.
20. Grossman, S. P. (1975): Role of the hypothalamus in the regulation of food and water intake. *Psychol. Rev.*, 82:200–224.
21. Grossman, S. P. (1978): Correlative analysis of ingestive behavior and regional amine depletions after surgical transections of neural pathway in the mesencephalon, diencephalon and striatum. In: *Central Mechanisms of Anoretic Drugs*, edited by S. Garattini and R. Samanin, pp. 1–38. Raven Press, New York.
22. Grossman, S. P. (1979): The biology of motivation. *Ann. Rev. Psychol.*, 30:209–242.
23. Grossman, S. P., Dacey, D., Halaris, A. E., Collier, T., and Routtenberg, A. (1978): Aphagia and adipsia after preferential destruction of nerve cell bodies in the hypothalamus. *Science*, 202:537–539.
24. Grossman, S. P., and Grossman, L. (1983): Iontophoretic injections of kainic acid into the rat lateral hypothalamus: effects on ingestive behavior. *Physiol. Behav. (in press)*.
25. Hales, C. N., and Kennedy, G. C. (1964): Plasma glucose, non-esterified fatty acid and insulin concentrations in hypothalamic hyperphagic rats. *Biochem. J.*, 90:620–624.
26. Hall, W. H., and Read, R. C. (1970): Effect of vagotomy and gastric emptying. *Am. J. Dig. Dis.*, 15:1047–1053.
27. Inoue, S., and Bray, G. A. (1977): The effects of subdiaphragmatic vagotomy in rats with ventromedial hypothalamic obesity. *Endocrinology*, 100:108–114.
28. Joseph, S. A., and Knigge, J. M. (1968): Effects on VMH Lesions in adult and newborn guinea pigs. *Neuroendocrinology*, 3:309–331.
29. King, B. M. (1980): A re-examination of the ventromedial hypothalamic paradox. *Neurosci. Biobehav. Rev.*, 4:151–160.
30. King, B. M., Carpenter, R. G., Stamoutsos, B. A., Frohman, L. A., and Grossman, S. P. (1978): Hyperphagia and obesity following ventromedial hypothalamic lesions in rats with subdiaphragmatic vagotomy. *Physiol. Behav.*, 20:643–651.
31. King, B. M., Phelps, G. R., and Frohman, L. A. (1980): Hypothalamic obesity in female rats in absence of vagally mediated hyperinsulinemia. *Am. J. Physiol.*, 239:E437–E441.
32. Kraly, F. S., Gibbs, J., and Smith, G. P. (1975): Disordered drinking after abdominal vagotomy in rats. *Nature*, 248:226–228.
33. Levitt, D. R., and Teitelbaum, P. (1975): Somnolence, akinesia and sensory activation of motivated behavior in the lateral hypothalamic syndrome. *Proc. Natl. Acad. Sci. U.S.A.*, 72:2819–2823.
34. Louis-Sylvestre, J. (1976): Preabsorptive insulin release and hypoglycemia in rats. *Am. J. Physiol.*, 230:56–60.
35. Louis-Sylvestre, J. (1978): Relationship between two states of prandial insulin release in rats. *Am. J. Physiol.*, 233:E103–E111.
36. Marshall, J. F., and Teitelbaum, P. (1974): Further analysis of sensory inattention following lateral hypothalamic damage in rats. *J. Comp. Physiol. Psychol.*, 36:375–395.
37. Marshall, J. F., Turner, B. H., and Teitelbaum, P. (1971): Sensory neglect produced by lateral hypothalamic damage. *Science*, 174:523–525.
38. Mayer, J. (1955): Regulation of energy intake and the body weight. The glucostatic theory and the lipostatic hypothesis. *Ann. N.Y. Acad. Sci.*, 63:15–43.
39. McDermott, L. J., and Grossman, S. P. (1979): Regulation of calorie intake in rats with rostral zona incerta lesions: Effects of caloric density or palatability of the diet. *Physiol. Behav.*, 23:1135–1140.
40. McDermott, L. J., and Grossman, S. P. (1980): Circadian rhythms in ingestive behavior and responsiveness to glucoprivic and osmotic challenges in rats with rostral zona incerta lesions. *Physiol. Behav.*, 24:575–584.
41. McDermott, L. J., and Grossman, S. P. (1980): Responsiveness to 2-deoxy-D-glucose and insulin in rats with rostral zona incerta lesions. *Physiol. Behav.*, 24:585–592.
42. Miselis, R. R., and Epstein, A. N. (1975): Feeding induced by intracerebroventricular 2-deoxy-D-glucose in the rat. *Am. J. Physiol.*, 229:1438–1447.
43. Nicolaidis, S. (1978): Mécanismé, nerve et l'équilibre énergétique. *Jour. Annu. Diabetol. Hotel Dieu*, 1:153–156.

44. Oltmans, G. A., and Harvey. J. A. (1972): LH syndrome and brain catecholamine levels after lesions of the nigrostriatal bundle. *Physiol. Behav.,* 8:69–78.
45. Oomura, Y. (1973): Central mechanisms of feeding. *Adv. Biophys.,* 5:65–142.
46. Oomura, Y. (1976): Significance of glucose, insulin, and free fatty acid on the hypothalamic feeding and satiety neurons. In: *Hunger: Basic Mechanisms and Clinical Implications,* edited by D. Novin, W. Wyrwicka, and G. A. Bray, pp. 145–156. Raven Press, New York.
47. Peterson, G. M., and Moore, R. Y. (1980): Selective effects of kainic acid on diencephalic neurons. *Brain Res.,* 202:165–182.
48. Ralph, T. L., and Sawchenko, P. E. (1976): Differential effects of lateral and ventromedial hypothalamic lesions on gastrointestinal transit in the rat. *Brain Res. Bull.,* 3:11–14.
49. Sclafani, A. (1978): Food motivation in hypothalamic hyperphagic rats reexamined. *Neurosci. Biobehav. Rev.,* 2:339–355.
50. Sclafani, A. (1981): The role of hyperinsulinemia and the vagus nerve in hypothalamic hyperphagia reexamined. *Diabetologia,* 20:402–410.
51. Shimazu, T. (1979): Nervous control of peripheral metabolism. *Acta Physiol. Pol.,* [*Suppl. 18*], 30:1–18.
52. Snowdon, C. T. (1970): Gastrointestinal sensory and motor control of food intake. *J. Comp. Physiol. Psychol.,* 71:68–76.
53. Steffens, A. B. (1970): Plasma insulin content in relation to blood glucose level and meal pattern in the normal and hypothalamic hyperphagic rat. *Physiol. Behav.,* 5:147–151.
54. Steffens, A. B. (1981): The modulation effect of the hypothalamus on glucagon and insulin secretion in the rat. *Diabetologia,* 20:411–416.
55. Stellar, E. (1954): The physiology of motivation. *Psychol. Rev.,* 61:5–22.
56. Stricker, E. M., Swerdloff, A. F., and Zigmond, M. J. (1976): Intrahypothalamic injections of kainic acid produce feeding and drinking deficits in rats. *Brain Res.,* 158:470–473.
57. Stricker, E. M., and Zigmond, M. J. (1976): Brain catecholamines and the lateral hypothalamic syndrome. in: *Hunger, Basic Mechanisms and Clinical Implications,* edited by D. Novin, W. Wyrwicka, and G. A. Bray, pp. 19–32. Raven Press, New York.
58. Stricker, E. M., and Zigmond, M. J. (1976): Recovery of function after damage to central catecholamine-containing neurons: A neurochemical model for the lateral hypothalamic syndrome. In: *Progress in Psychobiology and Physiological Psychology, Vol. 6,* edited by J. M. Sprague and A. N. Epstein, pp. 121–188. Academic Press, New York.
59. Ungerstedt, U., Ljundberg, T., and Steg, G. (1974): Behavioral, physiological, and neurochemical changes after 6-hydroxy-dopamine-induced degeneration of the nigro-striatal dopamine neurons. *Adv. Neurol.,* 5:421–426.
60. Walsh, L. L,, and Grossman, S. P. (1973): Zona incerta lesions: Disruption of regulatory water intake. *Physiol. Behav.,* 11:885–887.
61. Walsh, L. L., and Grossman, S. P. (1975): Loss of feeding to 2-deoxy-D-glucose but not insulin after zona incerta lesions in the rat. *Physiol. Behav.,* 15:481–486.
62. Walsh, L. L., and Grossman, S. P. (1976): Zona incerta lesions impair osmotic but not hypovolemic thirst. *Physiol. Behav.,* 16:211–215.
63. Walsh, L. L., and Grossman, S. P. (1977): Dislocation of responses to extracellular thirst stimuli following zona incerta lesions. *Pharmacol. Biochem. Behav.,* 8:409–416.
64. Wayner, M. J., Kantak, K. M., Barone, F. C., DeHaven, D. L., Wayner, M. J. III, and Cook, R. C. (1981): Effects of kainic acid infusions on ingestion and autonomic activity. *Physiol. Behav.,* 27:369–376.
65. Woodworth, R. S., and Sherrington, C. S. (1904): A pseudoaffective reflex and its spinal path. *J. Physiol. (Lond.),* 31:234–243.
66. Zeigler, H. F., and Karten, H. J. (1974): Central trigeminal structures and the lateral hypothalamic syndrome in the rat. *Science,* 186:636–638.

Eating and Its Disorders, edited by A. J. Stunkard and E. Stellar. Raven Press, New York © 1984.

Neurotransmitters in the Control of Feeding and Its Rewards: Monoamines, Opiates, and Brain-Gut Peptides

Bartley G. Hoebel

Department of Psychology, Princeton University, Princeton, New Jersey 08544

The outline of this chapter follows an outline of brain mechanisms in the control of feeding. It starts with taste and gut sensory signals ascending via adrenergic pathways to the hypothalamus for integration with local sensory systems. Next it follows the lateral hypothalamic (LH) output back down the medial forebrain bundle to the ventral tegmental area (VTA) in the midbrain where opiates and a new nonopiate are rewarding. Then it traces the ascending dopamine path from the VTA to the nucleus accumbens, which is important in the reinforcement of instrumental behavior.

This chapter is the second in a pair of presentations to the Association for Research in Nervous and Mental Disease. The first dealt primarily with catecholamine projections to the hypothalamus in the control of feeding and self-stimulation (43). The second presents new data on peptides in feeding and reward. The first paper also gave a detailed explanation of Fig. 1, which focuses on the hypothalamus. This chapter recapitulates Fig. 1 and then explains Fig. 2, which gives a framework for understanding hypothalamic interactions with other limbic areas. This schema becomes clearer as I explain the experimental basis for labeling each of the pathways. This useful diagram overemphasizes certain salient features to depict what we can see best at the moment. A number of authors have published other overviews (10,13,16,23,25,26,44,55,61,73,81,87,88,99,103,111, 112,116,120,139,150). New peptides and their functions are being discovered at such a rapid rate, that this chapter should be interpreted as a harbinger of the future, not a scientific steady state. In order to understand the information encapsulated in Fig. 2, it is first necessary to understand Fig. 1.

HYPOTHALAMIC MODULATION OF FEEDING BY MONOAMINE INPUTS

Figure 1A shows the classic LH feeding system where stimulation causes eating, and lesions cause the LH starvation syndrome (140) leading to a lower body weight level (Keesey and Corbett, *this volume*). The medial region represents the

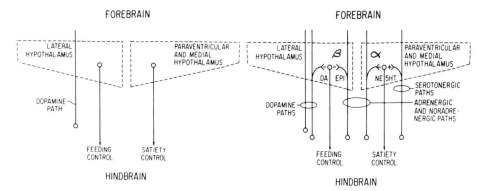

FIG. 1. A. Summary of hypothalamic lesion data. The lateral hypothalamus contains nigrostriatal dopamine fibers of passage and a feeding control output. The paraventricular and medial hypothalamic regions contain a satiety control system. **B.** The diagram is elaborated to include the beta-adrenergic and dopaminergic systems in the lateral hypothalamus. Note that epinephrine (EPI), or norepinephrine (NE), and dopamine (DA) have an effect on feeding which is inhibitory *(minus signs)*. In the paraventricular and medial region (on right-hand side of the diagram), the alpha-adrenergic and serotonergic systems are added to the scheme. Note that norepinephrine reduces satiety *(minus sign)*, whereas the predominant influence of serotonin is seen as facilitating satiety *(plus sign)*. GABA, endorphin, enkephalin and the "gut peptides", neurotensin, CCK and bombesin are not shown but may fit into this useful model. (See text for details.)

classic satiety system where stimulation interrupts feeding (36), and lesions cause the hypothalamic hyperphagia syndrome (14), which leads to an increased level of body weight maintainence (46). Stellar (135) made these feeding and satiety centers the core of a theoretical mechanism that controlled feeding motivation by the integration of internal signals, such as stomach fullness, and external signals, such as taste. This concept of centers has been much maligned because it was based on lesion and stimulation techniques which influence fibers of passage. However, other techniques such as neural recording and local drug injection have verified the original idea that cells in these regions integrate feeding signals. Therefore, Fig. 1 indicates that the lateral area is engaged in a "start feeding" decision process, and the medial area in a *stop feeding* process.

Several laboratories have recorded from hypothalamic single units that respond as if they integrate information in feeding control (95,96,100,116). Rolls (116) finds LH cells that alter their rate of firing in response to the taste of a palatable food and fire with a background rate that is correlated with food deprivation. These cells apparently combine internal homeostatic information with external food cues. Nishino et al. (96) also find LH cells that fire discriminately to food cues and vary their response with blood glucose level, and in addition, fire during operant bar press responses to obtain food. We can assume such cells participate in appetitive behavior for food.

Oomura et al. (100) report there are cells that respond to specific metabolic signals; these cells are *glucoreceptors* that fire to the combination of glucose plus

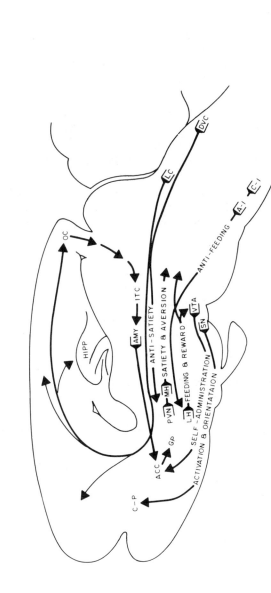

FIG. 2. Some of the regions, pathways and functions involved in feeding and its reinforcements are shown. 1. First is a system for preparedness: locus coeruleus (*LC*) to frontal cortex (*FC*), hippocampus (*HIPP*), and optic cortex (*OC*). 2. Sensory feature detection: optic cortex to infratemporal cortex (*ITC*) to the amygdala (*AMY*). 3. Activation and orientation: substantia nigra (*SN*) and other dopamine inputs to caudato-putamen (*C-P*) for response to stress and novelty. The following additional sequence would theoretically be sufficient (not necessary) for feeding to occur: 4. Anti satiety: increased activity in the dorsal vagal complex (*DVC*) and other noradrenergic inputs to the paraventricular nucleus (*PVN*) and medial hypothalamus (*MH*) which inhibit satiety. 5. Satiety and aversion: decreased PVN and MH output. 6. Antifeeding: decreased activity in an ascending pathway from norepinephrine, e.g., (*A-1*), or epinephrine (*C-1*) cell groups which otherwise inhibit LH feeding and reward. 7. Feeding and reward: augmented medial forebrain bundle, including lateral hypothalamic (*LH*), inputs to the ventral tegmental area (*VTA*) and other sites for enhancing food-related responses and their repetition. 8. Self-administration: VTA and other dopamine inputs to the nucleus accumbens (*ACC*) to facilitate other inputs, e.g., from the AMY, and outputs to the ventral globus pallidus (*GP*) for reinforcement. Recent findings from this laboratory include: (a) increased feeding and self-stimulation after 6-OHDA destruction of the antifeeding pathway; (b) neurotensin suppression of norepinephrine feeding in the PVN; (c) enkephalin-induced feeding in the PVN, presumably by suppression of satiety and aversion; (d) opiate and neurotensin-induced reward in the VTA; and (e) self-injection of amphetamine in the ACC.

insulin and are inhibited by free fatty acid. Such cells could theoretically play a role in either the physiological or behavioral aspects of glucostasis. Some cells along the medial-lateral border may fire in proportion to their metabolic rate and use ketone bodies as an alternate to glucose (95). New chemical stimuli for hypothalamic cells are still being discovered. Factors isolated from the blood of anorectic patients can alter the firing of selected hypothalamic cells in the rat (100).

The relative contributions of all these factors to feeding in everyday life is not known at the present, but the pivotal role of the hypothalamus is undeniable even if many fibers pass through without synapsing, and many others are involved in behaviors other than feeding. Even neurons that pass through may release neuromodulators from varicosities along their axons. For example, the fact that catecholamine fibers of passage can take up 6-hydroxydopamine in the LH and thereby deplete the anterior forebrain, suggests that they may normally release and take up catecholamines in the hypothalamus. Although recording studies suggest that the hypothalamic cells integrate factors related to feeding and glucostasis, it also seems that such cells are spread out along the anterior-posterior axis, not all clumped in neat, little hypothalamic nuclei.

Evidence supporting the traditional medial-to-lateral dichotomy comes from drug injection studies. Figure 1B shows that the pharmacological profile of the LH feeding system is distinguished by dopaminergic and β-adrenergic inhibitory influences (note the minus signs). The region within the LH area is specifically the perifornical LH region (67). The medial area, and more particularly the paraventricular nucleus (PVN), is characterized by *alpha*-adrenergic inhibition and possibly serotonergic excitation of the satiety system (Fig. 1B). Grossman (32) first demonstrated that local injection of putative neurochemicals could induce behavior, e.g., norepinephrine could induce feeding. Margules (74) and Leibowitz (58) found that norepinephrine could also have the opposite effect and cause satiety. Norepinephrine-induced feeding was localized to the PVN, and norepinephrine inhibition to the perifornical LH (60,61). In the 1960s many pharmacologists did not believe that locally injected neurotransmitters could act in a natural way. Some still do not believe it now. How, they asked, can drugs poured through a cannula possibly have physiological effects in synaptic junctions? The evidence is now very convincing. Norepinephrine in the PVN and norepinephrine or epinephrine in the perifornical LH come very close to satisfying the four formal criteria for a neurotransmitter (127). Rather than recording synaptic output by electrophysiology, the evidence is based on behavioral output, but the principles are the same:

1. Neuronal localization of the substance and its enzymes for synthesis and degradation (127). Histofluorescence shows dopamine, norepinephrine, and epinephrine in the perifornical LH and PVN (46,61,85,123,142). Modern immunofluorescence studies with antibodies against the enzymes which synthesize dopamine, norepinephrine, and epinephrine, not only trace the pathways for these catecholamines but also satisfy the criterion for enzyme localization. Varicosities along catecholamine axons and multiple terminations of finely branched endings

suggest that their natural mode of action may be to distribute catecholamines by leaking over a wide area. Electron microscopy of sympathetic ganglia and sympathetic innervation of smooth muscle has revealed receptor sites where there are no presynaptic classic vesicular release sites, as if catecholamines might in some cases act by diffusion from some distance (127). If catecholamines are naturally infused over a wide region, then neurotransmitter injection by cannula is not as unreasonable a technique as it once looked. In any case, physiological psychologists thought that the behavioral results provided sufficient rationale, and so they forged ahead (80).

2. Release of the substance by selective activation of a specific neuronal pathway. Push-pull cannula studies show that norepinephrine (and possibly epinephrine) is released during feeding. Myers and McCaleb (91) found that nutrient infused into a rat's stomach to cause satiety concomitantly caused inhibition of norepinephrine release in the PVN and enhancement of release in the LH. This agrees with the Leibowitz model as summarized in Fig. 1. Therefore, neural pathways activated by intragastric nutrients have predictable effects on norepinephrine (or epinephrine) release. Without knowing the specific pathways involved, they are nevertheless physiologically defined as appropriate pathways because they are stimulated by nutrients. Thus, the putative transmitter not only exists in the relevant hypothalamic regions, it is also released under the influence of relevant physiological factors.

3. Identical physiological response to exogenously applied transmitter and to activation of the pathway. Paraventricular nucleus injections of L-norepinephrine in the physiological range (1–4 mg) can lengthen a meal (60,61,113). In the LH, on the other hand, L-epinephrine (150 mg) inhibits ongoing feeding (67); norepinephrine requires an even higher dose. Therefore, if one were to judge by the necessary dose of exogenous transmitter, norepinephrine qualifies for the PVH system, and epinephrine is more likely than norepinephrine for the LH system.

4. Identical action of pharmacological agents (e.g., antagonists) when tested against the effects of exogenous transmitter or stimulation of the activated pathway (127).

(a) Pharmacological, postsynaptic blockers injected through cannulae have the opposite behavioral effects of the putative neurotransmitters. Alpha-adrenergic blockers reduce norepinephrine feeding; beta-adrenergic blockers reduce norepinephrine or epinephrine satiety, and dopamine blockers reduce dopamine satiety (61, see Fig. 1B).

(b) Presynaptic agonists, such as amphetamine, which release catecholamines have the same effect as the injected catecholamines (61).

(c) Presynaptic catecholamine depletion with locally applied drugs reduces the behavioral action of presynaptic acting agonists, such as amphetamine (61).

(d) Presynaptic catecholamine depletion by destruction of ascending catecholamine pathways causes a decrease in systemic amphetamine effectiveness (1,2,59) and in amphetamine's local effectiveness (64) with behavioral signs of receptor denervation supersensitivity (64, see the ascending paths in Fig. 1B).

(e) Food deprivation and food repletion cause changes in receptor binding to a radioactive α-adrenergic antagonist in the LH and PVN in accord with the feeding and satiety functions as labeled in Fig. 1. For example, PVN receptor binding decreased when rats were food deprived and then increased after *ad lib.* feeding (52,62). The opposite occurred in the LH where deprivation caused increased receptor binding (52). To understand this, one can imagine that during deprivation a lack of postingestional factors could lead to increased PVN release of norepinephrine resulting in receptor down regulation and hence to decreased binding as observed. Conversely, in the LH, the lack of postingestional factors would be accompanied by a lack of norepinephrine release, which in turn, would lead to receptor proliferation (up regulation) and increased binding.

Amphetamine may have similar direct postsynaptic effects, or more likely presynaptic effects, judging by a recent report that ^{3}H-amphetamine binds to receptors in much of the brain, but particularly in the hypothalamus (105). Time will tell whether the "brain's own amphetamine" is one of the catecholamines shown in Fig. 1B or some other endogenous phenethylamine or structurally related molecule.

In summary, criteria for a neurotransmitter were established after Loewi discovered that acetylcholine could modulate cardiac function. Norepinephrine in the PVN, and norepinephrine or epinephrine in the perifornical LH, meet these criteria as recently ennuciated by Siggins (127). In the present demonstration, instead of an organ system being modulated by a neurotransmitter from a nerve, a complete behavior pattern is modulated by nutrients acting by way of the brain. One of the ambiguities which remains is to distinguish between norepinephrine and epinephrine as the beta-adrenergic agonist.

Our part in this story was to show that the ascending ventral noradrenergic bundle contributes an inhibitory influence on feeding. Ungerstedt (143) had shown that the nigrostriatal dopamine system was necessary for eating and that its destruction accounted for part of the LH starvation syndrome (note nigrostriatal fibers of passage in Fig. 1B). The next question was what would happen if the noradrenergic bundles were destroyed without depleting dopamine. The result of ventral bundle destruction was hyperphagia and obesity (2). This was different from classic medial hypothalamic lesion-induced hyperphagia and obesity. For example the 6-OHDA rats only binged at night when they were awake and active (3). Leibowitz and Brown (64) replicated obesity after noradrenergic depletion, and they also obtained hyperphagia attributable to destruction of dopamine cells. We next confirmed that hyperphagia after 6-OHDA results from catecholamine depletion. This was done by preventing hyperphagia with drugs that protect the animal from 6-OHDA (33). These new animal models of obesity suggest that a deficit in the biosynthesis of catecholamines in components of the ventral pathway could cause obesity in humans.

Figure 1B shows why a catecholamine deficit in a pathway to the LH causes obesity that is different from medial hypothalamic lesion obesity. Catecholamine depletion disinhibits the LH by removing ascending inhibition. Medial lesions, on the other hand, destroy an outgoing satiety pathway and, thereby, disinhibit feeding by a different route. It is no wonder that obesity is difficult to treat, and that a variety of catecholaminergic, serotonergic, dietary, and exercise regimens are used. Obesity is a multivariate disease. In the rat, we now have a list of at least 16 models of chronic obesity:

1. Dietary obesity resulting from food palatability and variety (30,115,125).
2. Medial hypothalamic (MH) obesity produced by radio-frequency (35) or electrolytic lesions (46) which cause hyperinsulinemia (13,111), or MH obesity produced by local colchicine which blocks axonal transport (7).
3. Lateral hypothalamic, chronic stimulation-induced obesity (47,134).
4. Insulin-induced obesity due to chronic long-acting insulin treatment (46,104).
5. Gold-thio-glucose obesity which depends on insulin for uptake of the toxic glucose molecule (38).
6. Monosodium glutamate (MSG) obesity following injections near the PVN to kill cell bodies but not axons (128).
7. Adrenergic depletion obesity due to a catecholaminergic neurotoxin, 6-OHDA, injected in the ventral midbrain (1–3,33) or midbrain lesions (64).
8. Knife-cut obesity following damage to ascending pathways (29). Like MH lesion obesity, the effect of hypothalamic knife cuts depends on an intact vagus and is partly the result of vagally mediated hyperinsulinemia (30).
9. Dopamine depletion obesity following ventral midbrain lesions that in part disrupt input to the LH while sparing the nigrostriatal system (64).
10. Serotonin depletion obesity following ventricular parachlorophenylalanine (PCPA) (37) or hypothalamic 5,7-DHT (144,145).
11. Norepinephrine-induced obesity from chronic PVN injection (66).
12. Antidepressant-induced obesity as a consequence of noradrenergic agonists acting in the region of the PVN (63).
13. Antianxiety treatment (benzodiazepine)-induced hyperphagia (19,133,151).
14. Stress-induced obesity modeled by chronic tail-pinch (121) and attributed largely to nigrostriatal activation (5).
15. Amphetamine-overdose obesity as a long-lasting rebound following i.p., ventricular, or LH amphetamine injection (34,42).
16. Genetic obesity which could be an inborn tendency toward any of the above as well as peripheral effects (68).

Figure 1 helps to clarify these "animal models." Pharmacological agonists which induce feeding usually act in the MH, particularly the PVN. Agonists that cause satiety act in the LH, particularly the perifornical region. Number 15, amphetamine-overdose obesity is a new phenomenon discovered by Hernandez in this laboratory. A single, near fatal, i.p. dose of amphetamine caused anorexia as one would expect, but surprisingly this was followed by rebound overeating that lasted for months. The phenomenon seems to be due to LH abnormalities because it can be reproduced with 50 μg amphetamine delivered directly to the LH (34).

Amphetamine in the LH activates dopamine and beta-adrenergic receptors to inhibit feeding in the short run (Fig. 1), but we now know that a large dose can have the opposite effect in the long run. This chronic effect could hypothetically result from presynaptic terminal death, impairment in synthesis, impairment of release, or chronic down regulation of postsynaptic receptor sites for catecholamines or other unidentified amphetamine-like transmitters. Amphetamine can bind to LH receptors (105), but further work is necessary to identify the natural ligand and determine whether amphetamine binds pre- or postsynaptically. In any case, our results warn that an overdose of amphetamine may have an opposite effect to what was intended.

HYPOTHALAMIC OPIATE PEPTIDES THAT INITIATE FEEDING

Margules et al. (75) found abnormally high beta-endorphin associated with overeating in genetically obese animals. Other laboratories have found better correlations with leu-enkephalin (119) or dynorphin (88). To the extent pituitary beta-endorphin is involved, it may act by causing hyperinsulinemia (88). Many have found that the opiate blocker naloxone reduces food intake (8,12,15,18,51,89,101,122,154). With some exceptions (9), naloxone has been found to have little effect on its own, but it can block feeding induced by deprivation, stress, muscimol, the benzodiazepine diazepam, or 2DG (89). Grandison and Guidotti (31) and Leibowitz and Hor (65) discovered that feeding could be induced by injection of beta-endorphin or morphine directly into the PVN. Presumably chronically high opiate levels in the PVN might cause a tendency toward obesity, although this remains to be proven.

This laboratory found that an enkephalin might be an endogenous opiate involved in feeding. The evidence for enkephalin-induced feeding in the PVN is quite compelling. McLean and Hoebel (41,79) replicated PVN norepinephrine feeding and morphine feeding, then injected the long-acting enkephalin analogue, d-ala-met-enkephalinamide (DALA). The effect was an increase in food intake but not water intake. This suggests a specific behavioral role in appetite or homeostasis, and not just a general increase in consummatory behavior or nonspecific emotion. The feeding effect is strangely delayed for 30 min or more. Perhaps the time delay is required for PVN opiates to release another neurotransmitter, which in turn, induces the feeding (65,89,141), or perhaps opiates require time to release hormones, or they may simply cause an initial lethargy (89). With evidence pointing to multiple opiate receptors, the actual endogenous ligands for opiate-induced feeding remain to be determined.

It is interesting to compare norepinephrine feeding and DALA feeding. The amount of food eaten in response to PVN norepinephrine depends on corticosterone levels in the blood, suggesting a synergism between adrenal function and PVN noradrenergic function (61). Feeding that is DALA-induced did not show this synergism. Adrenalectomy reduced norepinephrine feeding without reducing opiate feeding (79,89). From this one would predict that sympathetic release of adrenal corticoids in the normal animal would potentiate PVN norepinephrine-mediated feeding but not PVN opiate-mediated feeding. Nevertheless, stress may release opiates that are themselves a separate source of stress-induced eating.

Diet selection studies suggest that norepinephrine feeding is preferential for carbohydrates (61). Opiates can also affect intake of sweet solutions (124,129), but morphine-treated rats given a choice tend to select fatty foods (76), and naloxone shifts intake away from fat (77). These studies are hard to interpret because the texture, taste, and composition of diets are confounded, but the idea that specific neurotransmitter systems trigger specific appetites adds another dimension to the analysis of feeding. It also adds another dimension to diagnosis and therapy. The foods a patient selects to overeat may someday provide a clue as to which neural system causes the overeating. There is also the possibility that the effect of diet on neurotransmitter levels may contribute to therapy (Wurtman and Wurtman, *this volume*).

In summary, the reader can add an arrow labeled "opiate" to Fig. 1B pointing to the PVN. Given that opiates induce feeding, the model suggests inhibition of satiety (a minus sign); however, there is no proof of cellular inhibition of satiety neurons except the circumstantial evidence that opiate peptides do inhibit the firing of some neurons in the PVN (90,110).

HYPOTHALAMIC "GUT PEPTIDES" THAT INHIBIT FEEDING

The next topic is *nonopiate* peptides. Cholecystokinin (CCK) is a gut peptide known to suppress feeding following peripheral injections (Smith, *this volume*). It can also cause aversion and sometimes illness (21,56). Its role in gastric-induced satiety and aversion seems assured by the fact that selective gastric vagotomy eliminates its feeding suppressive effect (130,131). The difference between gastric satiety and gastric malaise or aversion may be a matter of degree and may even involve the same neural system (36). In the clinic, CCK has sometimes been effective in reducing food intake (54). Cholecystokinin or octapeptide can also suppress feeding when injected in the PVN. Local injection of CCK along with norepinephrine suppressed norepinephrine-induced feeding (78), but again malaise was a potential problem. The problem was avoided by looking for an increase in food intake with CCK-antibody. It doubled food intake during continuous injection into the ventricles of sheep (20).

It is intriguing that this peptide might act both in the gut and brain with corresponding physiological and behavioral effects in both places. This is reminiscent of angiotension, which is secreted both by the kidney and by neurons in the brain to increase blood pressure through physiological adjustments and drinking behavior. Therefore, as an initial working hypothesis, we generalized from the case of CCK and angiotension to the case of neurotensin (40).

Neurotensin is a peptide secreted by the duodenum in response to food, particularly fat. Its physiological effects include slowing peristalsis to facilitate fat digestion and constricting capillaries in fatty tissue (117). Although peptides do not readily cross the blood-brain barrier, neurotensin is known to exist in the brain, including the hypothalamus, and to affect a number of physiological, sensory, and motor functions (94). If the CNS uses peptides for some of the same overall purposes in the brain as in the periphery, then CNS neurotensin might alter energy balance through feeding adjustments in the hypothalamus.

We injected neurotensin in the PVN with the following results. Neurotensin reduced norepinephrine-induced feeding just as CCK does (132). Norepinephrine feeding was blocked more effectively by neurotensin injected through the same PVN cannula than by neurotensin injected in the contralateral PVN; therefore, malaise or systemic endocrine effects cannot account for all of neurotensin's ability to suppress norepinephrine feeding.

Paraventricular nucleus injections of neurotensin also suppressed natural deprivation-induced feeding. Ingestive specificity was shown by neurotensin inhibition of liquid-diet drinking but not water drinking (41,132). Receptor specificity may be inferred by the lack of effectiveness of neurotensin fragments (NT_{1-8} and NT_{8-13}) compared with the whole peptide (NT_{1-13}).

Levine et al. (69) replicated neurotensin block of norepinephrine feeding using intraventricular injections. They found neurotensin also suppressed feeding induced by dynorphin but not insulin. Smith et al., (57,130) report that the gut peptide bombesin suppresses feeding when injected in the LH. What we need and do not have are drugs to selectively block the degradation of each of these peptides. Such drugs would potentiate endogenous peptides and conceivably be anorectic agents. Gut peptides are found in many parts of the brain, even the retina, so one would have to find a peptide configuration that recognized something unique about hypothalamic nonopiate receptors for satiety. The nonopiate peptide mechanisms can be tentatively added in Fig. 1B with another new arrow labeled "neurotensin, CCK," in the PVN and "bombesin" in the LH.

HYPOTHALAMIC CONNECTIONS WITH OTHER PARTS OF THE BRAIN

Figure 2 is a summary diagram of some hypothalamic connections. It ignores serotonin and numerous peptides, because we are not sure where the relevant cell bodies are located. Some of them are probably right in the PVN or MH where the arrow labeled satiety and aversion originates. In this figure the LH outflow is labeled feeding and reward. The prior discussion made it clear that the classic dual theory of hypothalamic function, i.e., LH feeding and MH satiety, is still at the core of our investigations, fibers of passage not withstanding. There has been a shift in emphasis from the MH to the PVN where there is maximum sensitivity to alpha-adrenergic feeding agents, and from the far LH to the perifornical LH where beta-adrenergic satiety is best obtained. These alpha- and beta-adrenergic modulations are shown in Fig. 2 by two ascending arrows, one to the PVN–MH for antisatiety and another to the LH for antifeeding. These pathways have been demonstrated both by histofluorescence and by retrograde transport of labeled compounds injected into the hypothalamus (123).

The antisatiety pathway, which arises in part from the dorsal vagal complex (DVC), is almost surely noradrenergic as already explained with reference to Fig. 1. Antisatiety refers to noradrenergic inhibition of satiety, i.e., norepinephrine-induced feeding. This pathway probably has other functions in addition to inhibiting feeding. The labels are not meant to be exclusive.

The antifeeding pathway is largely the ventral noradrenergic bundle, which arises in areas A-1 and C-1 containing cell bodies for norepinephrine and epinephrine fibers, respectively. Either of these two transmitters could be involved in the beta-adrenergic satiety effects in the LH. This pathway continues forward (not shown) to the PVN, where its function is presumably the opposite. The midbrain and hindbrain nuclei in Fig. 2 are known to interconnect with each other and to send sensory information to the hypothalamus from both the vagus nerve and taste inputs (137).

HYPOTHALAMIC REINFORCEMENT OF FEEDING AND SELF-STIMULATION

The labeled hypothalamic outputs in Fig. 2 suggest that the same two pathways which mediate feeding and satiety also mediate reward and aversion. We came to this conclusion because mid-lateral hypothalamic stimulation which induces feeding also supports self-stimulation that varies with feeding. Self-stimulation rate decreases with gastric and metabolic factors that cause satiety (36,39,45). Conversely, responses to escape from LH stimulation increase after a satiating meal (47). This suggests a shift from hypothalamic reward to hypothalamic aversion during satiety. Aversion is attributed to the MH region in Fig. 2 because this region contains a well-known satiety system and MH stimulation is aversive. Moreover, MH lesions disinhibit both LH self-stimulation and feeding (36,45) in parallel (39) suggesting that somewhere the MH outflow inhibits the LH outflow and, therefore, might be involved in both satiety and aversion labeled in Figure 2. Presumably mid-lateral electrodes which give both self-stimulation and stimulation-escape, either excite some of both the LH and MH types of pathways, or excite the reward path initially and the aversion path as disinhibitory rebound.

The idea that feeding and LH self-stimulation covary was confirmed in a new way when we found that 6-hydroxydopamine injected to destroy the ventral midbrain pathway labeled "anti-feeding", caused not only hyperphagia but also increased LH self-stimulation in most rats (39). Thus it appears that the ascending pathway from A1 and C1 cell groups normally inhibits not only feeding, but also inhibits the self-stimulation reward that is allied with feeding.

Where does the feeding reward pathway go? Presumably it projects to the hindbrain where it could facilitate reflexes for ingestion of food. It also projects to the ventral tegmental area (VTA) of the midbrain as shown in Fig. 2. Shizgal (126) demonstrated this projection of the LH reward system by stimulating with single pulses at two places along the path while recording in the VTA. The interval between pulses was varied until antidromic impulses from one stimulation site annihilated the orthordromic impulses from the other, then only one compound action potential arrived in the VTA instead of two. Simultaneously the rat responded for self-stimulation at about half its prior rate. The experiment is analogous to the classic demonstration that colliding antidromic and orthodromic nerve as impulses from a pair of stimulating electrodes on a peripheral nerve produce one-half as many downstream action potentials and a diminished muscle twitch (71,138). Thus, muscular behavior can be used to measure axonal properties in peripheral nerve trunks or in central nerve tracks (25,153). The evidence from 2-deoxyglucose radiographs (153) and lesion studies (136) corroborates the view that the self-stimulation reward path extends the full length of the medial forebrain bundle, including the LH, and descends to the ventral thalamic area (VTA) (126).

OPIATE REWARD IN THE VTA

The VTA was strongly implicated in reward processes by the discovery that rats would self-inject morphine directly into this region of the midbrain. Rats bar press for morphine at several limbic sites including the LH (97,98), but the VTA appears most sensitive (11,150,153). Not only can rats learn to work for local morphine, but they also can remember which end of a cage, bright or dark, they were in when they received morphine on prior days. This drug-induced conditioned preference for a particular place tells us that the drug was a memorable reinforcer capable of lending secondary reinforcing effects to a distinctive environment (118). Morphine injected in the VTA has this effect (107, 109).

The next question was which of the brain's own opiates is responsible. We obtained the conditioned place preference with VTA injections of an analog of enkephalin, DALA, then sought a means of potentiating the brain's own enkephalin. Fortunately, thiorphan, an enkephalinase inhibitor (i.e., enzyme blocker) had been made for the purpose, but it had never been used to potentiate brain reward.

Thiorphan was injected into the VTA while rats were confined on the bright side of a cage. After four such pairings of thiorphan with the bright side, the animals were given a choice the next day with no thiorphan injection; they only received saline injected as a control. Rats with prior VTA injection of thiorphan preferred to spend more time on the bright side than they had during baseline testing. Rats normally prefer the dark side, but thiorphan reversed this natural preference. Naloxone blocked the thiorphan effect, which confirms that endogenous opiates were involved (28). These new results suggest that endogenous enkephalin probably has rewarding effects on opiate receptors in the VTA.

NONOPIATE REWARD IN THE VTA: NEUROTENSIN

The VTA contains not only opiates, but also nonopiate peptides such as neurotensin. Injections of neurotensin into the VTA cause hyperactivity (93). This probably is the result of activating ascending dopamine neurons because the effect is altered by manipulations which affect dopaminergic transmission (53). In addition, neurotensin receptors have been identified on dopamine neurons (102), and iontophoretic application of neurotensin stimulates midbrain dopamine neurons (4). A large body of evidence links this mesolimbic-mesocortical dopamine system to reward processes (23,44,106,149,150); therefore VTA neurotensin might be expected to play a role in initiating reward.

Our hypothesis was confirmed by the finding that neurotensin injected in the VTA caused a conditioned place preference (27,41). Specificity of neurotensin receptor interaction was indicated by results showing that the neurotensin fragment containing the first 11 amino acids (NT_{1-11}) also produced the reward effect, but NT_{1-8} or NT_{8-13} did not (27). This is the first evidence that a nonopiate peptide can induce reward effects. It suggests that the VTA integrates a number of opiate and nonopiate inputs in the control of reward processes. On the basis of the results described, arrows to the VTA can be added to Fig. 2 with plus signs for enkephalin and neurotensin.

DOPAMINERGIC REWARD IN THE ACCUMBENS

The next step in tracking down a reward mechanism is to follow the major output of the VTA. Dopamine cells of the VTA project in the mesocortical pathway to limbic areas including the nucleus accumbens (85,92,147). Wise (149) has propounded the controversial theory that dopamine is a substrate for reward because dopamine blockers, such as pimozide, can decrease intravenous self-injection, self-stimulation, or feeding (23,24,50,106,148–150,152). Gallistel's group has done elaborate controls for locomotor impairments which suggest that pimozide blocks the payoff, not the ability to perform (146). Sometimes animals that will not bar press after injections of dopamine blockers will nevertheless perform simpler operant tasks (22). Rats can even perform simple operants for self-stimulation with most of the forebrain removed (49) or when they are only 3 days old (86), but there seems little doubt that intact dopamine systems are necessary both to perform and to reward the more dexterous operant tasks.

The nucleus accumbens is implicated in the reinforcement of bar pressing by the finding that LH self-stimulation or i.v. self-injection responses were impaired by lesions of the accumbens or 6-OHDA in the accumbens (17,72,114). If dopamine released in the accumbens reinforces bar presses, then rats should lever press to self-inject a dopamine releaser into their accumbens. Lenard visited this laboratory in 1976 and chose the nucleus accumbens for self-injection because of its heavy innervation by dopamine terminals where amphetamine could presumably act to release dopamine. The effort at Princeton was joined by Hernandez. Here are the findings:

1. Rats bar pressed to self-inject approximately 60 μl per injection of 10 μg/μl *d*-amphetamine-sulfate significantly more often than they would self-inject sodium chloride or sodium sulfate.

2. They responded at about 20 presses per hour during 4-hr daytime tests or 8-hr nighttime tests, although the rate varied from rat to rat. The procedure worked best if 2 days were allowed between tests.

3. Given two levers, one for amphetamine and one blank, the animals would switch from one to the other on different days, always learning to respond more on the amphetamine lever. This test rules out day to day perseveration and random hyperactivity.

4. The amount of amphetamine was self-regulated. When an individual animal's baseline rate of self-injection was determined on 3 test days, then averaged, and one-half that number of injections was programmed automatically, then the animal compensated by self-injecting half as often (83). Thus, animals accurately controlled their own dose.

5. Rats with both accumbens and ventricular cannulae showed response extinction on days when the same small injections were delivered into the lateral ventricle instead of the accumbens. Thus, accumbens injections acted locally near the accumbens, not by refluxing into the ventricles. Some animals learned to respond at approximately 10 times the normal rate, so we suspect they were pushing large quantities of the drug into the ventricles in such cases. Histological examination showed that effective cannulae were in the nucleus accumbens; ineffective sites were below the accumbens or in the ventricle or caudate. We did have one rat that self-injected through a cannula in the caudate, and one in the cortex as shown for monkeys by Phillips, Mora, and Rolls (108). At the present, the only site we have investigated in detail is the accumbens, medial to the anterior commissure.

6. When the dopamine blocker flupenthixol (10 $\mu g/\mu l$) was added to the amphetamine (10 $\mu g/\mu l$), self-injection was reduced. The active isomer of flupenthixol blocked self-injection significantly more than the inactive isomer. This control suggests that there is a true dopamine receptor interaction with the active isomer (Aulissi and Hoebel, *unpublished work*).

We conclude first that amphetamine self-injection is a positive reinforcer by the strict behavioral criteria cited above. Second, dopamine release is probably the primary mode of amphetamine action in producing the reinforcement. To double-check these points, we found that accumbens amphetamine injection could produce a conditioned place preference. This, too, was blocked by the active isomer of flupenthixol but not by the inactive one (Aulissi and Hoebel, *unpublished work*).

These results lend support to the theory that dopamine in the accumbens is involved in self-administration behavior requiring a complex operant response, and that neuroleptics diminish this reinforcement effect. We do not know how dopaminergic reward relates to feeding, but Wise (150) has reviewed evidence that neuroleptics can block responses for food. Mogenson (81,82) proposed that mesolimbic dopamine in the accumbens gates the flow of sensory information from the limbic system as it passes along to the globus pallidus (GP) and motor systems. Neill et al. (94) formulate this dopaminergic function in terms of willingness to exert effort, as opposed to reward. Fibiger and Phillips (23) suggest that dopaminergic innervation of the limbic system amplifies ongoing motivational processes such as feeding, including both homeostatic processes and external incentives. There is general agreement that this is different from nigrostriatal function, even though there is some overlap of nigral and VTA projections (70,84).

The nigrostriatal path is described in Fig. 2 as serving an activation and orientation function. This is the system that is debilitated in the classic Parkinson's Disease syndrome. The mesocortical projection to the accumbens is labeled self-administration as an operational description of its role in self-stimulation and self-injection. Complex feeding responses can be considered as a self-administrative behavior. Amphetamine and cocaine abuse clearly involve this system. Food abuse may also be linked to the accumbens in future studies.

OVERVIEW OF MOTIVATION

The remaining path in Fig. 2 is the noradrenergic dorsal bundle, which courses from the locus coeruleus (LC) to most parts of the forebrain. Its functions are still not understood, but electrophysiology has demonstrated that environmental feature detectors in the visual cortex are potentiated by LC stimulation (M. Segal, *unpublished work.*) Thus, environmentally significant stimuli are enhanced by this pathway, and it may play an overall role in focusing attention on external environmental events as opposed to internal autonomic factors (6). Visual feature detectors in the infratemporal cortex (ITC) project to the amygdala (AMY) and from there to parts of the cortex, hypothalamus, and nucleus accumbens as shown in Fig. 2. From the accumbens projections reach the LH, substantia nigra, and VTA thereby creating several loops (92,148) and to the ventral GP, which is part of the extrapyramidal motor system (92). The caudate and putamen (C-P) project to the more dorsal aspect of the GP.

Now we can run through the entire cartoon to get an overall feel for the neural basis of feeding and its reinforcement (Fig. 2). The first step is hippocampal and cortical arousal through the LC output for noradrenergic enhancement of environmentally significant features. With the animal awake and alert, we can next imagine a decrease in activity in the satiety and aversion system. Starting at the DVC, assume that the noradrenergic antisatiety pathway is activated by the taste of sugar in the mouth and a lack of nutrients in the gut and liver. This noradrenergic projection inhibits the PVN-MH region so as to reduce the satiety and aversion output. Simultaneously, any local MH glucoreceptors or other energy receptors involved in satiety would need to diminish their background activity, as occurs when fuel availability is low. In addition, one can presume that PVN opiate availability would be high and turnover of neurotensin, CCK, and bombesin would be low. As a result, the satiety and aversion output would be reduced. Thus, feeding would be disinhibited neurochemically, as it would by a PVN or MH lesion. This disinhibition of feeding by homeostatic needs plus taste could occur directly, for example in the midbrain, and/or by way of increased vagal output causing phasic insulin release.

Next assume that the "antifeeding" path from A-1 and C-1 cell groups is quiescent; this is presumably due in part to food deprivation and a lack of vagal satiety signals from the stomach, duodenum, and liver. This pathway provides the LH beta-adrenergic signal which can inhibit feeding. Its quiescence would disinhibit the LH output labeled feeding and reward; just as a 6-OHDA lesion of this ventral bundle disinhibits feeding and self-stimulation. As deprivation continued, there would be gradual up-regulation of the unstimulated beta-adrenergic receptors which would theoretically produce an augmented response to satiety factors when they were reintroduced. This could help explain poststarvation anorexia. In the deprived animal, we know some LH cells are firing with high baseline rates (116), due theoretically to the lack of ascending inhibition (43). These same cells respond vigorously to preferred taste stimuli and conditioned taste stimuli as recorded by Rolls (116). The evidence suggests that some LH neurons project to the VTA and help generate the reward of self-stimulation (126). Part of self-stimulation reward is related to feeding (36,39). We do not know how these feeding reward neurons affect the VTA, but some process in the VTA apparently releases enkephalin and neurotensin, which are rewarding as described above. Let us suppose that LH feeding reward is the reward normally triggered by good smells and tastes acting on the metabolically primed LH neurons and that this reward comes in part from the release of opiate or nonopiate peptides in the VTA.

As feeding starts, the next step in Fig. 2 is the pathway from the VTA to the accumbens, which carries a message necessary for self-administration. Presumably this message reinforces the link between stimuli and complex operant responses. This also requires that the nigrostriatal tract has simultaneously turned on activation and orientation for motor initiation. When the appropriate components of both of these ascending dopaminergic systems are active, then both multimodal sensory feature detection from the AMY and multimodal sensory choices from the cortex can move on to the last staging area in this diagram which is the GP. The GP activates ascending thalamic pathways and extrapyramidal motor pathways to potentiate the sensory-motor arcs which brought the animal into mental or behavioral proximity with the rewarding food. Thus, the animal homes in on the homeostatically sanctioned, environmentally exciting, hedonistic stimulus.

To repeat and simplify still further, the norepinephrine-alerted optic cortex and ITC encode a colorful shape (e.g., a yellow banana); the AMY encodes the stimulus features along with its positive or negative qualities (i.e., discriminative stimulus features and learned taste of a yellow banana), the altered hippocampus localizes it in space, and perhaps memory and the frontal cortex somehow makes its choice based on the firing of neurons which encode not only the quantitative physical features and qualitative experiential features but also the operant reinforcement history of the stimulus (116). The decision to act is apparently sent to the dorsal caudate to trigger appropriate motor programs (if dopamine is abundant) and to the ventral caudate and accumbens for carrying out successful programs (if dopamine has been released). Without C-P dopamine, the animal has trouble acting at all (Parkinson's Disease or aphagia or sensory neglect). Without accumbens dopamine, the animal seems to have trouble acting successfully (reward neglect, i.e., stimulus-response association neglect). Conversely, too much C-P dopamine potentiates circuits for unnecessary actions (Huntington's Chorea or stereotyped compulsive behavior), and too much accumbens dopamine may contribute to hyperactivity and excessive reinforcement (reward enhancement, i.e., stimulus-response association enhancement).

It has not yet been demonstrated that the accumbens is subdivided according to behaviors, feeding, sex, aggression, etc., but it must at least help gear the animal for success in matching the outcome of behaviors with the expected outcome. We do not know which pathways actually generate the good feelings or sharpened skills of success any more than we know the circuits for cognition of failure or pain. It is clear, however, that the dopaminergic systems are necessary for all complex self-administration behaviors, and that accumbens dopamine, released by amphetamine, is sufficient to reward lever pressing if the rest of the brain is intact.

Morphine is notoriously rewarding, and we have seen its reward duplicated by merely protecting VTA opiates from degradation. Neurotensin was also rewarding in the VTA, which demonstrates that nonopiate peptide can have such a function. Given that all three, accumbens dopamine, VTA enkephalin, and VTA neurotensin are likely to act, in part, on the ascending dopamine system labeled self-administration, simplicity would suggest that this is a major link in a system that reinforces behavior. Given that part of the LH self-stimulation reward system projects to the VTA and part is related to feeding, we predict that future research will find that the dopaminergic self-administration system is a major link in the control of food as a reinforcer.

ACKNOWLEDGMENTS

Preparation of this manuscript and peptide research in the author's laboratory was supported by U.S. Public Health Service grant MH-35740. Appreciation is expressed to Paul Glimcher for suggestions, to Kathy McGeady for typing, to the ARNMD for travel funds, and to the Neurobiology and Behavior Laboratory at the Salk Institute for sabbatical space while working on this chapter.

REFERENCES

1. Ahlskog, J. E. (1974): Food intake and amphetamine anorexia after selective forebrain norepinephrine loss. *Brain Res.,* 82:211–240.
2. Ahlskog, J. E., and Hoebel, B. G. (1973): Overeating and obesity from damage to a noradrenergic system in the brain. *Science,* 182:166–169.
3. Ahlskog, J. E., Randall, P. K., and Hoebel, B. G. (1975): Hypothalamic hyperphagia: Dissociation from noradrenergic depletion hyperphagia. *Science,* 190:399–401.
4. Andrade, A., and Aghajanian, G. K. (1981): Neurotensin selectively activates dopaminergic neurons of the substantia nigra. *Abstr. Soc. Neurosci.,* 7:573.
5. Antelman, S. M., Szechtman, H., Chin, P., and Fisher, A. E. (1975): Tail pinch-induced eating, gnawing and licking behavior in rats: Dependence on the nigrostriatal dopamine system. *Brain Res.,* 99:319–337.

6. Aston-Jones, G., and Bloom, F. E. (1981): Norepinephrine-containing locus coeruleus neurons in behaving rats exhibit pronounced responses to non-noxius envoronmental stimuli. *J. Neurosci.,* 1:887–900.
7. Avrith, D., and Mogenson, G. J. (1978): Reversible hyperphagia and obesity following intracerebral microinjections of colchicine into the ventromedial hypothalamus of the rat. *Brain Res.,* 153:99–107.
8. Baile, C. A., Keim, D. A., Della-Fera, M. A., and McLaughlin, C. L. (1981): Opiate antagonists and agonists and feeding in sheep. *Physiol. Behav.,* 26:1019–1023.
9. Belluzzi, J. D., and Stein, L. (1982): Endorphin mediation of feeding. In: *The Neural Basis of Feeding and Reward,* edited by B. G. Hoebel and D. Novin, pp. 479–484. Haer Institute, Brunswick, Maine.
10. Blundell, J. E. (1981): Bio-grammar of feeding: pharmacological manipulations and their interpretations. In: *Theory in Psychopharmacology,* edited by S. J. Cooper, pp. 234–276. Academic Press, London.
11. Bozarth, M. A. (1982): Opiate reward mechanisms mapped by intracranial self-administration. In: *Neurobiology of Opiate Reward Mechanisms,* edited by J. E. Smith and J. D. Lane. Elsevier Biomedical, New York.
12. Brands, B., Thornhill, J. A., Hirst, M., and Gowdey, C. W. (1979): Suppression of food intake and body weight gain by naloxone in rats. *Life Sci.,* 24:1773–1778.
13. Bray, G. A., and York, D. A., (1979): Hypothalamic and genetic obesity in experimental animals: An autonomic and endocrine hypothesis. *Physiol. Rev.,* 59:719–809.
14. Brobeck, J. R., Tepperman, J., and Long, C. N. H. (1943): Experimental hypothalamic hyperphagia in the albino rat. *Yale J. Biol. Med.,* 15:831–853.
15. Brown, S. R., and Holtzman, D. G. (1979): Suppression of deprivation-induced food intake and water intake in rats and mice by naloxone. *Pharmacol. Biochem. Behav.,* 11:567–573.
16. Collier, G. H. (1983): Life in a closed economy: The ecology of learning and motivation. In: *Advances in Analysis of Behavior, Vol. 3: Biological Factors in Learning,* edited by M. D. Zeiler and P. Harzem. Wiley, London *(in press).*
17. Cooper, B. R., Cott, J. M., and Breese, G. R. (1974): Effects of catecholamine depleting drugs and amphetamine on self-stimulation of the brain following various 6-hydroxydopamine treatments. *Psychopharmacologia,* 37:235–248.
18. Cooper, S. J. (1980): Naloxone: Effects of food and water consumption in the non-deprived and deprived rat. *Psychopharmacology,* 71:1–6.
19. Cooper, S. J. (1980): Benzodiazepines as appetite-enhancing compounds. *Appetite,* 1:7–19.
20. Della-Fera, M., Baile, C. A., Schneider, B. S., and Grinker, J. A. (1981): Cholecystokinin antibody injected in cerebral ventricles stimulates feeding in sheep. *Science,* 212:687–689.
21. Deutsch, J. A. (1982): Controversies in food intake regulation. In: *The Neural Basis of Feeding and Reward,* edited by B. G. Hoebel and D. Novin, pp. 137–165. Haer Institute, Brunswick, Maine.
22. Ettenberg, A., Koob, G. F., and Bloom, F. E. (1981): Response artifact in the measurement of neuroleptic-induced anhedonia. *Science,* 213:357–359.
23. Fibiger, H. C., and Phillips, A. G. (1983): Reward, motivation and cognition: Psychobiology of meso-telencephalic dopamine systems. In: *Handbook of Physiology: Intrinsic Regulatory Systems of the Brain,* edited by F. E. Bloom, American Psychiatric Society, Washington, D.C.
24. Franklin, K. B. J. (1979): Catecholamines and self-stimulation: reward and performance effects dissociated. *Pharmacol. Biochem. Behav.,* 11:71–75.
25. Gallistel, C. R. (1975): Motivation as a central organizing process: The psychophysical approach to its functional and neurophysiological analysis. In: *Nebraska Symposium on Motivation, 1974,* edited by J. K. Cole and T. B. Sonderegger, pp. 183–250. University of Nebraska Press, Lincoln, Nebraska.
26. Gallistel, C. R. (1980): *The Organization of Action: A New Synthesis.* Lawrence Erlbaum Associates, Hillsdale, New Jersey.
27. Glimcher, P., Margolin, D., Giovino, A. A., and Hoebel, B. G. (1983): Neurotensin: A new "reward" peptide. *Brain Res. (in press).*
28. Glimcher, P., Giovino, A. A., Margolin, D. H., and Hoebel, B. G. (1983): Endogenous opiate reward induced by an enkephalinase inhibitor, thiorphan injected into the ventral midbrain. *Brain Res., (in press).*

29. Gold, R. M. (1970): Hypothalamic hyperphagia produced by parasagittal knife cuts. *Physiol. Behav.*, 5:23–25.
30. Gold, R. M., Sawchenko, P. E., DeLuca, C., Alexander, J., and Eng, R. (1980): Vagal mediation of hypothalamic obesity, not of supermarket dietary obesity. *Am. J. Physiol.*, 238:R447–R453.
31. Grandison, L., and Guidotti, A. (1977): Stimulation of food intake by muscimol and beta-endorphin. *Neuropharmacology*, 16:533–536.
32. Grossman, S. P. (1960): Eating or drinking elicited by direct adrenergic or cholinergic stimulation of hypothalamus. *Science*, 132:301–302.
33. Hernandez, L., and Hoebel, B. G. (1982): Overeating after midbrain 6-hydroxydopamine: Prevention by central injection of selective reuptake blockers. *Brain Res.*, 245:333–343.
34. Hernandez, L., Parada, M., and Hoebel, B. G. (1983): Amphetamine-induced hyperphagia and obesity caused by intraventricular or lateral hypothalamic injections in rats. *J. Pharmacol. Exp. Therapeutics, (in press)*.
35. Hoebel, B. G. (1965): Hypothalamic lesions by electrocauterization: disinhibition of feeding and self-stimulation. *Science*, 149:452–453.
36. Hoebel, B. G. (1976): Brain-stimulation reward and aversion in relation to behavior. In: *Brain-Stimulation Reward*, edited by A. Wauquier, pp. 335–372. Elsevier, Amsterdam.
37. Hoebel, B. G. (1977): Pharmacologic control of feeding. *Annu. Rev. Pharmacol. Toxicol.*, 17:605–621.
38. Hoebel, B. G. (1977): The psychopharmacology of feeding. In: *Handbook of Psychopharmacology, Vol. 8*, edited by L. L. Iversen, S. D. Iversen, and S. H. Snyder, pp. 55–129. Plenum Press, New York.
39. Hoebel, B. G. (1979): Hypothalamic self-stimulation and stimulation escape in relation to feeding and mating. *Fed. Proc.*, 38:2454–2461.
40. Hoebel, B. G. (1982): The neural and chemical basis of reward: new discoveries and theories in brain control of feeding, mating, aggression, self-stimulation, and self-injection. *J. Sociol. Biol. Structures*, 5:397–408.
41. Hoebel, B. G., Hernandez, L., McLean, S., Stanley, B. G., Aulissi, E. F., Glimcher, P., and Margolin, D. (1982): Catecholamines, enkephalin and neurotensin in feeding and reward. In: *The Neural Basis of Feeding and Reward*, edited by B. G. Hoebel and D. Novin, pp. 465–478. Haer Institute, Brunswick, Maine.
42. Hoebel, B. G., Hernandez, L., Monaco, A. P., and Miller, W. C. (1981): Amphetamine-induced overeating and overweight in rats. *Life Sci.*, 28:77–82.
43. Hoebel, B. G., and Leibowitz, S. F. (1981): Brain monoamines in the modulation of self-stimulation, feeding, and body weight. In: *Brain, Behavior, and Bodily Diseases*, edited by H. Weiner, M. A. Hofer, and A. J. Stunkard, pp. 103–142. Raven Press, New York.
44. Hoebel, B. G., and Novin, D. (1982): *The Neural Basis of Feeding and Reward*. Haer Institute, Brunswick, Maine.
45. Hoebel, B. G., and Teitelbaum, P. (1962): Hypothalamic control of feeding and self-stimulation. *Science*, 135:375–377.
46. Hoebel, B. G., and Teitelbaum, P. (1966): Weight regulation in normal and hypothalamic hyperphagic rats. *J. Comp. Physiol. Psychol.*, 61:189–193.
47. Hoebel, B. G., and Thompson, R. D. (1969): Aversion to lateral hypothalamic stimulation caused by intragastric feeding or obesity. *J. Comp. Physiol. Psychol.*, 68:536–543.
48. Hokfelt, T., Fuxe, U., Goldstein, M., and Johansson, O. (1974): Immunohistochemical evidence for the existence of adrenaline neurons in the rat brain. *Brain Res.*, 66:239–251.
49. Huston, J. P. (1982): Searching for the neural mechanism of reinforcement (of "stamping-in"). In: *The Neural Basis of Feeding and Reward*, edited by B. G. Hoebel and D. Novin, pp. 75–84. Haer Institute, Brunswick, Maine.
50. Iverson, S. D., and Koob, G. F. (1977): Behavioral implications of dopaminergic neurons in the mesolimbic system. In: *Advances in Biochemical Psychopharmacology, Vol. 16*, edited by E. Costa and G. L. Gessa, pp. 209–214. Raven Press, New York.
51. Jalowiec, J. E., Panksepp, J., Zolovick, A. J., Najam, N., and Herman, B. H. (1981): Opioid modulation of ingestive behavior. *Pharmacol. Biochem. Behav.*, 15:477–484.
52. Jhanwar-Uniyal, M., Fleischer, F., Levin, B. E., and Leibowitz, S. F. (1982): Impact of food deprivation on hypothalamic alpha-adrenergic receptor activity and norepinephrine (NE) turnover in rat brain. *Abstr. Soc. Neurosci.*, 8:711.

53. Kalivas, P., Nemeroff, C. B., and Prange, A. J. (1982): Neuroanatomical sites of action of neurotensin. In: *Neurotensin, A Brain and Gastrointestinal Peptide,* edited by C. B. Nemeroff and A. J. Prange, pp. 307–315. Annals of the New York Academy of Sciences, New York, New York.

54. Kissileff, H. R., Pi-Sunyer, F. X., Thornton, J., and Smith, G. P. (1981): C-terminal octapeptide of cholecystokinin decreases food intake in man. *Am. J. Clin. Nutr.,* 34:154–160.

55. Kissileff, H. R., and van Itallie, T. B. (1982): Physiology of the control of food intake. *Ann. Rev. Nutr.,* 2:371–418.

56. Koob, G. F., Riley, S. J., Smith, S. C., and Robbins, T. W. (1978) Effects of 6-hydroxydopamine lesions of the nucleus accumbens septi and olfactory tubercle on feeding, locomotor activity, and amphetamine anorexia in the rat. *J. Comp. Physiol. Psychol.,* 92:917–927.

57. Kulkosky, P. J., Gibbs, J., and Smith, G. P. (1982): Behavioral effects of bombesin administration in rats. *Physiol. Behav.,* 28:505–512.

58. Leibowitz, S. F. (1970): Reciprocal hunger-relating circuits involving alpha- and beta-adrenergic receptors located, respectively, in the ventromedial and lateral hypothalamus. *Proc. Natl. Acad. Sci. U.S.A.,* 67:1063–1070.

59. Leibowitz, S. F. (1975): Amphetamine: Possible site and mode of action for producing anorexia in the rat. *Brain Res.,* 84:160–167.

60. Leibowitz, S. F. (1978): Paraventricular nucleus: A primary site mediating adrenergic stimulation of feeding and drinking. *Pharmacol. Biochem. Behav.,* 8:163–175.

61. Leibowitz, S. F. (1980): Neurochemical systems of the hypothalamus: Control of feeding and drinking behavior and water-electrolyte excretion. In *Handbook of the Hypothalamus, Vol. 3a: Behavioral Studies of the Hypothalamus,* edited by P. J. Morgane and J. Panksepp, pp. 299–437. Marcel Dekker, New York.

62. Leibowitz, S. F. (1982): Hypothalamic catecholamine systems in relation to control of eating behavior and mechanisms of reward. In: *The Neural Basis of Feeding and Reward,* edited by B. G. Hoebel and D. Novin, pp. 241–258. Haer Institute, Brunswick, Maine.

63. Leibowitz, S. F., Arcomano, A., and Hammer, N. J. (1978): Potentiation of eating associated with tricyclic antidepressant drug activation of alpha-adrenergic neurons in the paraventricular hypothalamus. *Prog. Neuropsychopharmacol. Biol. Psychiatry,* 2:349–358.

64. Leibowitz, S. F., and Brown, L. L. (1980): Histochemical and pharmacological analysis of catecholaminergic projections to the perifornical hypothalamus in relation to feeding inhibition. *Brain Res.,* 172:101–113.

65. Leibowitz, S. F., and Hor, L. (1980): Behavioral effect of beta-endorphin (B-EP) and norepinephrine (NE) in the hypothalamic paraventricular nucleus (PVN). *Abstr. Soc. Neurosci.,* 6:318.

66. Leibowitz, S. F., Marinescu, C., and Lichtenstein, S. S. (1982): Continuous and phasic infusion of norepinephrine (NE) into the hypothalamic paraventricular nucleus (PVN) increases daily food intake and body weight in rat. *Abstr. Soc. Neurosci.,* 8:711.

67. Leibowitz, S. F., and Rossakis, C. (1978): Pharmacological characterization of perifornical hypothalamic beta-adrenergic receptors mediating feeding inhibition in the rat. *Neuropharmacology,* 17:691–702.

68. Levin, B. E., Triscari, J., and Sullivan, A. C. (1980): Abnormal sympatho-adrenal function and plasma catecholamines in obese Zucker rats. *Pharmacol. Biochem. Behav.,* 13:107–113.

69. Levine, A. S., Kneip, J., Grace, M., and Morley, J. E. (1983): Effect of centrally administered neurotensin on multiple feeding paradigms. *Pharmacol. Biochem. Behav.,* 18:19–23.

70. Lindvall, O. (1979): Dopamine pathways in the rat brain. In: *The Neurobiology of Dopamine,* edited by A. S. Horn, J. Korf, and B. H. C. Westerink, pp. 319–342. Academic Press, New York.

71. Lucas, K. (1913): Effects of alcohol on the excitation, conduction, and recovery process in nerve. *J. Physiol. (Lond.),* 46:470–505.

72. Lyness, W. H., Friedle, N. M., and Moore, K. E. (1979): Destruction of dopaminergic terminals in nucleus accumbens: Effect on d-amphetamine self-administration. *Pharmacol. Biochem. Behav.,* 11:553–556.

73. Lytle, L. D. (1977): Control of eating behavior. In: *Nutrition and the Brain, Vol. 12,* edited by R. J. Wurtman and J. J. Wurtman, pp. 1–145. Raven Press, New York.

74. Margules, D. L. (1970): Alpha-adrenergic receptors in hypothalamus for the suppression of feeding behavior by satiety. *J. Comp. Physiol. Psychol,* 73:1–12.

75. Margules, D. L., Moisset, B., Lewis, M. J., Shibuya, H., and Pert, C. B. (1978): Beta-endorphin is associated with overeating in genetically obese mice (ob/ob) and rats (fa/fa). *Science,* 202:988–991.
76. Marks-Kaufman, R., and Kanarek, R. B. (1980): Morphine selectively influences macronutrient intake in the rat. *Pharmacol. Biochem. Behav.,* 12:427–430.
77. Marks-Kaufman, R., and Kanarek, R. B. (1981): Modifications of nutrient selection induced by naloxone in rats. *Psychopharmacology,* 74:321–324.
78. McCaleb, M. L., and Myers, R. D. (1980): Cholecystokinin acts on the hypothalamic "norepinephrine system" involved in feeding. *Peptides,* 1:47–49.
79. McLean, S., and Hoebel, B. G. (1982): Opiate and norepinephrine-induced feeding from the paraventricular nucleus of the hypothalamus are dissociable. *Life Sci.,* 31:2379–2382.
80. Miller, N. W. (1960): Motivating effects of brain stimulation and drugs. *Fed. Proc.,* 19:846–854.
81. Mogenson, G. J. (1982): Studies of the nucleus accumbens and its mesolimbic dopaminergic afferents in relation to ingestive behaviors and reward. In: *The Neural Basis of Feeding and Reward,* edited by B. G. Hoebel and D. Novin, pp. 275–288. Haer Institute, Brunswick, Maine.
82. Mogenson, G. J., Jones, D. L., and Yim, C. Y. (1980): From motivation to action: Functional interface between the limbic system and the motor system. *Prog. Neurobiol.,* 14:69–97.
83. Monaco, A. P., Hernandez, L., and Hoebel, B. G. (1981): Nucleus accumbens: Site of amphetamine self-injection, comparison with lateral ventricle. In: *The Neurobiology of the Nucleus Accumbens,* edited by R. B. Chronister, and J. F. DeFrance, pp. 338–343. Haer Institute, Brunswick, Maine.
84. Moore, R. Y., and Bloom, F. E. (1978): Central catecholamine neuron systems: Anatomy and physiology of the dopamine systems. *Annu. Rev. Neurosci.,* 1:129–169.
85. Moore, R. Y., and Bloom, F. E. (1979): Central catecholamine neuron systems: Anatomy and physiology of the norepinephrine and epinephrine systems. *Annu. Rev. Neurosci.,* 2:113–168.
86. Moran, T. H., and Blass, E. M. (1982): Organized response patterns and self-stimulation induced by intrahypothalamic electrical stimulation in 3-day-olds. *The Neural Basis of Feeding and Reward,* edited by B. G. Hoebel and D. Novin, pp. 59–66. Haer Institute, Brunswick, Maine.
87. Morgane, P. J. (1979): Historical and modern concepts of hypothalamic organization and function. In: *Handbook of the Hypothalamus, Vol. 1: Anatomy of the Hypothalamus,* edited by P. J. Morgane and J. Panksepp. pp. 000–000 Marcel Dekker, New York.
88. Morley, J. E., and Levine, A. S. (1982): Opiates, dopamine and feeding. In: *The Neural Basis of Feeding and Reward,* edited by B. G. Hoebel and D. Novin, pp. 499–506. Haer Institute, Brunswick, Maine.
89. Morley, J. E., Levine, A. S., Yim, G. K., and Lowy, M. T. (Submitted): Opioid modulation of appetite.
90. Muehlethaler, M., Gaehwiler, B. H., and Dreifuss, J. J. (1980): Enkephalin-induced inhibition of hypothalamic paraventricular neurons. *Brain Res.,* 197:264–268.
91. Myers, R. D. and McCaleb, M. L. (1980): Feeding: Satiety signal from intestine triggers brain's noradrenergic mechanism. *Science,* 209:1035–1037.
92. Nauta, W. J. H., Smith, G. P., Faull, R. L. M., and Domesick, V. B. (1978): Efferent connections and nigral efferents of the nucleus accumbens septi in the rat. *Neuroscience,* 3:385–401.
93. Nemeraff, C. B., and Prange, A. J. Jr. (1982): Neurotensin, a brain and gastrointestinal peptide. *Annals N.Y. Acad. Sci.,* New York.
94. Neill, D. B., Garr, L. A., Clark, A. S., and Britt, M. D. (1982): "Rate-free" measures of self-stimulation and microinjections: Evidence toward a new concept of dopamine and reward. In: *The Neural Basis of Feeding and Reward,* edited by B. G. Hoebel and D. Novin, pp. 289–298. Haer Institute, Brunswick, Maine.
95. Nicolaidis, S. (1983): *Role of the CNS in the control of metabolism and of feeding.* Third European Winter Conference on Brain Research. Les Arcs, France.
96. Nishino, H., Ono, T., Fukuda, M., and Sasaki, K. (1982): Lateral hypothalamic neuron activity during monkey bar press feeding behavior: Modulation by glucose, morphine and naloxone. In: *The Neural Basis of Feeding and Reward,* edited by B. G. Hoebel and D. Novin, pp. 355–372. Haer Institute, Brunswick, Maine.

97. Olds, M. E. (1979): Hypothalamic substrate for the positive reinforcing properties of morphine in rat. *Brain Res.,* 168:351–360.
98. Olds, M. E. (1979): Self-administration of morphine, levo-phanol, and DALA at hypothalamic and nucleus accumbens self-stimulation sites. *Abstr. Soc. Neurosci.,* 5:535.
99. Oomura, Y. (1980): Input-output organization in the hypothalamus relating to food intake behavior. In: *Handbook of the Hypothalamus, Vol. 2: Physiology of the Hypothalamus,* edited by P. J. Morgane, and J. Panksepp, pp. 557–620. Marcel Dekker, New York.
100. Oomura, Y., Shimizu, N., Miyahara, S., and Hattori, K. (1982): Chemosensitive neurons in the hypothalamus: Do they relate to behavior? In: *The Neural Basis of Feeding and Reward,* edited by B. G. Hoebel and D. Novin, pp. 551–566. Haer Institute, Brunswick, Maine.
101. Ostrowski, N. L., Rowland, N., Foley, T. L., Nelson, J. L., and Reid, L. D. (1981): Morphine antagonists and consummatory behaviors. *Pharmacol. Biochem. Behav.,* 14:549–559.
102. Palacios, J. M., and Khuar, M. J. (1981): Neurotensin receptors are located on dopamine containing neurons in rat midbrain. *Nature,* 294:587–589.
103. Panksepp, J. (1983): Hypothalamic integration of behavior: Rewards, punishments, and related psychological processes. In: *Handbook of the Hypothalamus, Volume 3b: Behavioral Studies of the Hypothalamus,* edited by P. J. Morgane and J. Panksepp, pp. 289–432. Marcel Dekker, New York.
104. Panksepp, J., Pollack, A., Krost, K., Meeker, R., and Ritter, M. (1975): Feeding in response to repeated protamine zinc insulin injections. *Physiol. Behav.,* 14:487–493.
105. Paul, S. M., Hulihan-Giblin, B., and Skolnick, P. (1982): (+)−Amphetamine binding in rat hypothalamus: Relation to anorexic potency of phenylethylamines. *Science,* 218:487–490.
106. Phillips, A. G., and Fibiger, H. C. (1978): The role of dopamine in maintaining intracranial self-stimulation in the ventral tegmentum, nucleus accumbens, and medial prefrontal cortex. *Can. J. Physiol.,* 32:58–66.
107. Phillips, A. G., and LePiane, F. G. (1980): Reinforcing effects of morphine microinjection into the ventral tegmental area. *Pharmacol. Biochem. Behav.,* 12:965–968.
108. Phillips, A. G., Mora, A., and Rolls, E. T. (1981): Intracerebral self-administration of amphetamine by rhesus monkeys. *Neurosci. Lett.,* 24:81–86.
109. Phillips, A. G., Spyraki, C., and Fibiger, H. C. (1982): Conditioned place preference with amphetamine and opiates as reward stimuli: Attenuation by haloperidol. In: *The Neural Basis of Feeding and Reward,* edited by B. G. Hoebel and D. Novin, pp. 455–464. Haer Institute, Brunswick, Maine.
110. Pittman, Q. J., Hatton, J. D., and Bloom, F. E. (1980): Morphine and opioid peptides reduce paraventricular neuronal activity: Studies on the rat hypothalamic slice preparation. *Proc. Natl. Acad. Sci. U.S.A.,* 77:5527–5531.
111. Powley, T. L. (1977): The ventromedial hypothalamic syndrome, satiety, and a cephalic phase hypothesis. *Psychol. Rev.,* 84:89–126.
112. Powley, T. L., Opsahl, C. A., Cox, J. E., and Weingarten, H. P. (1983): The role of the hypothalamus in energy homeostasis. In: *Handbook of the Hypothalamus, Vol. 3a: Behavioral Studies of the Hypothalamus,* edited by P. J. Morgane and J. Panksepp, pp. 211–298. Marcel Dekker, New York.
113. Ritter, R. C., and Epstein, A. N. (1975): Control of meal size by central noradrenergic action. *Proc. Natl. Acad. Sci. U.S.A.,* 72:3740–3743.
114. Roberts, D. C. S., Koob, G. F., Klonoff, P., and Fibiger, H. C. (1980): Extinction and recovery of cocaine self-administration following 6-hydroxydopamine lesions of the nucleus accumbens. *Pharmacol. Biochem. Behav.,* 12:781–787.
115. Rolls, B. J., Rowe, E. A., and Turner, R. C. (1980): Persistent obesity in rats following a period of consumption of mixed, high energy diet. *J. Physiol.,* 298:415–427.
116. Rolls, E. T. (1982): Feeding and reward. In: *The Neural Basis of Feeding and Reward,* edited by B. G. Hoebel and D. Novin, pp. 323–338. Haer Institute, Brunswick, Maine.
117. Rosell, S., Rokaeus, A., Mashford, M. L., Thor, K., Chang, D., and Folkers, K. (1980): Neurotensin as a hormone in man. In: *Neuropeptides and Neural Transmission,* edited by C. A. Marsan and W. Z. Traczyk, pp. 181–189. Raven Press, New York.
118. Rossi, N. A., and Reid, L. D. (1967): Affective states associated with morphine injections. *Physiol. Psychol.,* 4:269–274.
119. Rossier, J., Rogers, J., Shibasaki, T., Guillemin, R., and Bloom, F. E. (1979): Opioid peptide

and alpha-melanocyte-stimulation hormone in genetically obese (ob/ob) mice during development. *Proc. Natl. Acad. Sci. U.S.A.,* 76:2077–2080.

120. Routtenberg, A., editor (1980): *Biology of Reinforcement: Facets of Brain Stimulation Reward.* Academic Press, New York.

121. Rowland, N. E., and Antelman, S. M. (1976): Stress induced hyperphagia and obesity in rats: A possible model for understanding human obesity. *Science,* 191:310–312.

122. Sanger, D. J. (1981): Endorphinergic mechanisms in the control of food and water intake. *Appetite,* 2:193–208.

123. Sawchenko, P. E. (1982): Anatomic relationships between the paraventricular nucleus of the hypothalamus and visceral regulatory mechanisms: Implications for the control of feeding behavior. In: *The Neural Basis of Feeding and Reward,* edited by B. G. Hoebel and D. Novin, pp. 259–274. Haer Institute, Brunswick, Maine.

124. Sclafani, A., Avarich, P. F., and Xenakis, S. (1982): Dopaminergic and endorphinergic mediation of a sweet reward. In: *The Neural Basis of Feeding and Reward,* edited by B. G. Hoebel and D. Novin, pp. 507–516. Haer Institute, Brunswick, Maine.

125. Scalfani, A., and Springer, D. (1976): Dietary obesity in adult rats: Similarities to hypothalamic and human obesity syndromes. *Physiol. Behav.,* 17:461–471.

126. Shizgall, P., Kiss, I., and Bielajew, C. (1982): Psychophysical and electrophysiological studies of the substrate for brain stimulation reward. In: *The Neural Basis of Feeding and Reward,* edited by B. G. Hoebel and D. Novin, pp. 419–430. Haer Institute, Brunswick, Maine.

127. Siggins, G. R. (1981): Catecholamines and endorphins as neurotransmitters and neuromodulators. In: *Regulatory Mechanisms of Synaptic Transmission,* edited by R. Tapia and C. W. Cotman, pp. 1–27. Plenum Press, New York.

128. Simson, E. L., Gold, R. M., Standish, L. J., and Pellett, P. L. (1977): Axon-sparing brain lesioning technique: The use of monosodium-L-glutamate and other amino acids. *Science,* 198:515–517.

129. Siviy, S. M., Calcagnetti, D. J., and Reid, L. D. (1982): Opioids and palatability. In: *The Neural Basis of Feeding and Reward,* edited by B. G. Hoebel and D. Novin, pp. 517–524. Haer Institute, Brunswick, Maine.

130. Smith, G. P., Gibbs, J., and Kulkosky, P. J. (1982): Relationships between brain-gut peptides and neurons in the control of food intake. In: *The Neural Basis of Feeding and Reward,* edited by B. G. Hoebel and D. Novin, pp. 149–166. Haer Institute, Brunswick, Maine.

131. Smith, G. P., Jerome, C., Cushin, B. J., Eterno, R., and Simansky, K. J. (1981): Abdominal vagotomy blocks the satiety effect of cholecystokinin in the rat. *Science,* 213:1036–1037.

132. Stanley, B. G., Eppel, N., and Hoebel, B. G. (1982): Neurotensin injected into the paraventricular hypothalamus suppresses feeding in rats. In: *Neurotensin: A Brain and Gastrointestinal Peptide,* edited by C. B. Nemeroff and A. J. Prange, Jr., pp. 425–427. The New York Academy of Sciences, New York.

133. Stapleton, J. M., Lind, M. D., Merriman, V. J., and Reid, L. D. (1979): Naloxone inhibits diazepam-induced feeding in rats. *Life Sci.,* 24:2421–2426.

134. Steffens, A. B. (1975): Influence of reversible obesity on eating behavior, blood glucose, and insulin in the rat. *Am. J. Physiol.,* 228:1738–1744.

135. Stellar, E. (1954): The physiology of motivation. *Psychol. Rev.,* 61:5–22.

136. Stellar, J. R., and Nelley, S. P. (1982): Reward summation function measurements of lateral hypothalamic stimulation reward: Effects of anterior and posterior medial forebrain bundle lesions. In: *The Neural Basis of Feeding and Reward,* edited by B. G. Hoebel and D. Novin, pp. 431–442. Haer Institute, Brunswick, Maine.

137. Swanson, L. W., Sawchenko, P. E., Berod, A., Hartman, B. K., Helle, K., and Van Orden, L. S. (1981): An immunohistochemical study of the organization of catecholaminergic cells and terminal fields in the paraventricular and supraoptic nuclei of the hypothalamus. *J. Comp. Neurol.,* 196:271–285.

138. Tasaki, I. (1959): Conduction of the nerve impulse. In: *Handbook of Physiology, Section 1, Vol. 1, Chapter 3,* edited by J. Field, H. W. Magoun, and V. E. Hall, Amer. Physiol. Soc., Washington, D.C.

139. Teitelbaum, P. (1982): What is the "zero condition" for motivated behavior? In: *The Neural Basis of Feeding and Reward,* edited by B. G. Hoebel and D. Novin, pp. 7–24. Haer Institute, Brunswick, Maine.

140. Teitelbaum, P., and Epstein, A. N. (1962): The lateral hypothalamic syndrome: Recovery of feeding and drinking after lateral hypothalamic lesions. *Psychol. Rev.,* 69:74–90.

141. Tepperman, F. S., Hirst, M., and Gowdey, C. W. (1981): A probable role for norepinephrine in feeding after hypothalamic injection of morphine. *Pharmacol. Biochem. Behav.,* 15:555–558.

142. Ungerstedt, U. (1971): Adipsia and aphagia after 6-hydroxydopamine induced degeneration of the nigrostriatal dopamine system. *Acta Physiol. Scand. [Suppl.],* 367:95–122.

143. Ungerstedt, U. (1971): Stereotaxic mapping of the monoamine pathways in the rat brain. *Acta Physiol. Scand. [Suppl.],* 367:1–48.

144. Waldbillig, R. J., Bartness, T. J., and Stanley, B. G. (1981): Increased food intake, body weight and adiposity following regional neurochemical depletions of serotonin. *J. Comp. Physiol. Psychol.,* 95:391–405.

145. Waldbillig, R. J., Steel, D. J., and Clemmons, R. M. (1983): Hyperphagia following intra-hypothalamic microinfusion of 5,7-DHT: Potentional modulation of the estrogenic control of feeding. *(In preparation.)*

146. Wasserman, E. M., Gomita, Y., and Gallistel, C. R. (1982): Pimozide blocks reinforcement but not priming from MFB stimulation in the rat. *Pharmacol. Biochem. Behav.,* 17:783–787.

147. Williams, D. J., Crossman, A. R., and Slater, P. (1977): The efferent projections of the nucleus accumbens in the rat. *Brain Res.,* 130:217–227.

148. Wise, R. A. (1982): Common neural basis for brain stimulation reward, drug reward, and food reward. In: *The Neural Basis of Feeding and Reward,* edited by B. G. Hoebel and D. Novin, pp. 445–454. Haer Institute, Brunswick, Maine.

149. Wise, R. A. (1982): Neuroleptics and operant behavior: The anhedonia hypothesis. *Behav. Brain Sci.,* 5:39–87.

150. Wise, R. A. (1983): Brain neuronal systems mediating reward processes. In: *The Neurobiology of Opiate Reward Processes,* edited by J. E. Smith and J. D. Lane, pp. 405–437. Elsevier Biomedical Press, New York.

151. Wise, R. A., and Dawson, V. (1974): Diazepam-induced eating and lever pressing for food in sated rats. *J. Comp. Physiol. Psychol.,* 86:930–941.

152. Wise, R. A., Spindler, J., deWit, H., and Gerber, G. J. (1978): Neuroleptic-induced "anhedonia" in rats: Pimozide blocks reward quality of food. *Science,* 201:262–264.

153. Yeomans, J. S. (1982): The cells and axons mediating medial forebrain bundle reward. In: *The Neural Basis of Feeding and Reward,* edited by B. G. Hoebel and D. Novin, pp. 405–418. Haer Institute, Brunswick, Maine.

154. Yim, G. K. W., Martin, M. T., Davis, J. M., Lamb, D. R., and Malven, P. V. (1982): Opiate involvement in glucoprivic feeding. In: *The Neural Basis of Feeding and Reward,* edited by B. G. Hoebel and D. Novin, pp. 485–498. Haer Institute, Brunswick, Maine.

Eating and Its Disorders, edited by A. J.
Stunkard and E. Stellar. Raven Press,
New York © 1984.

Systems and Interactions: An Approach to the Pharmacology of Eating and Hunger

John E. Blundell

Department of Psychology, University of Leeds, Leeds LS2 9JT, United Kingdom

CONFRONTING A PARADOX

An examination of the field of pharmacology of feeding in animals and man reveals the existence of a paradox. In laboratory studies of experimental animals, hundreds of chemical compounds have been reported to adjust food consumption, and many produce long-term changes in body weight. The most frequent form of adjustment is a reduction in food intake, although a smaller number of chemical agents produce increases. This ready alteration of eating in animals is in contrast to the failure of researchers to produce effective drug treatments for human feeding disorders, particularly obesity. Indeed, in a survey carried out for the FDA in 1972, more than 10,000 patients in some 350 studies were assessed for changes in weight brought about by 11 anorexic compounds (118). The survey concluded that the drugs produced an advantage over placebo of 0.56 lb of weight lost per week, and the reviewer regarded this as clinically trivial. It may be debated whether such weight losses, if maintained for long periods of time, should be regarded as insignificant. However, the studies reviewed in the survey only lasted for a maximum of 20 weeks, and it is known that in the treatment of obesity creating small initial weight losses is not difficult; the problem is to maintain weight loss (31,129). Consequently, in the study of pharmacological inhibition of feeding, researchers are faced with a puzzle: Why can drugs inhibit with ease the food consumption of animals and yet fail to provide effective therapeutic aids in man?

This is not a rhetorical question raised merely for provocation since an inquiry into possible answers leads to a consideration of the methodology of drug administration and the interpretation of behavioral outcomes. Certainly, part of the disparity between animal and human studies can be accounted for by technical and procedural differences. For example, in animal studies, drugs are usually administered to severely food-deprived subjects, while in man this is rarely the case; animals are usually given a single, bland composite diet, whereas human subjects and patients are faced with a wide variety of foods; in animals, high doses of drugs sufficient to produce more than a 50% reduction in consumption are often given, while in man much lower doses are administered. Indeed, in man antiobesity drugs usually produce a fairly mild perturbation of the internal milieu

(28,29,105). If given in doses sufficient to cause the severe physiological disturbances associated with ileo-jejunal by-pass surgery, then drugs would surely bring
about marked changes in eating and body weight. These comments serve to indicate that the quantitative effects of drugs influencing eating depend on the circumstances and procedures operating at the time of administration. This notion
is central to an interpretation of drug action based on interactions.

A SYSTEMS VIEW

Many contemporary views of the control of food intake have developed from
the dual-center theory proposed by Stellar (126) and Brobeck (33) more than 20
years ago. In setting out this theory, Stellar was careful to stress that his use of
the term center implied functional rather than physical localization and that the
functional centers served to integrate multiple physiological factors (sensory and
metabolic) which influenced the motivation to eat. Despite these clear cautions,
many researchers in the pharmacology of feeding have made a literal interpretation of the dual-center idea as a reference to simple switches in the brain controlling the instigation and termination of eating. Drug effects on feeding have
frequently been explained as if they could *only* have arisen by an action at precisely localized neural control sites (see 23 for review). One of the main weaknesses of this view is that it fosters the belief that drugs exert purely quantitative
effects on eating by action on one or the other neural switches. Such a view unnec-
essarily restricts an understanding of the wide variety of effects which drugs may
exert on feeding behavior.

First, Stellar clearly stated that the highly sensitive hypothalamic sites formed
part of a much broader fabric of neural networks which linked limbic and midbrain structures with cortical areas. This concept of a system within the brain is
now more highly developed (see 64; Hoebel, *this volume*). Second, a much
broader system can be envisaged which incorporates the brain as one important
focus (Fig. 1). This system illustrates the interrelationships between behavioral
and physiological processes. Moreover, since shifts in food consumption (increases
or decreases) could arise from pharmacological manipulations at many points in
this system, the interpretation of the effects of drugs on food intake is not often
straightforward. For example, eating may be altered by drugs which act directly
on the brain, on gastrointestinal functions, on fat metabolism, or on energy expenditure. These considerations suggest that a theoretical framework for the interpretation of the mechanism of action of a drug should include reference to processes in the total system involved in feeding responses.

THE SYSTEM IS VULNERABLE

It is clear that the system which controls food consumption involves a complex
network in which metabolic, neural, and hormonal signals are integrated into a
coherent pattern within the physical and social environment in which the organism exists. One purpose of behavioral pharmacology is the use of drugs as tools to

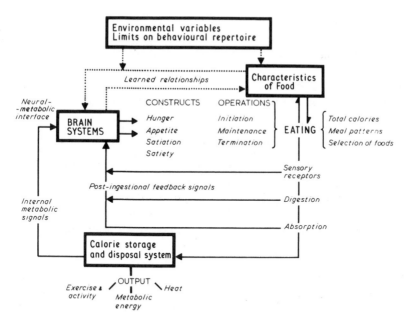

FIG. 1. Conceptualization of the brain as one component of a broad system influencing eating.

explore the relationship between physiological happenings and behavioral events. In this way, drugs can be used rationally as pharmacological scalpels to dissect the components of natural systems governing food consumption and to reveal the properties of this system. However, on the other hand, the system can be disrupted at many loci when a large variety of chemical agents are administered. Many of these agents have no obvious link with the mechanisms controlling food intake, but they adjust the system so as to produce changes in consumption. Acting within the brain, drugs may influence the tendency to feed by actions on a variety of processes. For example, the peripheral signals of the state of the body may be changed so that a certain distortion occurs when metabolic information is translated into neural activity. Additionally, the neural circuits which integrate different sources of information may be affected, sensory systems may be adjusted, and of course drugs may alter the neural coding of the motivational output for eating. Although not frequently mentioned, pharmacological manipulation could adjust in an unknown way the neural mechanisms which mediate in the learned relationships between food stimuli and feeding responses (Fig. 1). The overall complexity of the system and the interactions between various components—physiological and environmental—give the system a vulnerability to intruding agents.

Suppression of Feeding

The most frequent form of adjustment of intake is suppression, and an extensive range of agents have been reported to reduce food intake when injected, usually via a peripheral route, into experimental animals. These agents include neurotransmitters, hormones, amino acids and other precursors of transmitters, peptides and other neuromodulators, metabolites of digestion, certain chemical factions of blood and urine, and many synthetic compounds such as receptor blockers, reuptake blockers, and direct receptor agonists. Table 1 provides some examples of compounds which can reduce food consumption.

Enhancement of Food Intake

It is noticeable that whereas hundreds of chemical agents can reduce food intake, a much smaller number can increase intake. There are probably two major reasons for this discrepancy—one methodological and one theoretical. First, failure to eat is a passive response which may merely indicate a sort of abstinence by default. That is, any interference with the natural expression of behavior may lead to an observed decline in intake (particularly in short tests). Second, it is reasonable to suppose that a number of routes may mediate the inhibition of eating. It follows that the stimulation of any one of these routes by means of a pharmacological agent, centrally or peripherally applied, should inhibit eating. In other words, stimulation of one particular system will be a *sufficient* but not a *necessary* condition for inhibition. However, if one system is blocked by a pharmacological or direct neurochemical treatment, the other systems continue to function and to express an inhibitory capacity. Consequently, it may be difficult to observe an augmentation of food intake through a process of disinhibition. Alternatively, if a pharmacological agent acts on a facilitatory system to induce eating, this will be countered by the functioning inhibitory processes, and only a brief potentiation may be observed.

Despite these limitations, a number of notable instances illustrate that pharmacological agents can produce increases in eating and gains in body weight. Some of these phenomena are both sizable and robust, and they include the effects of clinically important groups of compounds such as antipsychotic drugs, antidepressant drugs, and minor tranquillizers (Table 2). Barbiturates (139) and the two most common categories of minor tranquillizers—meprobamate (123) and the benzodiazepines (98)—give rise to marked increases in food intake in animals tested in a wide variety of situations (35,99). Probably the most dramatic of these effects involves the widely used benzodiazepines, diazepam (Valium®) and chlordiazepoxide (Librium®). These drugs have been found to stimulate eating in mice (123), rats (141), cats (87), and horses (34) with an intensity sometimes bordering on voraciousness. It is possible that benzodiazepines may induce eating indirectly by altering emotional circumstances related to feeding (122,134), although it has been suggested that this class of compounds exerts specific action on central mechanisms influencing hunger or satiety (81). Indeed, it has been suggested that benzodiazepines can be considered as "hungermimetic" agents (42), although as noted previously there appear to be notable differences between various benzodiazepine compounds (54).

TABLE 1. *Various agents which reduce food intake*

Substance	Comments	Authors
Satiated blood	Blood from free-feeding rats. 26 ml injected in 2 ml portions reduces intake of sweetened milk (30 min test) of rats fed 30 min every day for 24 days.	Davis et al., 1967
Satietin	Peptide extracted from human plasma. Injected i.v. or intraventric. reduces food intake of rats deptived for 96 hr.	Knoll, 1980
Anorexic urine	Peptide (pyroGlu-His-Gly OH) extracted from urine of anorexia nervosa patients. Injected to female free-feeding mice. 50% decrease in daily food intake. Effect persists for year.	Trygstad et al., 1978.
Glucose and glycerol	40% glucose by gastric intubation decreases intake at 2, 7, and 24 hr. 40% glycerol decreases intake over 24 hr.	Glick, 1980
(−)-hydroxycitrate	Female rats, daily 3 hr feeding. 0.33 nm/kg. hydroxycitrate orally, twice daily. Decreased intake accounts for reduction in body weight and body lipids.	Sullivan et al., 1974
Threochlorocitrate	Slows gastric emptying. Oral administration reduces food intake in rats and dogs.	Sullivan et al., 1981
Atropine	Rats 17 hr deprived. Sham feeding with gastric fistula (liquid diet). Atropin methyl nitrate (2–250 μg/kg) —dose related decrease in intake.	Lorenz et al., 1978
Epinephrine/norepinephrine	Rats, high-carbohydrate diet for 1 hr/day. Epinephrine—0.1, 0.15, and 0.2 mg/kg. Norepinephrine—0.1, 0.15 mg/kg. 5 min before. 0.15 dose reduces intake by 71% and 34%, respectively.	Russek et al., 1967
Amphetamine (A)/mazindol (M)	Rats, 6 hr feeding per day, 2 hr test. Drugs given immediately before. A—1.25 mg/kg and M—7.5 mg/kg—effects blocked by ventral noradrenergic bundle lesions.	Samanin et al., 1980

TABLE 1. *Various agents which reduce food intake (continued)*

Substance	Comments	Authors
Mazindol, lisuride, piribidel, nomifensine, apomorphine	Rats, 4 hr per day feeding. Drugs injected i.p. at various times before start of 1 hr test. All drugs reduce intake—effect blocked by pimozide.	Carruba et al., 1980
Serotonin (5-HT)	Zucker fat and lean rats, VMH-lesioned rats. 14 g food/day between 9–2 5-HT—12.5 mg/100g—5 min prior to 2 hr test. Decreased eating in all groups.	Bray and York, 1972
Tryptophan (5-HTP)	50 mg/kg tryptophan i.p. Rats-eatometer-Noyes pellets. Free-feeding rats—decrease in meal size and 24 hr intake. 16 hr deprivation—decrease in size of first large meal and increase in postmeal interval.	Latham and Blundell, 1979
5-hydroxytryptophan	Rats 18 hr deprived 5-HTP—30/60/90 mg/kg i.p.—dose related decrease. Freefeeding with eatometer, 30 mg/kg decreases meal size and 24 hr intake.	Blundell and Latham, 1980
Fenfluramine, quipazine, ORG 6582, m—CPP (5-HT agonists and uptake blockers)	Rats, 4 hr feeding per day. Injections immediately before 1 hr test. All agents reduce intake.	Samanin et al., 1979, 1980 Garattini, 1978
Estrogens	Ovariectomized female rats—unrestricted access to food. Estradiol benzoate—2.0 μg and estrone benzoate—20.0 μg reduce daily intake.	Wade, 1975
Cholecystokinin	Rats—5.5 hr deprivation. CCK—2.5–40 Ivy Dog U/kg (15 min before test) decreases intake in first 30 min.	Gibbs, Young and Smith 1973
Bombesin	Rats—15 hr deprivation, liquid food sham feeding. Synthetic bombesin (2–256 μg/kg, decreases intake in first 15 min of 60 min test.	Martin and Gibbs, 1980
Enterogastrone	Mice—17 hr deprivation, liquid diet. Hormone given 10–15 min. after onset of feeding (0.1–1.0 mg) decreases intake for 30–60 min.	Schally et al., 1967

Compound	Description	Reference
Somatostatin (SS)	Rats deprived early in light part of cycle. 4/5 hr later given i.p. 1 μg SS. Decreases intake in 30 min test.	Lotter et al., 1981
Thryrotropin releasing hormone (TRH)	Rats, TRH (10–20 μg/kg i.p.) 20 hr deprivation, 1 hr test, 30 min data given. Injection immediately before test reduces intake.	Vogel et al., 1979
Calcitonin	Rats—25–50 U/kg decrease 24 hr food intake. Rats given 30 min period of eating/day—maximum inhibition when 12.5 U/kg given 4.5/8.3 hr before.	Freed et al., 1979
Prostaglandins	$F_{2\alpha}$—1 mg/kg i.p. to rats fed for 2 hr/day. Suppressed intake for 30 min. Also effective in satiated and partially satiated rats.	Doggett and Jawaharlal, 1977a
Prostaglandin precursors	Rats 22 hr deprived. Arachidonic, linolenic, and linoleic acids decrease intake for 30–60 min. Effect blocked by indomethacin and paracetamol.	Doggett and Jawaharlal
Cocaine and coca extracts	Rats 1 hr feeding/day on ground chow. Cocaine 3.45–27.6 mg/kg i.p. or p.o. reduces intake. Effect also of chloroform extraction layer of coca.	Bedford et al., 1980
	Rats 5 hr feeding period. Cocaine—10/15/15 mg/kg i.p. Dose-dependent decrease in first hours—no effect on total intake.	Balopode et al., 1979
Muscimol	Rats—condensed milk for 30 min each day. 0.5/1.0/2.0 mg/kg muscimol—dose related decrease.	Cooper et al., 1980
Naloxone	Rats 48 hr deprivation, 2 hr measurement. Food intake reduced by naloxone 1.0–10.0 mg/kg. No effect in mouse (24 hr deprived)	Holtzman, 1974
Tetrahydrocannabinol (THC)	Male rats, 6 hr feeding/day. THC (2.5 and 5.0 mg/kg) markedly decreases food intake in first 2 hr with carry over to next 4 hr.	Sofia and Barry, 1974

TABLE 2. *Various agents which increase food intake*

Substance	Comments	Author
Hyperphagic urine	Peptide fraction extracted from urine of anorexia nervosa patients. During posttreatment period mice overate and became obese.	Trygstad et al., 1978
Chloralose	Male rats, powdered diet.α-chloralose 2.5–50 mg/kg i.p. Increased intake at 15 and 25. Latency decreased during dark phase.	Booth and Nicholls, 1974
Meprobamate (M)	Rats—22 hr deprivation/2 hr feeding—isolated. M—100 mg/kg, oral administration, 17% increase in intake. Barbiturate and chlordiazepoxide also effective.	Bainbridge, 1968
Barbiturates	Male rats, fully satiated, 1 hr intake. Increased intake with sodium pentobarbital (9.5 mg/kg) and phenobarbital (40 mg/kg).	Watson and Cox, 1976
Benzodiazepines	Male rats, mice—liquid food. Diazepam, chlordiazepoxide, oxazepam, nitrazepam, lorazepam all increase latency. All decrease latency (except nitrazepam). Also barbiturates, meprobamate.	Soubrié et al., 1975
Neuroleptics Chlorpromazine (CPZ)	Rats—free feeding. CPZ 4 mg/kg s.c. or intragastric increases food intake on first day. So called *first day hyperphagia*.	Robinson et al., 1975
Promazine	0.5 mg/kg (250 mg) i.v. to adult horse. Eating within 30 min and increase in 1 hr intake.	Brown et al., 1976
Clozapine	Male rats, free-feeding—pellet food. Intragastric clozapine (10–20 mg/kg) increases intake in 2 hr test immediately after injection.	Antelman et al., 1977
5-HT antagonists Cyproheptadine	Rats, overnight deprivation, 6 hr feeding—continuous recording. 12.5 mg/kg increases size and duration of first meal.	Baxter et al., 1970
Methysergide	Rats, 16 hr deprivation then feed for 1 hr. Methysergide 2.0 mg/kg s.c. increases intake in following hours.	Blundell and Leshem, 1974

WA 335-BS	Cats 2.5 hr test. 2.5 mg/kg. p.o. increases intake.	Kahling et al., 1975
Opiate agonists	Free-feeding rats. Ethylketocyclazocine (Kappa receptor) 0–1/10.0 mg/kg and the enkephalin analogue. RX 783030 (mu receptor). Increase eating at 1, 2, 4 hr.	Sanger and McCarthy, 1981
Clonidine	Rats, *ad lib.* food—measures at 6, 24 hr. 300 µg/kg for more than 3 days increase eating at 6 hr period.	Akinson et al., 1978
	Rats—choice of diets. Tests in dark period—50 min, 60 min, 75 min. Clonidine 25, 50, 100 µg/kg i.p. increases food intake (and protein).	Mauron et al., 1980
	Stumptail macaques. 0.1 mg/kg intramuscularly for 7 days increased daily food intake.	Schlemmer et al., 1979
Yohimbine	Rats, diet choice. Mild (1 hr) deprivation before the dark period. Yohimbine (10 mg/kg) massive increase in intake during 50 min test.	Mauron et al., 1980
Insulin	Rats, protamine zinc insulin, 2 s.c. injections/day. 10 U/day doubles intake on chow and high fat diet.	Panksepp et al., 1975
2-deoxy-d-glucose	Rabbit, free-feeding, intravenous administration. Decreased latency to first meal and three-fold increase in food intake in first hour.	Gonzalez and Novin, 1974
5-thio-glucose	Rats, nondeprived, 6 hr test period. Intracardiac infusion. 5-TG increased intake at third of dose of 2-DG.	Susser and Ritter, 1980
Androgens	Gonadectomized male rats, free feeding, s.c. injections of testosterone, dihydrotestosterone, androstenidione daily for 10 days increase food intake and body weight.	Rowland et al., 1980
Formamidines	Rats. Formamidine (Amitraz®) and chlordimeform, normally pesticides, increase intake during daytime when potential to feed is low.	Pfister et al., 1978
Caffeine	Male mice, day time feeding, 2 hr test. Increased intake with 10, 20, 40 mg/kg	Dobrzanski and Doggett, 1976

Although not widely recognized, benzodiazepine-induced eating also occurs in man (62), and both chlordiazepoxide and diazepam have been reported to bring about increases in appetite and weight gain apparently unrelated to improvements in mental state (51). In addition, obesity in psychiatric hospital populations maintained on major tranquillizers is well known and considered to be a serious complication of drug therapy (1,65). Instances of severe weight gain are known to occur with the use of phenothiazines and butyrophenones linked to an increase in appetite (103). It has also been reported that patients who gain weight on phenothiazine medication display a markedly increased rate of eating (29). These observations are consistent with the results of animal studies showing changes in food intake following treatment with chlorpromazine (101,127). In addition, weight gain can occur following lithium treatment (135) and with amitryptiline therapy (96), an effect which seems to be associated with a preference for carbohydrates (see 28,89 for review).

A further class of compounds believed to increase food intake and weight gain are serotonergic antagonists. For example, the serotonin (and histamine) antagonist cyproheptadine (188) has been said to increase appetite in asthmatic children (11), in underweight adults (91), and in a patient with anorexia nervosa (10); it has also been reported to increase both weight and height (67). Although it has been suggested that cyproheptadine influences food intake only under special experimental conditions, definite increases in food consumption (8) and in body weight (58) have been demonstrated in rats. Taken together, these experiments illustrate that pharmacological manipulations not only suppress food intake but also lead to its enhancement.

Ambivalent Drug Effects on Food Intake

For more than 40 years, researchers have tacitly regarded amphetamine as the classic anorexic drug. It is of course true that amphetamine can reduce food intake, but in other domains of research, locomotor activity and stereotypy have been considered as the fundamental responses to amphetamine administration (e.g., 44). Moreover, it is obvious that amphetamine has an effect on a wide variety of physiological and behavioral parameters (see 43). However, in recent years evidence has revealed that amphetamine does not invariably produce a consistent effect on food consumption. For example, in deprived rats amphetamine usually increases the rate of eating while decreasing total food intake (e.g. 22). More importantly, amphetamine has been shown to produce paradoxical increases in food consumption. This has been observed when very low doses of the drug are administered to mice (48) or rats (19), that have not been subjected to usual food-deprivation regimes. In addition, this phenomenon has been shown to occur in cats (143) and rats (128) that have been subjected to sedating hypothalamic lesions, and it has occasionally been reported in food-deprived animals (66). Table 3 shows certain other agents whose effect on food intake varies with particular conditions. Consequently, in analysing a drug's action on feeding, it is necessary to

TABLE 3. *Agents producing equivocal effects*

Substance	Comments	Authors
Amphetamine	Incidental finding. Rats, 48 hr deprived, low dose (0.3 mg/kg) increased intake, higher doses gave anorexia.	Holtzman, 1974
	Male mice, free feeding. 0.5–1.0 mg/kg s.c. (2 hr test) decrease intake during nighttime, increase during day.	Dobrzanski and Doggett, 1976
	Rats, free feeding, eatometer; 1.0 mg/kg decreased intake over 24 hr; low dose (0.125 mg/kg) increased intake.	Blundell and Latham, 1978
	Zucker obese and lean rats. Liquid diet of sweet condensed milk. Low dose (1.5 mg/kg) increased daily intake of lean rats. High dose no effect.	Grinker et al., 1980
Apomorphine (A)	Rats either deprived (20 hr) or satiated (food removed for 4 hr then 1 hr feeding on sweet mash). A—0.02–0.6 mg/ml i.p. (1 ml/kg). Decrease under deprivation, increase under satiation.	Eichler and Antelman, 1977
Morphine (M)	M—1, 3, 10, 30 mg/kg. Rats deprived (24 hr) or free feeding. 10 and 30 dose reduce intake in deprived rats. Increase in satiated rats at 24 hr after injection.	Sanger and McCarthy, 1980
Bicuculline	Rats, intraventricular injection; 4 hr feeding regimen intake decreased. Free feeding, increase in 1 hr intake.	Olgiati et al., 1980

interpret not only increases or decreases in intake but also circumstances under which drugs may give rise to both effects.

INTERPRETATION OF DRUG ACTIONS

The sheer bulk of data on the effect of drugs on food intake, some of which is set out above, suggests that this research field is in a healthy state of development. However, this proliferation in numbers may be misleading for, as in other areas of psychopharmacology, it is relatively easy to obtain statistically significant effects by administering drugs, and consequently it is easy to demonstrate some relationship between a drug and food consumption. It is worth noting that not all occurrences of such events elucidate the action of a drug or the operation of systems controlling feeding. How is it possible to make sense of the numbers? Indeed, the problematic issue in this field is to provide appropriate interpretations for the ever-increasing number of grams of food eaten or left unconsumed by animals after drug treatment (15). The argument presented here is that it is possible to develop a cohesive theoretical framework to improve understanding of the pharmacological manipulations of hunger and eating. The argument is based on the following three major themes.:

1. Feeding is an expression of a total system rather than particular specialized physiological elements, although these elements may contribute to the final outcome (see above).

2. Explanatory power can be enhanced by a close examination of the structure of behavior (feeding patterns and preferences) and subjective experiences (feelings of hunger, fullness, and satisfaction) which occur in close association with eating (12,15). Emphasis on structure draws attention to the qualitative, rather than quantitative, features of eating which give character to ingestive behavior and illuminates the distinction between food intake—usually assessed by measuring the weight of food consumed—and feeding behavior which can only be understood through a close analysis of the topography of the feeding response. It follows that it is probably inadvisable to treat behavior as a unidimensional phenomenon in which only the total amount of behavior is measured. This caution has been expressed elsewhere (16,68), and it is worth considering the extent to which our understanding of certain other vital activities such as sleep, sexual behavior, and agonistic behavior have been enhanced by an examination of qualitative aspects. For example, although the total duration of sleep is often measured, it is the structure of sleep and the arrangement of stages which provide the most detailed explanations (69). Moreover, the effects of drugs on sleep are often described in terms of the adjustment of sleep stages. Similarly, an account of pharmacological actions on eating can be enriched by a description of qualitative aspects such as selection of commodities and the temporal pattern of feeding. Additionally, subjective experiences following drug administration can be examined to a greater degree than the measured intensity of global hunger feelings. The structure of conscious experiences can be analyzed as changes in food preference, perceived

bodily sensations, assessed intensity of sensory aspects of foods, and the temporal profile of these parameters (18).

3. The argument promotes a movement away from the notion of simple cause-effect relationships underlying the control of feeding and the design of experiments involving pharmacological agents (16). This strategy is in keeping with the encouragement which Waddington (137) has given to scientists to abandon the study of rigid causes and effects and instead to interpret the world in terms of interacting processes. Indeed, feeding behavior stands as a classic example of chains of interactions which only arbitrarily can be segmented into cause-response units.

Taken together, these themes have implications both for the design of drug studies and for the interpretation of pharmacological effects on feeding.

INTERACTIONS AND TRANSACTIONS

Eating is carried out by organisms, some of which are people, and eating is an activity which links alterations in a physiological domain with events taking place in a domain beyond the skin. The particular patterns of feeding observed at any time will represent an interaction between two constellations of stimuli (12,104). Figure 2 draws attention to the fact that feeding depends not only on the neurochemical and metabolic state but also on environmental features such as the taste, texture, novelty, accessibility and choice of food, and on other environmental features including the presence of other organisms. Moreover, subjective experiences or cognitions surrounding feeding can similarly be regarded as being constructed out of physiological signals and the characteristics of the external environment (25). Reynolds (100) has referred to these cognitions as culturally defined knowledge entering the mind to give contours to the world, thus making sense of phys-

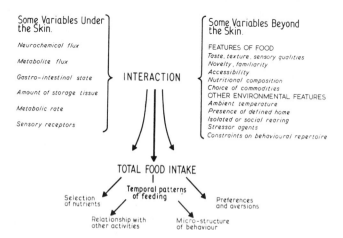

FIG. 2. Feeding behavior expressed as the outcome of an interaction between internal and external variables.

iological functioning. Contrary to the opinion popularly held that hunger is a reflection of bodily depletion, this view suggests that subjectively felt hunger may arise from nonphysiological happenings such as the appearance of food stimuli, the passage of time since a previous meal, or environmental cues indicating that hunger is an appropriate verbal label to attach to the current behavioral actions. In this way, reported hunger indicates one way of making sense of, or giving coherence to, the present behavioral state.

The notion of psychological states arising from interactions is not new, and the concept has been invoked to account for a varied range of phenomena. For example, at the most general level Lewin (77) regarded all behavior as a function of person-environment interactions, while Murray (90) argued that personality could be understood as the resultant of the confrontation between needs (in the individual) and press (in the environment). More recently, the usefulness of adopting an interactional approach to personality has received further attention (53,73). Elsewhere, emotional states (114) and anxiety in particular (124) have been considered as the outcome of interactions between internal conditions (needs or arousal level) and external events. In educational research, intellectual performance has been shown to depend on aptitude-treatment interactions (45,46). For psychosis, the widely encountered diathesis (constitutional disposition)-stress (adverse environmental circumstances) model (106) is supported by the notions of schizotypy, schizotoxia, and schizophrenia (86). A similar line of thinking has been proposed for eating control with the pathological condition of obesity at one time viewed as a consequence of the dominance of behaviour by salient external stimuli (112,113).

Many of these interactional views embody the idea that behavior results from a collision between internal and external forces with behavior being dominated by the strongest force arising out of the fragments of the condition. However, for feeding the interaction between internal and external events can be better interpeted as a rational relationship. Indeed, feeding behavior represents a particularly intimate form of interaction between organisms and their environments, for it involves consumption of part of the environment which in turn forms part of the organism and subsequently influences the intensity of the interaction. Accordingly, it seems appropriate to regard this process as a transaction. Consequently when drugs are administered to organisms (animal or human), they do not simply activate a specific set of receptors which induce specific responses, but they intervene into a complex transactional fabric. Perturbation of this dynamic system by a drug may adjust the network of interactions and lead to unanticipated outcomes.

CASE STUDIES OF DRUG-SYSTEM INTERACTIONS

Inspection of the recent literature on drugs and feeding, together with recent clinical and experimental findings from the author's laboratory, reveals a number of instances in which the alteration of some variable leads to a modification of drug action. Sometimes the modification is slight, while on other occasions there is a complete reversal of the drug's effect. Almost all of these phenomena are counterintuitive and could not have been predicted on the basis of known capacities of the drugs.

The Anorexic and Orexic Action of Amphetamine

Although amphetamine is the classic anorexic drug, locomotor activity and stereotopy have been considered its fundamental behavioral responses. Accordingly, there is no *prima facie* reason for believing that the decrease in food intake brought about by amphetamine is invariably achieved through an interaction with some primitive system which serves to match food consumption to nutritional requirements. Moreover, in recent years evidence has revealed that amphetamine does not invariably produce a consistent effect on parameters of food consumption. For example, in deprived rats amphetamine usually increases the rate of eating while decreasing total food intake (19,22). More importantly, amphetamine has been shown to produce paradoxical increases in food intake (see above). The explanation favored to account for these unexpected results implicates an intervening construct such as arousal or activation. Consequently, the effect of amphetamine on feeding will vary according to the internal state of the organism. This idea is quite similar to that put forward by Eichler and Antelman (52) to explain how apomorphine could give rise to feeding or anorexia depending on the nutritional status of the animal.

Amphetamine also has ambivalent effects in various other situations. For example, the drug normally antagonizes eating produced by electrical stimulation of the hypothalamus (125,132,142) but fails to block eating induced by certain forms of stress (3) believed to resemble brain stimulation (71). Additionally, amphetamine antagonizes eating induced by 2-deoxy-d-glucose but does not affect eating stimulated by insulin (36). This mixed array of effects is in keeping with interactions which have been observed between various behavioral measures of amphetamine's actions and deprivation conditions (40) and arena size (39).

What is the most appropriate explanation for the enhancement and suppression of food intake brought about by amphetamine under different circumstances? The model in Fig. 3 shows how different doses of amphetamine could give rise to varied or even opposite effects depending on the value of some state of the organism labeled construct x. At the present time it is not necessary to seek a deeper identity for this construct; although since the strongest evidence for contrasting behavioral actions is found with deprivation/satiation and hypothalamic damage, it is tempting to suggest that x represents some central arousal state embodied in catecholaminergic systems.

This explanation suggests that the effects of amphetamine on feeding are influenced by an interaction of the drug with internal systems only obliquely related to a nutritional control system. Even if amphetamine does exert a direct effect on endogenous neurochemical systems controlling eating (17,75) or some high-affinity hypothalamic receptor site (95), the final effect on eating will depend on an interaction with the state of the overall system.

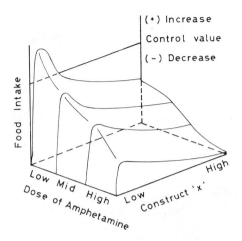

FIG. 3. Model to account for the orexic and anorexic actions of amphetamine. The final outcome is determined by the dose of drug administered and the value of certain other factors (labeled as construct *x*) such as deprivation state, level of arousal, etc.

Antidepressant Drugs and Food Palatability

Many reports on the use of antidepressant drugs (particularly amitriptyline) in clinical practice have reported that such compounds can lead to *weight gains* associated with a craving for carbohydrates (4,56,96,140,140a). Paradoxically, in animal studies the administration of amitriptyline has been associated with a decrease in food intake and a suppression of body weight (93). This discrepancy between the results of animal and human studies is itself interesting and may represent a type of drug-species interaction. This phenomenon is not unusual in the field of psychopharmacology and feeding (see above) and a similar discrepancy exists with regard to neuroleptics (antipsychotic drugs) and food intake (29). However, it is possible that the differences between the animal and human studies does not reflect a true species difference but depends on procedural variables associated with drug administration and the measurement of intake. For example, most pharmacological studies on food intake in animals are characterized by three particular experimental conditions: food-deprivation schedules, short measuring intervals, and high drug doses (17). These conditions are not normally encountered in studies in man. In addition, the quality of the diet needs to be considered, since animals are normally maintained on one single food (often a bland composite diet), whereas man eats an interesting and varied diet. However, when laboratory animals are given access to a range of highly palatable foods, hyperphagia occurs, followed by a rapid rise in body weight (117). Taken together, the combination of dietary differences, food deprivation, high doses, and short measurement periods could account for the observed differences between the effects of antidepressants in animals and humans. Accordingly, a study was designed to investigate the effects of antidepressant drugs on food intake in animals under conditions normally associated with human feeding viz. low drug doses, free access to food, repeated dosing, and opportunity to eat highly palatable foods (a cafeteria diet). The drugs chosen for study were amitriptyline, aloproclate, and zimelidine, all of which block the uptake of monoamines, although with different potencies (78).

The results of the study revealed that the drugs had quite different potencies to adjust food consumption of the bland diet or the array of palatable foods. However, the most marked and curious effects were observed for aloproclate. Figure 4 indicates that this drug increased the daily food intake of animals fed laboratory chow but decreased intake of the palatable foods. Zimelidine showed a similar but less noticeable tendency, whereas amitriptyline exerts equal but small effects on both diets. These findings indicate first that different antidepressant drugs can be expected to exert differing effects on food intake and body weight. This family of compounds is actually a heterogenous group of chemicals with differing neurochemical profiles and distinguishable behavioral actions. Second, and clearly demonstrated by the results with alaproclate, the action of the drug may interact with the sensory qualities of the diet. This interaction may actually give rise to an

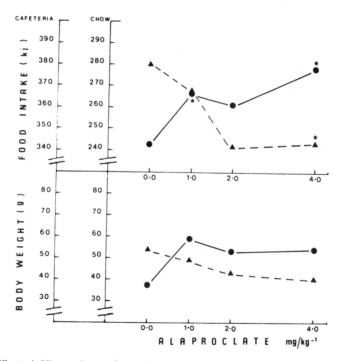

FIG. 4. Effect of different doses of an antidepressant drug on food intake and body weight of animals fed a cafeteria diet *(triangles)* or laboratory chow *(circles)*. The doses were administered daily for 3 weeks. Food intake values show average daily intakes (sampled at weekly periods) and the lower panel indicates body weight changes over the course of the 3 week period of drug administration.

amplification of eating or a suppression. Consequently, taste and textural qualities of food play an important role in the overall feeding system and may exert unexpected effects on pharmacological manipulations.

Anorexic Action and the Development of Obesity

In the investigation described above, a highly palatable diet was offered to rats to induce hyperphagia. Rats maintained on such a diet become obese. This dietary-induced obesity can be used as a model to test the anorexic and weight-reducing properties of antiobesity compounds. Additionally, it is of interest to investigate whether appetite-suppressant drugs have similar effects if given during the dynamic phase of obesity development (from the commencement of exposure to the palatable diet) and the static phase (once a plateau level of body weight has been reached). To investigate this possibility two anorexic compounds (actually DL-fenfluramine and the D-isomer alone) were administered daily over long periods of time to rats during the early development of obesity or after a large increase in body fat had been acquired. Drugs were also administered to control animals maintained on a normal laboratory diet. Table 4 indicates a number of interesting interactive effects. First, the drugs had a much more potent weight-reducing action in the fat animals than in the rats rapidly gaining weight. Second, the two drugs had equal suppressive actions for animals fed laboratory chow. Third, during the dynamic phase the *dl* form was significantly more active than the *d*-isomer, whereas the opposite tendency was observed during the static phase. Fourth, during the dynamic phase, the *dl* form exerted a significantly more potent effect on weight with the palatable food than with the chow diet. Taken together, these findings indicate that the effect of an antiobesity drug can be influenced both by the sensory qualities of the available food and by the stage of development of obesity.

TABLE 4. *Effect of the DL and D forms of an anorexic drug on body weight loss during the dynamic and plateau phases of dietary-induced obesity*[a]

	Phase of obesity development			
	Dynamic		Plateau	
Form of drug	D	DL	D	DL
Palatable diet	0.59	1.03[b]	2.57	2.22
Laboratory chow	0.60	0.63	0.76	0.73

[a]The figures in the body of the table are standardized values which represent the amount of weight loss in grams for every milligram of drug administered. Data for nonobese animals (fed laboratory chow) are also shown.
[b]$p < 0.05$, see text.

Pharmacological Action and Macronutrient Selection

Until quite recently, the testing of anorexic drugs was invariably carried out on rats given only a supply of laboratory chow (a balanced diet containing the major macronutrients protein, carbohydrate, and fat, plus essential vitamins and minerals). However, following the development of a hypothesis linking brain aminergic mechanisms to dietary intake of protein and carbohydrate (see Wurtman and Wurtman, *this volume*), pharmacological experiments began to be carried out on animals offered a choice of diets varying in macronutrient concentration (126,144). Interestingly, drugs which exerted a specific effect on serotoninergic neurotransmission tended to suppress carbohydrate intake more than protein consumption—an action which is usually labeled a protein-sparing effect (145). On the other hand, a drug like amphetamine, which acts mainly on the catecholamines noradrenaline and dopamine, tended to suppress protein intake (25,85). These findings indicate that the suppressive action of an anorexic agent on food consumption can be modified by the nutrient composition of the available diet. Moreover, this interesting interaction can be modulated by a further dietary dimension. If diets of similar nutrient composition are presented to rats in different physical forms—for example as a powder, in granulates, or a gel—then the action of an anorexic drug can be significantly modified (16,85).

Hunger Suppression and Eating

All of the above examples of interactions have been drawn from experiments on animals. However, similar effects do occur in man. For example, the preferential action of drugs on intake of specific macronutrients has been observed in short-term (28) and long-term studies (146). In addition, in man specific interactive effects involving subjective experiences can be demonstrated which are difficult to reveal in animals even if similar feelings exist. One example concerns the subjective experience of hunger. It has been demonstrated many times that anorexic drugs reduce subjective feelings of hunger and partially inhibit food consumption (105,119). The close association between these two effects and the measured correlation between them has suggested that the reduction in hunger causes the inhibition of eating. In an attempt to examine this causal relationship, subjects were given one or two different anorexic drugs (amphetamine or fenfluramine) and then ate a test meal. Before the meal started and periodically throughout the meal, subjects were asked to make ratings of the subjective hunger feelings (together with other sensations). The results revealed a curious and unexpected profile of hunger intensity. Before the meal began, both drugs displayed a marked capacity to suppress ratings of hunger in keeping with their anorexic capacity. It was expected that this initial low value of hunger would continue on a lowered trajectory during the course of the meal. However, as soon as eating commenced hunger was reinstated to control levels and remained at or above this value throughout the meal. This finding suggests that if the hunger-suppressant effect of anorexic drugs is important for the inhibition of eating, then the action must be limited to the premeal period. More importantly for the present discussion, the results indicate that the hunger-reducing property of anorexic drugs depends on whether the person is eating or not. This interaction between hunger sensations, eating, and drug action remains to be further investigated, but the findings so far revealed could not have been predicted on the basis of prior knowledge and may aid in explaining the rather weak therapeutic effect of anorexic agents in man.

IMPLICATIONS

The evidence quoted in the preceding section illustrates that drug effects can be modulated by a variety of conditions including intrinsic factors such as body weight and internal state of arousal, and extrinsic factors such as palatability, nutrient content, and physical state of the diet. In certain cases, the action of a drug may be reversed. Some of these effects have been demonstrated to occur in man, and further investigation will surely reveal an additional constellation of modulating influences involving cognitive mechanisms similar to those which underlie placebo effects. These findings do not mean that drug effects on feeding are either capricious or totally unpredictable, but they do indicate than an interpretation of pharmacological manipulations should extend beyond identified central mechanisms and embrace broader aspects of physiological-environmental interactions. Moreover, these findings do not in any way detract from the validity of specified neurochemical mechanisms of feeding (64; Hoebel, *this volume*) with which anorexic drugs are believed to engage. However, the action of drugs on these mechanisms probably should be interpreted with reference to the total system within which the brain mechanisms are embedded. Perhaps, instead of considering drug actions on target receptors as causes of behavior, this activity should be regarded as initiating dispositions toward actions; the ultimate behavioral outcome being modified according to the state of the system. Moreover, it should be kept in mind that this system extends beyond the boundaries of the body and incorporates the proximal social and physical environment.

Can the findings and arguments set out above go any way toward resolving the paradox outlined at the beginning of this chapter? Certainly, it seems that differences between drug effects in animals and man become understandable when a systems view is adopted and when neurochemical activity is interpreted against a background of interacting variables. Moreover, a systems approach is useful in another way. One problem in the field of behavioral pharmacology of feeding concerns the interpretation of unexpected effects on feeding and body weight of drugs specifically designed to act on mechanisms controlling nutritional intake, i.e., anorexic and orexic compounds. However, another problem—more pervasive and perhaps of greater social concern—implicates the many documented and unwanted adjustments in eating and body weight which are brought about by drugs administered for some purpose quite unrelated to nutrition. Such effects can be brought about by all common classes of psychotropic drugs including minor tranquillizers and hypnotics, antidepressants, and antipsychotic agents. Most of these drugs bring about an increase in food intake and, therefore, exacerbate the social problem of obesity. It is unlikely, although not impossible, that these drugs act on the neurochemical feeding sensitive zones within the hypothalamus. A more likely explanation is that these agents create perturbations within the feeding system which permits a more pronounced expression of the drive to eat. Perhaps this systemic effect may interact with some mild action at hypothalamic sites (76). Further research will undoubtedly disclose the disturbing effects of a wide variety of pharmaceutical agents on eating and body weight. However, the approach set out in this chapter serves to emphasize that the feeding system is not reserved for those agents specifically designed for it and intended to act on it. The system is vulnerable to nonspecific influences, and this vulnerability suggests the adoption of a cautious and more rigorous approach to the use of pharmaceutical agents lacking any intended action on eating or hunger.

ACKNOWLEDGMENTS

I am very grateful to Peter Rogers, Andy Hill, and Tim Kirkham for the discussion of the theoretical aspects of this chapter and to Mavis Walton for help with the preparation of the text.

REFERENCES

1. Amdisen, A. (1964): Drug-produced obesity. Experiences with chlorpromazine, perphenazine and clopenthixol. *Dan. Med. Bull.,* 11:182–189.
2. Antelman, S. M., Black, C. A. and Rowland, N. E. (1977): Clozapine induces hyperphagia in undeprived rats. *Life Sci.,* 21:1747–1750.
3. Antelman, S. M., Caggiula, A. R., Black, C. A. and Edwards, D. J. (1978): Stress reverses the anorexia induced by amphetamine and methylphenidate but not fenfluramine. *Brain Res.,* 143:580–585.
4. Arenillas, L. (1964): Amitriptyline and body weight. *Lancet,* 432–433.
5. Atkinson, J., Kirchertz, E. J. and Peters-Haefeli, L. (1978): Effect of peripheral clonidine on ingestive behaviour. *Physiol. Behav.,* 21:73–77.
6. Bainbridge, J. G. (1968): The effect of psychotropic drugs on food-reinforced behaviour and on food consumption. *Psychopharmacologia* (Berl.), 12:204–213.
7. Balopole, D. C., Hansult, C. D. and Dorph, D. (1979): Effect of cocaine on food intake in rats. *Psychopharmacology,* 64:121–122.
8. Baxter, M. G., Miller, A. A. and Soroko, F. E. (1970): The effect of cyproheptadine on food consumption in the fasted rat. *Br. J. Pharmacol.,* 39:229–230.
9. Bedford, J. A., Lovell, D. K., Turner, C. E., Elsohly, M. A. and Wilson, M. C. (1980): The anorexia and actometric effects of cocaine and two coca extracts. *Pharmac., Biochem. Behav.,* 13:403–408.
10. Benady, D. R. (1970): Cyproheptadine hydrochloride (Periactin) and anorexia nervosa: a case report. *Br. J. Psychiat.,* 117:681–682.
11. Bergen, S. S. (1964): Appetite stimulating properties of cyproheptadine. *Am. J. Dis. Children,* 108:270–273.
12. Blundell, J. (1979): Hunger, Appetite and Satiety—Constructs in search of identities. In: *Nutrition and Lifestyles,* edited by M. Turner, pp. 21–42. Applied Science Publ., London.

13. Blundell, J. E. (1980): Pharmacological adjustment of the mechanisms underlying feeding and obesity. In: *Obesity,* edited by A. J. Stunkard, pp. 182–207. Saunders, Philadelphia.

14. Blundell, J. E. (1981): Biogrammar of Feeding: Pharmacological manipulations and their interpretations. In: *Progress in Theory in Psychopharmacology,* edited by S. J. Cooper, pp. 233–276. Academic Press, London.

15. Blundell, J. E. (1981): Deep and surface structures: A qualitative approach to feeding. In: *The Body Weight Regulatory System: Normal and Disturbed Mechanisms,* edited by L. A. Cioffi, W. P. T. James and T. Van-Itallie, pp. 73–82. Raven Press, N.Y.

16. Blundell, J. E. (1983): Processes and problems underlying the control of food selection and nutrient intake. In: *Nutrition and the Brain Vol. 6,* edited by R. J. Wurtman and J. J. Wurtman pp. 164–221, Raven Press, New York.

17. Blundell, J. E. and Burridge, S. L. (1979): Control of feeding and the psychopharmacology of anorexic drugs. In: *The Treatment of Obesity,* edited by J. Munro, pp. 53–84. MTP Press, Lancaster.

18. Blundell, J. E. and Hill, A. J. (1982): Nutrients and Behaviour: research strategies for the investigation of taste characteristics, food preferences, hunger sensations and eating patterns in man. In: *Research Strategies for assessing the behavioural effects of food and nutrients,* edited by H. R. Lieberman and R. J. Wurtman, MIT, Cambridge.

19. Blundell, J. E. and Latham, C. J. (1978): Pharmacological manipulation of feeding behaviour: Possible influences of serotonin and dopamine on food intake. In: *Central Mechanisms of Anorectic Drugs,* edited by S. Garattini and R. Samanin, pp. 83–109. Raven Press, N.Y.

20. Blundell, J. E. and Latham, C. J. (1979a): Pharmacology of food and water intake. In: *Chemical Influences on Behaviour,* edited by S. Cooper and K. Brown, pp. 201–254. Academic Press, London.

21. Blundell, J. E. and Latham, C. J. (1979): Serotonergic influences on food intake: Effect of 5-hydroxytryptophan on parameters of feeding behaviour in deprived and free-feeding rats. *Pharmacology, Biochem. & Behav.,* 11:431–437.

22. Blundell, J. E. and Latham, C. J. (1980): Characterisation of the adjustments to the structure of feeding behaviour following pharmacological treatment: Effects of amphetamine and fenfluramine and the antagonism produced by pimozide and methergoline. *Pharmac., Biochem. & Behav.,* 12:717–722.

23. Blundell, J. E. and Latham, C. J. (1982): Behavioural Pharmacology of Feeding. In: *Drugs and Appetite,* edited by T. Silverstone, pp. 41–80.

24. Blundell, J. E. and Leshem, M. B. (1974): The effect of serotonin manipulation in rats with lateral hypothalamic lesions. In: *Proceedings, Fifth International Conference on Physiology of Food and Fluid Intake, Jerusalem.*

25. Blundell, J. E. and McArthur, R. A. (1979): Investigation of food consumption using a dietary self-selection procedure: Effects of pharmacological manipulation and feeding schedules. *Brit. J. Pharmac.,* 67:436P–438P.

26. Blundell, J. E. and McArthur, R. A. (1981): Behavioural flux and feeding: Continuous monitoring of food intake and food selection and the video-recording of appetitive and satiety sequences for the analysis of drug action. In: *Anorectic agents, mechanisms of action and of tolerance,* edited by S. Garattini, pp. 19–43. Raven Press, N.Y.

27. Blundell, J. E. and Rogers, P. J. (1978): Pharmacological approaches to the understanding of obesity. *Psychiatr. Clin. North Am.,* 1:629–650.

28. Blundell, J. E. and Rogers, P. J. (1980): Effects of anorexic drugs on food intake, food selection and preferences, hunger motivation and subjective experiences: Pharmacological manipulation as a tool to investigate human feeding processes. *Appetite,* 1:151–165.

29. Blundell, J. E., Tombros, E., Rogers, P. J. and Latham, C. J. (1980): Behavioural analysis of feeding: implications for the pharmacological manipulation of food intake in animals and man. *Prog. Neuropsychopharm.,* 4:319–326.

30. Booth, D. A. and Nicholls, J. (1974): Behavioural specificity of chloralose-induced feeding in the rat. *Psychopharmacologia (Berl.),* 39:145–150.

31. Bray, G. A. (1978): To treat or not to treat—that is the question? In: *Recent Advances in Obesity Research II,* edited by G. Bray, pp. 248–265, Newman, London.

32. Bray, G. A. and York, D. A. (1972): Studies on food intake in genetically obese rats. *Am. J. Physiol.,* 223:176–179.

33. Brobeck, J. R. (1960): Food and Temperature. *Rec. Prog. in Hormone Res.,* 16:439–459.

34. Brown, R. F., Houpt, K. A. and Schryver, H. F. (1976): Stimulation of food intake in horses by diazepam and promazine. *Pharmacol., Biochem. Behav.,* 5:495–497.

35. Cappell, H., Leblanc, A. E. and Endrenyi, L. (1972): Effects of chlordiazepoxide and ethanol on the extinction of a conditioned taste aversion. *Physiol. Behav.,* 9:167–169.
36. Carruba, M. O., Mantegazza, P., Müller, E. E. and Ricciardi, S. (1981): Effects of anorectic drugs on the hyperphagic response induced by insulin or 2-deoxy-d-glucose glucoprivation. *Br. J. Pharmacol.,* 72:161P.
37. Carruba, M. O., Ricciardi, S., Müller, E. E. and Mantegazza, P. (1980a): New findings in the neuropharmacological control of food intake. *Pharmacol. Res. Comm.,* 12:599–603.
38. Carruba, M. O., Ricciardi, S., Müller, E. E. and Mantegazza, P. (1980b): Anorectic effect of Lisuride and other ergot derivative in the rat. *Eur. J. Pharmacol.,* 64:133–141.
39. Cole, S. O. (1977): Interaction of arena size with different measures of amphetamine effects. *Pharmacol. Biochem. Behav.,* 7:181–184.
40. Cole, S. O. (1979): Interaction of food deprivation with different measures of amphetamine effects. *Pharmacol. Biochem. Behav.,* 10:235–238.
41. Cooper, B. R., Howard, J. L., White, H. L., Soroko, F., Ingold, K. and Maxwell, R. A. (1980): Anorexic effect of ethanolamine-O-sulphate and muscimol in the rat: Evidence that GABA inhibits ingestive behaviour. *Life Sciences,* 26:1997–2002.
42. Cooper, S. J. (1980): Benzodiazepines as appetite-enhancing compounds. *Appetite:* 1:7–19.
43. Costa, E. and Garattini, S. (1970): *Amphetamines and Related Compounds.* Raven Press, New York.
44. Creese, I. and Iversen, S. D. (1975): The pharmacological and anatomical substrates of the amphetamine response in the rat. *Brain Res.,* 83:419–436.
45. Cronbach, L. J. (1957): The two disciplines of scientific psychology. *Amer. Psychol.,* 12:670–684.
46. Cronbach, L. J. (1975): Beyond the two disciplines of scientific psychology. *Amer. Psychol.,* 30:116–127.
47. Davis, J. D., Gallagher, R. L. and Ladove, R. (1967): Food intake controlled by a blood factor. *Science,* 156:1247–1248.
48. Dobrzanski, S. and Doggett, N. S. (1976): The effects of (+)-amphetamine and fenfluramine on feeding in starved and satiated mice. *Psychopharm.,* 48:283–286.
49. Doggett, N. S. and Jawaharlal, K. (1977): Some observations on the anorectic activity of prostaglandin $F_{2\alpha}$. *Brit. J. Pharm.,* 60:409–415.
50. Doggett, N. S. and Jawaharlal, K. (1977b): Anorectic activity of prostaglandin precursors. *Brit. J. Pharm.,* 60:417–423.
51. Edwards, G. J. (1977): Unwanted effects of psychotropic drugs Part IV; Drugs for anxiety. *The Practitioner,* 219:117–121.
52. Eichler, A. J. and Antelman, S. M. (1977): Apomorphine: feeding or anorexia depending on internal state. *Commun. Psychopharm.,* 1:533–540.
53. Endler, N. S. and Magnusson, D. (1976): Toward an interactional psychology of personality. *Psychol. Bull.,* 83:956–974.
54. File, S. E. (1980): Effects of benzodiazepines and naloxone on food intake and food preference in the rat. *Appetite,* 1:215–224.
55. Freed, W. J., Perlow, M. J. and Wyatt, R. J. (1979): Calcitonin: Inhibitory effect on eating in rats. *Science,* 206:850–852.
56. Gander, D. R. (1965): Treatment of depressive illness with combined antidepressants. *Lancet,* 107–109.
57. Garattini, S. (1978): Importance of serotonin for explaining the action of some anorectic agents. In: *Recent Advances in Obesity Research: II,* edited by G. A. Bray, pp. 433–441.
58. Ghosh, M. N. and Parvathy, S. (1973): The effect of cyproheptadine on water and food intake and on body weight in the fasted adult and weanling rats. *Br. J. Pharmacol.,* 48:328–329P.
59. Gibbs, J., Young, R. C. and Smith, G. P. (1973): Cholecystokinin elicits satiety in rats with open gastric fistulas. *Nature,* 245:323–325.
60. Glick, Z. (1980): Food intake of rats administered with Glycerol. *Physiol. Behav.,* 25:621–626.
61. Gonzalez, M. F. and Novin, D. (1974): Feeding induced by intracranial and intravenously administered 2-deoxy-D-glucose. *Physiol. Psychol.* 2:326–330.
62. Goodman, L. S. and Gilman, A. (1970): *The Pharmacological Basis of Therapeutics.* 4th edition MacMillan, New York.
63. Grinker, J. A., Drewnowski, A., Enns, M. and Kissileff, H. (1980): Effects of d-amphetamine and fenfluramine on feeding patterns and activity of obese and lean Zucker rats. *Pharmac. Biochem. Behav.,* 12:265–275.

64. Hoebel, B. G. and Leibowitz, S. F. (1981): Brain monoamines in the modulation of self-stimulation, feeding, and body weight. In: *Brain, Behaviour and Bodily Disease,* edited by H. A. Weiner, M. A. Hofer and A. J. Stunkard, pp. 103–142. Raven Press, New York.
65. Holden, J. M. C. and Holden, V. (1970): Weight changes with schizophrenic psychosis and psychotropic drug therapy. *Psychosomatics,* 11:551–561.
66. Holtzman, S. G. (1974): Behavioural effects of separate and combined administration of naloxone and d-amphetamine. *J. Pharmacol. Exp.,* 189:51–60.
67. Idelshon, F. (1967): Experience with cyproheptadine hydrochloride as a nonhormonal anabolic: Its effect on the body weight of paediatric patients. *Oriental Med.* 185:824–826.
68. Jacobs, B. L., Mosko, S. S. and Trulson, M. E. (1977): The investigation of the role of serotonin in mammalian behaviour. In: *Neurobiology of Sleep and Memory,* edited by R. R. Drucker-Colin and J. L. McGaugh, pp. 99–133. Academic Press, New York.
69. Jouvet, M. (1967): Neurophysiology of the states of sleep. *Physiological Reviews,* 47:117–177.
70. Kahling, Von J., Ziegler, H. and Balhause, H. (1975): Zentrale Wirkungen von WA 335-BS, einer substanz mit peripherer Antiserotonin und Antihistamin-wirkung. *Arzneim.-Forsch. (Drug Res.)* 25:1737–1744.
71. Katz, R. J. (1978): Tail pinch versus brain stimulation: Problems of comparison. *Science,* 201:840–841.
72. Knoll, J. (1979): Satietin: A highly potent anorexigenic substance in human serum. *Physiol. Behav.,* 23:497–502.
73. Krauskopf, C. J. (1978): Comment on Endler and Magnusson's attempt to redefine personality. *Psychol. Bull.* 85:280–283.
74. Latham, C. J. and Blundell, J. E. (1979): Evidence for the effect of tryptophan on the pattern of food consumption in free feeding and food deprived rats. *Life Sciences,* 24:1971–1978.
75. Leibowitz, S. F. (1975): Amphetamine: possible site and mode of action for producing anorexia in the rat. *Brain Research,* 84:160–167.
76. Leibowitz, S. F. (1980): Neurochemical systems of the Hypothalamus. Control of feeding and drinking behaviour and water-electrolyte excretion. In: *Handbook of the Hypothalamus,* Vol. 3., pp. 299–437.
77. Lewin, K. (1939): Field theory and experiment in social psychology: concepts and methods. *Amer. J. Sociol.,* 44:868–897.
78. Lindberg, U. H., Thorberg, S-O and Bengtsson, S. (1978): Inhibitors of neuronal monoamine uptake.2. Selective inhibition of 5-hydroxy-tryptamine uptake by α-amino acid esters of phenethyl alcohols. *J. Med. Chem.,* 21:448–456.
79. Lorenz, D., Nardi, P. and Smith, G. P. (1978): Atropine methyl nitrate inhibits sham feeding in the rat. *Pharmacol. Biochem. Behav.,* 8:405–407.
80. Lotter, E. C., Krinsky, R., McKay, J. M., Treneer, C. M., Porte, D. and Woods, S. C. (1981): Somatostatin decreases food intake of rats and baboons. *J. Comp. Physiol. Psychol.,* 95:278–287.
81. Margules, D. L. and Stein, L. (1967): Neuroleptics v. Tranquillisers: evidence from animals of mode and site of action. In: *Neuropsychopharmacology,* edited by H. Brill, J. O. Cole., P. Deniker., H. Hippius and P. B. Bradley, pp. 108–120. Excerp. Med., Amsterdam.
82. Martin, C. F. and Gibbs, J. (1980): Bombesin elicits satiety in sham feeding rats. *Peptides,* 1:131–134.
83. Mauron, C., Wurtman, J. J. and Wurtman, R. J. (1980): Clonidine increases food and protein consumption in rats. *Life Sciences,* 27:781–791.
84. McArthur, R. A. The effect of varying diet texture on diet selection and response to fenfluramine. *Int. J. Obesity,* 7:87–88.
85. McArthur, R. A. and Blundell, J. E. (1983): Protein and carbohydrate self-selection: Modification of the effects of fenfluramine and amphetamine by age and feeding regimen. *Appetite,* 4: in press.
86. Meehl, P. E. (1962): Schizotaxia, schizotypy and schizophrenia. *Amer. J. Psychol.,* 17:827–838.
87. Mereu, G. P., Fratta, W., Gessa, P. and Gessa, G. L. (1976): Voraciousness induced in cats by benzodiazepines. *Psychopharmacology,* 47:101–103.
88. Miller, J. A. (1963): Serotonin antagonist cyproheptadine. *Ann. Allergy,* 21:588–592.
89. Morgan, R. (1977): Three weeks in isolation with two schizophrenic patients. *Brit. J. Psychiat.,* 131:504–513.

90. Murray, H. A. (1938): *Exploration in Personality.* Oxford University Press, New York.
91. Noble, R. E. (1969): Effect of cyproheptadine on appetite and weight gain in adults. *J. A. M. A.* 209:2054–2055.
92. Olgiati, J. R., Netti, C., Guidobone, F. and Pecile, A. (1980): The central GABA ergic system and control of food intake under different experimental conditions. *Psychopharmacology,* 68:163–167.
93. Opitz, K. and Akinlaja, A. (1966): Zur Beeinflussung der Nahrungsaufahme durch Psychopharmaca. *Psychopharmacologia* (Berlin) 9:307–319.
94. Panksepp, J., Pollack, A., Krost, K., Meeker, R. and Ritter, M. (1975): Feeding in response to repeated protamine zinc insulin injections. *Physiol. Behav.,* 14:497–493.
95. Paul, S. M., Hulihan-Giblin, B. and Skolnick, P. (1982): (+)-Amphetamine binding to rat hypothalamus: Relation to anorexic potency of phenylethylamines. *Science,* 218:487–490.
96. Paykel, E. S., Mueller, P. S. and De la Vergne, P. M. (1973): Amitriptyline, weight gains and carbohydrate craving: A side effect. *Brit. J. Psychiat.,* 123:501–507.
97. Pfister, W. R., Illingworth, R. M. and Yim, G. K. W. (1978): Increased feeding in rats treated with chlordimeform and related formamidines: A new class of appetite stimulants. *Psychopharmacol.,* 60:47–51.
98. Poschel, B. P. H. (1971): A simple and specific screen for benzodiazepine-like drugs. *Pscyhopharmacologia,* 19:193–198.
99. Randall, L. O., Schallek, W., Heise, G. A., Keith, E. F. and Bagdon, R. E. (1960): The psychoactive properties of methamino-diazepoxide. *J. Pharm. Exp. Ther.,* 129:163–171.
100. Reynolds, J. (1976): *The Biology of Human Action.* Freeman, Reading.
101. Reynolds, R. W. and Carlisle, H. J. (1961): The effect of chlorpromazine on food intake in the albino rat. *J. Comp. Physiol. Psychol.* 54:354–336.
102. Robinson, R. G., McHugh, P. R. and Bloom, F. E. (1975): Chlorpromazine-induced hyperphagia in the rat. *Psychopharmacol. Comm.,* 1:37–50.
103. Robinson, R. G., McHugh, P. R. and Folstein, M. F. (1975): Measurement of appetite disturbances in psychiatric disorder. *J. Psychiat. Res.,* 12:59–68.
104. Rodin, J. (1978): Has the distinction between internal versus external control of feeding outlived its usefulness? In: *Recent Advances in Obesity Research II,* edited by G. Bray, pp. 75–85. Newman Publications, London.
105. Rogers, P. J. and Blundell, J. E. (1979): Effect of anorectic drugs on food intake, and the micro-structure of eating in human subjects. *Psychopharmacology,* 66:159–165.
106. Rosenthal, D. and Kety, S. S. (1968): *The Transmission of Schizophrenia.* Pergamon, New York.
107. Rowland, D. L., Perrings, T. S. and Thommes, J. A. (1980): Comparison of androgenic effects on food intake and body weight in adult rats. *Physiol. Behav.,* 24:205–209.
108. Russek, M., Mogenson, G. J. and Stevenson, J. A. F. (1967): Calorigenic, hyperglycemic and anorexigenic effects of adrenaline and noradrenaline. *Physiol. Behav.,* 2:429–433.
109. Samanin, R., Caccia, S., Bendotti, C., Borsini, F., Borroni, E., Invernizzi, R., Patacini, R. and Mennini, T. (1980): Further studies on the mechanism of serotonin-dependent anorexia in rats. *Psychopharmacology,* 68:99–104.
110. Sanger, D. J. and McCarthy, P. S. (1980): Differential effects of morphine on food and water intake in food deprived and free-feeding rats. *Psychopharmacology,* 72:103–106.
111. Sanger, D. J. and McCarthy, P. S. (1981): Increased food and water intake produced in rats by opiate receptor agonists. *Psychopharmacology,* 74:217–220.
112. Schachter, S. (1971): Some extraordinary facts about obese humans and rats. *Amer. J. Psychol.,* 26:129–144.
113. Schachter, S. and Rodin, J. (1974): *Obese Humans and Rats.* Erlbaum/Halsted, Washington, D.C.
114. Schachter, S. and Singer, J. E. (1962): Cognitive, social and physiological determinants of emotional state. *Psychol. Rev.,* 69:379–399.
115. Schally, A. V., Redding, T. W., Lucien, H. W. and Meyer, J. (1967): Enterogastrone inhibits eating by fasted mice. *Science,* 157:210–211.
116. Schlemmer, R. F., Casper, R. C., Narasimhachari, N. and Davis, J. M. (1979): Clonidine induced hyperphagia and weight gain in monkeys. *Psychopharm.,* 61:233–234.
117. Sclafani, A. and Springer, D. (1976): Dietary obesity in adult rats: similarities to hypothalamic and human obesity syndromes. *Physiol. Behav.,* 17:461–471.
118. Scoville, B. (1975): Review of amphetamine-like drugs by the Food and Drug Administration.

In: *Obesity in Perspective, Part 2,* edited by G. A. Bray, pp. 441. U. S. Government Printing Office, Washington, D.C.

119. Silverstone, J. T. and Stunkard, A. J. (1968): The anorectic effect of dexamphetamine sulphate. *Brit. J. Pharmacol. Chemother.,* 33:513–522.
120. Slusser, P. G. and Ritter, R. C. (1980): Increased feeding and hyperglycaemia elicited by intracerebroventricular 5-thioglucose. *Brain Res.,* 202:474–478.
121. Sofia, R. D. and Barry, H. (1974): Acute and chronic effects of Δ^9-tetrahydrocannabinol on food intake by rats. *Psychopharmacologia,* 39:213–222.
122. Soper, W. Y. and Wise, R. A. (1971): Hypothalamically-induced eating: Eating from non-eaters with diazepam. *T. I. T. Jnl. Life Sci.,* 1:79–84.
123. Soubrie, P., Kulkarni, S., Simon, P. and Boissier, J. R. (1975): Effets des anxiolytiques sur la prise de nourriture de rats et de souris placés en situation nouvelle ou familière. *Psychopharmacologia,* 45:203–210.
124. Spielberger, C. D. (1966): *Anxiety and Behaviour.* Academic Press, New York.
125. Stark, P. and Totty, C. W. (1967): Effects of amphetamines on eating elicited by hypothalamic stimulation. *J. Pharm. Exp. Therap.,* 158:272–278.
126. Stellar, E. (1954): The Physiology of Motivation. *Psychol. Rev.,* 61:5–23.
127. Stolerman, I. P. (1970): Eating, drinking and spontaneous activity in rats after the administration of chlorpromazine. *Neuropharm.,* 9:405–411.
128. Stricker, E. M. and Zigmond, M. J. (1976): Recovery of function after damage to central catecholamine-containing neurons: A neurochemical model for the lateral hypothalamic syndrome. In: *Progress in Physiological Psychology,* edited by J. M. Sprague and A. N. Epstein, Vol. 6, pp. 121–188. Academic Press, New York.
129. Stunkard, A. J. (1978): Behavioural treatment of obesity: The first ten years. In: *Recent Advances in Obesity Research II,* edited by G. Bray, pp. 295–306. Newman, London.
130. Sullivan, A. C., Guthrie, R. W. and Triscari, J. (1981): Chlorocitric acid, a novel anorectic agent with a peripheral mode of action. In: *Anorectic agents, mechanisms of action and of tolerance,* edited by S. Garattini. Raven Press, New York.
131. Sullivan, A. C., Triscari, J., Hamilton, J. G. and Miller, O. N. (1974): Effect of (−)-hydroxycitrate upon the accumulation of lipid in the rat: II. Appetite. *Lipids,* 9:129–134.
132. Thode, W. F. and Carlisle, H. J. (1968): Effect of lateral hypothalamic stimulation on amphetamine-induced anorexia. *J. Comp. Physiol. Psychol.,* 66:547–548.
133. Trygstad, O., Foss, I., Edminson, P. D., Johansen, J. H. and Reichelt, K. L. (1978): Humoral control of appetite: A urinary anorexigenic peptide. Chromatographic patterns of urinary peptides in anorexia nervosa. *Acta. Endocrinol.,* 89:196–208.
134. Tye, N. C., Nicholas, D. J. and Morgan, M. J. (1976): Chlordiazepoxide and preference for free food in the rat. *Pharmacol. Biochem. Behav.,* 3:1149–1151.
135. Vendsborg, P. B., Bech, P. and Rafaelson, O. J. (1976): Lithium treatment and weight gain. *Acta Psychiat. Scand.,* 53:139–147.
136. Vogel, R. A., Cooper, B. R., Barlow, T. S., Prange, A. J., Mueller, R. A. and Breese, G. R. (1979): Effects of thyrotropin-releasing hormone on locomotor activity, operant performance and ingestive behaviour. *J. Pharm. Exp. Ther.,* 208:161–168.
137. Waddington, C. H. (1977): *Tools for Thought.* Paladin, St. Alban's.
138. Wade, G. (1975): Some effects of ovarian hormones on food intake and body weight in female rats. *J. Comp. Physiol. Psychol.,* 85:183–193.
139. Watson, P. J. and Cox, V. S. (1976): An analysis of barbiturate-induced eating and drinking in the rat. *Physiol. Psychol.,* 4:325–332.
140. Winston, F. (1971): Combined antidepressant therapy. *Brit. J. Psychiat.,* 118:301–304.
141. Wise, R. A. and Dawson, V. (1974): Diazepam-induced eating and lever pressing for food in sated rats. *J. Comp. Physiol. Psychol.,* 86:930–941.
142. Wishart, T. B. and Wall, E. K. (1974): Reduction of stimulus-bound food consumption in the rat following amphetamine administration. *J. Comp. Physiol. Psychol.,* 87:741–745.
143. Wolgin, D. L., Cytawa, J. and Teitelbaum, P. (1976): The role of activation in the regulation of food intake. In: *Hunger: Basic Mechanisms and Clinical Implications,* edited by D. Novin, W. Wyrwicka and G. Bray, pp. 179–191. Raven Press, New York.
144. Wurtman, J. J. and Wurtman, R. J. (1977): Fenfluramine and fluoxetine spare protein consumption while suppressing caloric intake by rats. *Science,* 198:1178–1180.

145. Wurtman, J. J. and Wurtman, R. J. (1979): Drugs that enhance central serotoninergic transmission diminish elective carbohydrate consumption by rats. *Life Sciences,* 24:895–904.
146. Wurtman, J. J., Wurtman, R. J., Growdon, J. H., Henry, P., Lipscomb, A. and Zeisel, S. H. (1982): Carbohydrate craving in obese people: suppression by treatments affecting serotoninergic transmission. *Int. J. of Eating Disorders,* 1:2–15.

Eating and Its Disorders, edited by A. J.
Stunkard and E. Stellar. Raven Press,
New York © 1984.

Gut Hormone Hypothesis of Postprandial Satiety

Gerard P. Smith

*Department of Psychiatry, Cornell University Medical College and Edward W. Bourne
Behavioral Research Laboratory, New York Hospital–Cornell Medical Center, White
Plains, New York 10605*

The gut hormone hypothesis of postprandial satiety proposes that gut hormones released by ingested food contacting the mucosal surface of the mouth, stomach, and/or small intestine are part of the physiological mechanism of postprandial satiety. This hypothesis predicts that gut hormones inhibit food intake and elicit the specific behavioral sequence that characterizes the initial period of postprandial satiety. The hypothesis was proposed in 1973 by Gibbs et al. (5) as the result of our initial observations of the inhibition of food intake by the small intestinal hormone cholecystokinin (CCK). The hypothesis has been tested extensively during the past decade. Most of the work has been concerned with the effect of CCK, but other gut hormones have been shown to inhibit food intake under at least one experimental condition (35). Without further testing, it is not possible to decide whether an inhibitory effect represents a physiological, pharmacological, or toxic effect of the peptide. The kinds of additional experimental tests that should be attempted are best illustrated by reviewing the investigation of the satiety effect of CCK.

EVIDENCE FOR THE SPECIFICITY OF THE SATIETY EFFECT OF CCK

An impure extract of CCK or the synthetic C-terminal octapeptide of cholecystokinin (CCK-8) inhibits food intake in rats, rabbits, chickens, pigs, sheep, rhesus monkeys, lean mice, genetically obese mice, genetically obese rats, neurologically obese rats, lean men and women, and obese men (36). The inhibition is dose related and occurs with solid or liquid food (5). The inhibitory effect of CCK has behavioral and molecular specificity.

Behavioral Specificity

There are three kinds of evidence for behavioral specificity: First, doses of CCK-8 < 8 μg/kg intraperitoneally inhibit food intake in food-deprived rats, but these doses do not inhibit water intake in water-deprived rats (5,26). Doses of 8 μg/kg or larger also inhibit water intake; thus, these doses are nonspecific (Table 1).

Second, doses of CCK in the range that are specific for inhibiting food intake do not disrupt the normal behavioral sequence that characterizes postprandial satiety in the mouse (42), rat (5), monkey (7), and human (15,31).

Third, doses of CCK specific for inhibiting normal food intake also terminate sham feeding and elicit the behavioral sequence of satiety in rats that are 17 hr food deprived (1,6). This is a striking result because when rats sham feed after 17 hr food deprivation, they do not satiate spontaneously (44). Thus, in the sham feeding preparation where endogenous satiety mechanisms are not active enough to terminate feeding and elicit satiety, the administration of CCK is sufficient to elicit an apparently complete satiety effect.

Molecular Specificity

All known biological actions and receptor binding of CCK depend on the presence of a sulfate group on the tyrosine moiety in the seventh position from the C-terminal end (13,28). Removal of the sulfate group abolishes or markedly reduces the classic visceral actions or receptor binding of CCK (28). Moving the sulfate group to the sixth position from the C-terminal end as occurs in the sulfated form of gastrin also markedly decreases the potency for many visceral actions and receptor binding (10). Both molecular constraints have been demonstrated for the satiety action of CCK. Desulfated CCK is essentially inactive in test conditions in which sulfated CCK is very effective (6). Sulfated gastrin is also inactive, even in very large doses (16). On the other hand, caerulein, an amphibian decapeptide that has a structure very similar to that of CCK including a sulfated tyrosine in the seventh position, mimics CCK's satiety effect (5,12,41).

TABLE 1. *Comparison of effect of CCK-8 on food and water intake[a]*

	Percent inhibition of intake dose of CCK-8 (μg/kg)				
	1	2	4	8	16
Food	22 ± 5^b	43 ± 6^b	44 ± 4^b	67 ± 4^b	NT[c]
Water	NT	5 ± 5	-2 ± 7	20 ± 7^b	21 ± 7^b

[a]Data (mean $\pm$ SE) are percent inhibition of food or water intake after 17 hr deprivation of food or water, respectively. The percent inhibition = $100 \times$ [1 − (30 min intake after CCK-8/30 min intake after saline)]. All rats were Sprague Dawley males weighing 300–450 g. There were 11 rats in the food intake experiment; their data were reported previously in Table 2 of ref. 38. There were 7 to 13 rats tested in the water intake experiment (C. Jerome and G. P. Smith, *unpublished data*).
[b]$p < 0.05$, matched pairs t-test.
[c]NT means not tested.

MECHANISM OF THE SATIETY EFFECT OF CCK

Since peptides have difficulty crossing the blood-brain barrier, the site of the satiety action of CCK has been assumed to be in the periphery. The occurrence of this peripheral action was postulated to be carried to the brain over visceral afferent fibers (38). Since the abdominal vagus nerve contains the majority of visceral afferent fibers gathered conveniently into two major trunks lying along the side of the esophagus (Fig. 1), the effect of abdominal vagotomy on the satiety action of CCK was investigated. The result was clear—abdominal vagotomy abolished or markedly reduced the satiety effect of CCK-8 (17,25,38, Fig. 2). Apparently, the spinal visceral afferents that course in the sympathetic fibers and have cell bodies in dorsal root ganglia make little or no contribution to the satiety effect of CCK-8 because when they were disconnected from the brain by a section of the spinal cord at a level between the second and third thoracic vertebrae, the potency of CCK-8 for satiety was normal (17).

Note that the effect of gastric vagotomy on the potency of CCK-8 for satiety does not prove that the critical lesion is of the afferent fibers because gastric vagotomy lesions affect both afferent and efferent gastric vagal fibers. It has not been possible to lesion the afferent or efferent fibers selectively in the abdominal vagal system. Peripheral anticholinergic blockade with atropine methylnitrate, however, provides a crude mimic of the loss of vagal efferent fibers. Therefore, we tested it. Prior treatment with atropine methylnitrate had no effect on the potency of CCK-

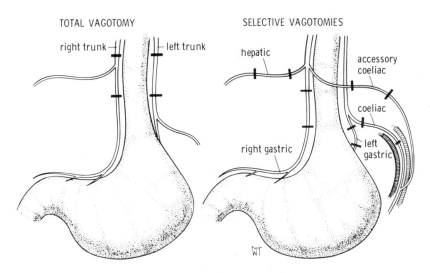

FIG. 1. Schematic of the abdominal vagal trunks and branches. The heavy black lines across the nerves indicate the sites of 3–0 silk sutures. The nerve between sutures is cut and removed en bloc or the ends are allowed to retract. All types of vagotomy are done under microscopic control. This is a revised and more accurate schematic than the one we published recently (14).

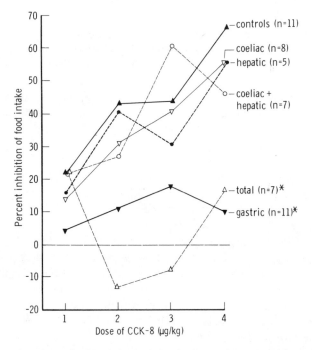

FIG. 2. Effect of total or selective abdominal vagotomies on the satiety effect of CCK-8. Total or bilateral gastric vagotomy markedly reduced or abolished the satiety effect of CCK-8; all other selective vagotomies did not produce a significant difference from controls. CCK-8 was administered intraperitoneally 15 min before presentation of liquid food to 17 hr food deprived, male Sprague Dawley rats. The number of rats is *n*. * different from controls, $p < 0.01$, Tukey HSD test. Percent inhibition of food intake = $100 \times [1 - (30 \text{ min intake after CCK-8} / 30 \text{ min intake after saline})]$. This graph represents the data from Table 2 in ref. 38.

8 for satiety (38). This suggests, but does not prove, that the critical lesion involves the gastric vagal afferent fibers.

The recent electrophysiological studies of Niijima (27) support this role of gastric vagal afferents. Niijima reported that CCK-8 stimulated gastric and coeliac vagal afferents, but CCK-8 inhibited hepatic vagal afferent activity.

If the gastric vagal afferents are involved, how do they respond to circulating CCK-8? There are at least two possibilities. First, gastric afferent fibers could respond to a smooth muscle effect of CCK-8. This possibility is consistent with the contractile effect of CCK-8 on gastric smooth muscle which, unlike that on intestinal smooth muscle (11), is direct and atropine resistant (9). It is also consistent with the sensitivity of gastric vagal receptors to gastric muscle tension and stretch (29).

Second, CCK-8 acts on the vagal afferents directly. This is consistent with two characteristics of abdominal vagal afferents: Blood-borne substances have access to the small terminal portions of the unmyelinated fibers (29), and the abdominal vagus has specific CCK-8 receptors (45).

Although both are plausible, there is no experimental evidence for either possibility at this time. Since this question is accessible to investigation, we should have an answer in the near future.

Note that if gastric vagal afferents carry the information for postprandial satiety encoded in CCK-8's effect on smooth muscle or vagal terminals, then the projection site of the gastric afferents in the nucleus tractus solitarius is the first site of central processing. The ability of CCK-8 to produce dose-related inhibition of feeding should facilitate the analysis of the synaptic events that transduce the peripheral cellular effect of CCK-8 into neural information for the central network controlling feeding that results in the inhibition of feeding and the onset of postprandial satiety. The fact that CCK inhibits the central system may make it a particularly useful analytic probe, because as Sherrington emphasized, inhibitory neural mechanisms are crucial for the central integration of behavior (32).

PHYSIOLOGICAL STATUS OF THE SATIETY EFFECT OF CCK

Although the evidence for CCK having a satiety effect is compelling, the physiological status of this effect is uncertain. Much more work must be done in order to find out if CCK satisfies the criteria for a physiological effect (Table 2). So far, only the first and second criteria have been satisfied. No unambiguous evidence has been reported that is relevant to the other three criteria.

The fifth criterion requires comment. The measurement of circulating levels of CCK has been a formidable problem. Recently, there have been preliminary reports that suggest such measurements may now be feasible and reliable. Such measurements are necessary to interpret the physiological status of the satiety effect of CCK, but they are not sufficient if CCK is synergistic for satiety with other neural and hormonal mechanisms activated by food. Three such interactions are already known to occur—CCK is synergistic with another gut peptide bombesin (8,43), with gastric filling (24), and with the satiety mechanism(s) activated by sham feeding (2). Thus, to evaluate the satiating potency of CCK released by a meal, it will be necessary to measure other neural and endocrine satiety mechanisms simultaneously in order to estimate the synergistic interaction of CCK with these other satiety mechanisms.

TABLE 2. *Criteria for a physiological satiety effect of a gut hormone*

1. The hormone is released during a meal.
2. Exogenous administration of the hormone produces a specific satiety effect.
3. Endogenous release of the hormone produces a specific satiety effect.
4. Treatments that block the satiety effect of the exogenous hormone block the satiety effect of the endogenous hormone.
5. The concentration of the hormone released during a meal is sufficient to have a satiety effect when acting alone or together with other neural and hormonal satiety mechanisms.

THERAPEUTIC POSSIBILITIES

CCK inhibits meal size in lean (15,40) and obese (31) humans and in genetically obese rodents (21–23, 30, 42). This suggests that CCK-8 may be useful in the treatment of bulimia and obesity (33). One of the reasons that makes CCK-8 an attractive therapy is that it produces satiety, not anorexia (1,15,31,39). All previous pharmacological treatments that inhibited food intake have not elicited the satisfactions of feeding in humans or, in the case of amphetamine, the satiety sequence in rats (1). But the ideal treatment should permit less food to produce the normal satisfaction and pleasure of feeding, and CCK-8 appears to do this. In some of the lean and obese subjects we have studied (15,31) subjects that ate as much as 30% less than control after CCK-8 reported feeling normally satisfied and, according to their feeding diaries, did not want to eat their next meal sooner. If instead of self-reports, one relies on behavior, the implication is the same. When CCK-8 inhibits meal size significantly, humans and animals still display the sequence of behaviors that characterizes postprandial satiety. The convergent evidence of the self-reports and behavioral sequence suggests that animals and humans respond to CCK-8 as if it represented a quantity of food. This is what the gut hormone hypothesis predicts. Thus, the therapeutic potential of gut hormones derives from their hypothesized natural function of encoding information about the nutrient contents of the small intestine. Therapeutic use of gut hormones would exploit this natural function by administering the hormone just prior to feeding so that an effective concentration of the hormone would be achieved at specific receptor sites sooner than normal. This would decrease the size of the meal by stopping it sooner. This is exactly what we have observed in our human studies (15,31).

Despite the attractive aspects of CCK-8 as a novel treatment for bulimia and obesity, recall that all the animal and human evidence for the satiety effect of CCK-8 is based on a single test meal. Thus, the efficacy and safety of repeated administration of CCK-8 are unknown. The fact that CCK-8 is not active when given orally is an additional therapeutic constraint.

Although I have discussed the therapeutic potential of CCK-8 in terms of exogenous administration, there is the alternative possibility of releasing endogenous CCK by calorically trivial and/or absorbable chemicals (34). This possibility has been tested by preloading monkeys (7) and humans (33) with L-phenylalanine, a potent, preabsorptive releaser of CCK from the small intestine. L-phenylalanine inhibited food intake in monkeys and humans. These results are consistent with the release of endogenous CCK inhibiting food intake, but they are not a critical test of this possible mode of treatment.

FORMULATION

The gut hormone hypothesis of postprandial satiety has been productive. It led to extensive testing of CCK and to the discovery that other gut peptides such as bombesin (8), glucagon (3,4,19), and somatostatin (18) have interesting satiety effects that are mediated by vagal (glucagon, ref. 20; somatostatin, ref. 25) and nonvagal (bombesin, ref. 37) mechanisms.

The work with CCK has established that under appropriate conditions and within an explicit range of doses, CCK produces a specific satiety effect in animals and humans. But the physiological status of this effect of CCK is far from proven.

The satiety effect of CCK suggests that CCK may be useful in the treatment of bulimia and obesity, but the efficacy and safety of CCK for this purpose is unknown.

Perhaps, the most useful result of the first decade of testing the gut hormone hypothesis has been to encourage physiological analysis of how food ingested during a meal terminates feeding and elicits the experiences and behaviors of postprandial satiety. This analysis led to a new view of the luminal surface of gut as a great sensory sheet extending from the mouth to the end of the small intestine that is sensitive to the chemical and physical stimuli of food.

It is now clear that understanding the sensory control and physiological mechanisms of postprandial satiety is a fundamental requirement of any explanation of feeding behavior proposed as a basis for effective treatment of hyperphagic syndromes. At present, the gut hormone hypothesis offers the most explicit concept of a mechanism for normal postprandial satiety, and it has generated the most attractive therapeutic possibility for those clinical conditions that may represent failures of postprandial satiety.

ACKNOWLEDGMENTS

I thank Mrs. Marion Jacobson and Mrs. Jane Magnetti for typing the manuscript and Dr. James Gibbs for criticizing it. This investigation was supported in part by a Research Scientist Award, MH00149 from the ADAMHA awarding Institute, National Institute of Mental Health.

REFERENCES

1. Antin, J., Gibbs, J., Holt, J., Young, R. C., and Smith, G. P. (1975): Cholecystokinin elicits the complete behavioral sequence of satiety in rats. *J. Comp. Physiol. Psychol.,* 89:784–790.
2. Antin, J., Gibbs, J., and Smith, G. P. (1978): Cholecystokinin interacts with pregastric food stimulation to elicit satiety in the rat. *Physiol. Behav.,* 20:67–70.
3. Geary, N., and Smith, G. P. (1982): Pancreatic glucagon and postprandial satiety in the rat. *Physiol. Behav.,* 28:313–322.
4. Geary, N., and Smith, G. P. (1982): Pancreatic glucagon fails to inhibit sham feeding in the rat. *Peptides,* 3:163–166.
5. Gibbs, J., Falasco, J. D., and McHugh, P. R. (1976): Cholecystokinin decreased food intake in rhesus monkeys. *Am. J. Physiol.,* 230:15–18.
6. Gibbs, J., Kulkosky, P. J., and Smith, G. P. (1981): Effects of peripheral and central bombesin on feeding behavior of rats. *Peptides [Suppl. 2],* 2:179–183.
7. Gibbs, J., Young, R. C., and Smith, G. P. (1973): Cholecystokinin decreases food intake in rats. *J. Comp. Physiol. Psychol.,* 84:488–495.

8. Gibbs, J., Young, R. C., and Smith, G. P. (1973): Cholecystokinin elicits satiety in rats with open gastric fistulas. *Nature,* 245:323–325.
9. Go, V. L. W. (1978): The physiology of cholecystokinin. In: *Gut Hormones,* edited by S. R. Bloom, pp. 203–207. Churchill Livingstone, New York.
10. Grossman, M. I. (1976): Gastrointestinal hormones. In: *Peptide Hormones,* edited by J. A. Parsons, pp. 105–116. MacMillan Press, London.
11. Hedner, P., Persson, H., and Rorsman, G. (1967): Effect of cholecystokinin on small intestine. *Acta Physiol. Scand.,* 70:250–254.
12. Houpt, T. R., Anika, S. M., and Wolff, N. C. (1978): Satiety effects of cholecystokinin and caerulein in rabbits. *Am. J. Physiol.,* 235:R23–R28.
13. Innis, R. B., and Snyder, S. H. (1980): Distinct cholecystokinin receptors in brain and pancreas. *Proc. Natl. Acad. Sci. U. S. A.,* 77:6917–6921.
14. Jerome, C., and Smith, G. P. (1982): Gastric vagotomy inhibits drinking after hypertonic saline. *Physiol. Behav.,* 28:371–374.
15. Kissileff, H. R., Pi-Sunyer, F. X., Thornton, J., and Smith, G. P. (1981): Cholecystokinin-octapeptide (CCK-8) decreases food intake in man. *Am. J. Clin. Nutr.,* 34:154–160.
16. Lorenz, D. N., and Goldman, S. A. (1982): Vagal mediation of the cholecystokinin satiety effect in rats. *Physiol. Behav.,* 29:599–604.
17. Lorenz, D. N., Kreielsheimer, G., and Smith, G. P. (1979): Effect of cholecystokinin, gastrin, secretin and GIP on sham feeding in the rat. *Physiol. Behav.,* 23:1065–1072.
18. Lotter, E. C., Krinsky, R., McKay, J. M., Treneer, C. M., Porte, D., Jr., and Woods, S. C. (1981): Somatostatin decreased food intake of rats and baboons. *J. Comp. Physiol. Psychol.,* 95:278–287.
19. Martin, J. R. and Novin, D. (1977): Decreased feeding in rats following hepatic-portal infusion of glucagon. *Physiol. Behav.,* 19:461–466.
20. Martin, J. R., Novin, D., and Vander Weele, D. A. (1978): Loss of glucagon suppression after vagotomy in rats. *Am. J. Physiol.,* 234:E314–E318.
21. McLaughlin, C. L., and Baile, C. A. (1980): Decreased sensitivity of Zucker obese rats to the putative satiety agent cholecystokinin. *Physiol. Behav.,* 25:543–548.
22. McLaughlin, C. L., and Baile, C. A. (1980): Feeding and drinking behavior responses of adult Zucker obese rats to cholecystokinin. *Physiol Behav.,* 25:535–543.
23. McLaughlin, C. L., and Baile, C. A. (1981): Obese mice and the satiety effects of cholecystokinin, bombesin and pancreatic polypeptide. *Physiol. Behav.,* 26:433–437.
24. Moran, T. H., and McHugh, P. R. (1982): Cholecystokinin suppresses food intake by inhibiting gastric emptying. *Am. J. Physiol.,* 242:R491–R497.
25. Morley, J. E., Levine, A. S., Kneip, J., and Grace, M. (1982): The effect of vagotomy on the satiety effects of neuropeptides and naloxone. *Life Sci.,* 30:1943–1947.
26. Mueller, K., and Hsiao, S. (1977): Specificity of cholecystokinin satiety effect: Reduction of food but not water intake. *Pharmacol. Biochem. Behav.,* 6:643–646.
27. Niijima, A. (1981): Visceral afferents and metabolic function. *Diabetologia,* 20:325–330.
28. Ondetti, M. A., Rubin, B., Engel, S. L., Pluščec, J., and Sheehan, J. T. (1970): Cholecystokinin-Pancreozymin: recent developments. *Am. J. Dig. Dis.,* 15:149–156.
29. Paintal, A. S. (1973): Vagal sensory receptors and their reflex effects. *Physiol. Rev.,* 53:159–227.
30. Parrott, R. F., and Batt, R. A. L. (1980): The feeding response of obese mice (genotype, ob ob) and their wild-type littermates to cholecystokinin (pancreozymin). *Physiol. Behav.,* 24:751–753.
31. Pi-Sunyer, F. X., Kissileff, H. R., Thornton, J., and Smith, G. P. (1982): C-terminal octapeptide of cholecystokinin decreases food intake in obese men. *Physiol. Behav.,* 29:627–630.
32. Sherrington, C. S. (1932): Inhibition as a coordinative factor. In: *Nobel Lectures, Physiology or Medicine, 1922–1941,* pp. 278–289. Elsevier, New York, 1965.
33. Smith, G. P. (1983): The place of gut peptides in the treatment of obesity. In: *Biochemical Pharmacology of Metabolic Disease States,* edited by R. B. Curtis-Prior, Elsevier, North Holland *(in press).*
34. Smith, G. P., and Gibbs, J. (1976): Cholecystokinin and satiety: theoretic and therapeutic implications. In: *Hunger: Basic Mechanisms and Clinical Implications,* edited by D. Novin, W. Wyrwicka, and G. Bray, pp. 349–355. Raven Press, New York.

35. Smith, G. P., and Gibbs, J. (1981): Brain-gut peptides and the control of food intake. In: *Neurosecretion and Brain Peptides: Implications for Brain Function and Neurologic Disease,* edited by J. B. Martin, S. Reichlin, and K. L. Bick, pp. 389–395. Raven Press, New York.
36. Smith, G. P., Gibbs, J., Jerome, C., Pi-Sunyer, F. X., Kissileff, H. R., and Thornton, J. (1981): The satiety effect of cholecystokinin: A progress report. *Peptides [Suppl. 2]*, 2:57–59.
37. Smith, G. P., Jerome, C., Cushin, B. J., Eterno, R., and Simansky, K. J. (1981): Abdominal vagotomy blocks the satiety effect of cholecystokinin in the rat. *Science,* 213:1036–1037.
38. Smith, G. P., Jerome, C., and Gibbs, J. (1981): Abdominal vagotomy does not block the satiety effect of bombesin in the rat. *Peptides,* 2:409–411.
39. Smith, G. P., Gibbs, J., and Kulkosky, P. J. (1982): Relationships between brain-gut peptides and neurons in the control of food intake. In: *The Neural Basis of Feeding and Reward,* edited by B. G. Hoebel and D. Novin, pp. 149–165. Haer Institute for Electrophysiological Research, Brunswick, Maine.
40. Stacher, G. H., Steinringer, H., Schnierer, G., Schneider, C., and Winklehner, S. (1982): Cholecystokinin octapeptide decreases intake of solid food in man. *Peptides,* 3:133–136.
41. Stacher, G. H., Steinringer, H., Schnierer, G., Schneider, C., and Winklehner, S. (1982): Ceruletide decreases food intake in non-obese man. *Peptides,* 3:607–612.
42. Strohmayer, A. J., and Smith, G. P. (1981): Cholecystokinin inhibits food intake in genetically-obese (C57BL-6J-ob) mice. *Peptides,* 2:39–43.
43. Woods, S. C., West, D. B., Stein, L. J., McKay, L. D., Lotter, E. C., Kenney, N. J., and Porte, D., Jr. (1981): Peptides and the control of meal size. *Diabetologia,* 20:305–313.
44. Young, R. C., Gibbs, J., Antin, J., Holt, J., and Smith, G. P. (1974): Absence of satiety during sham feeding in the rat. *J. Comp. Physiol. Psychol.,* 87:795–800.
45. Zarbin, M. A., Wamsley, J. K., Innis, R. B., and Kuhar, M. J. (1981): Cholecystokinin receptors: presence and axonal flow in the rat vagus nerve. *Life Sci.,* 29:697–705.

Eating and Its Disorders, edited by A. J.
Stunkard and E. Stellar. Raven Press,
New York © 1984.

Nutrients, Neurotransmitter Synthesis, and the Control of Food Intake

Richard J. Wurtman and Judith J. Wurtman

Laboratory of Neuroendocrine Regulation, Massachusetts Institute of Technology, Cambridge, Massachusetts 02139

My associates and I have found that some of the changes in plasma composition (notably those in the concentrations of amino acids and choline) which follow eating can have important secondary effects on the nervous system, selectively modulating the rates at which neurons convert the nutrients to neurotransmitters (14,15). Moreover, these effects can be amplified by administering the nutrients in pure form, as though they were drugs (14,15), and by mixing them with carbohydrates (9). The brain apparently uses this coupling of neurotransmission to plasma compositon as a source of information about the individual's metabolic state and as a basis for making decisions about subsequent food intake and about cyclic behavioral processes like sleeping. For example, if the first meal of the day is rich in carbohydrate and poor in protein, the changes it produces in plasma amino acid levels raise brain levels of the nutrient tryptophan; this, in turn, accelerates the production and release of trytophan's neurotransmitter product serotonin (3,4). The resulting changes in neurotransmission will predispose the individual to choose away from carbohydrates and towards protein at lunchtime. A protein-rich breakfast, which diminishes brain serotonin, may have opposite effects. The biochemical mechanisms underlying the nutritional control of neurotransmitter synthesis and food intake are discussed below.

The changes in brain serotonin induced by consuming foods of varying protein-to-carbohydrate ratios can also influence such behavioral phenomena as mood (Fig. 1), sleepiness, and pain sensitivity. Other neurotransmitters besides serotonin are also affected by nutrient availability, but behavioral effects have not clearly been shown to follow postprandial changes in their synthesis. In actuality, these other neurotransmitters (the catecholamines and acetylcholine) are affected by the availability of their nutrient precursors only under particular circumstances, i.e., only in particular catecholaminergic or cholinergic neurons that the brain is causing to fire relatively frequently. In contrast, serotonin-releasing neurons always seem to respond to having more or less tryptophan. Just the same, the ability of tyrosine or choline to act as amplifiers, increasing the amounts of their neurotransmitter products being released from physiologically active neurons, affords these compounds considerable potential use in the treatment of diseases or conditions thought to involve catecholamines or acetylcholine.

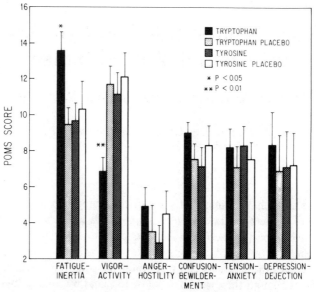

FIG. 1. Subjects received oral tryptophan (50 mg / kg) or tyrosine (100 mg / kg), using a double-blind, placebo-controlled crossover design. The substances were ingested at 0700 and behavioral testing began 0900. Mood, measured by the Profile of Mood States (POMS), was significantly altered. Specifically, tryptophan significantly decreased vigor ($p < .01$) and increased fatigue ($p < .05$) when compared to either placebo or tyrosine (7a).

FOOD CONSUMPTION AND PLASMA AMINO ACID PATTERN

Foods are, ultimately, mixtures of chemicals which are consumed electively at intervals during the day, partially metabolized within the gut, released into the bloodstream, and then taken up into the tissues. Some of these chemicals, the essential nutrients, are continuously required by cells; at times when foods are not being digested and absorbed, these compounds are released into the bloodstream from reservoirs in particular tissues. The rates at which major nutrients pass from the bloodstream into most tissues are controlled by hormones released postprandially, especially insulin, which facilitates the passages of glucose, fatty acids, and most amino acids. (The fall in plasma insulin that occurs when foods stop being absorbed causes the net flow of these nutrients to become tissue to plasma.) Brain is an exception: The passage of nutrients between its extracellular space and the plasma apparently is not controlled by hormones like insulin but depends instead on the kinetic characteristics of specific transport systems located in the endothelial cells lining the brain's capillaries. The macromolecules which comprise these systems physically carry the nutrient molecules in either direction across the blood-brain barrier (10). In most cases they are unsaturated with their circulating ligands, hence a postprandial increase (or decrease) in the plasma concentration of a nutrient like glucose, tyrosine, or choline will facilitate (or slow) the uptake of the compound into the brain.

Postprandial changes in plasma levels of most nutrients are relatively short-lived, since the compounds can be metabolized by the gut and liver before entering the systemic circulation (and during recirculations), or incorporated within the tissues into larger, water-soluble, *reservoir* molecules like glycogen, triglycerides, and proteins. Plasma levels of some nutrients (for example, calcium or glucose) are kept within a very narrow range postprandially, regardless of the composition of the food that was consumed, by homeostatic mechanisms; typically a small change in the plasma level is *sensed,* and processes are then activated which accelerate or slow the removal of the compound from the plasma by metabolism or tissue uptake. However, for other nutrients (the amino acids and choline) (5,7), it seems that no such feedback loops operate; hence, their plasma levels can vary across a wide range, depending solely on what is currently being digested. [For example, plasma valine levels may be as much as sixfold higher after a protein-rich breakfast than after a protein-free one (Fig. 2), and plasma choline is elevated threefold by a breakfast and lunch of eggs (Fig. 3).]

BRAIN SEROTONIN RESPONSES TO DIETARY CARBOHYDRATE AND PROTEIN

Consumption of a carbohydrate-rich, protein-free breakfast causes major changes in the pattern of amino acids in the plasma, largely because of the secre-

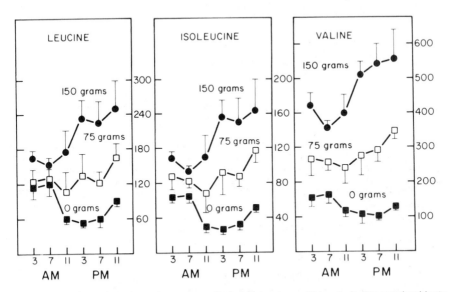

FIG. 2. Diurnal variations in plasma branched-chain amino acid levels in 7 normal subjects ingesting different levels of dietary protein for 5 consecutive days. (Plasmas were sampled on the fourth and fifth day of each treatment period.) Plasma amino acid levels are expressed in nanomoles per milliliter; *vertical bars* represent SD. In this and all other figures ■ = no-protein diet; □ = 75 g protein diet; ● = 150 g protein diet. Identical meals were served at 8 a.m., 12 p.m., and 5 p.m. (5).

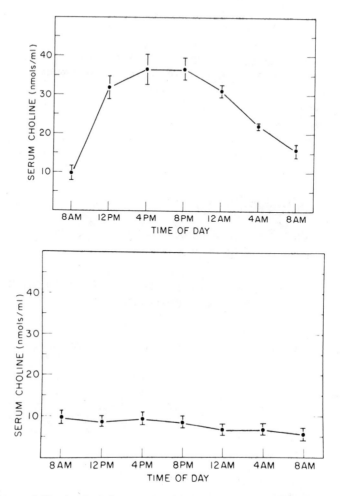

FIG. 3. Serum choline levels during consumption of a high-choline *(top)* and a low-choline *(bottom)* diet by 6 normal human subjects for 2 days. Each point represents the mean ± SEM. The high-choline diet contained 50 mg/day, or approximately 0.67 mg/kg. Meals were eaten starting at 8:30 a.m., 12 p.m., and 5 p.m. Blood samples were obtained at 8 a.m. on day 2 and every 4 hr. thereafter until 8 a.m. the following day. Data were analyzed by 2-way ANOVA and paired *t* test. *p<0.01 (7).

tion of insulin: The pancreatic hormone facilitates the uptake of most of the amino acids into tissues like skeletal muscle, thus lowering their plasma concentrations markedly. Plasma tryptophan levels, however, do not fall—primarily because the bulk of the tryptophan is loosely bound to circulating albumin, which retards its entry into peripheral tissues while allowing it to enter the brain (8). Hence, the ratio of plasma tryptophan to the plasma concentrations of other large, neutral amino acids (LNAA) like leucine, isoleucine, valine, tyrosine, and phenylalanine rises markedly. This ratio largely determines the concentration of tryptophan within the brain (4) because of the characteristics of the transport mechanism that carries tryptophan across the blood-brain barrier. This transport system is unsaturated with its amino acid ligand; hence, an increase or decrease in plasma tryptophan will rapidly alter the flux of tryptophan. Moreover, a single transport mechanicsm carries all of the LNAA—including tryptophan—competitively; thus an increase in the Tp/LNAA plasma ratio (caused postprandially, for example, by an insulin-mediated fall in the other LNAA) rapidly elevates tryptophan levels throughout the brain (3,4,10).

Within those relatively few brain neurons that convert tryptophan to serotonin and use the indoleamine as their neurotransmitter, the rise in tryptophan quickly increases the substrate saturation of the serotonin-forming enzyme tryptophan hydroxylase, thereby increasing synthesis of serotonin, absolute serotonin levels within nerve terminals, and serotonin release into synapses (and the extracellular space of the brain) each time the neurons fire (3,4).

If the initial meal is, instead, rich in protein, plasma tryptophan levels rise (5) (Fig. 4) because some of the tryptophan molecules in the protein are able to traverse the liver and enter the bloodstream: However levels of the other LNAA not only do not fall, as after a carbohydrate meal, but actually rise manyfold (Fig. 5). The difference between the responses of plasma tryptophan and other plasma LNAA to dietary protein reflects their relative abundance in the protein: Tryptophan (Tp) is scarce, comprising only about 1 to 1.5% of most proteins; the other LNAA, as a group, are not. It also reflects the fact that some of the other LNAA—leucine, isoleucine, and valine—are largely unmetabolized during their passage through the liver. Hence, the plasma Tp/LNAA ratio falls in response to protein ingestion, as do brain Tp and serotonin (4). Serotonin-releasing neurons can thus be conceived as *variable-ratio sensors,* emitting more or less of their signal, serotonin, depending on the chemicals being sensed (plasma concentrations of Tp and the other LNAA). These chemicals, in turn, vary predictably depending on the composition of the food currently being digested and absorbed.

SEROTONIN NEURONS AND THE CONTROL OF FOOD CHOICE

If animals are allowed to choose concurrently among two or more foods of differing composition, their observed behavior suggests that appetitive mechanisms are operating which allow them to regulate not only the mass of food that they eat and its number of calories but also the proportion of protein to carbohydrate (or carbohydrate to protein) within the meal. This can be demonstrated either by keeping the carbohydrate (and calorie) contents of the test foods constant and varying the percent protein, or by keeping the protein (and calories) constant and varying the percent carbohydrate. (That is, one can demonstrate regulation of both the protein and the carbohydrate components of the diet.) The ability to choose among foods so as to obtain a *desired* proportion of carbohydrates apparently is independent of the sweetness of the carbohydrate being tested: Regulation is as easy to demonstrate for dextrin as for dextrose or sucrose (12).

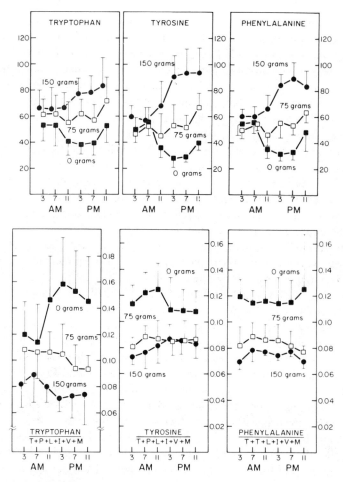

FIG. 4. *Top.* Diurnal variations in plasma aromatic amino acid levels in normal human subjects consuming different levels of dietary protein, as described in legend to Fig. 2 **(5)**. *Bottom:* Diurnal variations in plasma aromatic amino acid ratios in normal human subjects ingesting different levels of dietary protein, as described in legend to Fig. 2 **(5)**.

Serotonin-releasing neurons apparently are key components of the brain mechanisms underlying this regulation of food choice: Thus, rats can be manipulated to choose other than carbohydrates (i.e., to increase the protein/carbohydrate ratio of the test meal) either by giving them a carbohydrate-rich *pre-meal* (11), or by administering any of a large number of drugs which act at different loci to enhance serotonin-mediated neurotransmission (12). Moreover, dietary manipulations (like the chronic consumption of a carbohydrate-poor diet) which diminish the plasma Tp/LNAA ratio and, thus, reduce brain tryptophan and serotonin levels, sharply increase the proportion of carbohydrate that the animal subsequently eats when it is given the opportunity to choose (11). It seems not unlikely

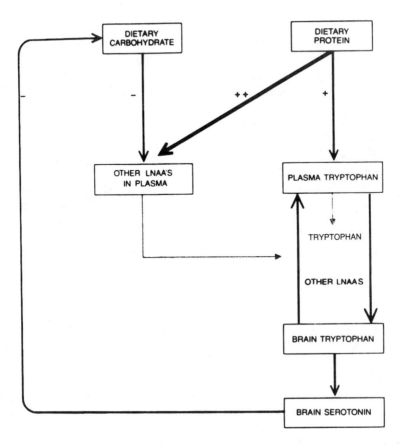

FIG. 5. Process by which food consumption may affect the synthesis of serotonin in the brain. Eating protein raises the plasma level of tryptophan, but it raises the plasma level of other large, neutral amino acids (LNAA) even further because each of them is more plentiful than tryptophan in proteins. Dietary carbohydrate induces the secretion of insulin, which moves most amino acids out of the bloodstream but has little effect on tryptophan. Because tryptophan must compete with the other LNAA for transport across the blood-brain barrier, the movement of tryptophan from the plasma to the brain is controlled by the plasma ratio of tryptophan to the other LNAA. When the ratio is high, tryptophan enters the brain; when it is low, tryptophan moves from the brain into the bloodstream. The release in the brain serotonin synthesized from the tryptophan appears to reduce a rat's (or a person's) carbohydrate intake (14).

that the tendency of humans to consume a more or less constant proportion of their calories as protein, and the relative stability of lean body mass, may reflect the operation of this mechanism; it diminishes the likelihood that meals imbalanced in one direction (too much protein or carbohydrate) will be immediately followed by others imbalanced in the same direction.

It also seems possible that some of the common abnormalities in eating behavior—including those that can lead to obesity—may have their origin in disturbances in the mechanism through which the brain *learns* about the composition of the last meal (by nutrient-induced variations in serotoninergic neurotransmission) and *decides* what to eat next. Such disturbances could exist at several loci: For example, the brain Tp/LNAA ratio might not respond appropriately to food-induced changes in the plasma Tp/LNAA ratio because of an abnormality in the blood-brain barrier transport system; the increase in brain tryptophan that follows a carbohydrate-rich, protein-poor meal might not have a sufficient effect on serotonin-mediated neurotransmission, because the unfortunate individual has a brain containing too few serotoninergic neurons; the functional activity of the serotoninergic neurons may be disturbed by pathological processes arising elsewhere in the brain. Although it is difficult to examine changes in brain chemicals using human subjects, it is relatively easy to determine whether, for example, obese individuals exhibit the same changes in the plasma Tp/LNAA ratio after a test meal as nonobese control subjects, and we are currently exploring such responses in collaboration with associates at the University of Lausanne. We have during the past few years identified a subset of obese people whose problem seems to be specifically related to an inappropriate desire for carbohydrates, especially at certain times of day (13). If such *carbohydrate cravers* compensate by diminishing their mealtime food intake or by increasing their energy output, they may avoid the development of obesity; however, if they eat normal-sized meals supplemented with multiple carbohydrate snacks, they become obese. We find that administration of subanorectic doses of drugs (like fenfluramine) which release brain serotonin can suppress the carbohydrate craving (13). It will be interesting to see whether supplemental Tp has a similar effect, especially in view of the evidence that the Tp/LNAA plasma ratio tends to be abnormally low in obese people (possibly as a consequence of peripheral insulin resistance) and that the protein-rich, carbohydrate-poor diet (the *PSMF diet*) with which many obese people are treated further lowers the Tp/LNAA ratio (6).

OTHER NUTRIENT-DEPENDENT NEUROTRANSMITTERS

As mentioned above, the rates at which physiologically active catecholaminergic neurons release their transmitter (dopamine, norepinephrine, or epinephrine) can be enhanced by giving the individual tyrosine and can be suppressed by administering other LNAA (which compete with tyrosine for uptake into the brain). The effect of a given tyrosine dose (or, for that matter, of a given dose of Tp) can be potentiated by giving it concurrently with a carbohydrate source (9). The resulting secretion of insulin lowers plasma levels of the competing LNAA and increases the proportion of administered molecules that are taken up into the brain (9,10). The reason that tyrosine levels affect catecholamine synthesis only when neurons are firing rapidly has to do with the properties of the key enzyme tyrosine hydroxylase that converts the amino acid to the catecholamines (14,15): When neurons fire frequently, the enzyme itself become phosphorylated; as a consequence, its affinity for its cofactor, tetrahydrobioperin, increases markedly so that it becomes limited by tyrosine. This phosphorylation is short-lived, hence soon after the neurons slow their firing, they become unresponsive to additional tyrosine. Tyrosine administration can, theoretically, be useful in any experimental or clinical situation in which it would be desirable to have more catecholamine molecules released at a particular locus, inside or outside the brain. [Its uses in these situations and the theoretical bases for such uses, have been reviewed extensively (15).]

Similarly, acetylcholine's production in and release from cholinergic neurons can depend on the availability of free choline when particular cholinergic neurons happen to be firing frequently: Any treatment that increases plasma choline, including oral choline chloride, dietary lecithin, or even eating eggs or liver, will have this effect. The primary reason that brain choline levels rise after choline consumption is not that more plasma choline enters the brain but that less leaves it. The brain is able to synthesize choline *de novo* (1,2); however, most of the choline is lost by secretion into the bloodstream via the operation of a bidirectional blood-brain barrier choline transport system. Raising plasma choline slows this loss, thereby allowing brain choline to accumulate. Choline is converted to acetylcholine by the enzyme choline acetyltransferase; the mechanism that couples the choline dependence of this process to neuronal firing frequency awaits identification. Choline (or lecithin) administration has been found to be useful in treating tardive dyskinesia, mania, and several neurological diseases (15); given chronically, it may also constitute a useful adjunct in the management of Alzheimer's disease or senility—if and when an effective drug is found that the choline can be an adjunct to—since the primary lesion in this disease appears to be a selective loss of acetylcholine-releasing brain neurons.

Although the effects of tyrosine and choline on brain function are less ubiquitous than those of Tp, when they do occur (i.e., in rapidly firing neurons) they can be of major health importance, for example, in memory, in control of mood, or in sustaining normal cardiovascular function. Hence, it seems prudent that care should be given to satisfying the brain's needs for these compounds—especially in formulating foods for people who might already have some disturbance involving catecholaminergic or cholinergic neurons (like the aged). The fact that tyrosine may not be an essential amino acid, nor choline an essential growth factor, for the young rat should not obscure our recognition that these compounds, like Tp, are absolutely essential for a normally functioning nervous system.

ACKNOWLEDGMENTS

These studies were supported in part by grants from the United States National Institute of Health, the National Aeronautics and Space Administration, and the Center for Brain Sciences and Metabolism Charitable Trust.

REFERENCES

1. Blusztajn, J. K., and Wurtman, R. J. (1982): Biosynthesis of choline by a preparation enriched in synaptosomes from rat brain. *Nature,* 290:417–418.

2. Blusztajn, J. K., and Wurtman, R. J. (1983): Choline and cholinergic neurons. *Science, (in press.)*

3. Fernstrom, J. D., and Wurtman, R. J. (1971): Brain serotonin content: Increase following ingestion of carbohydrate diet. *Science,* 174:1023–1025.

4. Fernstrom, J. D., and Wurtman, R. J. (1972): Brain serotonin content: Physiological regulation by plasma neutral amino acids. *Science,* 178:414–416.

5. Fernstrom, J. D., Wurtman, R. J., Hammarstrom-Wiklund, B., Rand, W. M., Munro, H. N., and Davidson, C. S. (1979): Diurnal variations in plasma concentrations of tryptophan, tyrosine and other neutral amino acids: effect of dietary protein. *Am. J. Clin. Nutr.,* 32:1912–1922.

6. Heraief, E., Burckhardt, P., Mauron, C., Wurtman, J., and Wurtman, R. J. (1983): Obesity and its dietary treatment may suppress synthesis of brain serotonin. *J. Neur. Trans. (in press).*

7. Hirsch, M. J., Growdon, J. H., and Wurtman, R. J. (1978): Relations between dietary choline intake, serum choline levels, and various metabolic indices. *Metabolism,* 27:953–960.

7a. Leiberman, H. R., et al. (1983): Mood, performance, and pain sensitivity: Changes induced by food constitutents. *J. Psychiatr. Res., (in press.)*

8. Madras, B. K., Cohen, E. L., Messing, R., Munro, H. N., and Wurtman, R. J. (1974): Relevance of serum-free tryptophan to tissue tryptophan concentrations. *Metabolism,* 23(12):1107–1116.

9. Mauron, C., and Wurtman, R. J. (1983): Co-administering tyrosine with glucose potentiates its effect on brain tyrosine levels. *J. Neur. Trans.,* 55:317–321.

10. Pardridge, W. M. (1977): Regulation of amino acid availability to the brain. In: *Nutrition and the Brain,* edited by R. J. Wurtman and J. J. Wurtman. Raven Press, New York.

11. Wurtman, J. J., Moses, P. L., and Wurtman, R. J. (1983): Prior carbohydrate consumption affects the amount of carbohydrate that rats choose to eat. *J. Nutr.,* 113:70–78.

12. Wurtman, J. J., and Wurtman, R. J. (1979): Drugs that enhance central serotoninergic transmission diminish elective carbohydrate consumption by rats. *Life Sci.,* 24:895–904.

13. Wurtman, J. J., Wurtman, R. J., Growdon, J. H., Henry, P., Lipscomb, A., and Zeisel, S. (1981): Carbohydrate craving in obese people: Suppression by treatments affecting serotoninergic transmission. *Int. J. of Eating Disorders,* 1:2–15.

14. Wurtman, R. J. (1982): Nutrients that modify brain function. *Scientific American,* 246:42–51.

15. Wurtman, R. J., Hefti, F., and Melamed, E. (1980): Precursor control of neurotransmitter synthesis. *Pharmacol. Rev.,* 32:315–335.

Eating and Its Disorders, edited by A. J.
Stunkard and E. Stellar. Raven Press,
New York © 1984.

Metabolic Defense of the Body Weight Set-Point

Richard E. Keesey and Stephen W. Corbett

Department of Psychology, University of Wisconsin, Madison, Wisconsin 53706

Although this volume focuses primarily on eating and eating disorders, the present chapter is concerned with how ingested energy is utilized and expended. Specifically, it deals with the adjustments in energy expenditure which aid in stabilizing an organism's body weight at a physiologically regulated level or "set-point."

ENERGY EXPENDITURE IN NORMAL WEIGHT ANIMALS AND MAN

The rate at which adult organisms ingest and expend energy can ordinarily be predicted from their body weight. Rats, pigeons, dogs, sheep, men, and steers obviously require different amounts of energy to maintain their widely differing body masses. Yet, Kleiber (12) has shown that all utilize energy at a rate proportional to their body weight. The logarithmic relationship between body weight and resting metabolism (Fig. 1) forms the basis of *Kleiber's rule* that the energy needs of many different animal species are proportional to the ¾ power of their body weight. Raising body weight to this ¾ power thus provides an estimate of an animal's "metabolic body size."

It is important to recognize, however, that this relationship between resting energy needs and metabolic size holds only when an animal is at its normally maintained body weight. Should intake be restricted and an animal's body weight caused to decline, metabolic body size no longer accurately predicts energy needs. This is because the rate of energy expenditure declines more quickly than would be predicted from the decline in metabolic body size (12,25). We have observed in food restricted lean Zucker rats, for example, that a weight loss of 5.8% was accompanied by a decline in resting metabolic rate of 14.7% (see Fig. 2). This reduction in resting metabolism is substantially greater than would be expected on the basis of the decline in metabolic body size. Similar findings have been reported in humans. The basal metabolic rates of men voluntarily submitting to a semistarvation diet during World War II declined such that, even when adjusted for the loss of metabolically active tissue, they were (after 24 weeks) nearly 16% below the initial level (11).

In a similar fashion, energy is apparently expended at rates exceeding those expected on the basis of changes in metabolic body size when body weight rises

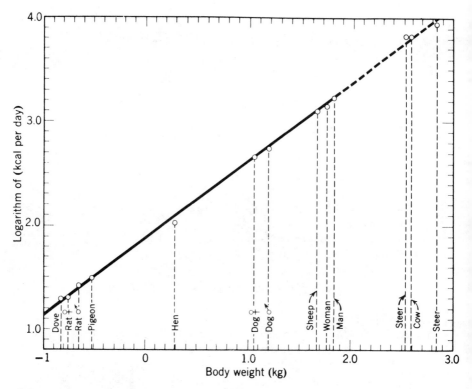

FIG. 1. Relation of log of metabolic rate to that of body weight. (From Kleiber, 1975, ref. 14.)

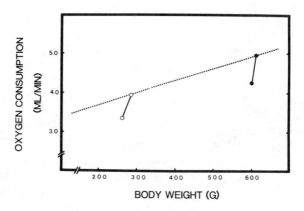

FIG. 2. Oxygen consumption as a function of body weight in lean *(open circles)* and obese *(closed circles)* Zucker rats. The *dotted line* connects the *ad lib.*-fed lean and obese groups. The *solid lines* connect the deprived lean and obese rats with their *ad lib.*-fed controls.

above the level normally maintained. Both animals and man display elevated rates of thermogenesis subsequent to overconsumption and/or weight gain. Overfeeding and weight gain induced by the feeding of a varied, palatable "cafeteria" diet produced a 28% increase in resting metabolic rate, even after scores had been corrected for differences in body size (16). We have seen similar, though quantitatively smaller, effects after feeding rats a palatable liquid diet (see Fig. 4). Human subjects who overconsume likewise display elevated rates of thermogenesis (14).

These adjustments in energy expenditure clearly contribute to the stability of body weight characteristic of most adult animals and man. Physiological mechanisms actively elevating or reducing rates of energy expenditure in response to weight increase or decline serve to blunt the effects of both overnutrition in times of food abundance and undernutrition in times of famine. These actions may likewise explain why most dieters are able to lose only a certain amount of weight even though they continue to restrict their intake, as well as why they regain their lost weight so rapidly when they forego the diet. They also contribute to an explanation of why the prisoners whom Sims and his coworkers (22) induced to ingest such large quantities of food gained so little weight, and why it was then necessary to continue eating so much just to maintain that added weight.

WEIGHT MAINTENANCE AT OBESE LEVELS

If these metabolic adjustments are so effective in restraining weight change, why do we see such wide variations in body weight within a species, and why is obesity so prevalent? Do the physiological mechanisms controlling these adaptive metabolic responses to weight gain fail to operate in the obese? The reported deficits in cold-induced thermogenesis in genetically obese rats (8) and in dietary-induced thermogenesis in humans (21) certainly raise this possibility. Or, is it the case that these mechanisms operate normally in the obese but are *set* to maintain and defend abnormally high body weights?

In addressing these questions, we have studied two animal preparations in which body weight is maintained at unusually high levels. One is the Zucker "fatty," a rat in which obesity is inherited as a single Mendelian recessive from the mating of two heterozygous lean rats. It is known that the fatty displays an effective behavioral defense of its elevated body weight. It remains obese, for example, when challenged with diets rendered unpalatable by the addition of quinine (4). Whether or not the Zucker fatty displays a metabolic defense of its elevated body weight, however, has not been determined. To examine this matter, we first restricted the daily intakes of a group of obese Zucker rats to 70% of normal, causing their body weights to decline over a 2-week period by 5.6%. The same procedure, as previously noted, caused a 5.8% weight decline in lean Zucker rats. It can be seen (Fig. 2) that just as the deprived leans, the deprived obese Zuckers displayed a marked decline in resting heat production. In fact, the decline in resting oxygen consumption in the obese and lean deprived rats was virtually identical (14.7 versus 14.5%, respectively). Note also that although the restricted obese rats still weighed nearly 600 g, their resting oxygen consumption declined to such an extent that it was only slightly higher than that of *ad lib.*-fed lean rats weighing one-half as much. We conclude from these observations that the Zucker fatty rat displays essentially the same pattern of energy conservation in response to food deprivation and weight loss as that of normal weight rats. The significant difference, of course, is that the adaptive metabolic adjustments in Zucker fatties are initiated at elevated body weights and thereby serve to sustain their obesity.

Another preparation maintaining body weight at abnormally high levels is the ventromedial hypothalamically (VMH) lesioned animal. Unlike the Zucker fatty rat, this rat does not display an effective behavioral defense of its obesity. Confronted with unpalatable diets or required to work for its food, the body weight of the obese VMH rat soon declines to levels of nonlesioned rats (6,7,20). One recent report suggests that their metabolic defense of these elevated weight levels may also be impaired. Specifically, VMH-lesioned rats seem not to display a hypermetabolic response to weight increases (24). It is as though the mechanisms adjusting thermogenesis in response to altered energetic status fail to respond normally following this lesion. We are thus inclined to believe that in the Zucker rat various adaptive metabolic responses play a significant role in maintaining its characteristic obesity. The VMH-lesioned rat, in a contrary fashion, may become fat because these metabolic adjustments to weight change are either blunted or fail to occur.

WEIGHT MAINTENANCE AT REDUCED LEVELS

Rats with lesions of the lateral hypothalamus (LH) maintain body weight at chronically reduced levels. They also make essentially the same behavioral adjustments to perturbations of energy balance as do nonlesioned animals in defending normal body weights. When confronted with experimentally induced over- or undernutrition, LH-lesioned animals make adjustments in food intake appropriate to maintaining body weight at a reduced level. That is, just as with non-lesioned animals, a metering of energy intake contributes to their stable regulation of body energy stores. Only the weight levels around which these behavioral adjustments occur has changed, suggesting that the LH lesion reduces the set-point for body weight (9).

Recently, our research has focused on features of energy expenditure that also contribute to the LH-lesioned rats' weight regulation at reduced levels. We have learned that immediately after lesioning, LH-lesioned rats display high rates of energy expenditure accompanied by rapid weight loss (10,23). We interpret this result by noting that, if LH lesions reduce the regulated level of body weight, the state of a recently LH-lesioned rat is analogous to that of a nonlesioned but overweight rat. Both are above their body weight set-point; both respond by increasing energy expenditure and rapidly depleting their energy stores. This episode of increased heat production persists in the overfed animals until their body weight returns to normal (16,17). Similarly, the hypermetabolic state of LH-lesioned rats persists until body weight declines to the reduced levels they will eventually maintain (10).

The physiological mechanisms responsible for the increased heat production of recently LH-lesioned and overfed rats also seem to be similar. Rothwell and Stock (18) have demonstrated the involvement of sympathetic nervous system activity in the hypermetabolic response to overfeeding. Specifically, the response involves β-adrenergic activation of heat producing systems, most importantly brown adipose tissue thermogenesis. LH lesion-induced thermogenesis appears also to depend on these systems. The heat increment following LH lesions is attenuated by the β-adrenergic blocker propranolol (2). It has also been determined that brown adipose tissue plays a role in this response to LH lesions. Local temperature changes in the interscapular brown fat depot precede the rise in core temperature following LH lesions and exceed the temperature changes in other tissues (1). Similar mechanisms in LH lesion-induced and diet-induced thermogenesis suggest that a similar function may be served, viz., the dissipation of excess calories.

Rats with lesions of the lateral hypothalamus eventually resume feeding and appear to regulate their body weights normally, although at a reduced level. Heat production in these animals is normal in that it is appropriate to the reduced body size they maintain (3). Thus, although nonlesioned animals are hypometabolic if their weight is lowered to the levels LH-lesioned animals maintain, LH-lesioned rats show normal rates of heat production at these reduced levels.

LH-lesioned rats also display an effective metabolic defense of their lowered body weight. In one experiment, we examined the metabolic response of both normal and LH-lesioned rats to elevations in body weight induced by a palatable diet. Nonlesioned and previously LH-lesioned rats maintaining stable, although reduced body weights, were fed either a standard chow diet or a highly palatable, liquid diet (Nutrament) for 3 weeks. As seen in Fig. 3, Nutrament promoted substantial weight gain in both the LH-lesioned and nonlesioned groups. In the case of the LH-lesioned rats, their weight rose to the level of nonlesioned chow-fed rats when fed this diet.

Daily rates of energy expenditure were then determined. Consistent with our earlier report (3), chow-fed LH-lesioned rats displayed normal rates of heat production at the reduced body weights they were maintaining. Fig. 4 shows that, when expressed with reference to body size, the daily heat production of chow-fed LH-lesioned rats (LHC) is the same as that of the heavier chow-fed nonlesioned rats (SHAMC). But, daily heat production is markedly elevated in both the lesioned and nonlesioned rats (LHN and SHAMN) induced to increase their weight by Nutrament. Clearly, LH-lesioned rats display the same hypermetabolic response to diet-induced weight gain as do nonlesioned animals (Fig. 4).

The preceding experiments establish that metabolic adjustments serve to defend the reduced body weights of LH-lesioned rats. LH-lesioned rats normally expend energy at a rate appropriate to the reduced body size they maintain. But,

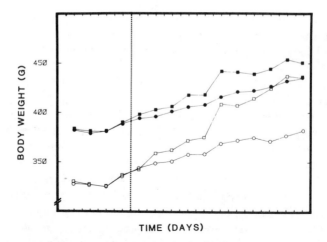

FIG. 3. Body weight of nonlesioned *(closed symbols)* and LH-lesioned *(open symbols)* rats fed either a Nutrament *(squares)* or a wet-mash *(circles)* diet.

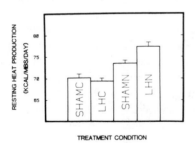

FIG. 4. Oxygen consumption, expressed relative to metabolic body size, of nonlesioned (SHAM) and lesioned (LH) rats fed either a Nutrament (N) or wet-mash (C) diet.

when their weight is raised (by the use of palatable diets) to the level of nonlesioned rats, they are markedly hypermetabolic, just as they are immediately following lesioning (10). At this body weight, nonlesioned animals are normometabolic, although they too become hypermetabolic if their weight is then elevated. Thus, both in their normal expenditure of energy at the lower body weights they maintain, and in their increased energy expenditure following overconsumption and weight gain, LH-lesioned rats give indication of defending a reduced body weight set-point.

DIET-INDUCED ALTERATIONS IN BODY WEIGHT SET-POINT

When rats are fed diets unusually high in fat content, a pronounced obesity often develops. The weight gain, due almost entirely to an accretion of fat (19), can be accompanied by increases in adipocyte number, both in young (13) and adult rats (5). Since such changes in adipose cellularity are nonreversible, they may account for the observation that body weights often fail to return to normal levels when rats are returned to regular diets (5,15). Apparently, this and/or other adaptations to the dietary treatment occur which then serve to sustain body weight at an elevated level.

This observation raises the question as to whether the physiological controls of energy expenditure have themselves been reset to operate at an elevated regulation level. That is, is energy expenditure in rats with irreversible obesity consistent with the pattern expected were the weight changes induced by long-term fat feeding to involve an upward displacement in the body weight set-point?

To answer this question we fed male rats a high-fat (50%) or low-fat (8%) diet for 6 months. The animals in each diet condition were then divided into groups fed 100, 75, or 50% of their *ad lib.* food intake for the next 3 weeks. Animals fed the high-fat diet *ad lib.* reached a body weight of 526 g, whereas those fed the low-fat diet *ad lib.* attained a weight of 414 g. Caloric restriction to 75 and 50% of *ad lib.* intake produced high-fat-fed groups weighing 459 and 456 g and low-fat-fed groups weighing 364 and 343 g, respectively. Resting heat production, expressed with reference to metabolic body size was then determined for each of these groups.

Two features of the high-fat-fed animals' energy expenditure suggest that long-term diet-induced obesity is indeed characterized by a shift in the regulated level of body weight. First, note in Fig. 5 that the high- and low-fat-fed rats show the same resting levels of energy expenditure. Resting expenditure for the obese, high-fat-fed animals may be considered *normal* in that when expressed with reference to their metabolic body size, it is the same as that of the low-fat-fed animals. Thus, although short-term overfeeding of a cafeteria diet causes an elevation in heat production (16), an adaptive response which serves to mitigate further weight gain, animals made obese by long-term high-fat feeding do not exhibit this hypermetabolic state. Rather, they display levels of heat production similar to animals regulating at normal body weight.

Second, the high- and low-fat-fed rats make similar adjustments to caloric privation. As seen earlier in both lean and obese Zucker rats (Fig. 2), a substantial

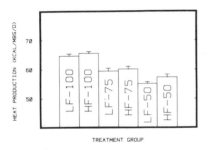

FIG. 5. Resting oxygen consumption, expressed relative to metabolic body size, of rats fed a low-fat (LF) or high-fat (HF) diet for 6 months. Two groups (LF-100 and HF-100) were then tested at the body weights (414 g and 526 g, respectively) each maintained when fed these diets *ad lib.* The LF-75 and HF-75 groups were tested after being restricted to 75% of their normal intake for 3 weeks, during which time their body weights declined to 364 g and 459 g, respectively. The LF-50 and HF-50 groups were tested following 3 weeks of restriction to 50% of their normal daily intake. Their weights at testing were 343 and 456 g, respectively.

reduction in resting energy expenditure occurs with caloric restriction and weight loss. The obese, fat-fed rats also make this compensatory energetic adjustment to caloric deprivation (Fig. 5). In as much as the adjustments in these animals serve to sustain them at a higher body weight, an elevated set-point is suggested.

SUMMARY AND CONCLUSIONS

The energy needs of an organism are a function of the tissue mass it maintains. Interspecific comparisons indicate that energy needs are a power function of body weight (12). Much of the work described here represents an effort to ascertain whether the function relating intraspecific energy expenditure to maintained body weight takes a similar form. The evidence to date from various rat preparations suggests that although some differences may exist, the form of the function for rats is not likely to differ substantially from the interspecific function derived by Kleiber (12). What has also emerged from this work, however is evidence that both the inter- and intraspecific functions accurately predict energy needs only when the organism is at the particular body weight it normally maintains and defends. This is because a rise in weight from the normal level causes energy needs to increase at a faster rate than the relationship would predict, whereas declines in weight from this level produce greater than predicted decreases in energy expenditure. We thus propose that an animal's body weight *set-point* be taken as the weight at which its daily energy needs can be accurately predicted from its metabolic body size. It is only at this one body weight that the animal is normometabolic.

It can then be asked whether organisms maintaining abnormally high or low body weights are suffering from regulatory dysfunctions or are regulating normally but at elevated or depressed set-points. We have seen that obese Zucker rats display the same adaptive metabolic adjustments to weight loss as normal weight rats. Since the exact form of the intraspecific body weight-metabolic needs relationship has not yet been determined, we must withhold judgment as to whether Zucker fatty rats are normometabolic at their elevated body weights. Since they display an effective metabolic defense of their obesity, however, an elevated set-point, rather than regulatory failure, seems to be the more probable cause of the Zucker fatty's condition. More compelling evidence of regulation at an altered body weight set-point is provided by the LH-lesioned rat. This preparation is normometabolic at the reduced body weight it maintains, and it becomes hypermetabolic when its weight is elevated to the level of nonlesioned littermates. The obesity of the VMH-lesioned rat, on the other hand, may well stem from primary regulatory impairments. This preparation appears to remain hypometabolic over a wide range of body weights, apparently failing to display the expected adjustments in energy expenditure to weight change.

Finally, a most interesting example of regulation at an altered set-point is the dietary obese animal. Rats, after months on a high-fat diet, display energy intakes and expenditures that are appropriate to the elevated body weight they then maintain. More importantly, they become hypometabolic when their weight is lowered from this level. Thus, the physiological controls which act to stabilize body weight at a particular level operate in these rats to sustain their body weight at an obese level. Clearly, we will want to study this preparation further with the aim of determining what physiological and/or anatomical changes might account for this elevation in the level of regulated body weight. An understanding of the mechanisms underlying such shifts in set-point could provide useful insights into the circumstances underlying the wide, natural variation between people in maintained body weight.

REFERENCES

1. Corbett, S. W. (1982): Energy metabolism in rats with lateral hypothalamic lesions. Doctoral Thesis, University of Wisconsin.
2. Corbett, S. W., Kaufman, L. N., and Keesey, R. E. (1983): Lateral hypothalamic lesion-induced heat production and its modification by beta-adrenergic blockade. *(Submitted.)*
3. Corbett, S. W., and Keesey, R. E. (1982): Energy balance of rats with lateral hypothalamic lesions. *Am. J. Physiol.,* 242:E273–E279.
4. Cruce, J. A. F., Greenwood, M. R. C., Johnson, P. R., and Quartermain, D. (1974): Genetic versus hypothalamic obesity: Studies of intake and dietary manipulations in rats. *J. Comp. Physiol. Psychol.,* 87:295–301.
5. Faust, I. M., Johnson, P. R., Stern, J. S., and Hirsch, J. (1978): Diet-induced adipocyte number increase in adult rats: a new model of obesity. *Am. J. Physiol.,* 235:E279–E286.
6. Ferguson, N. B. L., and Keesey, R. E. (1975): Effect of a quinineadulterated diet upon body weight maintenance in male rats with ventromedial hypothalamic lesions. *J. Comp. Physiol. Psychol.,* 89:478–488.
7. Franklin, K. B. J., and Herberg, L. J. (1974): Ventromedial syndrome: the rats "finickiness" results from the obesity, not from the lesions. *J. Comp. Physiol. Psychol.,* 87:410–414.
8. Godbole, V., York, D. A., and Bloxam, D. B. (1978): Developmental changes in the fatty (fa/fa) rat: evidence for defective thermogenesis preceding hyperlipogenesis and hyperinsulinemia. *Diabetologia,* 15:41–44.
9. Keesey, R. E., Boyle, P. C., Kemnitz, J. W., and Mitchel, J. S. (1976): The role of the lateral hypothalamus in determining the body weight set-point. In: *Hunger: Basic Mechanisms and Clinical Implications,* edited by D. Novin, W. Wyrwicka, and G. A. Bray, pp. 243–255. Raven Press, New York.
10. Keesey, R. E., Corbett, S. W., Hirvonen, M. D., and Kaufman, L. N. (1983): Heat production and body weight changes following lateral hypothalamic lesions. *(Submitted.)*
11. Keys, A., Brozek, J., Henschel, A., Mickelsen, O., and Taylor, H. C. (1950): *The Biology of Human Starvation.* University of Minnesota Press, Minneapolis.
12. Kleiber, M. (1975): *The Fire of Life.* Robert E. Krieger, New York.
13. Lemonnier, D. (1972): Effect of age, sex, and site on the cellularity of the adipose tissue in mice and rats rendered obese by a high fat diet. *J. Clin. Invest.,* 57:2907–2915.
14. Miller, D. S., Mumford, P., and Stock, M. J. (1967): Gluttony: thermogenesis in overeating man. *Am. J. Clin. Nutr.,* 20:1223–1229.
15. Rolls, B. J., Rowe, C. A., and Turner, R. C. (1980): Persistent obesity in rats following a period of consumption of mixed, high-energy diet. *J. Physiol. (Lond.),* 298:415–427.
16. Rothwell, N. J., and Stock, M. J. (1979): A role for brown adipose tissue in diet-induced thermogenesis. *Nature,* 281:31–35.
17. Rothwell, N. J., and Stock, M. J. (1979): Regulation of energy balance in two models of reversible obesity in the rat. *J. Comp. Physiol. Psychol.,* 93:1024–1034.
18. Rothwell, N. J., and Stock, M. J. (1981): Regulation of energy balance. *Ann. Rev. Nutr.,* 1:235–256.
19. Schemmel, R., Mickelsen, O., and Gill, J. L. (1970): Dietary obesity in rats: body weight and body fat accretion in seven strains of rats. *J. Nutr.,* 100:1041–1048.

20. Sclafani, A., Springer, D., and Kluge, L. (1976): Effects of quinineadulterated diets on the food intake and body weight of obese and nonobese hypothalamic hyperphagic rats. *Physiol. Behav.,* 16:631–640.
21. Shetty, P. S., Jung, R. T., James, W. P. T., Barrand, M. A., and Callingham, B. A. (1981): Postprandial thermogenesis in obesity. *Clin. Sci.,* 60:519–525.
22. Sims, E. A. H., Danforth, E., Horton, E. S., Bray, G. A., Glennon, J. A., and Salans, L. B. (1973): Endocrine and metabolic effects of experimental obesity in man. *Recent Progress in Hormone Research,* 29:457–496.
23. Stevenson, J. A. F., and Montemurro, D. G. (1963): Loss of weight and metabolic rate of rats with lesions in the medial and lateral hypothalamus. *Nature,* 198:92.
24. Vilberg, T. R., and Keesey, R. E. (1982): Metabolic contributions to VMH obesity. Poster presented at the North American Association for the Study of Obesity. Poughkeepsie, New York. Oct. 17–19.
25. Westerterp, K. (1977): How rats economize—energy loss in starvation. *Physiol. Zool.,* 80:331–362.

Eating and Its Disorders, edited by A. J.
Stunkard and E. Stellar. Raven Press, New York
© 1984.

Role of the Fat Cell in Energy Balance Physiology

Irving M. Faust

The Rockefeller University, New York, New York 10021

Why is it that some people with virtually unlimited access to all sorts of appealing foods maintain a moderate amount of body fat all of their lives with little or no effort, while millions of others maintain an immoderate, or very immoderate, amount of body fat in spite of great efforts to avoid doing so?

The answer to this question may be that some people are either pathologically overattracted to food or for some reason do not know when to stop eating. Another possibility is that obesity results from a defective mechanism for burning off excess calories. In this regard, brown fat has of late been repeatedly suggested as the site of such a defect (16).

However, there is a third possibility. Obesity may simply be the manifestation of a high equilibrium level for body fat mass created, as is the equilibrium level in normal weight individuals, by the interaction of a wide variety of factors such as hormones, hormone receptors, diet composition, exercise, ambient temperature, enzymes, and genetics. The appeal of this alternative is that it does not require us to postulate any pathology of food intake nor any pathology of energy expenditure in order to explain obesity. The logic behind the concept, as well as some of the reasons I am attracted to it, are illustrated by a few simple figures.

ENERGY BALANCE

Figure 1 presents a simple model of the normal weight individual. The lean body mass of the individual in this figure is represented by the unshaded area in the center. For the purpose of this example, as well as for the purpose of examples which follow, it is considered to be constant. It includes all of the body tissues except for the adipose tissue, which is shaded with stippling. The small black packets in the shape of the letter "E" represent total energy input on the left (i.e., the caloric value of the food consumed) and total energy expenditure on the right (which includes calories used for locomotion, heat production, digestion, cell replacement, and basic metabolism).

It is important to note one feature of the relationship between energy input and energy expenditure: In the freely feeding, normal weight individual, input and output are almost precisely equal, especially when our measures are made over

☐ Lean mass
▨ Fat mass

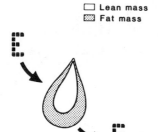

FIG. 1. Schematic representation of energy balance in the normal weight individual.

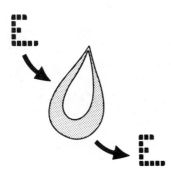

FIG. 2. High, balanced levels of energy input and output in the normal weight individual.

periods of weeks or months. To appreciate the degree of this precision, it is useful to consider that only a 5% positive error in me over the last 10 years would have caused my fat mass to be five times greater than it is now. Instead of creeping up from 165 to 175 lb, I would have raced up to 275 lb or more. Surely, the precise balance of energy input and output is not fortuitous, but rather is the result of the actions of physiological processes which function specifically to maintain the balance.

How might such a system work? One possibility is that input varies in relation to the opportunities and whims of the organism and that output is adjusted so that it varies accordingly. A second possibility is that output varies in relation to the needs and whims of the organism and that input is adjusted so that it varies accordingly. A third possibility, the one which I favor, is that both input and output are adjusted, as necessary, whenever the system is out of balance, one way or the other. If this notion is correct, a high level of input (represented in Fig. 2 by a few extra black packets on the left) would be balanced by an equally high level of output, shown by extra packets on the right, whereas the occurence of high output would be balanced by high input. The system stays in balance, and the fat mass does not change.

Likewise, low levels of input or output are also appropriately countered. In Fig. 3, subnormal energy input and output are represented by a few empty packets on each side of the organism. Net energy flow is low, but input and output are in balance so the fat mass does not change.

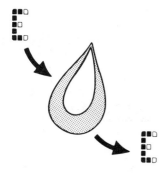

FIG. 3. Low, balanced levels of energy input and output in the normal weight individual.

There are many situations in which energy balance occurs at unusually high or low levels. For example, a rat housed in the cold requires vast amounts of energy to keep warm. Upon initial exposure to the cold, it must not only consume large amounts of food, it must also utilize some of its fat stores. However, after a sufficient period of adaptation, just the high levels of food intake are adequate to provide the rat's needs for heat production. The fat stores are at least partially replenished and the input/output balance is restored, although at a level that is far greater than normal. A rat adapted to living at 4°C may have twice the energy output matched by twice the energy input of a rat living at 23°C, while its body fat mass is stable at a level that is normal or somewhat less than normal (1,11).

ENERGY IMBALANCE

It is also important to consider that a physiological system which controls energy balance can be used to control energy imbalance as well.

Hibernating animals, such as the woodchuck and the golden-mantled ground squirrel, periodically go into either positive or negative energy balance and, thus, periodically gain and lose fat (14,19). In this manner, these animals satisfy their energy needs for hibernation. It is unlikely that this cycling is accomplished by the alteration, in isolation, of just energy input or just energy output. How much energy may have been consumed or expended in the recent past is of no consequence to these animals. What is of consequence is the size of the fat stores relative to the needs for hibernation. When one causes them to lose and then regain weight by temporarily restricting their food intake, the amount of weight they regain is a function only of the appropriate weight for that time of year. The particular body weight exhibited just prior to the period of deprivation is irrelevant. If they are prevented from hibernating (and are thus prevented from reducing energy expenditure), they nevertheless maintain the large amount of body fat appropriate for the time of year. They do this by eating a large amount of food during a time when their food intake is normally minimal (14).

The key concept is that body fat is kept constant at times as a result of physiologically controlled energy balance and altered at other times as a result of physiologically controlled energy imbalance. Thus, in pondering why a person may be

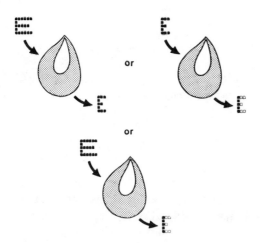

or

or

FIG. 4. The three states of energy imbalance which would cause the fat mass to increase.

gaining too much weight, it may be insufficient to ask why he is ingesting too many calories or why he is expending too few calories. It may be necessary to ask why input and output in this person are out of balance.

Theoretically, there are three combinations of energy input and output which can cause the fat mass to increase. These combinations are depicted in Fig. 4.

Obesity caused by high input alone is shown by the model in the upper left-hand corner of the figure; obesity caused by low output alone is shown by the model to the right; and obesity caused by high input plus low output is shown by the model at the bottom. Depending on the circumstance, an animal may use any one of these strategies. Indeed, when a preferred strategy is prevented, the animal may use another. A rat prevented from overeating often lowers energy expenditure and, thus, still gains weight (2). If the system is set for positive energy imbalance, the imbalance will still occur if it is at all possible.

ENERGY BALANCE IN OBESITY

A crucial feature of such physiologically controlled energy imbalance is that at some point the body fat mass plateaus and energy balance is restored. Excessive food intake or diminished energy expenditure during the weight gaining phase is not likely to represent a basic disorder if it disappears at the obese plateau.

Theoretically, there are three possible conditions of energy balance that may exist at the obese plateau. As depicted in Fig. 5, these are: high input matched by equally high output; normal input matched by equally normal output; and low input matched by equally low output.

To address the question of whether disorders of food intake are responsible for obesity, studies of food intake should surely be conducted at the obese plateau. However, in most studies of obese humans and animals that have been reported, it is unclear whether or not the subjects or animals studied were at the plateau.

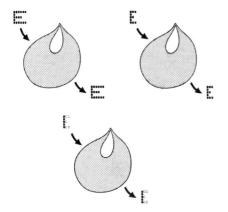

FIG. 5. The three states of energy balance which can theoretically exist at the obese plateau.

Do feeding disorders associated with obesity persist at the plateau? In particular, does overeating persist? If so, we should see the situation depicted by the model in the upper left-hand portion of the figure. If overeating persists, the obese plateau would only result when elevated expenditure finally matches the elevated food intake. The available evidence suggests that this condition does not occur in the rat (at least not in the most common obese models) (18). However, it does occur to some degree in severely obese people, perhaps because severe obesity in man is associated with an elevated resting metabolic rate (15).

What about disorders of energy output? Is there any evidence that they persist at the obese plateau? Do rats or people at the obese plateau still show disorders of thermogenesis? Is the activity of the brown fat (16) or of the sodium/potassium pump (3) still disordered at the obese plateau? If so, the condition in the lower portion of the figure should be seen. However, this condition has not been seen in the rat, and an extensive, recent study yielded no evidence for such a condition in obese man (20).

Has the condition schematized in the upper right hand portion of Fig. 5 (normal energy input balanced by normal energy output) been seen? Yes, it has.

Figure 6 shows the results of a 13-month experiment I conducted with lean Zucker (Fa/-) female rats fed a high-fat diet (5). The zero line represents both the level of caloric intake and the average body weight of control animals. The irregular solid line represents the daily caloric intake of the rats fed the high-fat diet, the dashed line represents the weight of these rats relative to controls. The left-hand side of the figure represents the first week of the experiment. This is the initial part of a long period of energy imbalance. During this week, caloric intake is very high and body weight increases rapidly.

The right-hand portion of the figure represents the final week of the experiment. Body weight of experimental rats is nearly twice that of their controls; body fat mass is nearly 10 times greater than in controls. But for the last 4 to 5 weeks, body weight has barely changed. This is the obese plateau. Calorie intake at the plateau is not significantly different from that of controls. It is certainly not

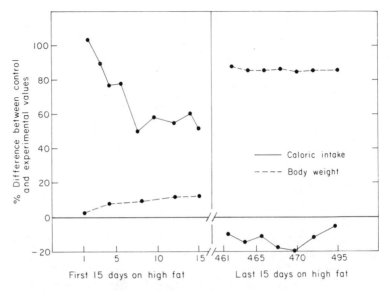

FIG. 6. Short- and long-term effects of feeding a high-fat diet to adult Lean Zucker (Fa/-) rats. (Reproduced with permission from ref. 5.)

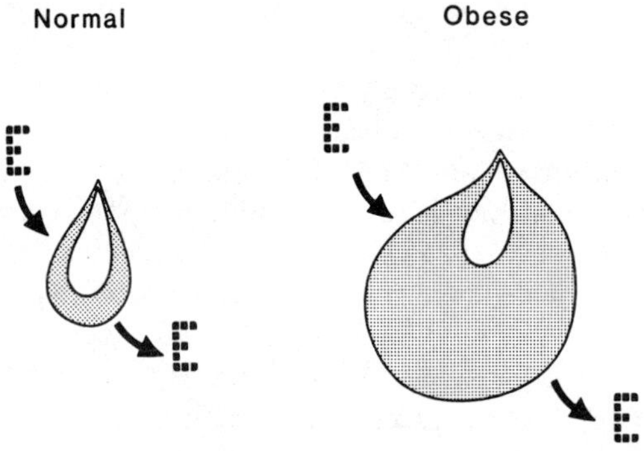

Normal   Obese

FIG. 7. Equal levels of energy input and output, but dramatically different amounts of body fat, in rats plateaued on chow *(left)* or on a diet high in fat *(right)*.

greater than in controls. As shown in Fig. 7, the system is in balance and energy input and output are normal. Perhaps other aspects of intake and output that are abnormal during weight gain also return to normal at the plateau.

Is this the condition to be found at the obese plateau in all types of obesity? I don't know, but I suspect that it would be found in at least a few of the most common obese models. Does the obese plateau itself occur in other types of obesity? Yes, it does. But not necessarily in all types. The important point is that there is much to be learned about causes and effects of obesity from examination of organisms at the obese plateau that cannot be learned during the period of weight gain.

What are the factors that determine the level at which the obese plateau occurs? From this experiment, we see that a major factor can be the composition of the diet. Although a low body weight plateau may occur in rats fed chow, an obese plateau occurs when the same rats are fed a diet high in fat. To test whether a dietary experience can have a permanent effect on the point at which body weight plateaus, I switched the high-fat fed rats back to the ordinary diet of chow. A dramatic drop in food intake occured immediately. For the first few weeks after the switch back to the chow diet, the experimental rats barely ate at all. Weight loss was precipitous.

Does this mean that rats will switch back and forth between the same two plateaus whenever the diet is switched back and forth between chow and high fat? Does the rat fed a high-fat diet for a period of months achieve energy balance only after body weight returns fully to the level seen in chow-fed controls? Apparently not. In another similar experiment with male rats fed high fat for just 6 months, my colleagues and I found that body weight plateaued following the switch back to chow at a level 15% (100 g) above normal. Body fat at the plateau was twice normal (4). It appears that a dietary experience that causes a period of overweight can have a lasting effect. The rats showed perfectly normal food intake at the elevated plateau, so normal energy balance was resumed but the original fat mass was not.

CELLULAR EFFECTS OF HIGH-FAT FEEDING

To understand the above phenomenon, we must consider that the adipose tissue of the rat is composed of millions of fat cells. In the adult, each fat cell may contain as little as a few tenths of a microgram of lipid or as much as two micrograms. Usually, fat cells of obese rats are filled with at least twice as much lipid as the fat cells of normal weight rats. This difference between obese and normal weight individuals is also true in man. In addition, if the obesity is severe enough, we also see more than the normal number of fat cells (see Fig. 8). In the most severe cases of human obesity, fat cells can be three or four times more plentiful than normal (10).

Is the overproduction of fat cells an underlying cause of severe obesity, or is it a response elicited by excessive weight gain? In rats fed high fat and then fed chow, what persists? Large fat cells or extra fat cells?

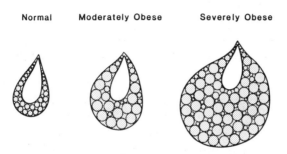

FIG. 8. Schematic representation of the size and number of fat cells in normal weight, moderately obese, and severely obese rats and man.

In a study designed to address these questions (7), my colleagues and I found that during the first few weeks of high-fat (HF) feeding, fat cells enlarge, rapidly reaching a peak size that is two to three times that of controls. In some depots, this peak was found to occur approximately 3 weeks after introduction of the diet, while in others it did not occur until approximately 6 weeks later. Nevertheless, in each depot, at about the time that the peak in fat cell size was attained, fat cell number began to increase rapidly and continued to increase for the rest of the 6 month period of the experiment. In one group of rats, 9 weeks of HF feeding caused fat cell size to be twice normal in retroperitoneal depots and three times normal in epididymal depots. However, after the rats had been refed on chow for 20 weeks, body weight returned to near normal levels and the increases in fat cell size were completely gone. There was no long-term trace of the increases whatsoever.

In contrast, the increase in fat cell number caused by 9 weeks of HF feeding persisted in its entirety. In the retroperitoneal depot, fat cell number doubled in just 9 weeks and remained doubled during the 20 weeks of chow refeeding.

It is thus clear why rats fed high fat for a few months have a higher fat mass plateau on chow than rats never fed high fat. They have an abundance of fat cells, and the abundance is not countered by a subnormal fat cell size. Indeed, their fat cells attain a size that is exactly the same as in controls. The HF diet has one effect that is permanent (increased fat cell number) and one that is reversed precisely (increased fat cell size).

A host of questions now beg to be asked: For example, since overeating and weight gain precipitated the increase in fat cell number, can undereating and weight loss cause fat cell number to decrease? What is the stimulus which causes the number of cells to increase? Is it the peak cell size? The composition of the diet? The amount of food that is eaten? What is the source of the newly apparent cells? Is there a pool of preadipocytes formed early in life waiting to be stimulated to differentiate, or are the cells formed *de novo* when they are needed?

Findings we have made over the past few years (9,12,13) bear directly on each of these issues and encourage us to believe that therapeutic control of fat cell production is a realistic objective. These experiments are reviewed elsewhere (8). Another set of questions suggested by these findings relate to the influence of fat cells on the behavior and metabolism of the organism.

BEHAVIORAL AND METABOLIC CHANGES IN THE HYPERPLASTIC, NONHYPERTROPHIC OBESE RAT

Consider the unusual condition that is created in the rat first fed an HF diet and then switched to chow. This animal is obese due to an abundance of fat cells alone. Fat cell size is perfectly normal. As far as I know, this is the only animal in which such a form of obesity exists. Furthermore, it is identical to its lean littermates in virtually every detail except for the extra fat cells. Surely, any peculiarity of metabolism or behavior that we may find in this rat is very likely due solely to the presence of the extra fat cells. Two simple observations my colleagues and I have made of this rat address the issue of altered metabolism and behavior and clearly illustrate the utility of the hyperplastic, nonhypertrophic (H,NH) obese model as a tool for further research in obesity and adipose tissue physiology. The first observation relates to the cause of hyperinsulinemia in obesity.

All other obese rats that have been examined show high levels of insulin, even when the obesity is at the plateau stage and food intake is normal. Does twice normal total body fat cause even a trace of an increase in plasma insulin levels in H,NH obese rats? The answer is no. Insulin levels seen in these rats are identical to those seen in their nonobese littermates (17). This observation argues strongly that the high insulin levels that are typically seen in obesity are at least partly the result of overly enlarged fat cells. Perhaps when a person or an animal is at the obese plateau, enlarged fat cells are the primary cause or the only cause of hyperinsulinemia.

A second observation I have made of the H,NH obese rat, relates to the question of whether the fat cells can influence food intake. Consider the fact that these hypercellular rats and their controls eat the same amount of chow. On a day to day basis, the chow consumption of the two groups is indistinguishable. Consider also that if both groups of rats were to be fed a diet less palatable than chow, food intake in both groups would decline for awhile until the body fat mass reached a new, lower plateau. If the rats were to be fed a more palatable diet, food intake would increase until the fat mass reached a new, higher plateau. But remember that the full increase in fat cell size is attained rapidly (in some depots within 3 weeks). Thus, it is of great interest to ask the following questions: Does the hypercellular rat achieve the same degree of decrease in fat cell size as its control in response to a less palatable diet? Does it achieve the same increase in response to a more palatable diet? Are such increases and decreases in fat cell size achieved at the same rate in the two animals? The answer to all three questions appears to be yes (4,6).

However, since the hypercellular rat has twice as many fat cells to accommodate, it must transfer twice as much energy to or from the fat mass in order to achieve the same degree of change in fat cell size as its control. If energy output does not change, the hypercellular rat must overeat twice as much of a highly palatable diet or undereat twice as much of an unpalatable diet in order to alter fat cell size as much as it is altered in control rats.

This is indeed what happens. In response to a tasty diet, H,NH and control rats overeat, but the hypercellular rat does so to a greater degree than the control rat. In response to the less-tasty diet, both rats undereat, but again the hypercellular rat does so to a greater degree than the control rat (4). The conclusion that there is a direct and positive relationship between fat cell number and change in food intake is compelling. It is thus very likely that the fat cells can influence food intake, and that this influence is part of the physiological process that serves to continually draw the mass of the body fat towards the equilibrium level dictated, in part, by the current diet.

CONCLUSION

At the beginning of this chapter, I suggested that an understanding of the problem of obesity will emerge from knowledge of the process which determines the equilibrium level for body fat, rather than from the discovery of a basic disorder of food intake or energy expenditure. Whether this notion is correct remains to be determined. However, it is certainly clear by now that the fat cell is an active participant in energy balance physiology and is not simply a passive receptacle for calories unwittingly overingested or underexpended. It exerts an influence, perhaps a major influence, both on metabolism and on feeding behavior. Therefore, knowledge of the fat cell is central to the understanding of body weight regulation. It may very well prove to be central to the understanding of obesity.

ACKNOWLEDGMENT

This research was supported in part by National Institutes of Health grant AM-20508.

REFERENCES

1. Brobeck, J. R. (1948): Food intake as a mechanism of temperature regulation. *Yale J. Biol. Med.,* 20:545–552.
2. Cox, J. E., and Powley, T. L. (1981): Intragastric pair feeding fails to prevent VMH obesity or hyperinsulinemia. *Am. J. Physiol.,* 240:E566–E572.
3. De Luis, M., Blackburn, G. L., and Flier, J. S. (1980): Reduced activity of the red-cell sodium-potassium pump in human obesity. *N. Engl. J. Med.,* 303:1017–1022.
4. Faust, I. M. (1980): Nutrition and the fat cell. *Int. J. Obes.,* 4:314–321.
5. Faust, I. M. (1981): Signals from adipose tissue. In: *The Body Weight Regulatory System: Normal and Disturbed Mechanisms,* edited by L. A. Cioffi, W. P. T. James, and T. B. Van Itallie, pp. 39–43. Raven Press, New York.
6. Faust, I. M., Johnson, P. R., and Hirsch, J. (1977): Surgical removal of adipose tissue alters feeding behavior and the development of obesity in rats. *Science,* 197:393–396.
7. Faust, I. M., Johnson, P. R., Stern, J. S., and Hirsch, J. (1978): Diet-induced adipocyte number increase in adult rats: A new model of obesity. *Am. J. Physiol.,* 235:E279–E286.
8. Faust, I. M., and Miller, W. H., Jr. (1983): Hyperplastic growth of adipose tissue in obesity. In: *The Adipocyte and Obesity: Cellular and Molecular Mechanisms,* edited by A. Angel, C. Hollenberg, and D. Roncari, pp. 41–51. Raven Press, New York.
9. Faust, I. M., Triscari, J., Sclafani, A., Miller, W. H., Jr., and Sullivan, A. C. (1980): Moderate adipocyte hyperplasia in the chow-fed VMH lesioned rat. *Fed. Proc.,* 39:887.
10. Hirsch, J., and Batchelor, B. R. (1977): Adipose tissue cellularity and human obesity. *Clin. Endocrinol. Metab.,* 26:607–614.
11. Miller, W. H., Jr., and Faust, I. M. (1982): Alterations in rat adipose tissue morphology induced by a low temperature environment. *Am. J. Physiol.,* 242:E93–E96.
12. Miller, W. H., Jr., Faust, I. M., Goldberger, A. C., and Hirsch, J. (1983): Effects of severe long-term food deprivation and refeeding on adipose tissue cells in the rat. *Am. J. Physiol.* 245:E74–E80.
13. Miller, W. H., Jr., Faust, I. M., Hirsch, J. Demonstration of *de novo* production of adipocytes in adult rats by biochemical and autoradiographic techniques. *(Submitted.)*
14. Mrosovsky, N. (1976): Lipid programmes and life strategies in hibernators. *Am. Zool.,* 16:685–697.
15. Ravussin, E., Burand, B., Schutz, Y., and Jequier, E. (1982): Twenty-four hour energy expen-

diture and resting metabolic rate in obese, moderately obese and control subjects. *Am. J. Clin. Nutr.,* 35:566–573.
16. Rothwell, N. J., and Stock, M. J. (1979): A role for brown adipose tissue in diet-induced thermogenesis. *Nature,* 281:31–35.
17. Schneider, B. S., Faust, I. M., Hemmes, R. B., and Hirsch, J. (1981): Effects of altered adipose tissue morphology on plasma insulin levels in the rat. *Am. J. Physiol.,* 240:E358–E362.
18. Vasselli, J. R., Cleary, M. P., Jen, K. C., and Greenwood, M. R. C. (1980): Development of food motivated behavior in free feeding and food restricted Zucker fatty (fa/fa) rats. *Physiol. Behav.,* 25:565–573.
19. Young, R. A., Salans, L. B., and Sims, E. A. H. (1982): Adipose tissue cellularity in woodchucks: effects of season and captivity at an early age. *J. Lipid Res.,* 23:887–892.
20. Leibel, R. L., and Hirsch, J. (1983): Diminished energy requirements in reduced-obese patients. *Metabolism, (in press).*

Eating and Its Disorders, edited by A. J.
Stunkard and E. Stellar. Raven Press,
New York © 1984.

The Enduring Storage Capacity for Fat: Implications for Treatment of Obesity

Theodore B. Van Itallie

Department of Medicine and Institute of Human Nutrition, College of Physicians and Surgeons, Columbia University, St. Luke's–Roosevelt Hospital Center, New York, New York 10025

About 120 years ago, a corpulent Englishman named William Banting decided that, with the help of his physician, William Harvey, he had solved the problem of obesity. The solution was simple: Follow a prescribed diet (in other words, eat less) and you can rid yourself of your corpulence. Banting was enthusiastic enough about his own "cure" to publish in 1863 an evangelical monograph (3) addressed to the public about his experience with Harvey's regimen, and his book promptly became a best seller. Clearly, Banting did lose weight on the diet; however, the long-term outcome of Banting's weight problem is not known—did he remain at his reduced weight or did he return to or even exceed his former corpulence? Whatever the case, he lived to be 81.

Since the time of Banting, the demonstration that it is possible to lose weight by dieting has been repeated countless times and numerous authors and their ghost writers have been generously remunerated for their initiative in formulating and publishing ingenious and sometimes bizarre variants of low-calorie diets for use by the public. Most successful diet books have been written by authors who were not professional nutritionists; indeed, one suspects that expertise in nutrition can be a serious handicap as regards the favorable outcome of such publishing enterprises.

For approximately 70 years after Banting's book was published, little progress was made in either the understanding or the treatment of obesity. Much was learned about energy metabolism, and the relationship between excessive calorie intake and fat gain was understood. Research conducted by Newburgh and Conn (14) half a century ago was designed to test the hypothesis that obese individuals might possess an unusually efficient mechanism for digesting, absorbing, and using dietary calories. When these investigators were unable to show that obese individuals were uniquely calorie-efficient, they concluded that, in man, the principal cause of obesity is simply overeating.

IS DEPOT FAT CONTENT REGULATED?

Following the demonstration in 1940 (10) that lesions placed in the ventromedial hypothalamus can induce obesity, and the observation in 1951 (1) that lesions placed in the lateral hypothalamus can induce hypophagia and weight loss, the concept evolved that a mechanism is present in the brain which normally regulates body fat content by controlling food intake. Presumably, this mechanism operates as a negative feedback system; however, the functional details of the system remain poorly understood (30). Embodied in this concept is the notion that the body acts as though it were attempting to maintain some "preferred" fat content; thus, if an animal (or a person) is deprived of food for some period of time and becomes depleted of fat stores, the control mechanism will attempt to rectify the situation by inducing a compensatory increase in energy intake. Conversely, after overfeeding has caused enlargement of the fat depot, a compensatory decrease in intake might be expected to occur. There is evidence from animal models and from clinical observations that some degree of regulation of body fat exists (12); however, if there were a truly effective "set point" for body fat in man, it should be able to compensate for a lowering in energy needs, whatever the cause, by reducing an individual's calorie intake. In that case, decreases in basal metabolic rate (BMR), physical activity, thermic response to meals and exercise, and a small improvement in the efficiency of digestion and absorption would not be expected to induce obesity. In other words, it would seem difficult to reconcile a belief in a fairly precise weight regulatory mechanism with a concurrent belief that obesity is inducible by a modest decrease in energy expenditure whatever the cause. Yet, although these beliefs appear to be mutually exclusive, the dilemma is resolvable if one decides arbitrarily that although there exists a regulatory mechanism, it may not be strong enough or sensitive enough to overcome the effects on body fat content of a subtle change in BMR, thermogenesis, or physical activity level.

RECIDIVISM AMONG FORMERLY OBESE INDIVIDUALS

During the first century after Banting, it was thought that the main problem in treating obesity was to eliminate the excess weight; consequently, little attention was paid to weight maintenance. It really was not until Stunkard and McLaren-Hume (26) in 1959 called attention to both the low success rate and the very high incidence of recidivism among obese patients that the problem of weight maintenance after weight loss began to be properly appreciated.

More recently, Schachter (21) has suggested that the available statistics on recidivism fail to take into account the fact that many persons have successfully controlled their weight for prolonged periods without recourse to professional assistance. However, the data derived from the samples studied by Schachter, namely a subgroup of people at Columbia University and certain inhabitants in Amagansett, New York, are too limited to permit one to estimate the number of Americans who fall into this category. But whatever the overall statistics on recidivism may prove to be, there is a lesson in the fact that so many weight losers regain their lost fat. Why is this so?

One explanation for the recidivism of reduced obese patients could turn out to be the same as the explanation for the existence of much obesity in the first place; namely, our culture predisposes to obesity by providing us with unlimited quantitites of readily available food that is calorically concentrated (high in fat and sugar), palatable, and varied (28). On the other hand, our culture does *not* provide us with an environment that requires us to expend many calories; indeed, we are encouraged to be sedentary. The recent preoccupation with jogging, running, tennis, etc., is certainly an antisedentary trend, but nationwide those involved in such activities remain a small minority. In any case, it is widely recognized that, although obese invididuals drastically reduce calorie intake during weight reduction, few really learn how to make appropriate changes in their eating and exercise behavior. And of those who do learn, few manage to apply what they have learned so as to avoid weight regain at some later time (27).

CAN DIETARY OBESITY PROMOTE FAT CELL PROLIFERATION?

The belief that obesity is to some extent culturally determined has received support from studies showing that lean, caged rats maintained on a nutritionally adequate, homogeneous, pelletized diet will become obese when exposed to a variety of snack foods from supermarket shelves (25) (Fig. 1). Moreover, Zucker rats that are already genetically obese become much more obese when offered a snack-food diet (8). It remains to be determined whether snack food- or (as it is sometimes called) cafeteria diet-induced obesity in rats is an adequate model for an appreciable proportion of human obesity; however, it is of interest that, when they are shifted back to a pellet diet, rats who had become obese on snack foods reduce their food intake and lose weight down to (or near to) control levels (20). Considerable effort has been expended by investigators to explain the hyperphagia and weight gain exhibited by rats who consume cafeteria diets, high-fat diets, or high-sucrose diets. This work has ranged from examination of the effect of certain "palatable" diets on endorphin secretion (2) to the studies of "sensory-specific satiety" conducted by Rolls and her associates (17). Apart from any consideration of the mechanism of dietary obesity, it is of great interest that, after snack-food obesity has been established for a sufficient period of time, a shift to a diet of rat pellets will cause weight loss but not necessarily back to the level of control animals (18). In other words, the experience of having been obese, if prolonged and severe enough, can induce a permanent biological change in the animal. What has changed and why may the formerly obese rat remain permanently heavier than its never-obese control? The change appears to result in large part from an increase in the number of fat cells in the formerly obese rat (I. Faust, this volume). The presence of these extra fat cells may explain why the formerly obese rat fails to return to control weight; the hypothesis being that although mean fat cell size returns to normal, total body fat content remains higher than before because now there are many more fat cells.

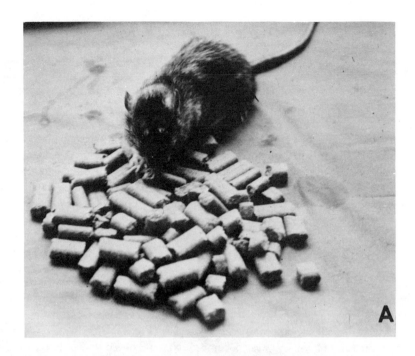

FIG. 1. Normal rat remaining lean on a diet of standard rat pellets (*A*), while previously lean sibling becomes obese on snack-food items (*B*). (From Am. J. Clin. Nutr. 31:543, 1978, with permission.)

This hypothesis is based on the prediction that when challenged by a monotonous, low-fat, nonsweet, calorically dilute diet, a rat with enlarged fat cells will spontaneously reduce food intake and lose weight until the fat cells shrink to a certain critical size. At that point, the rat is somehow impelled to consume sufficient amounts of this apparently unappetizing regimen to prevent further weight loss. Just how fat cell size might affect food motivated behavior is, of course, an intriguing subject but one that falls outside of the purview of this paper.

CYCLES OF HYPERPHAGIA: THE "RATCHET EFFECT" ON FAT CELL NUMBER

When the rat overeats, its fat cells at first grow larger. Then, at some point, the enlarging cells appear to generate a signal that initiates the formation of new fat cells—suggesting that, when the demand for more storage space for fat is sufficiently compelling, the body is programmed to increase its storage capacity (7).

Although the ability of the adipose tissue to proliferate is unquestioned, the precise nature of the stimulus for such proliferation is unknown. Also, it is not clear whether fat cell enlargement per se can trigger proliferation or whether some specific sequence of events associated with fat cell enlargement is required for proliferation; for example, high-fat feeding (13). In addition, the species of the rat (22), the duration of the hypertrophy, and the stage of the life cycle (23) may affect the ability of the adipose tissue to proliferate in response to a given stimulus.

If fat cell enlargement can trigger the formation of new fat cells, then cycles of hyperphagia leading to fat cell hypertrophy can be expected to have a ratchet effect on fat cell number. The term *ratchet effect* is used here to emphasize that, once formed, adipocytes appear to become a permanent part of the body's fat cell population. Thus, it is easy to visualize how repeated cycles of hyperphagia leading to fat cell enlargement can result in substantial and permanent adipose tissue hyperplasia (Fig. 2).

What happens once the body possesses an increased number of adipocytes? Obviously, its capacity to store fat is enlarged; however, it is important to keep in mind that the fat depot is not a passive receptacle for the storage of excess diet-derived fuel. There is evidence from studies of genetically obese Zucker rats that these animals are programmed to divert fuel from the circulation into the adipose tissue, leading to a vicious circle of hyperphagia and increasing obesity (23). If the obese Zucker rat is subjected to sufficient calorie deprivation after weaning, it may not weigh more than its lean sibling, but its growth will have been stunted and its proportion of body fat will be about as high (50% of body weight) as it would have been under conditions of unrestricted eating (6).

POSSIBLE ROLE OF PROTEIN DEPLETION IN RECIDIVISM

When nonobese rats and humans are subjected to semistarvation, their fat cells shrink, and concurrently their urge to eat increases. Also, when humans, whether

STAGES

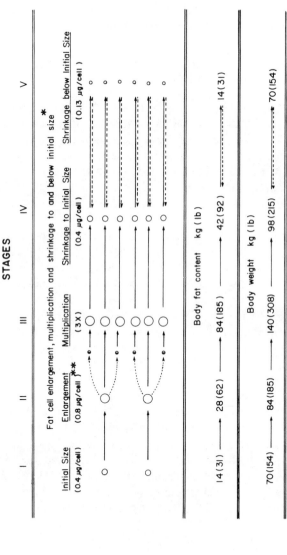

FIG. 2. Schematic representation of a sequence of stages ("ratchet effect") in which fat cells first enlarge and then proliferate, with development of hyperplastic-hypertrophic obesity. Once adipose tissue hyperplasia is established, return to "desirable" weight requires shrinkage of fat cells to below-normal size. The putative difficulty in maintaining this hypotrophic state is indicated by the *arrows* pointing *left*.

*For purposese of illustration fat cells are shown as homogeneous in size. Actually, they are not.

**The degree of fat cell enlargement needed to trigger proliferation is not known.

obese or nonobese, are placed on very-low-calorie diets, they lose more than body fat. For example, a good deal of protein can be lost from the body during semi-starvation depending in part on the size of the calorie deficit and in part on the initial supply of protein in the body. For example, one of our adult obese male patients lost 22% of his lean body mass while adhering faithfully to a 670 kcal diet for 64 days (32). When such an individual is returned to a weight mainte-nance diet, one wonders whether the need to replenish body protein generates a drive to overeat that can frustrate the patient's efforts to limit calorie intake and remain in energy balance at a reduced weight.

PHYSIOLOGIC VERSUS NONPHYSIOLOGIC EATING

It is hardly news that human beings are capable of restraining their intake of food, even if such restraint is biologically inappropriate. Witness the behavior of patients with anorexia nervosa, certain fashion models, ballet dancers, and polit-ical and religious fasters. However, for those of us interested in understanding obesity better, the concern is not simply whether restraint in eating is or is not being exercised, but to determine what it is exactly that is being restrained. Is it some biologically programmed urge within the person to maintain a certain body fat content, or is it an exaggerated appetitive response to the many inducements to overeat offered by the environment? In the latter case, it could be said that the rewarding qualities of food—those that stimulate and reinforce the appetite—like sweetness, creaminess, savoriness—are exaggerated far beyond the role they nor-mally play in promoting eating. Under these circumstances, the hedonic features of the available food and the pleasurable effects they cause may be totally discon-nected from the physiologic need to eat and become ends in themselves. In such situations, the calorie content of the food is irrelevant, and excess fat storage is the unwanted byproduct of gastronomic enjoyment.

Our group has tried to gain some leverage on the problem of distinguishing between physiologic and nonphysiologic eating. First, we admitted a series of non-obese and obese individuals to our metabolic ward and arranged to have them obtain all of their food as a vanilla- or chocolate-flavored liquid homogenate pro-vided on demand by an automatically monitored food dispensing device. Under these conditions, most obese individuals rarely ate more than 25% of the calories needed to maintain energy equilibrium and lost weight rapidly. In contrast lean, young men took sufficient liquid diet from the dispenser to maintain weight. Moreover, the nonobese men adapted spontaneously to covert changes in caloric density of the liquid diet; obese men did not (5).

After we became aware of the inability of the earlier described snack-food obese rats to maintain their obese weight when shifted from snack foods to labo-ratory food pellets, we wondered whether our obese patients were reducing food intake for a similar reason, a shift from a varied diet consisting of familiar foods to one offering the human equivalent of laboratory pellets (29).

Next, we admitted a series of nonobese and obese subjects to our metabolic ward and offered them a varied diet of appetizing foods which were made available to them at mealtimes from large, family style platters (15,16). We also kept their bedside refrigerators stocked with various snacks which they were encouraged to consume *ad lib.* On this type of regimen neither the nonobese nor the obese subjects had any problem maintaining weight. After an initial control period, we substituted in the diet foods that looked and, as far as we could tell, tasted exactly like the foods being replaced. However, the substitute foods were greatly reduced in calories because aspartame (a new, low-calorie synthetic sweetener) had been substituted for sucrose. In this way, we were able to reduce the caloric density of the diet by about 25% without materially changing the volume of food available or its taste. We reasoned that if obese people were eating solely for hedonic satisfaction and out of habit, they would not adapt to the reduced calorie density of the diet but, rather, would be satisfied with the reduced-calorie analogs, eat fewer calories, and lose weight. On the other hand, if the obese individuals were biologically programmed to be at their current weight, then they could be expected to adapt to the covert dilution of the diet by spontaneously eating more, thereby defending their proximate body composition.

As is so often the case in biological experiments, the answer we got was not clear-cut. First of all, most of the nonobese and obese subjects actually gained some weight initially when they were offered a normal, sugar-rich diet served family style. Second, when they were switched covertly to the calorically dilute diet, they ate correspondingly less during the first 4 days, but then they gradually increased spontaneous energy intake to a point where they had compensated (last 12 days) for approximately 40% of the aspartame-induced reduction in calorie intake. Thus, once intake had stabilized, covert aspartame substitution for sucrose resulted in a net decrease of 15% in overall calorie intake.

Oddly enough in these studies, both the nonobese and the obese subjects showed about the same degree of compensation (or lack of compensation) to covert calorie dilution.

The studies described so far have attempted to relate eating behavior to physiologic factors within the body rather than to focus on what might be called the psychodynamics of eating behavior. Although there is undoubted merit in explaining eating behavior in terms of mental or emotional forces, it seems important to explore first how bodily processes can influence such behavior, even though the precise pathways by which these effects are mediated are not presently known.

BIOLOGIC VERSUS PSYCHODYNAMIC DETERMINANTS OF EATING BEHAVIOR

The experimental psychologists have clearly demonstrated that there is a reward system in the brain which makes certain activities reinforcing at certain times (19). This reward system is frequently, if not invariably, related to activities that will help ensure survival of the individual or of the species. We must eat in order to survive; hence, food is rewarding when it is needed. For humans (and rats) a variety of foods is more rewarding than a single food, perhaps because consumption of a variety of foods makes it possible for us to obtain the wide spectrum of essential nutrients required for survival.

When the body is deprived of adequate food, whether by famine or by a deliberate attempt to restrain eating, fuel reserves diminish and food becomes more reinforcing. The conscientious objectors who were experimentally semistarved in the Minnesota Study (22) during World War II became bulimic during the refeeding phase. Early in rehabilitation after 24 weeks of semistarvation, they were able to eat large meals and yet feel hungrier at the end of the meal than at its beginning.

The binge eating that sometimes intersperses anorexia nervosa (24) could be a biologically appropriate response to a period of self-induced semistarvation. It is also possible that the cycles of weight loss and regain observed so often in the obese have, in some instances, a similar basis. It may be that as the inventory of stored fuel in the body is depleted in both obese and nonobese persons, the reduction in depot fat becomes known to the brain and, as a result, the satiety system becomes less responsive to satiety signals, leading to a larger intake of food (31). Attempts to restrain one's eating behavior could be frustrating under such circumstances.

What about the eating that is associated with boredom, depression, fatigue, etc. (4)? This type of overeating may be quite important. Not only does it lead to fat cell enlargement, but as we have already discussed, it may lead to fat cell proliferation, thereby laying the foundation for perpetuating the obesity.

CONCLUSIONS

Although it seems to be particularly difficult for many formerly obese patients with adipose tissue hyperplasia to maintain weight loss, it is by no means impossible. Nor is there evidence that the indefinite maintenance of one's fat cells at a below-normal size is physiologically harmful. However, in view of the difficulty so many reduced obese people experience in avoiding relapse, it makes sense to give more attention to preventing obesity rather than invest too high a proportion of available resources in seeking new treatments.

When one looks at the evolution of the biomedical/behavioral perspective on obesity since Harvey (9) devised the "Banting diet," it seems clear that we are now much more sophisticated and knowledgeable about the subject. However, this does not mean that we have solved the problem or that we have an adequate understanding of the ways in which physiologic state influences eating behavior and vice versa. Thanks to the multidisciplinary research that has been conducted in ever-increasing volume since 1940 (when it finally became crystal-clear that localized brain damage can produce obesity), we are now asking much better questions about the problems of excess fat storage. From studies with animal models, we know that obesity can be produced by dietary means and that it can also be hereditary. However, we have yet to identify a genetic marker for obesity in obese humans with a strong family history of adiposity. Studies of adipose tissue morphology have permitted us to distinguish at least three types of obesity; hyperplastic, hypertrophic, and a combination of these two. However, we are still not sure whether a certain fat cell size is really defended, and if it is, how such a defense is accomplished. As already mentioned in this discussion, there is preliminary evidence to indicate that patients with hyperplastic obesity may resist fat loss (beyond a certain point) more strongly than patients with the same amount of depot fat stored in enlarged adipocytes. Fortunately, it is possible to design experiments to answer this question and others of equal importance.

A major area for future research will be to understand better how certain types of eating behavior such as bulimia and finickiness might have a physiological basis. There is a tendency on the part of some workers to ascribe all aberrant eating behavior to emotional or psychologic factors; however, we know from studies of semistarved individuals, patients with adrenal insufficiency, or patients with uncontrolled diabetes mellitus or diabetes insipidus (and others) that certain ingestive behaviors and their emotional concomitants can arise from physiologic aberrations. Thus, we cannot afford to overlook the role of subtle, physiologic abnormalities any more than we can afford to overlook the role of cultural factors (such as composition and variety of the diet) in determining eating behavior and body fat content.

The era immediately ahead of us promises to be an exciting one insofar as obesity research is concerned. During the coming decade we shall find out whether some people are really biologically programmed to be obese and why. We shall learn much more about the attributes of food that promote hyperphagia. We shall identify with greater certainty the short-term signals that induce satiety and how they work. We shall learn much more about the mechanism by which the body endeavors to maintain its energy stores within certain limits. If there is such a thing as genetic obesity in man, we shall discover a way of identifying it reliably. It will be interesting to find out whether all this new information will appreciably strengthen man's ability to prevent and treat his own predisposition to accumulate an unwanted and often unhealthy excess of depot fat.

ACKNOWLEDGMENT

This study was supported in part by NIH grants AM-17624 and AM-26688.

REFERENCES

1. Anand, B. K., and Brobeck, J. R. (1951): Hypothalamic control of food intake in rats and cats. *Yale J. Biol. Med.,* 24:123–140.
2. Apfelbaum, M., and Mandenoff, A. (1981): Naltrexone suppresses hyperphagia induced in the rat by a highly palatable diet. *Pharmacol. Biochem. Behav.,* 15:89–91.
3. Banting, W. (1863): Letter on Corpulence, Addressed to the Public. London, Harrison.
4. Bruch, H. (1973): *Eating disorders: Obesity, anorexia nervosa and the person within.* Basic Books, Inc., New York.
5. Campbell, R. G. Hashim, S. A., and Van Itallie, T. B. (1971): Studies of food-intake regulation in man. Responses to variation in nutritive density in lean and obese subjects. *N. Engl. J. Med.,* 285:1402–1407.

6. Cleary, M. P. Vasselli, J. R., and Greenwood, M. R. C. (1980): Development of obesity in Zucker obese (fafa) rat in absence of hyperphagia. *Am. J. Physiol.,* 238:E284–E292.
7. Faust, I. M., Johnson, P. R., Stern, J. S. and Hirsch, J. (1978): Diet-induced adipocyte number increase in adult rats. A new model of obesity. *Am. J. Physiol.,* 235:E279–E286.
8. Gale, S. K., Van Itallie, T. B., and Faust, I. M. (1981): Effects of palatable diets on body weight and adipose tissue cellularity in the adult obese female Zucker rat (fa/fa). *Metabolism,* 30:105–110.
9. Harvey, W. (1872): *On Corpulence in Relation to Disease.* Henry Renshaw, London.
10. Hetherington, A. W., and Ranson, S. W. (1940): Hypothalamic lesions and adiposity in the rat. *Anat. Rec.,* 78:149.
11. Keys, A., Brozek, J., Henschel, A., Mickelsen, O., and Taylor, H. L. (1950): *The biology of human starvation.* Minneapolis: Univ. of Minnesota Press.
12. Kissileff, H. R., and Van Itallie, T. B. (1982): Physiology of the control of food intake. *Ann. Rev. Nutr.,* 2:371–418.
13. LeMonnier, D. (1972): Effects of age, sex and weight on cellularity of the adipose tissue in mice and rats rendered obese by a high fat diet. *J. Clin. Invest.,* 51:2907–2915.
14. Newburgh, L. H. (1944): Obesity; energy metabolism. *Physiol. Rev.,* 24:18–31.
15. Porikos, K. P., Booth G., and Van Itallie, T. B. (1977): Effect of covert nutritive dilution on the spontaneous food intake of obese individuals. A pilot study. *Am. J. Clin. Nutr.,* 30:1638–1644.
16. Porikos, K. P., Hesser, M. F., and Van Itallie, T. B. (1982): Caloric regulation in normal-weight men maintained on a palatable diet of conventional foods. *Physiol. Behav.,* 29:293–300.
17. Rolls, B. J., Rolls, E. T., Rowe, E. A., and Sweeney, K. (1981): Sensory specific satiety in man. *Physiol. Behav.,* 27:137–142.
18. Rolls, B. J., Rowe, E. A., and Turner, R. C. (1980): Persistent obesity in rats following a period of consumption of a mixed, high energy diet. *J. Physiol.,* 298:415–427.
19. Rolls, E. T. (1975): *The Brain and Reward.* Pergamon Press, Oxford.
20. Rothwell, N. J., and Stock, M. J. (1978): Mechanisms of weight gain and loss in reversible obesity in the rat. *J. Physiol.,* 276:60–61P.
21. Schachter, S. (1982): Recidivism and self-cure of smoking and obesity. *Am. Psychol.,* 37:4.
22. Schemmel, R., Mickelsen, O., and Gill, J. L. (1970): Dietary obesity in rats: body weight and body fat accretion in seven strains of rats. *J. Nutr.,* 100:1041–1048.
23. Schemmel, R., Michelsen, O., and Tolgay, Z. (1969): Dietary obesity in rats: influence of diet, weight, age and sex on body composition. *Am. J. Physiol.,* 216:373–379.
24. Schwartz, D. M. (1982): Anorexia nervosa and bulimia: The sociocultural context. *Int. J. Eating Disorders,* 1:20–36.
25. Sclafani, A., and Springer, D. (1976): Dietary obesity in adult rats: similarities to hypothalamic and human obesity syndromes. *Physiol. Behav.,* 17:461–471.
26. Stunkard, A. J., and McLaren-Hume, M. (1959): The results of treatment of obesity: a review of the literature and report of a series. *Arch. Int. Med.,* 103:79–85.
27. Stunkard, A. J., and Penick, S. B. (1979): Behavior modification in the treatment of obesity. The problem of maintaining weight loss. *Arch. Gen. Psychiatry,* 36:801–806.
28. Van Itallie, T. B. (1979): Obesity: The American disease. *Food Technology,* December, 43–47.
29. Van Itallie, T. B., and Campbell R. G. (1972): Multidisciplinary approach to the problem of obesity. *J. Am. Diet. Assoc.,* 61:385.
30. Van Itallie, T. B., Gale, S. K., and Kissileff, H. R. (1978): Control of food intake in the regulation of depot fat: an overview. In: *Advances in Modern Nutrition, Vol. 2: Diabetes, Obesity and Vascular Disease: Metabolic and Molecular Interrelationships,* edited by H. M. Katzen and R. J. Mahler, pp. 427–492. Hemisphere Publishing Corporation, John Wiley and Sons, New York.
31. Van Itallie, T. B., and VanderWeele, D. A. (1981): The phenomenon of satiety. In: *Recent Advances in Obesity Research: III,* edited by P. Bjorntorp, M. Cairella, A. N. Howard, pp. 278–89. John Libbey, London.
32. Yang, M-U., Barbosa-Saldivar, J. L., Pi-Sunyer, F. X., and Van Itallie, T. B. (1981): Metabolic effects of substituting carbohydrate for protein in a low-calorie diet: a prolonged study in obese patients. *Int. J. Obes.,* 5:231–236.

Eating and Its Disorders, edited by A. J. Stunkard and E. Stellar. Raven Press, New York © 1984.

What Constitutes a Sufficient Psychobiologic Explanation for Obesity?

Jules Hirsch and Rudolph L. Leibel

Rockefeller University, New York, New York 10021

Any consideration of the psychobiology of eating and its disorders should give obesity a place of special prominence; in the Western world, obesity must surely be the most prevalent disturbance related to food intake. Although there have been great advances in our understanding of the neurophysiology and psychology of food intake in man and animals, the pathogenesis of human obesity has not yet been rigorously described. A seemingly inexhaustible supply of changing concepts regarding both etiology and treatment attests to our fundamental ignorance of the pathogenesis of obesity in man. A great wave of excitement for theories related to defective thermogenesis has begun to ebb. But the theorists never weary—fat cells, endorphins, satiety signals from the gut, and lipoprotein lipase remain under scrutiny.

With regard to treatment, one must note that at one time or another, diets recommended for weight reduction have addressed nearly every imaginable possibility. Most recently we have witnessed intense interest in very-low-calorie diets which either do or do not spare lean body mass. We seem to be in the early stages of retreat from such diets and also from the hope that systematic behavior modification would obliterate obesity (2). We appear to be entering a period of enthusiasm for the use of drugs to treat obesity. Agents formerly promoted as anorectics are now emerging as stimulants of metabolism (1). Perhaps a better description of the pathogenesis of obesity will be a required prelude to the development of effective and lasting treatment. In this chapter, we examine what we believe to be necessary elements for a sufficient psychobiologic explanation of obesity.

Obviously, consuming fewer calories or expending more energy will lower body weight; most individuals maintain normal body weight by appropriate adjustment of these variables. Why is it so difficult for the obese to cure themselves by a permanent alteration in those same variables in the direction of thinness? There may be a clue in a review of data on the prevalence of obesity. The high prevalence of obesity in the United States has been abundantly documented (9). But, it will be particularly helpful for our analysis of the pathogenesis of obesity to examine the exact frequency distributions of weight on which decisions on the prevalence of obesity must be based.

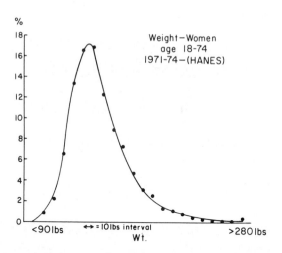

FIG. 1. A frequency distribution of the weights observed in women of all ages during the Health and Nutrition Examination Survey of 1971–74. The frequency distribution shows weights in 10-lb intervals from 90–280 lb.

Figure 1 shows the frequency of various body weights found in a large number of women, aged 18 to 74, during the Health and Nutrition Examination Survey (HANES) of 1971 to 1974 (11). Weight distribution is seen to be skewed to the right; thus, there is a greater probability of being overweight than being under-weight. Of course, there are so many subclasses of different-sized individuals within this distribution that it may not be possible to attribute skewness in weight solely to differences in fatness; but, in Fig. 2, it becomes clear that height, in this large group of women, was linear on a probit plot. This indicates that height was normally distributed, whereas weight showed signs of nonnormality. Using other data (10) on weight for individuals of known height, we made another probit plot as shown in Fig. 3. There can be no doubt that the frequency distributions of weight in women and in men are skewed. A typical case which illustrates this point is shown in Fig. 4: frequency of weight distribution in women, 62 inches in height, from the 1960 to 1962 HANES data base. Better indices of fatness than weight alone, such as weight divided by the square of height (body mass index) would show the same type of frequency distribution, since height is constant in this group. Thus, it is fair to consider the abscissa of Fig. 4 as representing body fatness. This being the case, body fatness can be treated as a variable with a mode, central tendency and a distribution as shown in this figure. The central tendency is a measure of the tightness of control of the variable around the mean. It would appear self-evident that up-side controls are less strictly exerted or less exact than down-side controls. Or, it is perhaps metabolically easier to maintain fatness than an equivalent degree of leanness; certainly obesity is more prevalent than leanness in this population of women 62 inches in height. The same is true in other height groups as well.

Another interpretation of these findings derives from the most robust of clinical observations on human obesity; namely, those who are obese tend to remain obese in spite of our best therapeutic efforts, and those who in adult life are not obese are unlikely to become so. If we perturb any individual by moving relative fatness to the right or the left in Fig. 4, the likelihood that an individual might return to initial fatness is much greater than one would predict on the basis of the shape of the population distribution. As is well known, weight tends to remain within a very narrow range over months and years. If weight were to change with illness or other misfortune, then on recovery from illness, weight would return to its starting point. In this respect, weight or fatness appears to be set. Each set within a population should have a mean and central tendency determined by a set of controlling factors or variables. We will consider that skewness to the right in a large population is likely to be the result of combining many subpopulations rather than some general looseness of control on the upside. This model is shown in the freehand drawing of Fig. 5. The dotted line is taken from the data used in Fig. 4, but the various distributions of fatness are totally hypothetical. As shown, each population has its own mean and any deviations from the mean will provoke reciprocal forces tending to restore the individual to his or her initial weight.

If we are to carry this premise to a stage which will be meaningful to the understanding of obesity, we must ask what the nature of these controlling forces might

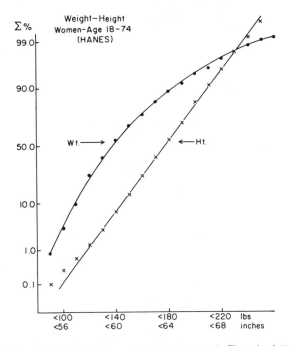

FIG. 2. The weight and height of the same population shown in Fig. 1 is plotted here as cumulative frequency distributions with a probability or probit transformation (*ordinate*).

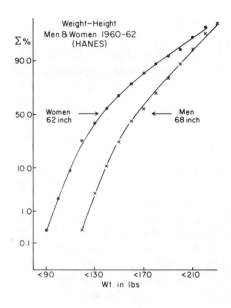

FIG. 3. Cumulative frequency distribution in probit plot of weights or men and women from the Health and Nutrition Examination Survey (HANES). Note the curvature, hence nonnormality of both curves of weight.

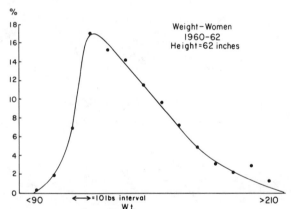

FIG. 4. Cumulative frequency distribution of weight of women from HANES as shown in another plot (Fig. 3).

be. Individuals at stable weight will, on perturbation of that weight, change food consumption, physical activity, and resting metabolic rate in directions appropriate to restoration of initial weight. Indeed, it is the operation of these regulations which has made it so difficult to induce obesity in adult man (7). These forces or biochemical alterations might be most aptly termed restorative forces. The sum of their activity is dependent on the degree of perturbation of weight. The least arguable assumption about such forces is that they operate so as to generate the probability of weight function shown as Fig. 4. This being the case, it must follow that the strength of the restorational force at any weight is reciprocally related to

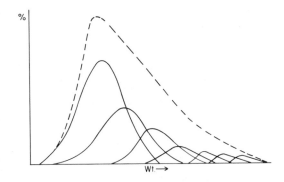

FIG. 5. A theoretical series of curves. The sum of these theoretical curves are meant to be equal to the dotted line which is the same as the curve of weight distribution as shown in Fig. 4 (see text).

the probability that an individual will be found in that weight class. The shape of this theoretical curve of restorational forces for the entire population is shown in Fig. 6. If this were the entire story, then we might end simply by noting how praiseworthy are the extremely obese or the extremely lean, since they maintain their weight in the face of great, opposing forces. A model taking subpopulations into consideration is probably closer to reality.

A combination of concepts of restorational forces and subpopulations is schematized in Fig. 7. This figure shows four modal weights, each defended by forces which act to maintain that weight. The restorational forces appear to be nonlinear functions of the distance that weight is perturbed from its initial or usual position. Modal weight for an individual is by definition that weight at which restorational forces are minimal. That Fig. 4 shows a skewed curve of weight probabilities might indicate that there are more individuals in lower channels of weight than in higher weight channels. How many channels or modes of weight there are for any given population is unknown. Obviously, the curve of weight probability can be made by many combinations of modal weights and central tendencies. If restorational forces were very strong and were closely controlling a precise level of weight, then we would require a large number of modal weights for a smooth curve of weight prevalence. There is enough variability in any individual's weight to suggest the following compromise: a fairly small number of modal weights and some give in restorational forces at least over short terms. Surely, one can briefly starve or overeat and yet return over time to very close to the initial state.

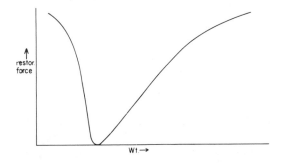

FIG. 6. An inversion of Fig. 4 with special labeling of axes (see text).

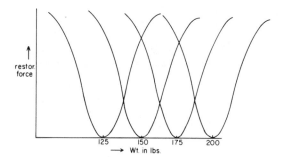

FIG. 7. A theoretical set of curves each of which is an inverted normal distribution (see text for explanation).

We wish to note that there are, of necessity, important elements of behavior included among the effector mechanisms for this regulatory model of weight control. Obviously, prolonged over- or undereating can override any regulatory mechanism that might be proposed. In fact, in some animal models such as hypothalamic obesity, a simple regulatory element appears to have been altered or removed from the system, and extraordinary changes ensue. The ultimate effector is food intake and to lesser degrees physical activity and thermogenesis. The latter are lesser only in the sense that longer periods of variation in physical activity or thermogenesis are required to moderate the effects of brief periods of over- or undereating. Whatever physiologic or regulatory explanations one wishes to invoke, they can be overridden in man by voluntary alterations in food intake. For some reason, such voluntary actions are experienced as being exceedingly difficult, even dysphoric, when they are opposed to other restorational forces. Thus, any complete explanation for obesity in man must include the mechanism for the discomfort or dysphoria that attends volitional behavior which would correct biological disturbances in energy metabolism. In short, no matter what is wrong, why do the obese not eat appropriately less, thereby adjusting body weight to more average levels? What is it that makes such corrective behavior so difficult for the obese? Let us now examine some of the usually suggested etiologies for obesity, in the context of the regulatory scheme we have described.

Our further considerations will repeatedly use the scheme shown in Fig. 7. In this figure, note that there are four modal weights: 125, 150, 175, and 200 lb. Each weight is at the nadir of a U-shaped curve or channel of weight probabilities about the mode. For convenience we will refer to these curves as channels 1,2,3, and 4. If an individual who has been maintaining body weight at 150 lb were suddenly to gain weight to 175 lb, there would be at least two ways of viewing this event using the model shown in Fig. 7. We might consider the weight change to be due to a change in channel from 2 to 3. Or we might say that some new force has perturbed the regulation within channel 2, either increasing upside pressure or reducing upside resistance, resulting in a new equilibrium position at 175 lb high on the upper limit of the curve. These and other possibilities can be tested.

The most common view of the etiology of obesity in man is that of altered hedonism. Either for personal psychological reasons or due to psychosocial influ-

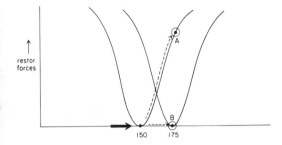

FIG. 8. A theoretical set of curves. The influence of a factor exogenous to regulation (*large arrow*) propels weight to either position *A* or position *B* (see text).

ences, the obese person perturbs his otherwise normal physiology by attempting to satisfy a greater need for the pleasure that comes from food intake. Much dietary therapy is based on this notion, i.e., taking the calories out of food, but returning to the food sufficiently pleasant qualities so as to placate the drive for food pleasure by artificial tastes or other noncaloric additives. If this theory of obesity were correct, then one would expect that the obese individual who is not abnormal in regulatory capacity but only in need for pleasure would be always on the upside of a curve in one of the channels of Fig. 7. This possibility is shown in Fig. 8. The large arrow just to the left of 150 is a drive exogenous to the regulatory system, which is driving weight upward. Weight advances to 175, but in terms of restorational forces, the weight is at position *A* rather than *B*. This being the case, one would find no diminution in thermogenesis or in other potential mechanisms for adjusting body fat content downward. Quite the reverse would be the case: All regulatory forces would be actively at work propelling weight downward but opposed by the need for hedonic pleasure. Similarly failure of satiety signals from the gut (3) or elsewhere would, if they were to cause obesity, drive the obese into the upper levels of the curve of regulation. One would then expect to find that obese individuals have elevated rates of resting thermogenesis (6), a very active and abundant brown fat organ (12) if this is present in adult man, higher than average levels of plasma triiodothyronine, and perhaps a concomitant reduction in plasma reverse T_3 (8), the noncalorigenic derivative of thyroxine. The evidence that these events occur on a regular basis in human obesity is not particularly convincing. What is more often noted is the starvational metabolic state of the formerly obese. When weight is lowered, they do not move quickly to an equilibrium at the nadir of restorational force but rather to declines in thermogenesis and T_3 levels, suggesting that they were in a nadir of restorational force to begin with and have moved into the left limb of the curve with forces tending to conserve calories. To account for these findings we need believe, as conceptualized in Fig. 8, that a weight increase from 150 to 175 lb is the result of a move to point *B*.

A simple hedonic or similar unitary explanation for obesity does not fit with all the facts. In respect to hedonic factors in obesity, one must comment on the fact that the hedonism of obesity is most often clinically observed after weight reduction rather than before. Hyperphagia, sudden erratic departure from prescribed diets, and unusual attention to food are all seen. Perhaps it is this aspect of human obesity that has lured us into ornate theoretical constructs relating obesity to inattentiveness to inner signals for food (5) or even the idea that hedonic drive is preeminent in producing obesity. Hedonism for food may be more related to protection from starvation, here conceptualized as motion into the left limb of the curve of restorational forces.

It can be argued that the series of events with hedonic or psychosocially-induced obesity may not be so simple as described above. There may be instances in which the driving of weight upward in the face of restorational forces which tend to lower weight, leads over time, to atrophy of those forces which defend against weight increase. This would mean that an obese subject was so long harassed by hedonism, that restorational forces permitted a shift in channels. This possibility is shown in Fig. 9. The dotted lines eventually disappear and the weight position (175 lb), initially high on the dotted line, sinks to a new position reduced or absent restorational force.

A change of channels as shown in Figs. 8 and 9 is an attractive hypothesis for the regulatory changes in obesity. Abrupt changes in channels seem to occur when brain lesions lead to obesity. With hypothalamic obesity, body weight is still defended at a set, but the set is different from that of the sham-operated animal. Also, the gradual growth of body fat stored during development and maturation, as well as the more abrupt physiological changes that occur with premigration or prehibernation in some animals (4) speak for the biological possibility of rapid shunting from one channel to another. Therefore, it could be that a hedonic factor long at work might propel one into a higher channel. If this were the case, one would expect to find that the obese have completely normal thermogenesis and food intake and all other controllers of energy metabolism are at a normal level when in the obese state. One should see abnormalities only when weight is elevated or lowered from a set-point, within the higher channel. One might also anticipate changes in the shape of the curves of restorational forces if restorational forces atrophied with long-term hedonic bombardment. The normal, nonobese, nonhedonically driven individual might have a U-shaped curve, but the hedonically driven individual who is pushed to a new channel of regulation would ultimately develop a different U-shape with a greatly flattened bottom. Ultimately,

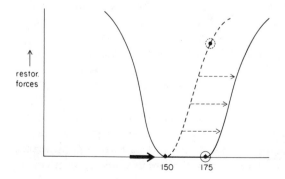

↑
restor.
forces

150   175

FIG. 9. A theoretical set of curves showing the motion of weight to a new high as pushed upward by the *large arrow*. Eventually the new weight on the *dotted line* "sags" as upward defenses weaken. A new curve of restorational forces is thereby described (see text).

defense against even higher levels of weight comes into action, but since downside controls were left unaltered, they would not be active until weight drops below 150 lb as shown in Fig. 9.

In another chapter in this book, our colleague, Dr. Irving Faust, argues for a role of adipose cellularity in the development and maintenance of the level of fat storage in rodents and perhaps in man. Extending our reasoning to include regulatory possibilities generated by adipose cellularity would call for fat cell size to be a regulator within each channel and would consider fat cell number as a marker for the channel itself, i.e., channel 4 contains individuals with more fat cells than channel 3. Faust's work, suggests that prolonged perturbation of cell size may lead to an ineradicable increase in cell number, which would fit well with the concept of escalation to a higher channel, under prolonged pressure to become obese. Skipping to higher channels could be developmental events modified by genetic influences as well as overnutrition.

The advantage of considering systems such as those described by Faust is that regulatory systems are invoked in explaining both the development and maintenance of obesity. There are many dividends to developing such systematic approaches. For example, abnormalities associated with obesity can be conceptually categorized within the system and experimental approaches developed to test each possibility. If increases in fat cell number are important in moving individuals from one channel of regulation to another, then one might consider that factors permissive of cell division and hyperplasia are essential ingredients or participants in the development of obesity but not necessarily causal nor even functional within the regulatory arms of each U-shaped channel. Thus, insulin or growth hormone may be essential for bursts of adipose tissue hyperplasia but not function in within-channel regulation. The use of adipose tissue morphology to understand obesity is rich in theoretical possibilities but as yet impoverished in a detailed understanding of chemical and other links between adipocyte size and number and energy homeostasis. The work of Faust and his colleagues strongly suggests the existence of such links, but they are yet to be described in concrete terms.

Any finding, whether in the psychological, social, or cellular domain, should be evaluated within a regulatory scheme if it is believed to have a role in the pathogenesis of human obesity. Some findings in obese subjects may be purely secondary to the presence of obesity. Skin striae, like the stretched clothing of the obese have no integral function in either the production or maintenance of obesity, but are markers. Whether changes in serum insulin levels, fat cell size, or thermogenesis are merely inner, more obscure markers of obesity or whether they play some more dynamic role in obesity is yet to be decided. Clearly, any system or simple abnormality whether in brown fat, white fat cell size, or the level of endorphin can only excite our interest insofar as it explains obesity within the functioning of a regulatory system as shown in Fig. 7. Ultimately, the coupling of whatever abnormalities are found to the powerful behavioral display which occurs when weight is lost will be a necessary feature for any total explanation of obesity.

The richness of present day observations in obesity research ranging from the molecular level to psychosocial forces gives promise for full understanding. However, momentary enthusiasm for any new finding must not deflect our insistence on rigorously evaluating any putative factor for the cause of obesity within the confines of a complete regulatory system. The demonstration of a simple enzymatic or cellular defect or a particular behavioral or psychologic observation found in the obese cannot be considered a sufficient description of the pathogenesis of obesity.

ACKNOWLEDGMENT

This work was supported in part by NIH grant AM 30583.

REFERENCES

1. Cawthorne, M. A., and Arch, J. R. S. (1982): The search for peripherally acting drugs for the treatment of obesity—A Review. *Int. J. Obes.*, 6:1–10.
2. Craighead, L. W., Stunkard, A. J., and O'Brien, R. M. (1981): Behavior therapy and pharmacotherapy of obesity. *Arch. Gen. Psychiatry*, 38:763–768.
3. Gibbs, J., Young, R. C., and Smith, G. P. (1973): Cholecystokinin decreases food intake in rats. *J. Comp. Physiol. Psychol.*, 84:488–498.
4. Jameson, E. W., and Mead, R. A. (1969): Seasonal changes in body fat, water and basic weight in Citellus lateralis, Eutamias Specioseus, and E. amoenus. *J. Mammal.*, 45:359–365.
5. Rodin, J. (1981): Current status of the internal-external hypothesis for obesity. *Am. Psychol.*, 36:361–371.
6. Rothwell, N. J., and Stock, M. J. (1982): Effect of chronic food restriction on energy balance, thermogenic capacity, and brown-adipose-tissue activity in the rat. *Biosci. Rep.*, 2:543–549.
7. Sims, E. A. H., Danforth, E., Horton, E. S., Bray, G. A., Glennon, J. A., and Salans, L. B. (1973): Endocrine and metabolic effects of experimental obesity in man. *Recent Prog. Horm. Res.*, 29:457–487.
8. Spaulding, S. W., Chopra, I. J., Sherwin, R. S., and Lyau, S. S. (1976): Effect of caloric restriction and dietary composition on serum T_3 and reverse T_3 in man. *J. Clin. Endocrinol. Metab.*, 42:197–200.
9. Van Itallie, T. B. (1979): Obesity: Adverse effects on health and longevity. *Am. J. Clin. Nutr.*, 32:2723–2733.
10. *Weight by Height and Age of Adults, U.S.—1960–1962.* May, 1966: Vital and Health Statistics. Series II, #14.
11. *Weight by Height and Age of Adults 18–74, U.S.—1971–1974.* November 30, 1977: Vital and Health Statistics Advance Data #14.
12. Young, J. B., Saville, E., Rothwell, J. J., Stock, M. J., and Landsberg, L. (1982): Effect of diet and cold exposure on norepinephrine turnover in brown adipose tissue of the rat. *J. Clin. Invest.*, 69:1001–1071.

Eating and Its Disorders, edited by A. J. Stunkard and E. Stellar. Raven Press, New York © 1984.

Is Obesity a Disease of Inactivity?

Judith S. Stern

Department of Nutrition and the Food Intake Laboratory, University of California, Davis, California 95616

There are numerous reports that some obese people living in highly industrialized nations have lower caloric intakes than lean individuals. In one study conducted in Zutphen, The Netherlands, middle-aged men in the highest quartile of body fat consumed on the average of 300 to 400 kcal less than men in the lowest quartile (1). In one survey of 14-year-old adolescents in Glasgow in 1964 and 1971, all of the food eaten by each individual was measured over a period of 7 consecutive days (2). Adolescent boys between 1964 and 1971 showed an average decrease in daily energy intake from 2,795 to 2,610 kcal. The boys in 1971 had an increased percent body fat, from 16.3 to 18.4%, while height and weight were similar between 1964 and 1971. The most likely explanation for the increase in body fat was a decrease in physical activity.

Today, in the United States, the incidence of obesity is higher than it was in the early part of the 20th century, yet according to figures published by the U.S. Department of Agriculture, the U.S. per capita caloric intake is approximately 5% less now than it was in 1910 (3). A major difference is that today we live in a more automated world and as a consequence require fewer calories to maintain body weight. In some cases, the decrease in activity may be slight, but when viewed over the course of months or years plays a significant role in the development and maintenance of obesity in some individuals. A simple example: The Illinois Bell Telephone Company has estimated that in the course of 1 year, an extension phone saves an individual approximately 70 miles of walking. For some people, this could be the caloric equivalent of 2 to 3 lb of fat or 7,000 to 10,500 kcal.

The following chapter will present data illustrating the point that obese individuals are generally less active than normal weight individuals and will discuss the relationship between exercise and food intake, how exercise affects body composition, energy metabolism, its psychological benefits, and finally its possible role in maintenance of a reduced body weight.

ACTIVITY AND THE OBESE INDIVIDUAL

Although obese individuals are not always less active than those of normal weight, inactivity is often associated with obesity in individuals of all ages. In one study of adult-onset obesity, Greene (4) was able to trace the onset of obesity to forced inactivity in 68% of his patients. A history of increased food intake was obtained in only 3%. When obese adolescent girls in summer camp were observed using time-lapse photography during periods of mandatory physical activity, they were also less active than normal-weight girls (5). For example, during swimming period obese girls spent less time swimming and more time floating. While playing tennis, obese girls were inactive 77% of the time compared with 56% of the time for the normal-weight girls. Similar findings were reported for obese and nonobese boys at summer camp (6). Not all studies of obese boys, however, report decreased activity and food intake (7). In terms of routine daily activity, obese men and women walk less than normal-weight adults, and this difference is relatively greater for women than for men (8). Obese men walked on the average of 4 miles/day, compared with 6 miles/day for those of normal weight. Obese women walked on the average of 2 miles/day, compared with 5 miles/day for those of normal weight. These findings suggest that inactivity may play a greater role in maintenance of obesity in women than in men.

Inactivity in experimental animals is more precisely documented and may actually promote obesity in normally lean rats (9). With respect to genetically obese rodents, both the obese hyperglycemic mouse (ob/ob) and the obese Zucker rat (fa/fa) are spontaneously less active than their lean littermates (10,11). At 1 to 2 weeks of age, ob/ob mice were less active when given a brief, 5-min motor test (12). In the case of the Zucker rat, the onset of inactivity is coincident with weaning and occurs before the obese animal is markedly heavier than the lean one (11). When these morbidly obese rats and mice are forced to exercise, excessive weight gain is slowed but not normalized (11,13–15). Only when forced exercise is combined with caloric restriction is weight gain comparable to genetically lean rats. In contrast, when obesity is more moderate, exercise can play a more impressive role. Such is the case when obese yellow mice (Ay/a) are given access to activity wheels at 5 weeks of age. Body weight is normalized in 50% and weight and fat gain are decreased in all of them (16). In this particular study obese and lean mice were comparably active.

EXERCISE AND FOOD INTAKE

The relationship between exercise and food intake is not as clear as that between exercise and obesity, and exercise has been reported to increase, decrease, or have no effect on food intake (for review, see 17). These differences may be explained in part by differences in sex and age of the individual as well as the duration and intensity of the exercise training and the type of exercise. The results are perhaps clearest in experimental animals. Typically, in comparison with sedentary controls, exercised male rats do not gain as much weight and food intake may be decreased (18–20). On a similar exercise program, female rats are more resistant than males to change and usually maintain their body weight and do not change or may even increase their food intake (18,19).

On the same treadmill exercise program (0.25 miles/day for 8 weeks), young rats did not change food intake and body weight continued to increase (21). In contrast, mature rats decreased their food intake and actually lost weight (21).

In adult rats isolated bouts of exercise, ranging in duration from 2 to 6 hr, served to decrease food intake on the day of the exercise (22). The decrease was greatest for the longest exercise period. Furthermore, the closer the next meal time was to the termination of the exercise, the greater the anorexia. With long-term exercise this situation was reversed; the rats that exercised the longest had the largest food intake. When energy expenditure was held constant and intensity was varied, the reduction in food intake of male rats was greatest in the high-intensity group within the first 24 hr and lasted up to 3 days postexercise (23). Finally, there is some evidence that, after the termination of a long-term exercise program, food intake is increased for at least 2 weeks and that this increase is seen as early as 60 hr after exercise termination (24,25). The mechanism for this increase is unclear. However, in this particular study an increase in plasma insulin preceded the increase in food intake. Also associated with exercise termination are increased lipogenesis and rapid regaining of body weight and body fat (24,26).

The type of exercise may also influence food intake. In one study, the decrease in food intake was less when rats were forced to swim than when they ran on a treadmill (22). The authors proposed that since the heat produced during exercise was more readily dissipated in water than in air, swimming would constitute a smaller physiological stress. Thus, in experimental animals it is clear that the effects of forced exercise on food intake are influenced by duration, intensity, and type of exercise in addition to sex and age.

In humans, the effect of exercise in the short term are to decrease food intake immediately after exercise. In a 14-day study of military cadets, food intake was carefully measured and energy expenditure was calculated from diaries (27). Food intake was depressed on exercise days, and increased on rest days. While there was no correlation between food intake and energy expenditure in the same day, they were correlated 2 days later. For moderately active humans, long-term exercise promotes increased caloric intake. For example, in one study middle-aged male joggers who ran approximately 65 km/week consumed more calories than sedentary controls (2,959 versus 2,361 kcal/day, respectively) (28). Similarly, middle-aged female joggers who ran approximately 55 km/week consumed more calories than sedentary controls (2,386 versus 1,871 kcal/day, respectively). Sedentary controls were actually slightly shorter and heavier.

In contrast, in two studies by Mayer and colleagues (14,29), sedentary men and rats actually ate more than those that were engaged in light activity. For example, men working in sedentary occupations in a jute mill in West Bengal had higher food intakes and weighed more than individuals in less sedentary jobs (29). In a similar study, female rats forced to exercise 1 hr daily ate less than sedentary controls (14). Finally, in one study with six obese men, subjects walked vigorously on a treadmill for 90 min (1,100 kcal/day), 5 days/week for 16 weeks (30). Although no attempt was made to influence food intake, monitored food intake initially increased and then progressively decreased so that by week 16 it was actually below pretraining levels. While these studies are often cited to encourage sedentary, obese individuals to increase their activity in hopes of decreasing their food intake, these findings are not universal (31).

The bulk of the evidence points to lower food intakes in sedentary obese individuals in comparison with those of normal-weight individuals engaging in moderate or heavy physical activity. Some of the differences between studies may be a result of the variabilities and inaccuracies associated with recording caloric intake, especially when working with obese subjects (32). In self-reports of food intake the obese may underreport their actual food intake. With this qualification, there are a number of studies in which obese individuals were less active than normal-weight controls and their food intake was not greater than, and in some studies was actually less than, normal. This was observed with infants (33), schoolchildren (34), and adults (35,36).

EXERCISE AND ITS EFFECTS ON FATNESS AND ENERGY METABOLISM

The amount of exercise engaged in by humans and other animals is of major importance in regulating the fat content of the body. There have been numerous studies documenting the observation that exercise results in decreased total body fat and may increase lean body mass, although the magnitude of this change depends on the duration and intensity of the exercise and the age of the individual (for review, see 17). A normal-weight adult male is expected to be between 15 and 20% body fat, a female between 20 and 25% body fat. In contrast, a highly trained athlete, engaging in an endurance sport such as marathon running, may be only 5% body fat. In experimental animals, Crews et al. (37) have shown a specific lipid-mobilizing effect of exercise since trained rats had significantly less fat than did pair-weighed controls.

For some obese individuals increased physical activity can promote spontaneous weight loss and presumably decreased body fat. In the aforementioned study in which six sedentary obese men completed 16 weeks of a vigorous walking program, body weight loss averaged 5.7 kg—the majority of the weight loss was probably fat tissue (30). In another study obese women who walked at least 30 min/ day lost an average of 20 lb at the end of 1 year (38).

The amount of exercise needed to decrease body fat is related to duration and intensity of the exercise (39). In one study subjects exercised three times a week for 6 weeks (39). Included in the exercise period were three 5-min periods of cycling on an ergometer just below maximal working capacity. Body fat of non-obese and obese subjects decreased by approximately 1 kg. This approached significance in the nonobese subjects ($p < 0.10$). In another study of patients who suffered a myocardial infarction, body fat decreased by approximately 7 kg over a 9-month period without restriction of energy intake (40). Bjorntorp (41) suggested that provided the exercise is strenuous enough, at least 2 months of training are necessary to significantly reduce body fat.

Obese individuals on a standard weight reduction diet often lose some lean tissue as well as fat. However, when exercise is combined with caloric restriction, lean body mass is preserved or even increased. Adolescent boys attending a 7-week summer camp to lose weight were placed on a 1,200 kcal/day diet and participated in at least 6 hr of supervised exercise/day (42). Weight loss averaged 29.2 lb and percent body fat dropped from 39.0 to 27.5% while lean body mass was unchanged (107.5 $\pm$ 4.7 versus 106.9 $\pm$ 5.1 lb; $p > 0.05$). In another study, adults (a) reduced their caloric intake by 500 cal/day and kept their physical activity constant, (b) increased their physical activity to provide a comparable caloric deficit, or (c) reduced caloric intake by 250 cal and increased caloric output by 250 cal (43). Weight loss was similar in all three groups. However, the group that only dieted lost lean tissue as well as fat, while the exercise groups lost more fat and maintained lean body mass.

Exercise helps contribute to the caloric deficit of the dieting individual by increasing caloric output in two ways. First, there is the caloric cost of the actual exercise. For example, an individual weighing 120 lb would burn up approximately 165 kcal when walking 2 miles for 1 hr; this increases to 195 kcal for an individual weighing 175 lb.

Second, although this point remains controversial, there is evidence that the effects of physical activity on metabolism can last for a number of hours after the exercise is completed, thus adding to the caloric deficit (44–46). In one study of Harvard football players, basal metabolic rate was elevated by as much as 25% 15 hr after a strenuous game or workout (44). Furthermore, this effect was in part dependent on the duration and the intensity of the exercise. In another study, when obese women walk for 45 min before and after a test meal of 750 kcal, metabolic rate in response to this meal was enhanced for up to 5 hr after physical activity (45). However, this response was actually greater in nonobese individuals.

Finally, numerous authors have reported that with caloric restriction (i.e., dieting) basal metabolism decreased in both lean and obese individuals and that this decline was greater than the decrease in body weight (46–50). In one study of obese individuals, when caloric intake was reduced from 3,500 to 450 kcal/day, oxygen consumption fell by 15% after 2 weeks while body weight decreased by approximately 7% (49). In a study in our laboratory, we have reported that when obese individuals were placed on a 500 kcal/day diet, over a 2-week period they showed a gradual reduction in basal heat production/hr/75% body weight to 91% of their predieting levels (46). When they exercised for 20 to 30 min/day at approximately 60% of their VO_2max, basal heat production rose to the precontrol level within 3 to 4 days and continued to increase over a 2-week period to approximately 107% of predieting levels. In contrast, in sedentary individuals four weeks of similar caloric restriction resulted in a reduction of basal heat production to 81% of predieting levels. In obese individuals on calorically restricted diets these findings can be of practical importance and could explain why actual weight loss on a diet is often less than the predicted weight loss.

PSYCHOLOGICAL BENEFITS

In addition to the physiological benefits, exercise is also associated with feelings of well-being and even euphoria (for review, see 50). In one study, 20 min of treadmill running was associated with elevations in plasma concentrations of β-endorphins (51). This may be a partial explanation for the euphoria anecdotally associated with exercise. In some individuals who were distressed, anxious, or physically unfit, exercise training was associated with improvements of mood (52). In obese adolescent boys, it improved self-concept (53). When combined with a weight reduction program, exercise was associated with a shift toward a more internal locus of control or feelings of self-control over one's life (42).

WEIGHT MAINTENANCE

In 1959, Stunkard and McLaren-Hume reviewed the results of treatment for obesity in the preceding 30 years (54). They concluded that the majority of individuals in obesity treatment programs do not lose any significant amount of weight and those that do lose weight tend to regain this lost weight over time. Changes in eating and exercise patterns instituted during a weight loss program are often short-lived. In experimental animals, exercise termination is associated with rapid weight and fat gain (24,26).

Studies have attempted to characterize what therapies and what types of individuals increase success in weight maintenance. In one study, Gormally and colleagues interviewed 21 participants in a weight reduction program 7 months after the end of the program (55). Seven of the eight people (86%) who were successful at maintenance reported that they exercised frequently. In contrast, 54% of unsuccessful participants engaged in very little or no exercise during follow-up. Those who relapsed also reported that they were unable to cope with stressful events that occurred during follow-up.

The benefits of exercise in weight maintenance may go beyond its effects on food intake, lipogenesis, and body composition. As previously mentioned, in obese adolescent boys exercise can improve self-concept (53) and is associated with increased feelings of self-control (42). Studies by Cohen and colleagues demonstrated that children who maintained lost weight reported more self-regulation than children who regained weight (56).

CONCLUSIONS

In conclusion, the answer to our original question "Is obesity a disease of inactivity?" is: "Definitely maybe!" In reviewing the obesity literature one is impressed with the observation that obesity is not a single disorder. For those obese individuals who are considerably less active than lean individuals, for those who have low caloric requirements, and for those who respond to a modest increase in activity by decreasing food intake, obesity can be considered a disease of inactivity. In these cases, rational treatment and long-term maintenance should include increased physical activity.

ACKNOWLEDGMENT

This work was supported by grant no. AM 18899 from the National Institutes of Health.

REFERENCES

1. Kromhout, J. (1983): Changes in energy and macronutrients in 871 middle-aged men during 10 years of follow-up (the Zutphen study). *Am. J. Clin. Nutr.*, 37:287–294.
2. Durnin, J. V. G. A., Lonergan, M. E., Good, J., and Ewan, A. (1974): A cross-sectional nutritional and anthropometric study, with an interval of 7 years, on 611 young adolescent schoolchildren. *Br. J. Nutr.*, 32:169–179.
3. Friend, B. (1977): *Changes in Nutrients in the U.S. Diet Caused by Alterations in Food Intake Patterns.* Prepared for The Changing Food Supply in America Conference, May 22, 1974, sponsored by the Food and Drug Administration.
4. Greene, J. A. (1939): Clinical study of the etiology of obesity. *Ann. Intern. Med.*, 12:1797–1803.
5. Bullen, B. A., Reed, R. B., and Mayer, J. (1964): Physical activity of obese and non-obese adolescent girls appraised by motion picture sampling. *Am. J. Clin. Nutr.*, 4:211–233.
6. Stefanik, P. A., Heald, F. P., Jr., and Mayer, J. (1959): Caloric intake in relation to energy output of obese and non-obese adolescent boys. *Am. J. Clin. Nutr.*, 7:55–62.
7. Waxman, M., and Stunkard, A. J. (1980): Caloric intake and expenditure of obese boys. *J. Pediatr.*, 96:187–193.
8. Chirico, A. M., and Stunkard, A. J. (1960): Physical activity and human obesity. *N. Engl. J. Med.*, 263:935–940.
9. Ingle, D. J. (1949): A simple means of producing obesity in the rat. *Proc. Soc. Exp. Biol. Med.*, 72:604–605.
10. Mayer, J. (1953): Decreased activity and energy balance in the hereditary obesity-diabetes syndrome of mice. *Science*, 117:504–505.
11. Stern, J. S., and Johnson, P. R. (1977): Spontaneous activity and adipose cellularity in the genetically obese Zucker rat (fafa). *Metabolism*, 26:371–379.
12. Joosten, H. F. P., and Van der Kroon, P. H. W. (1974): Growth pattern and behavioral traits associated with the development of the obese hyperglycemic syndrome in mice (ob/ob). *Metabolism*, 26:1141–1147.
13. Stern, J. S., and Johnson, P. R. (1978): Size and number of adipocytes and their implications. In: *Advances in Modern Nutrition, Vol. 2: Diabetes, Obesity and Vascular Disease*, edited by H. Katzen and R. Mahler. Hemisphere, New York.
14. Mayer, J., Marshall, N. B., Vitale, J. J., Christensen, J. H., Mashayekhi, M. B., and Stare, F. J. (1954): Exercise, food intake, and body weight in normal rats and genetically obese mice. *Am. J. Physiol.*, 177:544–548.
15. Walberg, J. L., Mole, P. A., and Stern, J. S. (1982): Effect of swim training on development of obesity in the genetically obese rat. *Am. J. Physiol.*, 242:R204–R211.
16. Stern, J. S., Dunn, J. R., and Johnson, P. R. (1977): Spontaneous activity and adipose cellularity in the genetically obese yellow (Ay/a) mouse. *Fed. Proc.*, 36:1150.
17. Oscai, L. B. (1973): The role of exercise in weight control. *Exerc. Sports Med.*, 1:103–123.
18. Applegate, E. A., Upton, D. E., and Stern, J. S. (1982): Food intake, body composition and blood lipids following treadmill exercise in male and female rats. *Physiol. Behav.*, 28:917–920.

19.   Nance, D. M., Bromley, B., Barnard, R. J., and Gorski, R. A. (1977): Sexually dimorphic effects of forced exercise on food intake and body weight in the rat. *Physiol. Behav.,* 19:155–158.

20.   Oscai. L. B., and Holloszy, J. O. (1969): Effects of weight changes produced by exercise, food restriction or overeating on body composition. *J. Clin. Invest.,* 48:2121–2128.

21.   Ahrens, R. (1972): Effect of age and dietary carbohydrate source on the response of rats to forced exercise. *J. Nutr.,* 102:241–247.

22.   Stevenson, J. A. F., Box, B. M., Feleki, V., and Beaton, J. R. (1966): Bouts of exercise and food intake in the rat (fafa). *J. Appl. Physiol.,* 21:118–122.

23.   Katch, V. L., Martin, R., and Martin, J. (1979): Effects of exercise intensity on food consumption in the male rat. *Am. J. Clin. Nutr.,* 32:1401–1407.

24.   Applegate, E. A., and Stern, J. S. (1983): Food intake, adiposity and adipose tissue lipoprotein lipase activity associated with exercise and its termination. *Fed. Proc. (in press).*

25.   Applegate, E. A., Upton, D. E., and Stern, J. S. (1983): Effects of exercise and detraining on food intake, adiposity, lipoprotein lipase, and *in vivo* lipogenesis in Osborne-Mendel rats made obese on high fat diets. *Am. J. Physiol. (submitted).*

26.   Tsai, A. C., Rosenberg, R., and Borer, K. T. (1982): Metabolic alterations induced by voluntary exercise and discontinuation of exercise in hamsters. *Am. J. Clin. Nutr.,* 35:943–949.

27.   Edholm, O. G., Fletcher, J. G., Widdowson, E. M., and McCance, R. A. (1955): The food intake and individual expenditure of individual men. *Br. J. Nutr.,* 9:286–300.

28.   Blair, S. N., Ellsworth, N. M., Haskell, W. L., Stern, M. P., Farquhar, J. W., and Wood, P. D. (1981): Comparison of nutrient intake in middle aged men and women runners and controls. *Med. Sci. Sports Exerc.,* 13:310–315.

29.   Mayer, J., Roy, P., and Mitra, K. P. (1956): Relation between caloric intake, body weight, and physical work. Studies in an industrial male population in West Bengal. *Am. J. Clin. Nutr.,* 4:169–175.

30.   Leon, A. S., Conrad, J., Hunninghake, D. B., and Serfan, R. (1979): Effects of a vigorous walking program on body composition and carbohydrate and lipid metabolism of obese young men. *Am. J. Clin. Nutr.,* 32:1776–1787.

31.   Blulbulian, R., and Grunewald, K. (1983): Protein and fat composition of male Swiss albino mice: The effect of exercise duration. *Med. Sci. Sports Exerc.,* 15:139.

32.   Beaudoin, R., and Mayer, J. (1953): Food intakes of obese and non-obese women. *J. Am. Diet. Assoc.,* 29:29–33.

33.   Rose, H. E., and Mayer, J. (1968): Activity, caloric intake, fat storage and the energy balance of infants. *Pediatrics,* 41:18–29.

34.   Corbin, C. B., and Pletcher, P. (1968): Diet and physical activity patterns of obese and non-obese elementary school children. *Q. Res.,* 39:922–928.

35.   Curtis, D. E., and Bradfield, R. B. (1971): Long-term energy intake and expenditure of obese housewives. *Am. J. Clin. Nutr.,* 24:1410–1417.

36.   Maxfield, E., and Konishi, F. (1966): Patterns of food intake and physical activity in obesity. *J. Am. Diet. Assoc.,* 49:406–408.

37.   Crews, E. L., III, Fuge, K. W., Oscai, L. B., et al. (1969): Weight, food intake and body composition: Effects of exercise and of protein deficiency. *Am. J. Physiol.,* 216:359–363.

38.   Gwinup, G. (1975): Effects of exercise alone on the weight of obese women. *Arch. Intern. Med.,* 135:676–680.

39.   Bjorntorp, P., Holm, G., Jacobsson, B., Schiller-de-Jounge, K., Lundberg, P., Sjostrom, L., Smith, U., and Sullivan, L. (1977): Physical training in human hyperplastic obesity. IV. Effects on the hormonal status. *Metabolism,* 26:319–328.

40.   Bjorntorp, P., Berchtold, P., Grimby, G., Lindholm, B., Sanne, H., Tibblin, G., and Wilhelmsen, L. (1972): Effects of physical training on glucose tolerance, plasma insulin and lipids and on body composition in men after myocardial infarction. *Acta Med. Scand.,* 192:439–443.

41.   Bjorntorp. P. (1975): Exercise in the treatment of obesity. *Clin. Endocrinol. Metab.,* 5:431–453.

42.   Speaker, J. G., Schultz, C., Grinker, J. A., and Stern, J. S. (1983): Body size estimation and locus of control in obese adolescent boys undergoing weight reduction. *Int. J. Obes.,* 7:73–80.

43.   Zuti, W. B., and Golding, L. A. (1976): Comparing diet and exercise as weight reduction tools. *Physician Sport Med.,* 4:49–53.

44.   Edwards, H. T., Thorndike, A., and Dill, D. B. (1935): The energy requirements in strenuous muscular exercise. *N. Engl. J. Med.,* 213:532–536.

45. Bradfield, R. B., Curtis, D. E., and Margen, S. (1968): Effect of activity on caloric response of obese women. *Am. J. Clin. Nutr.,* 21:1208–1210.
46. Schultz, C., Bernauer, E., Mole, P. A., et al. (1980): Effects of severe caloric restriction and moderate exercise on basal metabolic rate and hormonal status in adult humans. *Fed. Proc.,* 39:783.
47. Benedict, F. G., Miles, W. R., Roth, P., and Smith, H. M. (1919): *Human Vitality Under Restricted Diet.* Carnegie Institute of Washington Publication No. 280.
48. Grande, F., Anderson, J. T., and Keys, A. (1958): Changes of basal metabolic rate in man in semistarvation and refeeding. *J. Appl. Physiol.,* 12:230–238.
49. Bray, G. A. (1969): Effect of caloric restriction on energy expenditure in obese patients. *Lancet,* 2:397–398.
50. Keys, A., Brozek, J., Hanschel, A., and Michelson, O. (1950): *The Biology of Human Starvation.* University of Minnesota Press, Minneapolis.
51. Gambert. S. R., Garthwaite, T. L., Pontzer, C. H., et al. (1981): Running elevates plasma β-endorphin immunoreactivity and ACTH in untrained human subjects. *Proc. Soc. Exp. Biol. Med.,* 168:1–4.
52. Folkins, C. H., and Sime, W. E. (1981): Physical fitness training and mental health. *Am. Psychol.,* 36:373–389.
53. Collingwood, T. R., and Willett, L. (1971): The effects of physical training upon self-concept and body attitudes. *J. Clin. Psychol.,* 27:411–412.
54. Stunkard, A., and McLaren-Hume, M. (1959): The results of treatment for obesity. *Arch. Intern. Med.,* 103:79–85.
55. Gormally, J., Rardin, D., and Black, S. (1980): Correlates of successful response to a behavioral weight control clinic. *J. Counseling Psychol.,* 27:179–191.
56. Cohen, E. A., Gelfand, D. M., Dodd, D. K., Jensen, J., and Turner, C. (1980): Self-control practices associated with weight loss maintenance in children and adolescents. *Behav. Ther.,* 11:26–37.

Eating and Its Disorders, edited by A. J.
Stunkard and E. Stellar. Raven Press,
New York © 1984.

A Boundary Model for the Regulation of Eating

C. Peter Herman and Janet Polivy

University of Toronto, Department of Psychology, Toronto, Canada M5S   1A1

One of the major perplexities facing researchers interested in the study of eating is the seeming incongruity of so much of the research that has been conducted to date. Not that any given study is necessarily incongruous in an absolute sense; rather, much of the inherently cogent research is incongruous only in the context established by other research enterprises. The very terms of reference encountered in one study may have no applicability whatsoever in other studies, although all the studies in question presumably share a common devotion to uncovering the determinants of eating. In the field of psychology alone, a survey of the major journals will often produce a sense that there are at least two schools of thought regarding eating research, and that these schools differ not only in their conclusions but in their very premises.

One school may be characterized as primarily physiological: Its essential premise is that eating—or feeding, as it is more typically called when rats, rather than people, are the subjects of concern—is basically a biological activity. Organisms start eating when they are hungry; they stop when they are full; and these basic events are controlled by signals emanating either from the brain or from the periphery.

A second school of thought tends to focus primarily on nonphysiological factors affecting eating. Examples of such factors would be social influence—e.g., the observation that people eat more when others around them are eating prodigiously—or cognitive considerations—e.g., an individual postponing consumption so as not to spoil his dinner. This sort of research assumes that eating is under the control of a wide variety of influences, many of which serve no evident biological purpose.

In the present chapter, we wish to outline what we consider to be the first steps toward a resolution of the incongruity fostered by these two schools of thought. We—along with our colleague, Lynn Kozlowski—are attempting to refine what we call a boundary model for the regulation of eating. This model attempts to provide an explicit place for both physiological and nonphysiological determinants of eating. Indeed, its very purpose is to provide a way of thinking coherently about both sorts of influences on eating.

By way of preface, we should mention that this model, as applied to eating, represents a special case of a more general boundary model that we have applied to all sorts of consummatory behaviors, at least in humans (2). This model, for instance, has recently been applied to smoking (7), another sort of behavior where debate rages over the relative importance of physiological and nonphysiological influences.

THE BOUNDARY MODEL

The crux of the boundary model is the notion that consumption is regulated within boundaries, rather than at a point. In terms of eating, this proposition amounts to the assertion that eating normally occurs so as to maintain the organism within the boundaries corresponding to hunger and satiety. We assume— prompted by the multitude of studies in which caloric regulation is remarkably imprecise, at least in the short run—that nature is not terribly concerned about consummatory regulation occurring at a precise point. Rather, nature cares that it occurs within a range; as long as consumption (or its physiological correlates) is maintained within that range, nature is satisfied. We designate that range as the range of biological indifference.

If we think of this range spatially, then at its lower end (at the left of Fig. 1), we may identify a boundary that we designate as hunger. If consumption is inadequate to maintain the organism within the range of biological indifference, then the organism falls below the boundary into an aversive zone that we call hunger. All of the various activators, or negative reinforcers, that we associate with hunger, are experienced by the organism when it enters this suboptimal zone. The organism feels uncomfortable (or worse), and eating becomes a much more pleasant activity than usual. Ordinarily, when the organism experiences hunger, it will seek out and consume enough food so as to escape from this aversive condition.

Note three qualifications to the foregoing scenario: First, the purpose of eating, in this instance, is to escape from the aversive zone back into the zone of biological indifference; we make no assumptions about how much additional eating will occur once the hunger boundary has been recrossed and the aversive pressure of hunger has been relieved. Indeed, the question of how much additional eating will occur is entirely independent of considerations of hunger at this point in the sce-

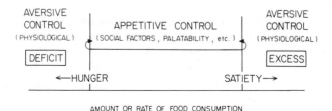

AMOUNT OR RATE OF FOOD CONSUMPTION

FIG. 1. The basic boundary model.

nario and requires our exploration of other sorts of determining factors, which we shall address later.

Second, the aversive nature of hunger provides a strong incentive for the organism to eat, but it is not absolutely compelling. Some organisms can tolerate hunger; some have no choice; others (e.g., compulsive dieters) seem to luxuriate in hunger and regard it as desirable if not exactly pleasant. Our point here is simply that hunger usually provokes eating, but the onset of hunger is no guarantee of eating, even in the presence of palatable food. We must distinguish between degrees of influence. Immediately below the range of biological indifference, the extent of hunger (and the experience of hunger) is weaker than at levels further removed to the left in the figure. Correspondingly, the aversive pressure to eat increases as we move to the left in Fig. 1, and it approaches zero as we move to the right, toward what is labeled the hunger boundary; above that boundary, there are no biologically aversive pressures to eat.

A third consideration, related to the second, involves the possibility that organisms may learn to anticipate the transgressions of boundaries and take appropriate action beforehand so as to minimize the disruption of their caloric economy. People learn to eat more than is required simply to eliminate hunger; otherwise, they would soon be facing the prospect of hunger once again and feeding would become tantamount to a continuous drip, orally self-administered. When we say that above the hunger boundary there is no biological pressure to eat, then we are technically correct but are ignoring the pressure exerted by the anticipation of biological pressure.

Just as the organism ordinarily learns to eat more than the absolute minimum necessary to preclude immediate hunger, so it learns not to eat the absolute maximum it can stomach. Although such a strategy would maximally forestall the onset of hunger, it nevertheless clashes with the second major feature of the boundary model—the upper, or satiety, boundary. We regard this boundary as more or less equivalent to the hunger boundary, at least insofar as it demarcates an aversive zone that the organism ordinarily strives to avoid. The particular aversive experiences encountered in this zone are not clearly the opposite of those experienced in the aversive hunger zone; nevertheless, considerable discomfort may be attached to an incursion into this zone, as most of us can recall. Escape from this zone is in some respects more problematic than is escape from the hunger zone. Although the sufferer need not seek out food—which is, of course, a serious problem for some organisms suffering from hunger—he or she rarely has any immediate recourse short of vomiting to relieve the pressure. The absorption and disposition of ingested food takes time; thus, although the organism can stop eating precipitately, escape from the aversive zone of satiety may be delayed.

The boundary model as delineated so far corresponds fairly well to what we all know about eating. It is worth dwelling on a couple of its more theoretically important features. First, as has been emphasized, the model involves two boundaries, rather than one regulated level. This separation of boundaries implies that hunger and satiety are separate processes, rather than opposite sides of the same coin, as they are occasionally viewed in single-level models of regulation. Accordingly, we are released from whatever obligation single-level thinking may impose on us to interpret hunger and satiety processes as inextricably linked; the physiological bases of these two regulatory processes may well be quite distinct, and investigations of one process may tell us little about the operation of the other. This amounts to a loss of parsimony, but there are gains, as we shall see.

A second major feature of the boundary model is that it provides by definition a zone of biological indifference, as we have termed it. This zone, as we have seen, is an area—we think spatially—in which aversive biological pressures are absent. The amount of food consumed by an organism located in the zone of biological indifference is not constrained by hunger or satiety. However, we should not therefore conclude that consumption within this range is simply random; rather, we believe that it is precisely within the range of biological indifference that nonphysiological factors manifest their influence. The organism is indifferent to biological pressures; but as a consequence, it is all the more susceptible to social, cognitive, and other psychological influences. As is the case in the aversive zones, there is no absolutely compelling pressure to eat; indeed, in the zone of biological indifference, the pressures are more likely to be appetitive—as opposed to aversive—and consequently weaker. Nevertheless, such psychosocial and cognitive pressures are demonstrably effective in influencing, if not absolutely controlling, eating.

Cognitive and social pressures may spill over into the aversive zones of hunger and satiety. For instance, the serious dieter may inhibit her consumption so as to remain in the hunger zone, and this inhibition is best described as cognitively achieved. Likewise, social contagion may induce the sort of group overeating that propels the group members into serious overindulgence to their gastric regret. By the same token, physiological factors may encroach on the zone of indifference; as we have suggested, anticipatory reactions—which may involve cephalic phase reactions or other physiological modulators—may operate within the zone of indifference so as to preclude actual transgressions of the boundaries and consequent suffering. In general, however, we may identify the aversive zones as the domains of physiological pressures, and the zone of biological indifference as the territory where psychological factors are most likely to exert their influence.

We have now arrived at a point where it may be more clearly seen how physiological and nonphysiological factors may coexist within a field theory of eating. Our boundaries serve to demarcate their respective zones of influence. Neither sort of factor is relegated to inferior conceptual status. The question does not become "Which factor really controls eating?" but "Under what conditions are we likely to observe physiological controls, and when will nonphysiological factors predominate?" Obviously, as we indicated when first outlining the problem, social factors will be relatively impotent when the subject is either famished or stuffed; but when the subject is neither famished nor stuffed, social factors may be the most powerful factors of all.

Notice that this view gives equal scientific status to physiological and nonphysiological factors. There is no attempt to reduce one sort of factor to another (e.g., to assume that social factors are best understood in terms of their biological substrates, if such could be discovered). Our only assumptions are that manipulation of either sort of factor may be seen to affect eating on some occasions, and that our science requires more than anything else the depiction of lawful regularities in the influence of any sort of specifiable and measurable variable on the behavior of interest—eating.

INDIVIDUAL DIFFERENCES IN BOUNDARY PLACEMENT

One question that immediately arises on contemplation of the boundary model as we have proposed it concerns individual differences in boundary placement. Specifically, might it be the case that people differ, for example, in the width of the zone of biological indifference? In our opinion, such differences do exist, and they can help make sense of some otherwise confusing observations.

In our laboratory, we have long been concerned with contrasts between dieters and nondieters. One apparent difference between these two groups of individuals is that dieters seem to act as if they have a larger spread between their hunger and satiety boundaries. On the one hand, it seems that it takes more food deprivation to get them to admit to the sensation of hunger; by and large, after an equivalent period of deprivation, the dieter will be less likely to eat than will the nondieter. This finding may be represented as the dieter having a lower hunger boundary than does the nondieter. It may be explained in terms of conditioning, such that the dieter gets used to eating less and/or experiencing hunger. (This explanation is not particularly compatible with the notion that dieters are below set point, and presumably subject to greater hunger and pressures to eat more; but it is the behavior of the dieters, not the boundary model, that is at the root of this apparent discrepancy with the set point analysis.)

While under some normal circumstances, our dieters tend to eat less than do nondieters, there are some circumstances under which they eat considerably more. (It is these instances wherein they eat considerably more that lead us to wonder whether our average dieter really does manage to reduce her weight significantly below set point. Perhaps dieters are best characterized by the attempt to lose weight, rather than by weight loss per se.) The evident ability of dieters to eat more than nondieters while showing no signs of discomfort leads us to the conclusion that their upper (satiety) boundary may be elevated relative to that of the nondieters. Of course, the elevated satiety boundary observed in dieters is quite compatible with the notion that they have managed to reduce their weight below some optimal level or set point; an elevated satiety boundary would conduce to the restoration of weight, as demanded by long-term weight regulatory considerations. This interpretation, however, cannot account for the observed lowering of the hunger boundary, which appears to exacerbate the problem of an organism below set point.

Overall, then, dieters are characterized by a lower hunger boundary and a higher satiety boundary. In our view, they may be seen as in some sense under reduced physiological control, compared to nondieters. (Of course, this is precisely

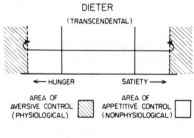

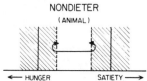

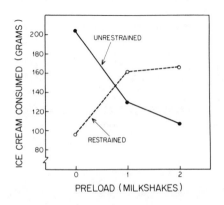

FIG. 2. Dieter/nondieter differences in hunger and satiety boundaries.

what dieting is all about—namely, the attempt to replace normal physiological controls with a cognitive agenda extracted from the latest diet book. If dieters were satisfied with the operation of their physiological boundaries, they would not have had to undertake dieting in the first place.) We call our dieters transcendental to acknowledge their attempt to defy the physiological controls that have left them with a weight that does not suit their personal preference.

We call our nondieters, by contrast, animal. The nondieter is much more responsive to the pressures of hunger and satiety and acts as if those pressures were impinging on him even within the zone of biological indifference. We represent this situation by showing these boundaries as pulled together in the nondieter rather than pushed apart, as in the dieter (Fig. 2).

THE DISINHIBITED DIETER

A severe challenge to the boundary model as described so far is posed by some data from our own laboratory (3). In Fig. 3, we may observe the response, in terms

FIG. 3. *Ad lib.* consumption following a forced preload.

of *ad lib.* consumption of ice cream, to a milkshake preload, in dieters and non-dieters. In this study, subjects believed that they were engaged in an exercise in taste perception, examining the influence of taste experiences on subsequent taste ratings.

The initial taste experience consisted of milkshakes, with subjects in the three experimental conditions receiving either zero, one, or two tastes corresponding, respectively, to zero, one, or two milkshakes. Since "for purposes of experimental control" subjects were required to consume all of the "initial taste," this consti-tuted a preload manipulation. Immediately after the preload, subjects were given three flavors of ice cream to taste and rate. Ice cream consumption was *ad lib.;* subjects were told that they could have as much as was "needed" to make accu-rate ratings, and that after the ratings were completed, they could have additional ice cream to whatever extent they wished. Naturally, unbeknownst to the subject, our true interest was not in the ratings but in the amount of ice cream consumed; we surreptitiously weighed the ice cream before and after the subject ate.

The data for the nondieters, or unrestrained eaters, corresponds well to common sense, previous experience, and the boundary model. With increasing amounts of forced preload, subjects ate less and less ice cream *ad lib*. Although we have no direct evidence on this point, we may assume that greater amounts of milkshake preload carried the subjects further to the right within the zone of biological indif-ference, so that there was less room available for further consumption without encountering satiety pressures. These data are certainly compatible with our view of nondieters as highly susceptible to physiological constraints on eating.

The dieters, in marked contrast, reacted to the forced preload in a fashion rarely encountered in lower animals or other sensibly regulating creatures. With increases in the size of the forced preload, we note an increase in the amount of ice cream consumed *ad lib*. We have called this effect, purely descriptively, coun-terregulation, and speculated that it arises from the peculiar cognitive calculus of the dieter.

Our inclination to interpret the behavior of the dieters in this study as cognitive rather than physiological is based on a number of considerations. First, the response of the dieter does not conform in any straightforward way to the negative feedback assumption that underlies most physiological models of eating. It is as if the dieter were engaged in a positive feedback loop, which does not lend itself easily to physiological interpretation.

Second, when the dieter is merely *told* that the preload is high calorie, greater subsequent *ad lib.* consumption is observed, regardless of whether the preload is actually high calorie or not (8). When the preload, be it high or low calorie, is presented as low calorie, dieters tend not to overindulge subsequently. Thus, it is the dieter's belief about the caloric value of the preload, rather than the actual caloric value of the preload, that determines subsequent *ad lib.* consumption.

It is conceivable, of course, that some bizarre physiological process might pro-duce the correspondingly bizarre behavior of the dieters in this and similar studies. For instance, it may be that dieters have some sort of hypoglycemic reaction to the milkshakes, so that the more of them they eat, the more they need. This explanation and other variations on the theme of eating-induced hunger do not cope well with the studies in which it has been shown that perceived rather than actual calories are the truly determining factor. Nor does the positing of increased hunger explain in a cogent way how satiety pressures are to be dealt with. Our dieters are eating surprisingly large amounts; if they are sated in the zero milkshake condition, what has become of satiety in the two milkshake condition?

We consider the perceived-calorie studies to be the best argument in favor of a cognitive interpretation of these data. However, it is always arguable that even the perception of calories may somehow elicit a physiological reaction that provokes further eating. Although the logic of this proposal is somewhat suspect, we nevertheless did our best to test it by investigating the hormonal reactions of dieters and nondieters to the prospect of high-calorie, palatable food. We have found (5) that dieters salivate much more than do nondieters when anticipating eating pizza; salivation, it has been argued (12) is a useful measure of appetite. Still, Wooley and Wooley have demonstrated rather convincingly (12) that the prospect of a forced, high-caloric load actually inhibits salivation in dieters. It is only when dieters can decide for themselves how much they will eat that the prospect of eating is appealing. Thus, applying these findings to our milkshake situation, we must conclude that the prospect of a forced, high-calorie milkshake preload would not serve to elicit strong appetitive reactions at the physiological level.

Other indices of differential physiological reactivity in dieters and nondieters have proved no more helpful in understanding why dieters react as they do to high-calorie preloads. Measures of insulin, motilin, pancreatic polypeptide, gastrin, and a variety of other hormones involved in eating and digestion have occasionally showed dieter/nondieter differences (e.g., elevated motilin levels in dieters), but these differences do not appear specifically in response to the ingestion or anticipated ingestion of food (6). The validity of our measures is corroborated somewhat by our finding the expected obese/normal weight differences on some of these variables; but when normal weight dieters and nondieters are compared, their physiology simply does not map onto the behavior that we are trying to explain in the milkshake preload studies.

The counterregulatory effect that we have been discussing has been replicated many times, in a number of laboratories other than our own (10). As we have seen, we consider it to be primarily a cognitively determined phenomenon; but how, precisely, are we to understand it?

Certainly, the boundary model as we have presented it to this point, despite its provision for the operation of cognitive factors, does not easily accommodate the data portrayed in Fig. 3. The contention that dieters may have a larger distance between their hunger and satiety boundaries in no way explains why these dieters ought to show reverse regulation. A minor adjustment to our model, however, will provide a neat resolution of our paradox.

In Fig. 4, we add one more boundary to the model—what we call the diet

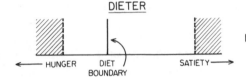

FIG. 4. Modified boundary model for dieters.

boundary. This boundary, as its name implies, characterizes dieters but not non-dieters. Moreover, unlike the hunger and satiety boundaries, this diet boundary is not physiological; that is, aversive physiological reactions do not defend the boundary by punishing transgressions of it. On the contrary, this boundary is entirely psychological—or more precisely, cognitive—and represents the dieter's self-imposed quota for consumption on a given occasion. The actual specification of where this boundary lies in any given dieter poses some interesting problems in measurement; for the time being, it suffices to note that the diet boundary characteristically falls well short (i.e., to the left) of the satiety boundary. This is the case almost by definition, since if the satiety boundary itself were to inhibit consumption at a point that was low enough to satisfy the dieter, then she would have no need to impose a diet boundary. The diet boundary, in effect, reflects the dieter's conclusion that satiety alone provides an inadequate (or at least overly delayed) brake on consumption.

But how does this cognitive diet boundary account for counterregulation? In Fig. 5 we see how we might plot the data from a counterregulation study in terms of the modified boundary model. For the nondieter, the situation is fairly simple. In the absence of a preload, the nondieter is well to the left within the zone of indifference. Given highly palatable ice cream, she can—and usually does—eat a great deal before satiety pressures are encountered (or anticipated). After a sizable preload, however, she begins her *ad lib.* eating from a position displaced to the right within the zone of indifference; she is closer to satiety, and has less room for eating. (Of course, this way of putting it corresponds to the phenomenology

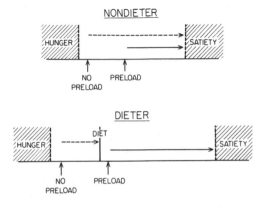

FIG. 5. A boundary explanation for counterregulation.

of the eater and reflects the common tendency to think of hunger and satiety in spatial terms.)

It should probably be noted at this point that if we were to make the available ice cream less palatable, the nondieter would undoubtedly eat less, independent of the effect of the preload. In short, we have presented the boundary model to this point as if eating always proceeds until satiety is reached; this assumption in all likelihood is untenable. The fact that palatability can dramatically affect the amount of food eaten by subjects within the zone of biological indifference reinforces the need to take nonphysiological factors operating within this zone into consideration.

To further complicate matters, we might note as well that some researchers, such as Barbara Rolls (9), regard the influence of alterations in palatability as direct influences on the satiety boundary itself, though Rolls does not use our terminology. Rolls, in effect, sees palatability as determining the satiety boundary; we regard the inhibiting effects of decreased palatability as operating before satiety is reached. Our view of satiety is thus more closely linked to calories than hers and, thus, to physiology as ordinarily conceived. Whether we view the satiety boundary as fixed (and palatability as a perceptual influence occurring to its left) or whether we regard palatability as a direct determinant of the satiety boundary location, we must acknowledge that palatability is a major influence on eating and that its influence is not essentially physiological. We make this statement even while cognizant of the fact that physiological alterations—e.g., severe changes in body weight—can affect palatability as well (1). The effect of palatability on eating, in short, is more than that of a mediator between physiological state and behavior, although such mediation may comprise some of its function.

To return to Fig. 5, we may now consider the psychodynamics of the dieter located within the zone of indifference. As long as she remains to the left of the diet boundary, her self-imposed diet quota remains in effect. Thus, after a small preload, there is still every prospect of maintaining her diet goal for the immediate future. Accordingly, *ad lib.* eating is likely to proceed so as to maintain total (i.e., forced plus *ad lib.*) consumption at or below the diet quota.

After a large preload, however, the dieter may well find herself already compromised. The preload itself may have caused the dieter to transgress (albeit unwillingly) the diet boundary. In the perceived-calorie studies, the dieter only *thinks* that the boundary has been transgressed; but in this case, since the boundary itself is cognitive, thinking is all that matters. In either case, the dieter who has consumed (or thinks she has consumed) a high-calorie preload finds herself to the right of the diet boundary. There is no immediate point to restraining further consumption, since the purpose of such restraint—maintaining diet goals— has been undercut. Consequently, the dieter tends to eat substantial amounts of palatable food *ad lib.*, up to the point where true satiety pressures begin to inhibit consumption; and, as we have seen, the true satiety boundary for dieters often seems to be displaced to the right, allowing, if not guaranteeing, occasionally prodigious *ad lib.* consumption. We have termed this psychological state the what-the-hell effect, in an attempt to capture the dieter's subjective state of caloric abandon.

A couple of details are worth mentioning. First, we do not believe that the behavior of dieters following a large or high-calorie preload is unregulated. Rather, the boundary model makes explicit that consumption of the large preload changes the basis for regulation, not its presence. As long as the diet boundary has not been breached, it provides the upper boundary for regulation. But once it has been surpassed, it no longer serves a regulatory purpose; rather, the satiety boundary becomes the boundary of reference, just as it is at all times for the nondieter. Accordingly, we prefer not to formulate our counterregulatory effect as implying that the larger the preload, the more subsequent *ad lib.* consumption. That formulation is an artifact, so to speak, of crossing the diet boundary. Once the boundary has been crossed, we believe that it is more accurate to suggest that the larger the preload, the less the subsequent *ad lib.* consumption. Note in Fig. 3 that the largest preload did not produce significantly more eating than did the intermediate size preload. The study depicted in Fig. 3 (3) was not a particularly clear case of post-diet-boundary regulation, since, we believe, the intermediate preload size was only partially successful in breaching the diet boundary, all dieters considered. Likewise, the largest preload may have been too large to permit maximal consumption, given that the diet boundary had been breached. Currently, research in our laboratory (V. Esses, *unpublished M.A. thesis*) is investigating the effects of forcing dieters to consume large and extralarge preloads. We expect, as would any subscriber to regulatory sanity, that even dieters will inhibit their consumption when the forced preload brings them to a point just short of the aversive satiety zone. (Parenthetically, we should note that this research requires very strict attention to palatability effects, which can mask caloric regulation if they are not taken into account.)

Another consideration worth mentioning is the logically fallacious reasoning implicit in the what-the-hell effect. The dieter thinks and behaves as if dieting were best considered in diurnal units. Once the daily diet quota has been surpassed, there is no point in further restraint. Of course, from our perspective, a calorie consumed on Saturday night probably counts just as much as one consumed on Sunday morning; abandoning calorie counting because the diet boundary has been breached does not make much sense if we take a broader perspective. Still, the narrow perspective, fostered no doubt by diets that emphasize daily quotas, remains rampant in dieters, and provides the cognitive substrate for dramatic disinhibition. Recently, diet counselors have been urging their clients to take a broader view and to make allowance for the occasional splurge; we believe that such advice, if taken seriously, would diminish the incidence of the what-the-hell effect as we encounter it in everyday life.

In our previous research, we have contrived situations wherein the dieter believes herself to have transgressed the diet boundary. In such cases, the diet boundary is rendered irrelevant as a guide to eating, since it is thought to have been calorically surpassed. We believe that factors other than forced preloading can also render the diet boundary (temporarily) irrelevant to the dieter. For instance, one study currently underway in our laboratory (11) involves what we call a postload paradigm: the dieter is told that she will consume a forced high-calorie load, but the *ad lib.* consumption is measured before the load is actually consumed. If the what-the-hell effect operates as we have postulated, then the dieter in the forced postload situation will be equally resigned to caloric sin, even if the sin has not yet occurred. We expect, according to this formulation, that the mere anticipation of a forced load may produce disinhibited eating in dieters.

There are other situations, we believe, in which the diet boundary is rendered irrelevant or at least ineffective. These situations need not involve caloric loads at all. For instance, we have shown that emotional upheaval (4) can lead to greater *ad lib.* consumption in dieters. (Stress makes nondieters eat less, generally.) We have argued that the effect of stress on dieters is best interpreted as the imposition of a more urgent concern (i.e., how to cope with the stressor) than even dieting. The diet quota then and the boundary that it sustains are rendered relatively less important to the dieter facing a more urgent stress; as a consequence, eating may proceed as if the diet boundary had been knocked down. The nondieter, being more responsive than the dieter to physiological pressures, reacts to stress as to any other sympathomimetic experience—namely, by decreasing consumption. The dieter, basically unresponsive to such physiological subtleties, proceeds to eat more than usual, since the diet boundary is inoperative. We believe that much the same sort of dynamic underlies the differential response of dieters and nondieters to alcoholic intoxication: Nondieters eat less *ad lib.*, whereas dieters eat more.

EXTENSIONS OF THE BOUNDARY MODEL

As we have tried to convince the reader, the boundary model with suitable amendations can help us interpret or at least systematically depict the behavior of dieters and nondieters. Perhaps most importantly, it can help us to understand the seemingly bizarre behavior of dieters; it can render this behavior sensible by demonstrating that it is not simply unregulated (i.e., unresponsive to controlling factors) but rather regulated in terms of a series of boundaries. In our view, there has been a dearth of constructive thinking about the determinants of overeating and especially about the factors that control it while it is occurring. Indeed, we are often led to believe that this is eating that is out of control. As scientists, we remain wedded to the notion that behavior is always controlled; our task is to discover the controlling factors and the manner in which they exert themselves.

Another virtue of the boundary model is that it permits, by extension, a consideration of eating behaviors even more abnormal than those displayed by the garden-variety dieter. In Fig. 6, we display some other types of problem eaters in terms of the boundary model.

In the top panel of Fig. 6, we may observe the dieter as we have been discussing her throughout this chapter. This panel depicts the dieter with her diet boundary intact or perhaps breached by a forced load. Immediately below, we may observe

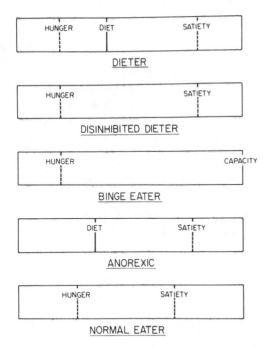

FIG. 6. Comparison of various types of eaters.

the dieter whose diet boundary, for one reason or another, has been eliminated from immediate consideration. Such, we believe, is an appropriate way to imagine the dieter who has become disinhibited in virtue of a momentary disinclination to adhere to her diet goals, either because they do not seem important (as may be the case in intoxication) or because they are not sufficiently important to attend to right at the moment (as may be the case in stressful situations). The only difference between these two panels is the presence/absence of the diet boundary itself.

In the next panel, we encounter a binge eater on a binge. Although we have occasionally discussed our disinhibited dieters as if they were bingers, we hasten to note an important difference. Our dieters, even when engaged in a bout of caloric abandon, are nevertheless still constrained, as we have seen, by the pressures of satiety. They regulate at the satiety boundary, and they experience the aversive consequences of overindulgence as sufficiently unpleasant to prevent any major transgression of the satiety boundary. Not so the binger. The binger, for whatever psychodynamically complex reasons she might have, does transgress the satiety boundary. She stops not when eating more becomes unpleasant but when it becomes impossible (i.e., when she reaches her limit of physical capacity). Of course, some binges may stop short of absolute physical capacity; indeed, some theorists regard bingeing as a state of mind, so that it may be observed to start (and even stop) even before satiety is reached. But what is most notable about bingers at the behavioral level is their apparent willingness to tolerate the discomfort of the upper aversive zone in their quest for whatever it is that eating does for them.

At the other end of the scale, the anorexic is notable for her willingness to tolerate the discomforts of the lower aversive zone. For her, it is not the satiety boundary that is irrelevant; it is the hunger boundary. The anorexic has a very stringent diet boundary, of course; but it seems that almost any amount of consumption (or nonconsumption) below that boundary is tolerable; indeed, the less, the better. Many anorexics claim not to experience aversive consequences of hunger; but such claims are usually discredited by those patients who eventually recover.

The major difference, then, between our normal dieter and patients with eating disorders is that the normal dieter does not make regular excursions into the aversive zones. Her behavior within the zone of indifference may be affected bizarrely by the operation of the diet boundary; but severe hunger or satiety remain as effective determinants of behavior. For those with the more serious eating disorders, even these natural guides to behavior are overridden. How the individual contends with such aversive experiences remains an important research question. Can people learn to tolerate being famished or bloated? Or do these aversive experiences simply seem like a small price to pay for compulsive eating or not eating?

Our final panel in Fig. 6 depicts what we consider to be a normal eater. Superficially, this individual resembles the disinhibited dieter; this resemblance, however, is misleading. For one thing, the disinhibited dieter's lack of a diet boundary is a temporary condition, whereas for the normal eater it is chronic. Second, the hunger and satiety boundaries tend to be closer together for the normal eater than for the dieter (disinhibited or otherwise). We believe that these two features are interrelated. In our view, it is the dieter's continuing attempt to live with the diet boundary, which in turn forces her to adopt a predominantly cognitive orientation to the question of when and how much to eat, that forces the hunger and satiety boundaries apart. To the extent that the dieter attempts to operate in terms of cognitive considerations, and eats in response to an agenda derived from a source other than her own body's demands, she is bound to become less sensitive to the physiological pressures that might otherwise help her regulate her consumption. Indeed, in the dieter's view, these physiological pressures (especially hunger) are not helpful guides to consumption, but bothersome pressures to be overcome. If, however, the temporary abandonment of the diet boundary that we see in the second panel were to become permanent—which is to say, if the dieter would give up dieting—then we suspect that normal hunger and satiety pressures reflecting the natural physiological needs of the body would reassert themselves. At least we would hope so.

CONCLUSIONS

In the previous section, we attempted to demonstrate the utility of the boundary model as a way of comparing and contrasting different types of eaters and eating disorders intelligibly. We believe that the boundary model with suitable revisions is capable of incorporating most if not all of the significant factors affecting both normal and abnormal eating. Indeed, one of our major goals is to provide a bridge from normal to abnormal eating so that they are no longer treated as two separate disciplines obeying separate rules of their own. (For example, normal eating responds to normal physiological and psychological factors, whereas abnormal eating responds to an almost nonoverlapping set of abnormal physiological and psychological factors.)

By the same token, we hope to offer the boundary model as a bridge from physiological to nonphysiological determinants of eating. As we noted at the outset, there has often seemed to be an essential incompatibility between physiological and nonphysiological models of eating, with each model unsure how (or even whether) to incorporate the other model's factors. In our discussion of preload effects in dieters and nondieters, it soon became evident that the discussion could not proceed at all unless a way were found to involve both sorts of factors. Moreover, the boundary model suggests more specifically how these two types of factors might be discussed intelligently, without demeaning the role of either.

Obviously, the boundary model at present is simply a skeleton. The sorts of interpretations that it permits and the sorts of research that it suggests remain a task for us to undertake in the future. The present chapter is tentative both with respect to the model itself and perforce to how it explains dieters' behaviors. Nevertheless, we believe that such an effort is long overdue and are optimistic that our thinking about eating may yet become more harmonious and illuminating.

ACKNOWLEDGMENT

The research reported herein is supported by Grant A7078 from the Natural Sciences and Engineering Research Council of Canada.

REFERENCES

1. Cabanac, M. (1971): Physiological role of pleasure. *Science,* 173:1103–1107.
2. Herman, C. P., and Kozlowski, L. T. (1982): Indulgence, excess, and restraint: Perspectives on consummatory control in everyday life. In: *Control Over Intoxicant Use,* edited by N. E. Zinberg and W. M. Harding, pp. 77–88. Human Sciences Press, New York.
3. Herman, C. P., and Mack, D. (1975): Restrained and unrestrained eating. *J. Pers.,* 43:646–660.
4. Herman, C. P., and Polivy, J. (1975): Anxiety, restraint, and eating behavior. *J. Abnorm. Psychol.,* 84:666–672.
5. Klajner, F., Herman C. P., Polivy, J., and Chhabra, R. (1981): Human obesity, dieting, and anticipatory salivation to food. *Physiol. Behav.,* 27:195–198.
6. Klajner, F., Herman, C. P., Polivy, J., Marliss, E. B., and Greenberg, G. R. (1981): Elevated postprandial motilin secretion in normal weight and obese dieters, and elevated postprandial insulin response after cephalic exposure to food. Paper presented at International Symposium on the Brain-Gut Axis, Florence, Italy.
7. Kozlowski, L. T., and Herman, C. P. (1983): Controlled smoking. *J. Drug Iss. (in press).*
8. Polivy, J. (1976): Perception of calories and regulation of intake in restrained and unrestrained subjects. *Addict. Behav.,* 1:237–243.

9. Rolls, B. J., Rolls, E. T., and Rowe, E. A. (1982): The influence of variety on human food selection and intake. In: *The Psychobiology of Human Food Selection,* edited by L. M. Barker, pp. 101–122. Avi Publishing, Westport, Connecticut.
10. Spencer, J. A., and Fremouw, W. J. (1979): Binge eating as a function of restraint and weight classification. *J. Abnorm. Psychol.,* 88:262–267.
11. Stotland, S. (1983): Effect of anticipated loads on restrained and unrestrained eaters. M.A. Thesis, University of Toronto (*in progress*).
12. Wooley, O. W., and Wooley, S. C. (1981): Relationship of salivation in humans to deprivation, inhibition and the encephalization of hunger. *Appetite,* 2:331–350.

Eating and Its Disorders, edited by A.J.
Stunkard and E. Stellar. Raven Press,
New York © 1984.

The Current Status of Treatment for Obesity in Adults

Albert J. Stunkard

University of Pennsylvania, Philadelphia, Pennsylvania 19104

Two new developments make it possible to discuss treatment for obesity in a way that has not previously been possible. These are a theory of obesity that has therapeutic revelance and a classification of obesity that has therapeutic consequences.

The theory which can now inform our treatment of obesity is described in several of the chapters of this book. It states, in brief, that obesity is a result of regulated, homeostatic processes that act to maintain body weight and body fat at a constant level and that attempts to lower them are opposed by powerful biological processes. This theory has been expounded by Keesey *(this volume)* and Faust *(this volume)* and it underlies Herman's *(this volume)* concept of restrained eating, the idea that reducing diets have lowered the body weight of many people below their body weight set point, with various unfortunate consequences.

The theory that body fat is a regulated function is relevant to the treatment of obesity. The clinician already knows how difficult it is to help patients lose weight and to maintain their weight losses. This theory now provides a rationale for this difficulty. For it makes clear that much of the doctor's job is to help patients to exercise cognitive controls over powerful biological systems, in effect, learning to live in a semistarved manner. Occasionally, as we shall see, the physician may be able to change the system and ease the burden of the patients, but in either case, the doctor's job is not an easy one, and as the Wooley's (*this volume*) point out, the risks of treatment may frequently not be worth the benefits.

An ideal classification of a disease derives from an understanding of etiology and pathogenesis, and we are far from such an understanding of obesity. But the major goal of classification for the clinician is more limited—to tell us what to do when we are faced with a patient. And for this purpose, the classification proposed here is quite useful. It is, quite simply, a classification based on the severity of obesity, a classification only slightly modified from that recently proposed by Garrow (10).

The classification is a simple threefold one, of mild, moderate, and severe obesity, characterized by body weights that are, respectively, 20 to 40% overweight, 41 to 100% overweight, and more than 100% overweight. Table 1 shows that the percentage of obese women falling into these three categories is, respectively, 90.5,

TABLE 1. *A classification of obesity together with prevalence, pathology, complications, anatomy, and treatment of the three types*

Type	Classification of Obesity		
	Mild	Moderate	Severe
Percentage overweight	20–40%	41–100%	> 100%
Prevalence (among obese women)	90.5%	9.0%	0.5%
Pathology	Hypertrophic	Hypertrophic, hyperplastic	Hypertrophic, hyperplastic
Complications	Uncertain	Conditional	Severe
Treatment	Behavior therapy (lay)	Diet and behavior therapy (medical)	Surgical

9, and 0.5% (39). Comparable data for men are not available. It should be emphasized that these are percentages of the *female obese* population, not of the total population, of which about 35% is considered to be obese. The complications of obesity depend on the severity. Severe obesity is clearly a health hazard, with a 12-fold increase in mortality for persons 25 to 34 years of age (7). Much of this increased mortality is due to the precipitation or exacerbation of other diseases—hypertension, diabetes, hyperlipidemias, arthritis, operative mortality, and so forth. In addition, there are serious disorders unique to severe obesity such as the compromised pulmonary function of the Pickwickian syndrome (1). Finally, there is growing evidence that severe obesity, particularly when associated with hypertrophic adipose tissue cells, gives rise to proliferation of adipose tissue cells and to an increase in the severity of the obesity (26).

The health hazards of mild and moderate obesity derive also from the conditions precipitated or exacerbated by obesity that have been noted. They are less prevalent among moderately obese persons and still less prevalent among mildly obese ones.

This classification has, as we have noted, therapeutic implications. Severe obesity is best treated by surgical measures. Moderate obesity is probably best treated by diet and behavior modification under medical auspices, whereas for mild obesity, diet and behavior modification under lay auspices are indicated.

SEVERE OBESITY

Severe obesity is an uncommon disorder with a prevalence of only 0.5% of the *obese* population (39). Nevertheless, in a country the size of the United States, this percentage means that at least 200,000 persons suffer from severe obesity, and physicians will encounter them in their practices. Severe obesity is the one form which presents unequivocal medical complications in almost every person who suffers from it. Many of these complications are decreased or even abolished by weight reduction. But, until recently, severely obese persons have rarely lost weight and have even more rarely maintained that weight loss (38).

The advent of surgical treatments for obesity nearly 20 years ago has radically changed this picture of therapeutic impotence (3,20). Large amounts of weight—up to 100 kg—can be lost by severely obese patients, and furthermore, they can often maintain these large weight losses. The first extensively used surgical treatment for obesity was jejunoileal bypass in which the absorptive surface of the intestine was decreased to 18 inches in order to decrease the amount of food that could be absorbed (3). Continuing severe complications of this operation have resulted in its replacement by other procedures (36) but not, as we will see, before teaching us some surprising things about the mechanisms of action of this surgery. The procedures which have replaced intestinal bypass surgery consist of a variety of gastric restriction procedures designed to radically reduce the volume of the stomach—to as little as 50 ml and the passageway from this restricted stomach to no more than 1.2 cm in diameter (20). The surgery is more complicated than intestinal bypass and is associated with the usual complications of major surgery on severely obese persons. But problems during the first postoperative years are far fewer than those following intestinal bypass.

From the point of view of treatment, gastric restriction procedures are clearly a promising development. From the point of view of theories of the regulation of body weight, they are of even greater interest. This interest began with the recognition of the apparently benign social and emotional course of many severely obese patients following surgery (27). Almost all accounts agree on this benign course. The early studies, however, almost certainly underestimated the benefits of this surgery. For in assessing the emotional sequelae of surgery, they used an inappropriate control period—the period just before the surgery. The appropriate control period is *not* this period just before surgery, but rather previous periods when the patient was losing without surgery.

Reducing diets are associated with a high degree of untoward emotional responses. In the general obese population, such responses occur in as many as half of all persons undertaking reducing diets (35). They are more common in severe obesity. A recent study noted a high incidence of untoward emotional responses among severely obese people during attempts at weight reduction by the usual therapies—drugs, diets, fasting, and so forth (15). Figure 1 shows that 15% of patients experience severe depressive reactions and another 26% moderately depressed. Only a minority of patients had not experienced some degree of depression during earlier attempts at weight loss, and even fewer reported no anxiety, irritability, or preoccupation with food.

By contrast, the emotional response of patients to gastric bypass surgery was far more benign, even though they were losing far more weight than in their earlier efforts. Figure 2 shows that approximately half the patients reported a "much less" dysphoric mood following bypass surgery and another 5 to 15% reported "less" dysphoria.

The benefits of gastric bypass surgery were not confined to a lessening of negative emotions. Table 2 shows that half of the patients reported "much more" elation and self-confidence and 75% reported "much more" feelings of well-being.

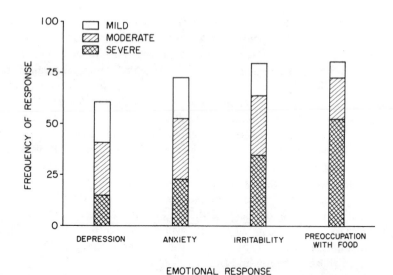

FIG. 1. Untoward responses to previous weight loss by dieting. The percentage of patients who reported severe, moderate, and mild symptoms are indicated on the *bars* representing depression, anxiety, irritability and preoccupation with food. Only a minority of patients reported no symptoms. (Figure drawn from data in Halmi et al. ref. 15.)

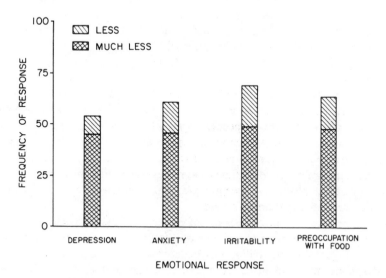

FIG. 2. Comparison of untoward response after gastric bypass with those during dieting. The percentage of patients reporting differences in untoward responses to weight loss after gastric bypass compared to those during dieting. Nearly half reported that their symptoms were much less severe after surgery, and very few reported that they were more severe. (Figure drawn from data in Halmi et al., ref. 15.)

TABLE 2. *Favorable emotional consequences of gastric bypass surgery.*
Differences in response to weight loss

	Much more	More	Same	Less	Much Less
Elation	46	6	36	3	4
Self-confidence	53	10	24	5	3
Well-being	75	8	13	1	3

Satiety was also affected by the surgery. Before surgery, 91% of the patients reported that it required "much" willpower to stop eating; after surgery, this number fell to 10%. Similarly, when patients were asked how much more they could eat after having finished a meal there were marked differences. Before surgery, 33% said that they could eat another full meal, and only 14% said that they could not eat any more. After surgery, 1% could eat a full meal, and 94% could eat no more. These differences are even more remarkable in the light of what a full meal meant before and after surgery.

Body image disparagement was also affected by surgery. This troublesome and intractable disorder which afflicts many severely obese persons is characterized by a feeling that one's body is grotesque and loathsome and that others must view one with hostility and contempt (34). Before surgery, 70% of patients reported severe body image disparagement, and only 11% reported its absence. By contrast, no more than 4% reported severe disparagement after surgery, and nearly half were symptom free. This result is particularly striking since it occurred before the patients had lost more than a small amount of weight and when they still appeared to others as grossly obese.

Another striking change in behavior following gastric bypass surgery occurred in the area of food likes and dislikes (14). Fifty per cent of the patients reported that high-density fat and high-density carbohydrates were no longer enjoyable, with smaller percentages reporting a lack of enjoyment of breads, high-fat meats, high-calorie beverages, and "alternative sources of protein" such as eggs, cheese, and peanut butter. The development of dislikes for these foods was highly correlated with decrease in the frequency with which they were consumed ($r = 0.687$, $p < 0.06$). The changes in frequency of eating various food types is illustrated in Fig. 3. In this figure, increased frequency of consumption is depicted above the 0 line, decreased frequency of consumption below it. As might be expected from reports of foods no longer found enjoyable, patients also reported that there was a marked decrease in frequency of consumption of high-density fats, high-density carbohydrates, high-calorie beverages, and high-fat meats. An added measure of the reliability of these responses is the high correlation ($r = 0.865$, $p < 0.01$) between changes in the frequency of eating various types of food and reports of reductions in food intake.

This surprising series of changes in behavior following gastric bypass surgery does not exhaust the list. Changes in eating patterns of a similar striking nature have been observed by clinicians, although they have not yet been documented in

CHANGE IN EATING

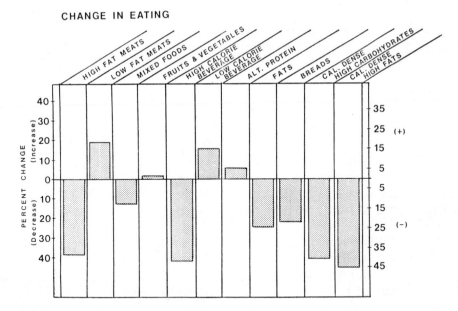

FIG. 3. Changes in the frequency of eating of the different food categories. Increased frequency of consumption is depicted above the 0 line, decreased frequency of consumption below it. Note marked decrease in frequency of consumption of high-density fats, high-density carbohydrates, high-calorie beverages, and high-fat meats. There are few instances of greater frequency of consumption, and all are in the low-caloric density categories (From Halmi et al., ref. 14, by permission.)

a systematic manner. For such documentation, we may turn to the results of jejunoileal bypass surgery, in which many of the favorable sequelae of gastric bypass have also been found.

In a retrospective study of 80 patients following jejunoileal bypass surgery, we discovered a remarkable normalization of eating patterns (22), a result that was confirmed by a prospective study (2). Before surgery, most of these patients reported chaotic patterns of excessive food intake. Surgery was followed by a striking normalization of eating patterns—marked decrease in binge-eating, night eating, excessive snacking, and difficulty in stopping eating. One finding of this study was particularly striking. Before surgery, a very large percentage of these severely obese patients—as is true of many such persons—ate no breakfast. Following surgery and even during a period of rapid weight loss, these patients began to eat breakfast!

As striking as the change in these eating patterns was the fact that it occurred without voluntary effort on the part of the patients.

These phenomena are sufficiently dramatic to suggest that surgery does far more than simply alter the functioning of the gastrointestinal tract; it produces major changes in the biology of the organism. A parsimonious explanation of these changes is that surgery has brought about a lowering of the set point about which body weight is regulated. Such an explanation can help to explain the paucity of dysphoric reactions to weight loss, the normalization of eating patterns, and the minimal effect that obese persons must exercise in order to lose weight. For with a lowered body weight set point, they need no longer struggle against biological pressures to support a higher weight and can easily limit their food intake until a new, lower set point is reached.

MODERATE OBESITY

Moderate obesity, from 41 to 100% overweight as noted in Table 1, afflicts about 9% of the obese population. The adipose tissue of these persons is usually of the hypertrophic type and may be, in addition, hyperplastic, particularly among those at the upper range of weight. Complications depend on the presence of the several conditions which can be precipitated or aggravated by obesity. Treatment consists of diet and behavior modification under medical auspices.

Diet

Dietary management of moderate obesity is a special case which will be discussed here, leaving until later a more general discussion of diets. The large amount of excess weight of moderately obese persons sets the primary goal of dietary treatment as the establishment of the largest caloric deficit that the patient can tolerate with safety and comfort. Fasting produces large caloric deficits but is limited in safety and comfort. Conventional reducing diets of 1,200 to 1,500 calories are safe and comfortable but produce too slow a weight loss to be practical for many moderately obese persons. For them, a recent compromise between the two extremes is promising; it is the very-low-calorie diet (41).

Also called the protein-sparing modified fast, these diets provide from 400 to 700 calories, largely or exclusively protein, in the form of either formula or of natural foods such as fish, fowl, or lean meat. As contrasted with the earlier liquid protein diets, which were associated with a number of fatalities, these diets appear to be safe when administered under careful medical supervision for periods of up to 3 months, and weight losses achieved in this way are striking.

Figure 4 shows the results of the eight major reports on very-low-calorie diets (41). Note the linear relationship between time on the diet and weight loss. Patients lose 1.5 to 2.3 kg/week on these diets, with the extent of weight loss depending on the initial amount of excess weight, that is, body fat.

The big question in all dietary treatment is how well is the weight loss maintained. At the present time, the answer must be, "not very well." The large clinical series which have provided most of our information on this topic have reported poor maintenance of weight loss (11). One exception has been a report by Lindner and Blackburn (18). They treated a selected sample of patients on very-low-calorie diets combined with behavior therapy, and many of these patients *did* maintain their weight loss.

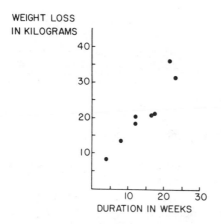

FIG. 4. Relationship between treatment duration and weight loss in the eight major studies that utilized very low-calorie diets. (From Wadden et al. ref. 41, by permission).

This finding brings us to the second modality of treatment of moderate obesity—behavior modification.

Behavior Modification

Behavior modification will be introduced together with a treatment that will not be recommended—pharmacotherapy. A major reason for this negative view of pharmacotherapy of obesity comes from a recent large-scale clinical trial (6). That trial firmly established the efficacy of behavior modification, particularly in terms of maintenance of weight loss, and at the same time, cast doubt on the ability of patients to maintain weight lost with the aid of medication. The results were definitive enough to warrant a description of the trial.

The study enrolled 145 persons with moderate obesity (60% overweight), who were treated for 6 months. Follow-up information was obtained 1 year after the end of the treatment on 99% of those who completed it. The three major treatments were (a) behavior modification in groups that used Ferguson's (8) Learning to Eat manual; (b) medication (fenfluramine) administered to patients who also met in groups to control for the effects of group contact in the behavior modification condition; and (c) combined treatment of behavior modification and medication, as administered in the previous two conditions. In addition, there was a doctor's-office medication condition and a no-treatment control condition. The doctor's-office medication condition was an effort to approximate the standard medical-office treatment of obesity, utilizing primarily medication and diet.

Figure 5 shows the results of this treatment and of the follow-up. The patients in the behavior modification condition lost 11.4 kg, perhaps the largest weight losses yet reported in a controlled clinical trial of this modality. The patients in the medication condition lost 14.5 kg. Adding the two treatments had no effect on weight loss: Patients in the combined treatment condition lost 15.0 kg.

The results 1 year after the end of the treatment throw a completely different light on this picture. The patients in the behavior modification condition main-

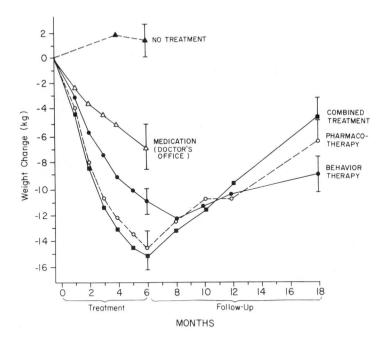

FIG. 5. Weight changes during 6-month treatment and 12-month follow-up. The three major treatment groups lost large amounts of weight during treatment: behavior therapy (*closed circles*), 10.9 kg; pharmacotherapy (*open circles*), 14.5 kg; and combined group (*squares*), 15.3 kg. Among control groups, no-treatment (waiting list) group (*closed circles*) gained weight; physician's office medication group (*open triangles*) lost 6.0 kg. Patients in control groups received additional treatment at 6 months and so were not available for follow-up. *Vertical lines* represent 1 SEM. (From Craighead et al. ref. 6, by permission.)

tained their weight losses quite well, regaining only 1.8 kg during the course of the year. Those in the group medication condition, not unexpectedly, regained 8.6 kg. The combined treatment group showed the most surprising and disappointing results. They regained no less than 9.5 kg during the course of the year, ending it weighing only 4.5 kg less than the weight at which they started treatment!

The addition of medication can increase the rate of weight loss of persons receiving behavioral treatment for obesity. This benefit, however, is more than outweighed by the deleterious effects of medication on the maintenance of weight loss. Over the long run, behavior therapy clearly outperformed the most potent alternative treatment with which it has yet been compared. This most recent study provides grounds for optimism as to the future of behavioral treatment of obesity.

These findings are of interest in terms of the regulation of body weight. For an appealing interpretation of the findings is that the drug acted by lowering a body weight set point, thereby making it easier for patients to control their food intake. The drug did, as it is supposed to do, suppress appetite. But this suppression of appetite appears to be secondary to the lowering of a body weight set point. When the drug is discontinued, set point rises and so does body weight. These findings, plus considerable support from research with experimental animals (31), has led us to believe that any benefits derived from starting of medication are lost when the medication is stopped. And that the use of appetite-suppressant medication may be contraindicated in the treatment of obesity unless one is prepared to continue the medication indefinitely. By contrast, a great strength of behavior modification is its relatively good record in maintaining weight loss.

At the present time, treatment of moderate obesity is the most problematic of the three types of obesity. It appears that one must either use diets that produce good weight loss and poor maintenance or behavior modification that produces good maintenance but relatively poor weight loss. The ideal would appear to be a combination of the two modalities and just such a combination is under active investigation at the University of Pennsylvania today.

MILD OBESITY

Mild obesity, from 20 to 40% overweight, is by far the most common form of the disorder, afflicting 90.5% of obese persons. The adipose tissue of mildly obese persons is usually hypertrophic, and it is hyperplastic only in those rare persons who maintain their body weight lower than it would otherwise be, by means of constant dieting. As in the case of moderate obesity, complications depend on the presence of conditions that can be precipitated or aggravated by obesity. Although these conditions are less prevalent among mildly obese people than among the moderately obese, they still occur with some frequency and they are still benefited by weight reduction. There are two basic forms of treatment—diet and behavior modification. The major vehicle for delivery of treatment is the lay-led group, although professionals do play a role and lay-led treatment at the work site is being explored.

Treatment—Diet

As noted above, dietary treatment of moderate obesity is a special case since it may require the rapid weight loss for which very-low-calorie diets are indicated. Such diets are not indicated for mildy obese persons with smaller amounts of excess weight. Instead, such persons have the luxury of choosing from among a wide variety of diets. And there is a wide variety!

There are diets high in protein and low in protein, high in fat and low in fat, high in carbohydrate and low in carbohydrate and, quite recently, a special diet from Beverly Hills that is high in papayas and mangos (21). A discussion of dietary treatment could easily fill this volume without exhausting the topic, even though the general principal is simple—any diet that reduces calorie intake below caloric expenditure will produce weight loss. In this sense, all treatments for obesity are dietary. But diets today have become far more than simply a means of producing a caloric deficit. They have acquired all manner of magical properties in the minds of the lay public as is clear from the above list. How does one choose among them?

The effective agent in many, if not most, popular diets (which emphasize one dietary constituent) is probably boredom or its more elegant cognate "sensory specific satiety" (24,25). Almost anyone will become tired of almost any kind of food if that is all there is to eat, and high-protein diets can become every bit as boring as low-protein diets. This is not necessarily a bad thing. In fact, it can be a real advantage while patients are *on* a diet. But it becomes a problem when patients go off their diets and resume their old eating patterns and all too frequently their former caloric intakes. Indeed, the whole concept of dieting can be criticized on psychological grounds: Going on a diet implies going off it and the resumption of old eating habits. For this reason, one can argue that the most effective diet is not a diet at all but rather a gradual change in eating patterns and a shift to foods that the patient can continue to eat indefinitely. This means increasing the intake of complex carbohydrates, particularly in fruits, vegetables, and cereals, and decreasing the intake of fats and concentrated carbohydrates. It means voluntarily adopting the pattern that we have seen occurring in persons following gastric bypass. This course of action probably gives the best chance of maintaining the weight that is lost, and it is an eminently safe one. A diet that consists primarily of sensible eating habits does not require medical monitoring and is particularly well suited to use by the lay organizations that are assuming the dominant role in the treatment of mild obesity.

Treatment—Behavior Modification

Traditional behavioral treatment of obesity is based on classic applied behavioral analysis which considers in great detail the behavior to be changed, its antecedents, and its consequences (30). The primary behavior to be changed is eating, and a number of exercises are designed to slow the rate of eating and allow physiological mechanisms of satiety to exert their effect. An even greater focus is placed on the antecedents of eating behavior. Efforts extend from the control of relatively remote antecedents such as shopping for food to more proximate ones such as the ready availability of high-calorie food. Patients are helped to remove from their environment such stimuli that might elicit eating, to plan strategies to control eating when such stimuli are present, and to avoid television and reading materials that might distract their attention from their efforts at stimulus control. The third element in applied behavioral analysis is the consequences of behavior, with rewards for carrying out the various prescribed behaviors, primarily those involving stimulus control.

In addition to this basic behavior analysis, behavioral treatment of obesity includes four other elements.

The first element is self-monitoring, or the recording in exquisite detail, of a large number of the behaviors to be modified. This kind of careful record-keeping makes it possible to determine quite accurately what aspects of behavior should be modified, to develop programs to modify them, to monitor the effectiveness of these programs, and to use this information to make necessary corrections.

The second element consists of nutrition education. It is not possible to make sensible choices among foods without a clear idea of their nutritional value, and simple, didactic exercises comprise an important part of behavioral programs.

The third element is a program to increase physical activity. Increasing physical activity serves several purposes. As is well known, it increases caloric expenditure. As is not as well known, it probably counteracts the fall in metabolic rate that is induced by dieting, and it probably also decreases appetite and food intake among sedentary obese persons (4).

The fourth element of a behavioral program is cognitive restructuring, designed to overcome the self-defeating and maladaptive attitudes toward weight reduction and toward themselves of so many obese persons (19).

A key aspect of behavior therapy is that it is easy to specify and therefore easy to learn. Many of the key elements are readily packaged in easy-to-use treatment manuals. As a result, it has been administered by persons with progressively less formal, professional training—from the doctoral to the master's level and, finally, to persons with no professional background. There is, accordingly, a technology at hand that can promise modest weight losses at minimal risk.

An important early exploitation of this situation was that of Penick et al. (23) who showed that behavior modification, conducted by a team with little clinical experience, was more effective in the treatment of obesity than was the best alternative traditional program that could be devised by highly skilled professionals. Lesser increases in effectiveness have brought about major changes in the management of other disorders. The question now becomes—how can this technology be applied? There are at least three potential vehicles, and they lead us far beyond the boundaries of medicine.

Treatment Vehicles—Professional Auspices

An obvious vehicle for the application of these treatment measures is the physician's office. Although few physicians themselves carry out behavioral weight control programs, more and more of them are hiring nutritionists and nurses to conduct weight reduction groups within their practices. Hospitals are also beginning to establish such programs in their outpatient departments, and behavioral psychologists have carried out such programs for some years. By far the largest number of obese persons, however, is being treated under the auspices of lay-led groups.

Treatment Vehicles—Lay-Led Groups

Lay-led groups for obesity antedate the development of behavioral weight control by several years. The self-help movement itself has been traced back to 19th-century England (16), and in the early years of our nation, Tocqueville (37) could already point out the tendency for Americans to organize in informal groups to achieve ends that are the responsibility of government in other societies. Nowhere has the proclivity been more clearly expressed than in the organization of patients to cope with illness. Alcoholics Anonymous led the way and many of the current lay-led groups have been modeled after it. Prominent among them are Take Off Pounds Sensibly (TOPS), the largest of the nonprofit groups, and Weight Watchers, the largest commercial group.

TOPS, founded in 1948, was the first self-help group for obesity, and it now enrolls more than 300,000 persons (9,33). The key elements of TOPS are weekly meetings that provide group support, weekly weigh-ins that are high points of the meeting, and policy supervision from the national headquarters. The membership of TOPS is almost exclusively female, middle-aged and of lower middle-class socioeconomic status; the average member is 60% overweight.

The effectiveness of self-help groups is difficult to assess becasue of the very high drop-out rates—67% in one careful study (17)—and because those who dropped out were persons who had lost lesser amounts of weight (33). Reports of weight loss based on a select sample of treatment survivors such as this may be highly biased. Valid estimates of weight loss require cohort studies which consider all persons who enter the program. Subject to this caution, it can be noted that the most extensive study of TOPS found an average weight loss of 6.8 ± 6.8 kg (33). Persons losing more than 9 kg totalled 29%, and 6.4% lost more than 18 kg. The results of TOPS were improved by an experimental program in which behavior modification was introduced into ongoing TOPS chapters, with a significant reduction in the drop-out rate—from 67% to 40% and a small increase in weight loss (17). Take Pounds Off Sensibly did not capitalize on this demonstration of the value of adding behavior modification to a self-help group, but the commercial weight loss organizations did.

The commercial weight loss organizations appeal to much the same clientele as do the nonprofit ones, and with somewhat greater success—in 1976, 1,655,000 new and rejoining members used the services of just one such organization, Weight Watchers (28,29). The commercial organizations have added three important elements to the programs pioneered by the nonprofit groups—behavior modification, inspirational lecturers drawn from successful members, and a carefully designed nutritional program. They are readily available to persons with even a casual interest in weight reduction. But they, too, suffer from drop-outs, even more severely than the nonprofit organizations. One recent study revealed that 50% of the members of one such group had dropped out in 6 weeks and 70% in 12 weeks (40). Furthermore, similar drop-out rates have been reported from four other studies conducted on three continents (40). In the face of drop-out rates of this magnitude, reports of the weight lost by the survivors are of questionable value.

Despite these serious problems, the low cost and ready availability of lay-led groups makes them an important resource for the control of mild obesity. First is the very large number of persons that can be reached by these measures. Second, as noted by Stuart and Mitchell, even the high drop-out rates are not necessarily a weakness (29). Instead, the ease of withdrawal from treatment with a parallel ease of reentry is a benefit in that members can easily avail themselves of service when needed. Finally, despite the limited effectivness of these programs, their very low costs result in favorable cost/effectiveness ratios. Yates (42), for example, has shown that it cost far more to lose comparable amounts of weight in an exemplary university clinic than in a neighboring commercial program, even with its high drop-out rate.

Recent reports from Norway suggest that the serious problems afflicting Anglo-American self-help groups are not innate to this modality of treatment. Grimsmo and Borchgrevink (13) and Grimsmo et al. (12), for example, have described a nationwide weight control program enrolling 80,000 persons, a sizeable proportion of the (4 million) Norwegian population, with drop-out rates of less than 10% in 8 weeks. Furthermore, weight losses averaged 6.5 kg and, with the aid of follow-up sessions, were relatively well maintained for periods of as long as 5 years. The reasons for this superior performance are not clear but may result from the close nature of Norwegian society as well as from the management skills of the director of the program (C. F. Borchgrevink, *personal communication*). These results suggest that the full potential of self-help groups has not been realized in the English-speaking countries and that efforts to improve their performance are indicated.

Treatment Vehicles—The Work Site

A third vehicle for the delivery of treatment for mild obesity is the work site. Most people spend more of their time at work than at any other activity, and the support of their fellow workers should be able to help them improve their health behaviors. Furthermore, weight loss programs at the work site can be carried out by nonprofessionals just as effectively as by professionals and at far lower cost. As a result of these favorable circumstances, health promotion at the work site is attracting a large and growing number of industries. How effective is it?

In comparison with the obvious potential, the results leave much to be desired. The problem is the same as that of the self-help groups—the high drop-out rates. The four work-site programs for obesity that have reported their results had drop-out rates approaching those of the self-help groups.

The most intensive effort to develop work-site treatment for obesity is that conducted by Brownell and me over the past 4 years with the United Store Workers Union in New York (5,32). During this time we have treated 172 patients in three sequential cohorts, using the results of each program to improve the results of the next. In the first cohort, we encountered a drop-out rate of 57%. By hard work over 4 years this drop-out rate was reduced to 34%, and weight losses were slightly increased from their very low initial value of 1.2 kg to 2.7 kg. These results are disappointing, but as with the self-help groups, costs are low and cost/effectivness ratios favorable.

SUMMARY AND CONCLUSIONS

This review has considered the current status of the treatment of obesity from the point of view of a new theory and a new classification. The theory states that obesity is the result of regulated, homeostatic processes that maintain body fat at an elevated level. The classification divides obesity into three categories—mild, moderate, and severe.

Severe obesity, more than 100% overweight, which afflicts 0.5% of the female obese population is most effectively treated by surgical measures, particularly ones that reduce the size of the stomach and of its opening into the lower gastrointestinal tract. Such surgery may produce very large weight losses with relatively few untoward consequences, suggesting that it acts by lowering a body weight set point. Moderate obesity, 41 to 100% overweight, afflicts 9% of the female obese population. It is currently treated under medical auspices either by diets that may achieve satisfactory weight loss but poor maintenance of this loss, or by behavior modification that achieves good maintenance, but only modest weight loss. Medication is of limited value because of its continued efficacy, rather than because, as was thought, tolerance develops to its effects. It appears to lower a body weight set point and cessation of medication is followed by a rapid rebound in body weight. For this reason, medication should probably be used either for an indefinite period of time or not at all. Mild obesity, 20 to 40% overweight, afflicts 90% of the female obese population and today is larely managed by large organizations, both commercial and nonprofit. The basis of treatment is behavior modification in groups, a liberal, balanced diet, and exercise. Despite very high drop-out rates from these organizations, their low costs result in favorable cost/effective ratios, and they are continuing to increase the number of obese people that they treat.

ACKNOWLEDGMENTS

This research was supported in part by grant #MH31050 and a Research Scientist Award from the National Institute of Mental Health.

REFERENCES

1. Bierman, E. L. (1980): Obesity. In: *Cecil Textbook of Medicine,* 16th ed., edited by J. B. Wyngaarden and L. H. Smith, pp. 1372–1379. Saunders, Philadelphia.
2. Bray, G. A., Dahms, W. T., and Atkinson, R. L. et al, (1980): Factors controlling food intake: A comparison of dieting and intestinal bypass. *Am. J. Clin Nutr.,* 33:376–382.
3. Bray, G. A., Greenway, F. L., Barry, R. E. et al. (1977): Surgical treatment of obesity: A review of our experience and an analysis of published reports. *Int. J. Obes.,* 1:331–367.
4. Brownell, K. D., and Stunkard, A. J. (1980): Physical activity in the development and control of obesity. In: *Obesity,* edited by A. J. Stunkard, pp. 300–324. Saunders, Philadelphia.
5. Brownell, K. D., Stunkard, A. J., and McKeon, T. (1983): Treatment of obesity at the work site: A promise half fulfilled *Am. J. Publ. Health (in press).*
6. Craighead, L. W., Stunkard, A. J., and O'Brien, R. (1981): Behavior therapy and pharmacotherapy of obesity. *Arch. Gen. Psychiatry,* 38:763–768.

7.   Drenick, E. J., Bale, G. S., Seltzer, F., and Johnson D. G. (1980): Excessive mortality and causes of death in morbidly obese men. *J. A. M. A.*, 243:443–445.
8.   Ferguson, J. M. (1975): *Learning to Eat: Leaders Manual and Patients Manual.* Bull Publishing, Palo Alto, California.
9.   Garb, J. R., and Stunkard, A. J. (1974): Effectiveness of a self-help group in obesity control: A further assessment. *Arch. Intern. Med.*, 134:716–720.
10. Garrow, J. S. (1982): *Treat Obesity Seriously: A Clinical Manual.* Churchill Livingston, London and New York.
11. Genuth, S. M., Castro, J. H., and Vertes, V. (1974): Weight reduction in obesity by outpatient semistarvation. *J. A. M. A.*, 230:987–991.
12. Grimsmo, A., Helgesen, G., and Borchgrevink, C. F. (1981): Short-term and long-term effects of lay groups on weight reduction. *Br. Med. J.*, 283:1093–1095.
13. Grimsmo, A., and Borchgrevink, C. F. (1982): Langtidsresultater ved behandling av overvekt i selvhjelpsgrupper. *Tidsskr. Norsk. Laegeforen.*, 102:163–165.
14. Halmi, K. A., Mason, E., Falk, J., and Stunkard, A. J. (1981): Appetitive behavior after gastric bypass for obesity. *Int. J. Obes.*, 5:457–464.
15. Halmi, K. A., Stunkard, A. J., and Mason, E. E. (1980): Emotional responses to weight reduction by three methods: Diet, jejunoileal bypass, and gastric bypass. *Am. J. Clin. Nutr.*, 33:446–451.
16. Katz, A. H., and Bender, E. L., editors (1976): *The Strength in Us: Self-help Groups in the Modern World.* New Viewpoints, New York.
17. Levitz, L. S., and Stunkard, A. J. (1974): A therapeutic coalition for obesity: Behavior modification and patient self-help. *Am. J. Psychiatry*, 131:423–427.
18. Lindner, P. G., and Blackburn, G. L. (1976): Multidisciplinary approach to obesity utilizing fasting modified by protein-sparing therapy. *Obes. Bariatric Med.*, 5:198–216.
19. Mahoney, M. J., and Mahoney, K. (1976): *Permanent Weight Control.* Norton, New York.
20. Mason, E. E. (1981): *Surgical treatment of obesity.* Saunders, Philadelphia.
21. Mazel, J. (1982): *The Beverly Hills Diet Lifetime Plan.* Macmillan, New York.
22. Mills, M. J., and Stunkard, A. J. (1976): Behavioral changes following surgery for obesity. *Am. J. Psychiatry*, 133:527–531.
23. Penick, S. B., Filion, R. D. L., Fox, S., and Stunkard, A. J. (1971): Behavior modification in the treatment of obesity. *Psychosom. Med.*, 33:49–55.
24. Rolls, G. J., Rolls, E. T., Kingston, B., Megson, A., and Gunary, R. (1981): Variety in a meal enhances food intake in man. *Physiol. Behav.*, 26:215–221.
25. Rolls, G. J., Rolls, E. T., Rowe, E. A., and Sweeney, K. (1981): Senory specific satiety in man. *Physiol. Behav.*, 27:137–142.
26. Sjöström, L. (1980): Fat cells and body weight. In: *Obesity,* edited by A. J. Stunkard, pp. 72–100. Saunders, Philadelphia.
27. Solow, C., Silberfarb, P. M., and Swift, K. (1974): Psychosocial effects of intestinal bypass surgery for severe obesity. *N. Engl. J. Med.*, 290:300–304.
28. Stuart, R. B. (1977): Self-help for self-management. In: *Behavioral Self-Management,* edited by R. B. Stuart. pp. 278–305. Brunner/Mazel, New York.
29. Stuart, R. B., and Mitchell, C. (1980): Self-help groups in the control of body weight. In: *Obesity,* edited by A. J. Stunkard, pp. 345–354. Saunders, Philadelphia.
30. Stunkard, A. J. (1975): From explanation to action in psychosomatic medicine: The case of obesity. *Psychosom. Med.*, 37:195–236.
31. Stunkard, A. J. (1982): Appetite suppressant agents lower body weight set point. *Life Sci.*, 30:2043–2055.
32. Stunkard, A. J., and Brownell, K. D. (1979): Work site treatment for obesity. *Am. J. Psychiatry*, 137:252–253.
33. Stunkard, A. J., Levine, H., and Fox, S. (1970): The management of obesity: Patient self-help and medical treatment. *A.M.A. Arch. Int. Med.*, 125:1067–1072.
34. Stunkard, A. J., and Mendelson, M. (1967): Obesity and the body image: I. Characteristics of disturbances in the body image of some obese persons. *Am. J. Psychiatry*, 123:1296–3000.
35. Stunkard, A. J., and Rush, A. J. (1974): Dieting and depression reexamined: A critical review of reports of untoward responses during weight reduction for obesity. *Ann. Intern. Med.*, 81:526–533.
36. Symposium (1980): Surgical treatment of morbid obesity. *Am. J. Clin. Nutr.*, 33:353–530.

37. Toqueville, A. de (1966): *Democracy in America: A New Translation.* Harper and Row, New York.
38. Van Itallie, T. B. (1980): "Morbid obesity" a hazardous disorder that resists conservative treatment. *Am. J. Clin. Nutr.,* 33:358–363.
39. Vital and Health Statistics. Obese and overweight adults in the United States. National Center for Health Statistics, Series II, No. 230, Feb., 1983.
40. Volkmar, F. R., Stunkard, A. J., Woolston, J., and Bailey, B. A. (1981): High attrition rates in commercial weight reduction programs. *Arch. Intern. Med.,* 141:426–428.
41. Wadden, T. A., Stunkard, A. J., and Brownell, K. D. (1983): Very low calorie diets: A critical review. *Ann. Int. Med.* (*in press*).
42. Yates, B. T. (1978): Improving the cost-effectiveness of obesity programs: Three basic strategies for reducing the cost per pound. *Int. J. Obes.,* 2:249–266.

Eating and Its Disorders, edited by A. J.
Stunkard and E. Stellar. Raven Press,
New York © 1984.

New Developments in the Treatment of Obese Children and Adolescents

Kelly D. Brownell

University of Pennsylvania, Philadelphia, Pennsylvania 19104

Obesity is a serious and prevalent problem among children in industrialized societies. Approximately 25% of American children are overweight (23). Their obesity is associated with decreased growth hormone release, hyperinsulinemia, hyperlipidemia, hypertension, and carbohydrate intolerance (4,14,20,27,31,32). Kannel and Dawber (29) claim that many atherogenic serum lipid disorders originate in childhood, and there is some evidence that obesity in children is an independent risk factor for later coronary heart disease (35,36).

The medical concomitants of obesity have occupied the attention of the professional community, but the psychological and social perils are the primary concern of those afflicted by the problem. Most persons seek treatment for cosmetic and social reasons because they are tormented by a condition which they and their culture do not accept. The effects on a person's self-concept and psychological functioning has been described in a book by Stunkard (46), aptly titled *The Pain of Obesity.*

The psychological and social burdens of obesity are particularly troublesome for children. Children as young as age 6 rate pictures of obese children as less likeable than pictures of normal weight children, underweight children, and children with a variety of serious physical handicaps (38,44). Obese children are at increased risk for disturbed family interactions, disapproval from peers, academic discrimination, and poor self-image (10,11,13,33,41). The labels attributed to obese children by their peers (lazy, sloppy, forgetful, stupid, etc.) imply overindulgence and personal failing. Clearly, obese children are blamed for their condition. It is an unusual person who does not fashion this into serious self-doubt and a persistent concern with dieting (2,7,37).

Waiting for an obese child to "grow out of it" is to wait for an unlikely event. Fully 80% of obese children become obese adults (1). If an obese child has not slimmed down by the end of adolescence, the odds against him or her doing so as an adult are 28 to 1 (47). The problem requires early identification and aggressive action.

ARGUMENTS FOR EARLY INTERVENTION

There are many compelling reasons to deal with obesity in children. These extend far beyond the usual notion that an ounce of prevention is worth a pound of cure. The benefits of early intervention may occur for both psychological and physiological reasons.

Childhood is when most persons develop and solidify eating and activity patterns. Food preferences are acquired early (40). Children learn how fast to eat, whether eating is associated with specific mood states, whether eating beyond satiety is acceptable, whether eating too much or too little evokes a positive or negative response from the family, whether physical activity is encouraged or discouraged, and so forth. Work with children and their families may help the child make positive changes before the habits become firmly ingrained.

Children also develop attitudes about eating, exercise, and dieting which can greatly facilitate or hinder later attempts at weight control. As an example, most obese persons feel very negative about exercise (7). Those who were overweight during childhood have suffered from being picked last for teams and being ridiculed about poor athletic performance, and most have developed methods for avoiding situations in which physical activity is required. Weight loss as an adult is easier to accomplish when exercise is combined with diet than when diet alone is used, so these negative attitudes can help perpetuate obesity once it develops. This problem may be remedied either by helping children reduce so they can perform better physically or by teaching them ways to be active within the limits of their excess weight.

Early intervention may help curtail fat cell proliferation, thus preventing the hyperplasia which is associated with the most pronounced cases of obesity. The vast majority of a person's fat cells develops by adolescence (28,43). There are probably certain ages at which fat cell proliferation is most likely to occur. The most frequently cited periods are during the prenatal months, during the first year after birth, between ages 7 and 9, and then again early in adolescence, although these periods are not definite and are based more on speculation than on research. Whatever the ages, dietary moderation and weight control (to keep the *size* of the fat cells at normal levels) may help prevent a problem (hyperplasia) which predisposes a person to adult obesity and to difficulty with weight reduction.

Most obese persons lose weight and regain many times during their dieting career. Although imperfectly documented, it is possible that weight fluctuations make subsequent dieting more difficult, both psychologically and physiologically. If children can be taught the necessary habits and attitudes to control their weight without the large fluctuations, later weight control may be easier.

One of the most distressing psychological aspects of obesity is body image disparagement (46,48). Many obese persons detest their bodies and feel that others view them with contempt and hostility. This is most common among persons who were obese as children (46). Studies by Stunkard and Burt (47), Stunkard and Mendelson (48), and Grinker et al. (25) have shown that weight loss in adult-onset obese persons is accompanied by corresponding improvement in body image; such is not the case for juvenile-onset obese persons. This negative body image may undermine a person's motivation to lose weight, and it almost certainly increases the chances for relapse because a person who loses weight still feels obese. Early intervention many help children control their weight during the critical years when body image develops.

EXCESSIVE INTAKE OR LOW OUTPUT?

There has been continued debate about whether obesity in children is due to excessive ingestion of energy or to low levels of energy expenditure. Early studies by Bullen et al. (12) and Stephanic et al. (45) suggested that obese children eat no more than their thin peers but that they are far less active. Others have reported conflicting findings on this issue (6,49,52), suggesting that the nature of the measurement (e.g., self-report vs observations) influences the findings. To further complicate matters, low levels of activity and/or high levels of intake could be either the cause or the consequence of obesity.

Waxman and Stunkard (50) attempted to remedy the problems in the earlier studies by carrying out an intensive study of eating and activity patterns in obese boys and their thin brothers. Four such pairs were studied using observers in the home and in the school. The nonobese brothers served as controls for the obese boys. The obese boys consumed more calories than the nonobese boys at home and consumed far more calories at school. The obese boys were far less active inside the home, slightly less active outside the home, and equally active at school. By virtue of their extra weight, the obese boys were actually expending more energy via activity than the thin boys.

This observation study by Waxman and Stunkard (50) is noteworthy for several reasons. First, it underscores the conflict in existing studies and argues for more intensive research. Second, it introduces an innovative and powerful method for measuring eating and activity in children in their natural environment. Third, it points to the importance of situational variables in determining intake and expenditure; and obese/nonobese comparisons varied greatly depending on whether the measurements were made in the home or the school. This is a very important area for research.

AVAILABLE TREATMENTS

Conventional Approaches

Until recently, the most frequently used treatments for obese children have not been effective (10,11,16,18). These have included inpatient starvation, appetite suppressants, nutrition counseling, and exercise prescriptions. The problems with these approaches have been limited weight loss, high attrition, high relapse rates, and untoward emotional affects (10,11,16,18).

Behavior Modification

Behavioral approaches with children are now in their second generation. The first generation involved the application of techniques used in the treatment of obese adults (3,26,39,51). The results were very encouraging compared to the gloomy results reported from traditional approaches. Children in the behavioral programs tended to remain in the programs and average weight losses ranged from 4 to 13 lb.

The second generation of behavioral studies have been more comprehensive and have been more effective. Procedures designed specifically for children have been employed and greater attention has been paid to family involvement, exercise, and cognitive factors. These studies show weight losses which approach 20 lb and the long-term maintenance (when evaluated) has been quite good (9,15,17,21,22). These results are most promising, especially considering the poor long-term results of most treatments.

One thing common to the successful studies in this area has been the concern with social factors. Involvement of the parents has been considered central to the success of overweight children. Some experimenters have looked to the schools as another social system in which long-term behavior change can be promoted. These two issues, school programs and parent involvement, are both promising avenues for inquiry and will be discussed in detail below.

TREATMENT IN THE SCHOOLS

There are several important advantages to treating obesity in the schools. First, large numbers of children can be screened and treated. Second, cost to the family can be minimized, particularly if the program is administered by school personnel. Third, contact with the children can be continuous, concentrated, and enduring. Fourth, it removes obesity from the medical arena and makes the child a partner in an educational experience. Fifth, long-term assessment is possible. Sixth, children can be reached before their weight problem becomes sufficiently serious to warrant professional attention.

The most thoroughly evaluated school programs have been reported by Collipp (19), Seltzer and Mayer (42), Botvin et al. (5), and Brownell and Kaye (8). The first three reported significant weight losses in programs combining behavior modification, nutrition, exercise, and psychological support. However, the weight losses tended to be small and long-term evaluation was not undertaken.

Brownell and Kaye (8) conducted a program for obese children in a school in Florida. The program was for children ages 5 through 12 and involved instruction in nutrition, exercise, and eating habits. The model for the program (Fig. 1) shows that behavioral techniques were used but that behavioral principles were emphasized as a means for encouraging changes in nutrition and activity patterns. The program also emphasized social support, i.e., the context in which the program was administered was considered as important as what the children were taught.

During the 10-week program, 95% of the program children lost weight, compared to 21% of control children. The program children averaged a loss of 9.7 lb, a surprising result considering that children at this age are expected to gain weight due to developmental growth. The weaknesses in the study were that it was done in only one school and that no long-term evaluation was done.

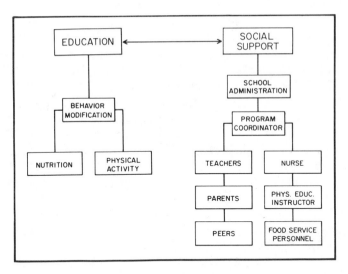

FIG. 1. The conceptual model for a program of weight control in the schools. The model emphasizes the process by which the program is implemented (social support), as well as the program components (education). (Adapted from Brownell and Kaye, 1982, ref. 8.)

To summarize the results of school programs, the initial findings are promising, but far too little work has been done to justify embracing this approach. Experimental control has not been demonstrated in most cases, and only short-term results are available. Considering the potential benefits of intervention in the schools, along with the promising initial results, more work in this area would be a positive move for the field.

PARENTAL INVOLVEMENT

Most researchers and clinicians agree that parents exert a powerful influence on the eating, activity, and attitude patterns of their children (34). Children with two obese parents have a 3 to 8 times greater chance of being obese than do children with two thin parents (24,34). Parents help control a child's weight by determining the nature and amount of food that enters the house, by encouraging or discouraging specific patterns of eating and activity, and by exerting specific pressures for a child to maintain a given physical appearance. These factors have led some researchers to study the role parents play in the treatment of their overweight children.

The first controlled study in this area was reported by Kingsley and Shapiro (30). Their study included 10- and 11-year-old children and tested the effects of involving or not involving mothers in a treatment program. The results indicated that weight losses were similar in groups in which only the child attended, only the mother attended, or both the mother and child attended. Reports of satisfaction with the program were highest in the groups in which both mother and child attended, but this did not translate into greater weight losses.

Epstein and colleagues conducted two intensive studies in which parents and their children were both involved in treatment (21,22). The first study (22) found a strong relationship between weight changes in mothers and their children (ages 6–12) when both wanted to lose weight and when both earned back deposited money for losing weight. The second study (21) found no differences in weight loss in groups where the parents and child were both reinforced for weight loss, only the child was reinforced, or money was refunded for attendance. Parent and child weights were correlated after treatment but not at follow-up. These two studies were nice demonstrations that a program involving the parents could produce significant weight losses.

Brownell et al. (9) made a direct test of whether parents would help or hinder their child's efforts to lose weight. Forty-two obese adolescents, ages 12 to 16, were assigned randomly to one of three experimental conditions: (a) Child Alone: children attended groups alone—mothers were not involved; (b) Mother-Child Together: the children and mothers met together in the same group; and (c) Mother-Child Separately: the children and mothers both attended treatment sessions but met in separate groups. The mothers were not required to be overweight (73% were more than 20% overweight, and 42% were more than 50% overweight). The program included behavior modification, nutrition, exercise, cognitive restructuring, and a special emphasis on family support.

The weight losses for the study by Brownell et al. (9) are displayed in Fig. 2. After a 16-week treatment program, the Mother-Child Separately group had lost more weight (8.4 kg, 18.5 lb) than the Mother-Child Together (5.3 kg, 11.7 lb) and the Child Alone (3.3 kg, 7.3 lb) groups. At a 1-year follow-up, the latter two

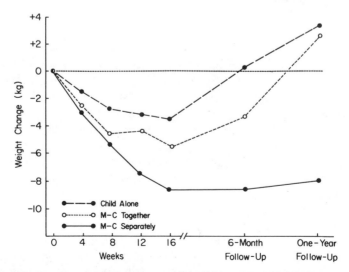

FIG. 2. Weight change in kilograms for children treated alone (Child Alone), children treated in the same group with their mothers (M-C Together), and children who met in a child group while the mothers met in a separate group (M-C Separately). (From ref. 9.)

groups had regained to above their baseline levels, while the Mother-Child Separately group had essentially maintained their loss (mean loss at 1 year = 7.7 kg, 16.9 lb).

These losses rank among the highest reported in the treatment of obese children and adolescents. Most encouraging is the success of the children in the Mother-Child Separately group in keeping their weight off during the year following treatment. Most importantly, the study demonstrated that a subtle change in the approach used with the parents (having the mother meet together with or separately from their child) had a powerful effect on weight loss. In fact, having the mothers involved offered no advantage to having the children meet alone, except when the mother and children were involved in separate meetings. This was only a first trial of this important issue, but it does point to the need for more research on parental factors.

CONCLUSIONS

Obesity in children is a serious public health problem. It merits attention in its own right, but it is particularly troubling considering that it predisposes a child to some of the most serious medical disorders of adult life. For most obese persons, the psychological and social consequences of being fat are more disabling than the medical conditions. The problem must be taken seriously, because most obese children become obese adults and because even heroic treatments like inpatient starvation have not been effective.

Behavior modification has shown new promise in the treatment of overweight children. Recent programs have been increasingly sophisticated and have yielded encouraging short-term results. More and more attention has been given to the important issue of long-term maintenance. There is much more to be learned in this area, and there is great potential here for testing innovative treatment approaches.

Two exciting developments in the field have been treatment in the schools and involvement of the parents in the treatment process. Although neither area has received the attention needed to draw firm conclusions, preliminary results are encouraging. Both areas highlight the need for considering social factors in both the genesis of obesity and its treatment.

ACKNOWLEDGMENT

This work was supported in part by Research Scientist Development Award MH00319 from the National Institute of Mental Health.

REFERENCES

1. Abraham, S., and Nordsieck, M. (1960): Relationship of excess weight in children and adults. *Public Health Rep.*, 75:263–273.
2. Allon, N. (1979): Self-perceptions of the stigma of overweight in relationship to weight-losing patterns. *Am. J. Clin. Nutr.*, 32:470–480.

3. Aragona, J., Cassady, J., and Drabman, R. S. (1975): Treating overweight children through parental training and contingency contracting. *J. Appl. Behav. Anal.,* 8:269–278.
4. Berenson, G. S. (1980): *Cardiovascular Risk Factors in Children.* Oxford University Press, New York.
5. Botvin, G. J., Cantlon, A., Carter, B. J., and Williams, C. L. (1979): Reducing adolescent obesity through a school health program. *J. Pediatr.* 95:1060–1062.
6. Bradfield, R., Paulos, J., and Grossman, H. (1971): Energy expenditure and heart rate of obese high school girls. *Am. J. Clin. Nutr.,* 24:1482–1486.
7. Brownell, K. D. (1982). Obesity: Understanding and treating a serious, prevalent, and refractory disorder. *J. Consult. Clin. Psychol.,* 50:820–840.
8. Brownell, K. D., and Kaye, F. S. (1982): A school-based behavior modification, nutrition education, and physical activity program for obese children. *Am. J. Clin. Nutr.,* 35:277–283.
9. Brownell, K. D., Kelman, J. H., and Stunkard, A. J. (1983): Treatment of obese children with and without their mothers: changes in weight and blood pressure. *Pediatrics,* 71:515–523.
10. Brownell, K. D., and Stunkard, A. J. (1978): Behavioral treatment of obesity in children. *Am. J. Dis. Child.,* 132:403–412.
11. Brownell, K. D., and Stunkard, A. J. (1980): Behavioral treatment for overweight children and adolescents. In: *Obesity,* edited by A. J. Stunkard, pp. 415–437. Saunders, Philadelphia.
12. Bullen, B. A., Reed, R. B., and Mayer, J. (1964): Physical activity of obese and nonobese adolescent girls appraised by motion picture sampling. *Am. J. Clin. Nutr.,* 14:211–233.
13. Canning, H., and Mayer, J. (1966): Obesity-Its possible effect on college acceptance. *N. Engl. J. Med.,* 275:1172–1174.
14. Clarke, R. P., Morrow, S. B., and Morse, E. H. (1970): Interrelationships between plasma lipids, physical measurements, and body fatness of adolescents in Burlington, Vermont. *Am. J. Clin. Nutr.,* 23:754–763.
15. Coates, T. J., Jeffery, R. W., Slinkard, L. A., Killen, J. D., and Danaher, B. G. (1982): Frequency of contact and contingent reinforcement in weight loss, lipid changes, and blood pressure reduction with adolescents. *Beh. Ther.,* 13:175–185.
16. Coates, T. J., and Thoresen, C. E. (1978): Treating obesity in children and adolescents: a review. *Am. J. Public Health,* 68:143–151.
17. Coates, T. J., and Thoresen, C. E. (1981): Behavior and weight changes in three obese adolescents. *Behav. Res. Ther.,* 12:383–399.
18. Collipp, P. J. (editor) (1980): *Childhood obesity, 2nd edition.* PSG Publishing Company, Massachusetts.
19. Collipp, P. J. (1980): Obesity programs in public schools. In: *Childhood Obesity, 2nd edition,* edited by P. J. Collipp, pp. 297–308. PSG Publishing Company, Massachusetts.
20. Drash, A. (1973): Relationship between diabetes mellitus and obesity in the child. *Metabolism,* 22:337–344.
21. Epstein, L. H., Wing, R. R., Koeske, R., Andrasik, F., and Ossip, D. J. (1981): Child and parent weight loss in family-based behavior modification programs. *J. Consult. Clin. Psychol.,* 49:674–685.
22. Epstein, L. H., Wing, R. R., Sternachak, L., Dickson, B., and Michelson, J. (1980): Comparison of family-based behavior modification and nutrition education for childhood obesity. *J. Pediatr. Psychol.,* 5:25–36.
23. Forbes, G. B. (1975): Prevalence of obesity in childhood. In: *Obesity in Perspective,* Vol. 2, edited by G. A. Bray. DHEW Publication No. (NIH) 75-708, U.S. Government Printing Office, Washington, D.C.
24. Garn, S. M., and Clark, D. C. (1976): Trends in fatness and the origins of obesity. *Pediatrics,* 57:443–456.
25. Grinker, J., Hirsch, J., and Levin, B. (1973): The affective response of obese patients to weight reduction: a differentiation based on age at onset of obesity. *Psychosom. Med.,* 35:57–63.
26. Gross, I., Wheeler, M., and Hess, R. (1976): The treatment of obesity in adolescents using behavioral self-control. *Clin. Pediatr.,* 15:920–294.
27. Heald, F. P. (1971): Biochemical aspects of juvenile obesity. *Practitioner,* 206:223–226.
28. Hirsch, J., and Knittle, J. L. (1970): Cellularity of obese and nonobese human adipose tissue. *Fed. Proc.,* 29:1516–1521.
29. Kannel, W. B., and Dawber, T. R. (1972): Atherosclerosis as a pediatric problem. *J. Pediatr.,* 80:544–554.

30. Kingsley, R. G., and Shapiro, J. (1977): A comparison of three behavioral programs for control of obesity in children. *Beh. Ther.,* 8:30–36.
31. Lauer, R. M., Conner, W. E., Leaverton, P. E., Reiter, M. A., and Clarke, W. R. (1975): Coronary heart disease risk factors in school children. *J. Pediatr.,* 86:697–706.
32. Lauer, R. M., and Shekelle, R. B., (editors) (1980): *Childhood Prevention of Atherosclerosis and Hypertension.* Raven, New York.
33. Lerner, R. M., and Schroeder, C. (1971): Kindergarten children's active vocabulary about body build. *Dev. Psychol.,* 5:179.
34. Mayer, J. (1968): *Overweight: Causes, Cost, and Control.* Prentice-Hall, Englewood Cliffs, New Jersey.
35. McLain, L. G. (1976): Hypertension in childhood: a review. *Am. Heart J.,* 92:634–644.
36. Miller, R. A., and Shekelle, R. B. (1976): Blood pressure in tenth-grade students. *Circulation,* 54:993–1000.
37. Millman, M. (1980): *Such a Pretty Face: Being Fat in America.* Norton, New York.
38. Richardson, S. A., Hastorf, A. H., Goodman, N., and Dornbusch, S. M. (1961): Cultural uniformity in reaction to physical disabilities. *Am. Sociol. Rev.,* 26:241–247.
39. Rivinus, T. M., Drummond, T., and Combrinck-Graham, L. (1976): A group-behavior treatment program for overweight children: results of a pilot study. *Ped. Adol. Endocrinol.,* 1:212–218.
40. Rozin, P. (1980): Acquisition of food preferences and attitudes to food. *Int. J. Obes.,* 4:356–363.
41. Sallade, J. (1973): A comparison of the psychological adjustment of obese and nonobese children. *J. Psychosom. Res.,* 17:89–96.
42. Seltzer, C. C., and Mayer, J. (1970): An effective weight control program in a public school system. *Am. J. Public Health,* 60:679–689.
43. Sjöström, L. (1980): Fat cells and body weight. In: *Obesity,* edited by A. J. Stunkard, pp. 72–100. Saunders, Philadelphia.
44. Staffieri, J. R. (1967): A study of social stereotype of body image in children. *J. Pers. Soc. Psychol.,* 7:101–104.
45. Stephanic, P. A., Heald, F. P., and Mayer, J. (1959): Caloric intake in relation to energy output of obese and nonobese adolescent boys. *Am. J. Clin. Nutr.,* 7:55–62.
46. Stunkard, A. J. (1976): *The Pain of Obesity.* Bull Publishing, Palo Alto, California.
47. Stunkard, A. J., and Burt, V. (1967): Obesity and the body image. II. Age at onset of disturbances in the body image. *Am. J. Psychiatry,* 123:1443–1447.
48. Stunkard, A. J., and Mendelson, M. (1967): Obesity and body image: I. Characteristics of disturbances in the body image of some obese persons. *Am. J. Psychiat.,* 123:1296–1300.
49. Stunkard, A. J., and Pestka, J. (1962): The physical activity of obese girls. *Am. J. Dis. Child.,* 103:812–817.
50. Waxman, M., and Stunkard, A. J. (1980): Caloric intake and expenditure of boys. *J. Pediatr.,* 96:187–193.
51. Weiss, A. R. (1977): A behavioral approach to the treatment of adolescent obesity. *Behav. Res. Ther.,* 8:720–726.
52. Wilkinson, P., Parklin, J., Pearloom, G., Strang, H., and Sykes, P. (1977): Energy intake and physical activity in obese children. *Br. Med. J.,* 1:756.

Eating and Its Disorders, edited by A. J.
Stunkard and E. Stellar. Raven Press,
New York © 1984.

Should Obesity Be Treated At All?

Susan C. Wooley and Orland W. Wooley

Psychiatry Department, University of Cincinnati Medical Center, Cincinnati, Ohio 45267

This chapter is entitled with a surprising question: "Should we treat obesity at all?" The title was suggested by the organizers of this volume and the fact that it can be asked at all reflects, I think, a shared unrest within the profession. The question is whether the generally modest benefits of successful obesity treatment clearly outweigh the negative effects of unsuccessful treatment and the general impact on an already weight-obsessed society of our continuing efforts to prevent or eradicate fatness. The unrest stems from the fact that the more we learn, the more nagging the doubts that obesity is, in fact, a behavioral disorder and that it is inherently so undesirable.

For many years, treatments of obesity were derived from the assumption that fatness was due to some potentially remediable abnormality of behavior: The intake of unusually large amounts of food, subnormal physical activity, or both. Treatments thus sought to correct psychological causes of excessive eating, to educate people on proper diet and exercise, and most recently, to use learning theory techniques to gradually and systematically modify behavior. The results of these efforts have been, on the whole, frankly discouraging.

One rarely reads a volume such as this without some renewed hope about the apparent promise of a new technique or combination of techniques, but in the dissemination process, the marginal gain of these innovations is often lost. We shouldn't be surprised that experts in the field are better than others in achieving cures. Expertise implies unusual knowledge, resourcefulness, flexibility, and effort. Occasional reports of unusual success should not blind us to the fact that techniques based on insight, education, and behavior modification have a very modest success rate (2,30). We significantly change only a small minority of those we treat.

These results are understandable in view of the fact that, in many cases, the obese patient has little or no abnormality of behavior to be corrected by these interventions. Although occasional studies have found overeating by the obese, the majority have found no difference in the food intakes of obese and lean infants, children, adolescents, and adults (38). This can be taken to mean that the majority of obese people do not overeat in comparison to others, or do so only for short periods of time, difficult to capture in time-limited experiments. Whether or not obesity is typically caused by a period of overeating is a question we cannot answer at this time. However, obesity can certainly be maintained without overeating, even with undereating. This fact is simply incompatible with the concept of curing obesity by normalizing eating behavior.

And if, through sufficiently extreme and sustained undereating, an obese person succeeds in losing weight, we must acknowledge the growing evidence of a strong physiological pressure toward regain, frequently conceptualized as regulation around a set point. We have what will surely some day be regarded as a very primitive understanding of this process, but there are many suggestive data. Metabolic rate is depressed by food restriction (38), and the restoration of normal eating required to correct it seems to lead inevitably to fat replenishment and weight gain. Increased efficiency following weight loss has been demonstrated in lean humans reduced to subnormal weights (15,28), in obese patients subjected to restriction (26), and in laboratory animals (5,9,12). This effect appears to be due to reduced thermogenesis and to altered hormonal responses favoring fat storage (38).

It would be a cruel trick of nature to thwart the best efforts of a substantial segment of the population to reach and stay in a weight range necessary to survival. However, the most fundamental assumption of obesity treatment—that to become thinner is to become healthier—is also now the focus of increasing skepticism, particularly for women. Keys' 1980 review (14) of 13 prospective studies on obesity and mortality concluded that risk of early death increases only at the extremes of under- and overweight, with weight having no impact on health of women in the middle 80%. Data from the Framingham study (27) indicated that underweight was more dangerous than overweight and found no relationship between fatness and mortality for women in the middle 60% of the weight range.

In a study of the Pima Indians of Arizona, a population subject to high rates of obesity and diabetes mellitus, it was found that the lowest mortality rate occurred in a body mass index range that would be considered extremely obese by most standards. The safest range was equivalent to 167 to 190% of desirable weight for women and 145 to 176% of desirable weight for men based on the Society of Actuaries standards (21). Finally, in one of the few studies concerned specifically with women, Noppa et al. found an inverse relationship between death from all causes and degree of obesity (19).

Admittedly, these findings do not negate the health problems, or even simple discomfort, of the massively obese. But these data do raise very serious questions about the rational basis for treatment of the great majority of patients who are mildly to moderately obese.

Taking all these facts into account, it seems increasingly difficult to make a case that the benefits to the few patients we call therapeutic successes are so compelling as to warrant the enormous efforts involved. Schachter (25) recently reported a surprisingly high rate of well-maintained weight losses in an untreated sample of university personnel and residents of a resort town. The casual sampling procedure makes it difficult to interpret these findings, but if true, they could be taken to mean that those people who can lose weight will do it without professional help. Perhaps these spontaneous cures include many of the simple overeaters who gain weight during transitory periods of stress or indulgence and who are able to return to a lower natural weight without undue difficulty. Occasionally, one sees such a patient in a clinical setting, and the experience of effortless success is heady indeed.

But most patients who seek professional help belong to a refractory group who have tried and failed to achieve a lasting weight loss many times. I share Hilde Bruch's (6,7) skepticism as to whether those who are eventually helped are really that much better off. Many treatment successes are in fact condemned to a life of weight obsession, semistarvation, and all the symptoms produced by chronic hunger. We have often encountered and have recently begun studying successful maintainers from commercial weight loss programs and have been more impressed by their fortitude than the quality of their life. Caught in a metabolic rut, to use the term coined by Vincent (33), some consume as few as 800 calories per day, struggle constantly to ward off or compensate for losses of control, and seem precariously close to developing a frank eating disorder. Perceptible beneath the visible pride is often an unmistakable bitterness over the price they pay to have a socially acceptable body. If this is, indeed, a better fate than being fat, it only shows how miserable we have made the world for fat people.

If this is the dubious reward of the treatment successes, what of the treatment failures? Their story is of course well known to all who treat obesity. Again and again they have invested their time, money, and energy in treatments which fail, each time feeling less worthy. Seemingly almost no one takes seriously the risks to health said to be caused by repeated weight fluctuation (32), perhaps because in their eagerness to obtain our help, patients are so persuasive in their assurances that this hospitalization, this program, this fast—will be the one which changes them for good.

A recent review by McReynolds (18) concludes that obese patients undergoing medical or psychiatric treatment show evidence of psychological disturbance and those in the general population show comparable or better mental functioning than nonobese people. A conservative interpretation of this finding is that disturbed fat people, like thin ones, tend to seek professional help. A radical interpretation is that the obesity treatment process fosters psychological problems. In either case, it is clear that obese people can be well adjusted despite a social handicap, something we tend to forget when exposed only to the disturbed patients who seek our help. We might wonder whether it is always wisest to unquestioningly accept the patient's opinion that losing weight is the route to an improved quality of life and consider instead how to maximize their adjustment. It is interesting that there are no studies of the attitudes, life styles, and coping strategies of well-adjusted obese people.

So far, we have considered only the direct effects of obesity treatment on patients. There is a larger issue to be considered: namely, the impact of the attitudes and activities of experts on the millions of people who are never themselves recipients of treatment, but who are lifelong witnesses of it. Medicine's demand for universal slenderness may not have caused the weight obsession of our society, but I can think of nothing that would go further toward defusing it than a refusal by medicine to define fatness per se as a disease or to so treat it. It is very hard to maintain that there is little intrinsic harm in a condition to which we continue to direct such limitless and heroic efforts for cure.

At this point there is a formidable transmission of prejudice concerning body size. The literature on attitudes about body types has been reviewed elsewhere (36,38), but a couple recent studies are of particular relevance to the development of antifat attitudes in children. In a study of expectant parents, Sherman (*unpublished thesis*) found an overwhelming aversion to fat children of varying ages. For children beyond the age of 12, obesity was seen as being worse for a girl than a boy. It is little wonder that by an early age children regard fat as bad. These findings also reflect the lesser cultural tolerance for fatness in females as they move into adolescence.

In a detailed study of antifat attitudes, Harris (*unpublished manuscript, p. 22*) found "Both males and females, ranging in age from preschool through adulthood, from four different cultural and ethnic groups, including both underweight and overweight subjects, all viewed the drawings of fat boys and girls, and men and women more negatively than similar drawings of normal weight stimulus persons." Perhaps the most thought-provoking finding of this study was that although kindergartners fully shared the overall antifat prejudice of older subjects, they made a minimal distinction between fat and thin people on the dimension of appearance. The judgement that fat is ugly evidently develops later than the judgement that fat is socially undesirable and indicative of negative personality traits. Thus, the dislike of fatness cannot be ascribed to an innate aesthetic preference, a fact already well-supported by the enormous cultural and historical variability in preferred body types.

The effects of cultural fact aversion appear to be increasingly reflected in dieting efforts among the young. Nylander (20) found 80% of Scandinavian women to have dieted by the age of 18. Among a sample of college women, Thompson and Schwartz (31) found 31 out of 77 to show anorexic-like behaviors. They noted that virtually all of the anorexic-like women and many of the problem-free ones reported that they were "always dieting," the mean age of the first diet being 13.8 years and 15.1 years, respectively.

In view of our current epidemic of eating disorders, we need to consider more carefully what happens to people who diet. Since the classic study of Keys et al. (15) of starved conscientious objectors in World War II, it has been known that a period of starvation leads to gorging when food is again made available. Innovative work of Polivy et al. (22) on restraint has shown a repeated connection between chronic dieting and the tendency to binge, findings confirmed by Wardle's report (34) that among normal subjects, restrained eaters were more likely to crave food and go on binges. Thompson and Schwartz (31) found that of the 40% of college women who showed anorexic-like behavior without actually being anorexic, half reported binge-eating. Of course, eating binges which bring diets to an abrupt end are so characteristic of overweight patients that we have tended to see them as part of the psychopathology of obesity rather than as a natural consequence of voluntary weight loss.

Although hunger caused by starvation seems natural enough, explanations advanced for the mechanism of this phenomenon are quite intriguing. Based on observations of high rates of insulin release and consequent hyperlipogenesis in VMH-lesioned animals, genetic obesity, and following starvation, Stricker (29) advanced the hypothesis that it is the diversion of foodstuffs to fat stores which creates hunger. This is like being cash poor when one's salary is garnisheed to pay off old debts. Stricker argues that the animal does not get fat because it overeats, but rather overeats because it is getting fat. Similar theories have been advanced by Booth (3).

Others, including Powley (23), have stressed the appetite-stimulating effects of a general anticipatory response to food which includes salivation, insulin release, and the secretion of digestive enzymes. There responses are quite sensitive to weight change and could account for heightened appetite following restriction. Finally, Polivy et al. (22) have argued that dieting leads to a weakening of physiologic satiety mechanisms so that when cognitive controls are set aside, the dieter who gorges is not ignoring his body but responding to a revised set of commands.

Attempting to maintain a weight loss in the face of overwhelming appetite would certainly appear to constitute a condition of high risk for the development of a clinical eating disorder. In fact, it may be precisely the increased hunger and faltering control which so dramatically intensifies fear of fatness. Anorexia nervosa, of course, always begins as a weight loss diet, generally indistinguishable from those without such a calamitous conclusion. So, too, do most cases of bulimia begin with diets. Pyle et al. (24) found 30 out of 34 cases of bulimia began after a diet; Boskind-Lodahl (4) found this to be almost universal. In an analysis of 10 cases of longstanding bulimia, Wooley and Wooley (3) found that the first episode of vomiting nearly always followed a simple diet infraction, often on a holiday or other special occasion. Instances of gorging and purging usually continued in this way for some time before the advent of planned binges. Thus, what begins as a way of undoing a lapse of otherwise tight control eventually allows the regular abandonment of control. At this point, bulimics have usually developed dependence on binge purging for relief of tension and hunger, and (in many cases) for nutritional needs.

Among the 40% of college women found by Thompson and Schwartz (31) to have anorexic-like characteristics, fully half reported vomiting. All of these knew another woman who vomited and many had been taught by them. Lacey (16, p. 60) in a description of his series of bulimic women without prior history of anorexia nervosa asserts, "What marks out patients in the bulimic syndrome is that the development of progressive and massive obesity which would otherwise have been their destiny is prevented by either abstinence or laxative abuse or . . . vomiting or by a combination of methods."

The truth is that bulimia is probably the most effective method of weight control available today, and it should not surprise us that intelligent, young women seize upon it. In fact the number one bestseller last year—outselling the nearest competitor more than 2 to 1—was the *Beverly Hills Diet Book* (17) in which Judy Mazel advocates a form of bulimia in which binges are "compensated" (her term) by eating massive quantities of raw fruit in order to produce diarrhea (35).

If one has not seen bulimic patients, it is easy to wonder what really is wrong with the system. What is wrong, of course, is the unexpected progression of appetite which can leave the victim eating almost continually, and the depression and self-hatred which usually ensue. Johnson et al. (13) found that 50% of his sample of bulimics (only half of whom had sought treatment) had a history of suicidal ideation. Ninety per cent reported that their thoughts and feelings about themselves were "totally influenced by eating difficulties."

The argument here, of course, is that cultural weight obsession is in large part responsible for the current epidemic of eating disorders. The development of these disorders is a perfectly predictable response to the social demand to maintain a body weight at which extreme hunger is to be expected. Bruch (8, p. 212) writes "The moralistic social pressure aggravates the inner psychological problems and conflicts of youngsters whose weights deviate from the stereotypic picture of a desirable figure. The pressure to be thin seems to be on the rise, and increasingly often parents, even physicians, condone or encourage excessive thinness."

That standards of thinness have become increasingly stringent is documented in the Garner et al. (11) study of historical trends. The impact of such pressures is also illustrated in Garner and Garfinkel's findings of high rates of anorexia nervosa among dancers, which developed after being in dance (10).

It is perhaps too obvious to mention, but it should be remembered that the victims of this process are not drawn evenly from society but are virtually all females. These are problems deeply rooted in sexism. A 1975 report of the American Psychological Association Task Force on Sex Bias and Sex-Role Stereotyping in Psychotherapeutic Practice (1, p. 1122) states "Psychologists should recognize the reality, variety, and implications of sex-discriminatory practices in society and should facilitate client examination of options in dealing with such practices." Interestingly, when this group published a book examining the impact of sexism in the development and treatment of various psychological disorders (e.g., depression, agoraphobia), the section on eating disorders was a last minute inclusion. How easily we take for granted the fact that it is women who worry about weight. How easily weight obsession is dismissed as an inevitable phase of female development. Would things be different if our hospitals and clinics were filled with young men whose educations and careers were arrested by the onset of anorexia nervosa, bulimia, or the need to make dieting and body shaping exercise a full-time pursuit?

Returning to the original question, "Should we treat obesity at all?," the relevant facts seem to be these: (a) obesity treatment with the exception of surgical techniques carrying high physical risks are generally ineffective; (b) individual differences in body size appear to have a strong basis in biology, helping to account for the extreme measures required to maintain a successful weight loss, and the high number of therapeutic failures; (c) mild to moderate obesity does not appear to constitute a significant health risk for women, and possibly not for men; (d) an increasingly stringent cultural standard of thinness for women, largely supported by the medical and psychological professions, has been accompanied by a steadily increasing incidence of serious eating disorders in women.

It is very hard to construct a rational case for treating any but massive, life-endangering obesity. At the same time, it is clear that we must vigorously treat weight obsession and its manifestations, namely, (a) poor self and body image, (b) disordered eating patterns created by dieting, (c) metabolic depression produced by dieting, (d) inadequate nutrition due to constricted eating behavior, and (e) disordered lifestyles, often marked by excessive or inadequate exercise.

Body weight and the particulars of weight control strategies are no more the real issue than age and occupation are the real issues in depression. Weight change may, in some cases, be a worthwhile and attainable goal, but it cannot be the major goal of treatment and its appropriateness and feasibility can only become apparent as other problems are corrected. When these are corrected, weight will usually be seen to be less important than it first appeared. Patients treated from this perspective are generally able to reach their own conclusions.

There remains, of course, the problem of the massively obese or others whose health is genuinely endangered. Unfortunately, these patients are often among the most difficult to successfully treat by conservative methods. The issue of appropriate treatment for this group is a strictly medical one. Any treatment which can be demonstrated to increase health and longevity, without undue negative impact on lifestyle or psychological functioning, should be considered appropriate. However, the same stringent criteria applying to the use of any other medical or surgical procedure should be retained. Risky procedures should not be employed simply because there is a patient demand for them. We should not try to solve social problems in operating rooms.

REFERENCES

1. American Psychological Association Task Force (1975): Report of the task force on sex bias and sex-role stereotyping in psychotherapeutic practice. *Am. Psychol.,* 30:1169–1175.
2. Ashby, W. A., and Wilson, G. T. (1977): Behavior therapy for obesity: Booster sessions and long term maintenance of weight loss. *Behav. Res. Ther.,* 15:451–464.
3. Booth, D. A. (1976): Approaches to Feeding Control. In *Appetite and Food Intake,* edited by T. Silverstone, pp. 417–478. Dahlem Konferenzen, Berlin.
4. Boskind-Lodahl, M. (1976): Cinderella's stepsisters: A feminist perspective on anorexia nervosa and bulimia. *Signs: Jounral of Women in Culture and Society,* 2:342–356.
5. Boyle, P. C., Storlien, H., and Keesey, R. E. (1978): Increased efficiency of food utilization following weight loss. *Physiol. Behav.,* 21:261–264.
6. Bruch, H. (1973): *Eating Disorders: Obesity, Anorexia, and the Person Within.* Basic Books, New York.
7. Bruch, H. (1980): Thin fat people. In *A Woman's Conflict: The Special Relationship Between Women and Food,* edited by J. R. Kaplan, pp. 17–28. Prentice-Hall, Inc., Englewood Cliffs, New Jersey.
8. Bruch, H. (1981): Developmental considerations of anorexia nervosa and obesity. *Can. J. Psychiatry,* 26:212–217.
9. Coscina, D. V., and Dixon, L. (1981): *Body weight regulation in starving females: Insights from an animal model.* Paper presented at the Anorexia Nervosa Conference, Toronto, Canada, September 12–13.

10. Garner, D. M., and Garfinkel, P. E. (1980): Socio-cultural factors in the development of anorexia nervosa. *Psychol. Med.,* 10:647–656.
11. Garner, D. M., Garfinkel, P. E., Schwartz, D., and Thompson, M. (1980): Cultural expectations of thinness in women. *Psychol. Rep.,* 47:483–491.
12. Hamilton, C. L. (1969): Problems of refeeding after starvation. *Ann. N.Y. Acad. Sci.,* 157:1004–1017.
13. Johnson, C. L., Stuckey, M. K., Lewis, L. D., and Schwartz, D. M. (1982): Bulimia: A descriptive survey of 316 cases. *Int. J. Eating Disorders,* 2:3–16.
14. Keys, A. (1980): Overweight, obesity, coronary heart disease and mortality. *Nutr. Rev.,* 38:297–307.
15. Keys, A., Brozek, J., Henschel, A., Mickelson, O., and Taylor, H. (1950): *The Biology of Human Starvation.* University of Minnesota Press, Minneapolis.
16. Lacey, J. H. (1982): The bulimic syndrome at normal body weight: Reflections on pathogenesis and clinical features. *Int. J. Eating Disorders,* 2:59–66.
17. Mazel, J. (1981): *The Beverly Hills Diet.* MacMillan Publishing Co., Inc., New York.
18. McReynolds, W. T. (1982): Toward a psychology of obesity: Review of research on the role of personality and level of adjustment. *Int. J. Eating Disorders,* 2:37–57.
19. Noppa, H., Bengtsson, C., Wedel, H., and Wilhelmsen, L. (1980): Obesity in relation to morbidity and mortality from cardiovascular disease. *Am. J. Epidemiol.,* 111:682–692.
20. Nylander, I. (1971): The feeling of being fat and dieting in a school population. *Acta Sociomed. Scand.,* 1:17–26.
21. Pettitt, D. J., Lisse, J. R., Knowler, W. C., and Bennett, P. H. (1982): Mortality as a function of obesity and diabetes mellitus. *Am. J. Epidemiol.,* 115:359–366.
22. Polivy, J., Herman, C. P., Olmsted, P., and Jazwinski, C. (1983): Restraint and Binge Eating. In: *Binge-Eating: Theory, Research and Treatment,* edited by R. C. Hawkins II, W. Fremouw, and P. Clement. Springer, New York, *(in press).*
23. Powley, T. (1977): The ventromedial hypothalamic syndrome, satiety, and a cephalic phase hypothesis. *Psychol. Rev.,* 84:89–126.
24. Pyle, R. L., Mitchell, J. E., and Eckert, E. D. (1981): Bulimia: A report of 34 cases. *J. Clin. Psychiatry,* 42:60–64.
25. Schachter, S. (1982): Recidivism and self-cure of smoking and obesity. *Am. Psychol.,* 37:436–444.
26. Shetty, P. S., Jung, R. T., James, W. P. T., Barrand, M. A., and Callingham, B. A. (1981): Post-prandial thermogenesis in obesity. *Clin. Sci.,* 60:519–525.
27. Sorlie, P., Gordon, T., and Kannel, W. B. (1980): Body build and mortality. *J. A. M. A.,* 243:1828–1831.
28. Stordy, B. J., Marks, V., Kalucy, R. S., and Crisp, A. H. (1977): Weight gain, thermic effect of glucose and resting metabolic rate during recovery from anorexia nervosa. *Am. J. Clin. Nutr.,* 30:138–146.
29. Stricker, E. M. (1978): Hyperphagia. *N. Engl. J. Med.,* 298:1010–1013.
30. Stunkard, A. J., and Penick, S. B. (1979): Behavior modification in the treatment of obesity: The problem of maintaining weight loss. *Arch. Gen. Psychiatry,* 36:801–806.
31. Thompson, M. G., and Schwartz, D. M. (1982): Life adjustment of women with anorexia nervosa and anorexic-like behavior. *Int. J. Eating Disorders,* 1:47–60.
32. U.S. Department of Health, Education, and Welfare (1966): *Obesity and Health: A Sourcebook of Information for Professional Health Personnel.* U.S. Government Printing Office, Arlington, Virginia.
33. Vincent, L. M. (1979): *Competing with the Sylph.* Andrews and McMeel, New York.
34. Wardle, J. (1980): Dietary restraint and binge eating. *Behav. Anal. Modification,* 4:201–209.
35. Wooley, O. W., and Wooley, S. C. (1982): The Beverly Hills eating disorder: The mass marketing of anorexia nervosa. *Int. J. Eating Disorders,* 1:57–69.
36. Wooley, O. W., Wooley, S. C., and Dyrenforth, S. R. (1979): Obesity and women II: A neglected feminist topic. *Women's Stud. Int. Quart.,* 2:81–92.
37. Wooley, S. C., and Wooley, O. W. (1981): Overeating as a Substance Abuse. In: *Advances in Substance Abuse, Vol. 2,* edited by N. Mello, pp. 41–67. JAI Press, Greenwich, Connecticut.
38. Wooley, S. C., Wooley, O. W., and Dyrenforth, S. R. (1979): Theoretical, practical, and social issues in behavioral treatments of obesity. *J. Appl. Behav. Anal.,* 2:3–25.

Eating and Its Disorders, edited by A. J. Stunkard and E. Stellar. Raven Press, New York © 1984.

The Treatment of Anorexia Nervosa: Do Different Treatments Have Different Outcomes?

W. Stewart Agras and Helena C. Kraemer

Department of Psychiatry and Behavioral Sciences, Stanford University School of Medicine, Stanford, California 94305

Over the last few years, a consensus has begun to emerge concerning the aims of treatment of anorexia nervosa, based on the observations of Crisp and others (7,8) that the anorexic is phobic, of adult body weight and shape, and the associated social and interpersonal demands. Thus, the goal of treatment has come to be seen as the restoration of normal body weight, which, in turn, leads to exposure to and experience with normal adolescent or adult social and interpersonal demands (8). To accomplish this goal usually requires hospitalization to facilitate weight gain, combined with various approaches to facilitate social readjustment, such as psychotherapy, family therapy, and social skills training.

The general outcome of such treatment appears to be well established as indicated both in reviews of the literature (2,18,32) and from reports of large clinical series (8), although no long-term controlled treatment study exists. Follow-up studies reveal that nearly two-thirds of a previously hospitalized anorexic population will be at normal weight and that the majority of these individuals will have resumed regular menstruation (8,18). However, about one-half of the population will continue to have eating difficulties and will show social and psychiatric impairment (2,18). A small number of anorexics will become obese, and from 2 to 6% will have died from complications of the anorexia or by suicide. Predictors of poor outcome appear to be longer duration of illness, severity of weight loss, and bulimia (18,32).

Despite these general conclusions concerning the efficacy of treatment, much less is known about the differential effectiveness of different treatment approaches to this difficult and not infrequently refractory disorder. Treatment programs have been developed based on clinical experience and tend to be multicomponent in nature, with the contributions of each component to therapeutic outcome being uncertain. This is obviously a somewhat unsatisfactory state of affairs, contributed to in part by the relative rarity and chronic nature of the disorder, which makes long-term controlled outcome studies of convincing size difficult if not impossible to carry out.

To attempt to clarify the differential effectiveness of different treatments for anorexia nervosa, two approaches are taken in this chapter. The first approach was to establish a data base of treated cases of anorexia nervosa with identical information for each case. The data base was derived from 21 studies published in English between 1954 and 1982 and included 193 cases of women below the age of 30 years (1,3–6,11–14,16,19–28,30,31). To be included in this data set, the study from which data were drawn had to report more than one case and to include the sex and age of each patient as well as height or ideal weight, admission weight, discharge weight, and length of treatment. The second approach was to review the published controlled studies of the treatment of anorexia nervosa, focusing particularly on the few studies comparing different treatments.

These sources of information are used to address two questions. Has the treatment of anorexia nervosa improved over the last 50 years?, and What is the differential effectiveness of various approaches to the treatment of anorexia nervosa?

TREATMENT OVER THE LAST 50 YEARS

To answer the first question, we arrayed the results of treatment without reference to the type of treatment by decade from 1930, using the date of admission to hospital rather than the study date to classify cases. Plotted in Fig. 1 are the body mass indices on admission and on discharge for the subjects in each decade. One surprising finding is immediately apparent, namely that the body mass index of patients on admission has shown a marked decline over time. There is no sig-

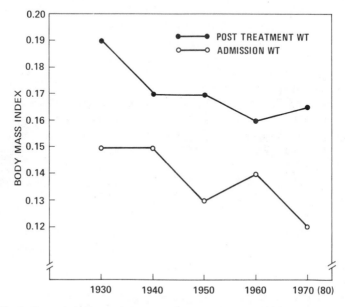

FIG. 1. The body mass indices of patients with anorexia nervosa before and after treatment by decade from 1930.

nificant increase in height over time or in ideal or goal weight, but there is a statistically significant decline in entry weight [F $(21,151)$ = 8.3, p <0.001]. Since a lower admission weight predicts poorer outcome, these data suggest that patients with more severe anorexia nervosa are being admitted to hospital today than was the case 50 years ago. Whether this is due to later recognition of the disorder, to longer outpatient treatment, or to worsening of the disorder in the general population is, of course, not answerable from these data. However, the latter explanation would seem the most likely since there is a reported increase in the prevalence of anorexia nervosa and a strengthening of societal factors predisposing toward thinness (9).

As can also be seen in Fig. 1, there is no evidence that the weight increment attributable to treatment has increased over time. This suggests that the overall treatment outcome of anorexia nervosa, at least as reflected in these data, has not improved over the last 50 years.

THE DIFFERENTIAL EFFECTIVENESS OF TREATMENT

Despite the possibility that the treatment of anorexia nervosa has not shown improvement over the decades, it may be that a particular form of treatment applied to a subset of patients is more effective than other forms of treatment. To attempt to answer this question, the treatment methods used in the 21 studies comprising the data set were classified, for the purposes of this study, into a general category termed medical treatment, behavior therapy, and drug therapy. Medical treatment included hospitalization, often combined with confinement to bed, supervised eating, psychotherapy, family therapy, and occasionally tube feeding. Behavior therapy consisted of the structured use of reinforcement for weight gain in a hospital setting. Usually activities in which patients liked to engage were made contingent on small increases in daily weight (1,2,11,14). This was sometimes combined with systematic caloric and weight feedback, and also the serving of large meals (1). Drug therapy consisted of the use of a pharmacologic agent including, in the studies selected, amitriptyline (26), clomipramine (21), lithium carbonate (17), and L-DOPA (20).

While the clumping together of somewhat different treatment approaches into just three general categories is less precise than might be desired, particularly in the case of pharmacologic agents, such clumping was necessitated by the small sample sizes involved in individual studies. The three main treatment categories are distributed quite differently over the decades. From 1930 to 1959, all patients were treated with medical therapy. In the 1960s, drug therapy accounted for nearly 20% of cases and behavior therapy for a slightly smaller proportion. In the last decade, drug therapy accounted for a quarter of all cases and behavior therapy for some 45%.

The mean age of the sample is 18.1 years, and there are no significant differences in the age of patients at admission between the three treatment conditions. One major contrast between the three treatments is illustrated in Fig. 2. As

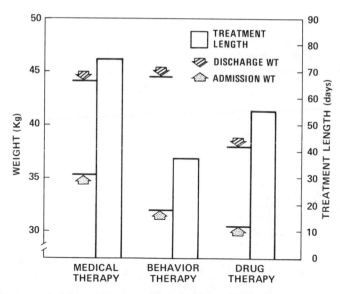

FIG. 2. Admission weights *(stippled arrows)*, discharge weights *(shaded arrows)*, and treatment lengths, for medical therapy, behavior therapy, and drug therapy.

shown, patients treated with medical therapy have a higher admission weight than those treated with behavior therapy or drug therapy [$F(2,151) = 8.3, p<0.005$]. However, posttreatment weights differentiate only drug therapy (37.6 ± 8.0 kg) from behavior therapy (44.3 ± 6.5 kg) or medical therapy (44.1 ± 5.8 kg) [$F(2,151) = 8.6, p <.05$]. Thus, we must conclude, in accord with previous reviews, that there appears to be no difference in the effectiveness of behavior and medical therapy. This conclusion must be tempered by the fact that patients in medical therapy were primarily those treated from 1930 to 1970 when entry weights were higher, whereas behavior and drug therapy patients were all treated from 1960 to 1980.

A second major contrast is the unexpected finding, as indicated in Fig. 2, that the mean length of treatment is 37.0 ± 22.3 days for behavior therapy, 75.8 ± 50.5 days for medical therapy, and 44.0 ± 32.8 days for drug therapy, a difference which is highly significant [$F(2,151) = 16.7, p <0.001$]. Although the mean weight gains in the three groups are similar, it appears that the efficiency of behavior therapy, in terms of rate of weight gain, is significantly better than that of either medical therapy or drug therapy: Behavior therapy (8.0 ± 6.4 kg/month), medical therapy (4.7 ± 8.9 kg/month), and drug therapy (4.2 ± 3.7 kg/month) ($F = 9.3, p <0.001$). The superior efficiency of behavior therapy as compared with medical therapy and drug therapy is also seen in the relationship of rate of weight gain for subjects treated for comparable periods of time as shown in Fig. 3. This result also held when patients were matched in terms of entry weight.

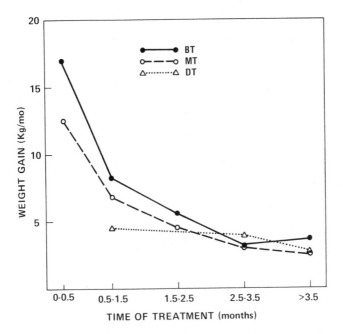

FIG. 3. Rates of weight gain for medical therapy, behavior therapy, and drug therapy, for various treatment durations.

To illustrate the importance of such increased efficiency of therapy, the average weight gain over the treatment period in this study was 10 kg. With a rate of weight gain of 4 kg/month, this would mean a treatment period of 2.5 months or 75 days. However, with a rate of weight gain of 8 kg/month, the treatment period would be only 38 days. A difference of 37 days of treatment represents a savings of several thousand dollars in costs. Of course, such enhanced efficiency must not be at the cost of longer-term disadvantages. However, as noted in previous reviews (2) and in an analysis of the present data set, there are no significant differences in weight between medical treatment and behavior therapy at follow-up.

Controlled Studies: Overview

During the past few years, as indicated in Table 1, nine controlled studies of various approaches to the treatment of anorexia nervosa have appeared, including those with quasi-experimental designs, randomized designs, and single-case controlled experiments. As can be seen, the majority has been published since 1977. These studies have varied in scope with experimental group size ranging from 7 to 42. Admission weight varied from a mean of 30.9 to 40.6 kg, as compared with 33.7 ± 5.6 kg for the pooled data described above. Nine of the 13 groups had a mean admission weight higher than pooled sample. Weight gain ranged from 3.3 to 14.7 kg as compared with 9.7 kg for the pooled sample. Ten of 15 groups

TABLE 1. *Controlled studies of the treatment of anorexia nervosa*

Study	Treatment	N	Admission wt. (kg)	Discharge wt. (kg)	Δ	Length of hospitalization (days)	Wt. gain kg/month	Follow-up	Methodologic problems
Dally and Sargent (1966)	Chlorpromazine and insulin	30	—	—	10.4	36	8.7	33% readmitted	Nonrandom
	Insulin	8	—	—	8.1	59	4.2	(2 years)	
	Standard therapy	27	—	—	5.4	44	3.6	30% readmitted	Retrospective
Moldofsky and Garfinkel (1977)	Behavior therapy	7	34.1	44.3	10.2	46.2	6.18	28.5% readmitted in 18 months	Nonrandom, Retrospective Own controls
	Standard therapy	7	—	—	3.3	—	—		
Vigersky and Loriaux (1977)	Cyproheptadine	13	34.9	—		56	—	—	Baseline differences
	Placebo	11	33.6	—		56	—	—	No weight data presented
Eckert et al. (1979)	Behavior therapy	40	35.96	—		35	4.2	—	Limited treatment period
	Standard therapy	41	—	—		35	3.6	—	
Goldberg et al. (1979)	Cyproheptadine	42	35.96	—	5.1	35	4.5	—	Limited treatment period
	Placebo	39	—	—	4.3	35	3.6	—	
Lacey and Crisp (1980)	Clomipramine and standard therapy	8	40.6	53.9	13.3	78.2	5.1	19 months	
	Placebo and standard therapy	8	37.7	52.4	14.7	70	6.3		
Gross et al. (1981)	Lithium and behavior therapy	8	35.7	42.5	6.8	28	7.3	—	Limited treatment period Baseline differences
	Placebo and behavior therapy	8	32.7	37.9	5.2	28	5.6	—	
Pertschuk et al. (1981)	Parenteral treatment and behavior therapy	11	31.5	41.9	10.4	63	4.95	—	Nonrandom, Retrospective
Pillay and Crisp (1981)	Behavior therapy	11	30.9	38.1	7.4	51.6	4.19		
	Social skills training and standard therapy	11	41.0	48.0	7.0	122.8	1.7	1 year	
	Standard therapy	12	40.2	47.4	7.2	114	1.9		

showed a lower mean weight gain than the pooled sample, and 10 of 16 groups showed a lower rate of weight gain than the pooled sample. This suggests that the controlled studies population may have been somewhat less severe at admission and gained about the same amount of weight at a slightly slower rate than the pooled sample. The three highest rates of gain in the controlled studies were the combination of chlorpromazine and insulin (8.7 kg/month), behavior therapy plus lithium carbonate (7.3 kg/month), and behavior therapy alone (6.18 kg/month). The five lowest rates were social skills training (plus standard therapy), standard therapy alone, or placebo treated patients, none of which groups was higher than 3.6 kg/month.

QuasiExperimental Studies

The earliest of these studies, and the first attempt to evaluate the effectiveness of two treatments in common use at the time, namely the administration of chlorpromazine and the use of a modified insulin regimen, was reported by Dally and Sargant (10). These investigators used a retrospectively chosen control group of 27 patients treated with bed rest and a steadily increasing number of calories, to compare with a group of 30 patients receiving a combination of chlorpromazine and insulin in addition to the standard treatment, and with 8 patients receiving insulin alone. The groups were well matched on baseline characteristics such as age, weight, and duration of illness. However, those receiving drug therapy had been treated between 1957 and 1962, whereas those receiving standard therapy were treated between 1939 and 1959. Thus, the historical control was inadequate.

Chlorpromazine was given orally in doses up to 1,600 mg/day, and insulin was given daily before breakfast in doses up to 60 units. The group receiving the combination of chlorpromazine and insulin gained weight at a rate of 8.7 kg/month, compared with rates of 4.2 and 3.6 kg/month for the groups receiving insulin alone and standard therapy, respectively. Length of hospitalization varied from 36 days for the combined treatment to 59 days for insulin alone. Since the combination therapy was significantly superior to standard therapy ($p < .01$) and insulin alone was comparable to standard therapy, the authors concluded that chlorpromazine was the most effective treatment agent. However, no differences were found between groups at 3 years follow-up in terms of weight with approximately two-thirds being regarded as satisfactory. Unfortunately, bulimia was present in 45% of those treated with chlorpromazine as compared with 12% in the usual care group, although this finding may have been due to the inadequate historical control, e.g., a higher prevalence of bulimia in the general and/or anorexic population in the later years of the study, rather than to a true pharmacologic effect.

In the second investigation (14), the effectiveness of behavior therapy was evaluated by comparing the progress made in inpatient treatment, using reinforcement of weight gain, with the progress made in previous hospitalizations using a variety of other treatment approaches. Each patient was her own control, although behavior therapy was always the second treatment. Thus, there was a confounding of treatment with order of treatment. The series reported involved 7 patients. Weight gain was 10.2 kg in 42 days for the behaviorally treated admissions (6.18 kg/month) and 3.3 kg for the other treatments. In a later paper (25), the authors report on a larger series using a retrospectively arranged control group treated with various methods to compare with a group treated with behavior therapy. No weight data were reported, but on a global scale assessing various aspects of functioning, the 17 patients treated with behavior therapy did not differ significantly from the 25 patients treated by other methods.

Finally, Pertschuk and his colleagues (28) reported a comparison between 11 patients receiving parenteral nutrition and a similar number treated with behavior therapy, using retrospective matching of the two groups. Total parenteral nutrition was associated with a number of complications, including transient transaminase elevations in 5 cases, pneumothorax in 1 case, joint pains and effusion in 1 case which cleared when therapy was discontinued, and hypophosphatemia leading to muscle weakness, numbness, and pneumonia in 2 cases, with death ensuing in 1 of these patients. As noted by the authors, this therapy is not to be entered lightly.

When the overall outcome of parenteral nutrition was compared with that of behavior therapy, no differences in absolute weight gain were found, and as shown in Table 1, rates of weight gain were fairly similar. However, while receiving parenteral nutrition, patients gained weight at a rate of 10.8 kg/month as compared with 5.4 kg/month for behavior therapy at a comparable time during hospitalization. The former rate of weight gain is, thus, the most efficient of all therapies examined. However, the complications of therapy more than offset this advantage.

Randomized Controlled Studies

The most ambitious controlled study of different approaches to the treatment of anorexia nervosa was designed to compare the relative effectiveness of behavior therapy and milieu therapy, the latter essentially a standard therapy, and cyproheptadine and placebo. These comparisons were reported separately. The study involved 81 anorexic young women who participated for 35 days each, at one of three collaborating clinical centers. Thus, the conclusions based on this study are limited to short-term outcome, and with weight gain averaging 5.0 kg, few patients could have reached ideal body weight.

In the first comparison (11), 40 patients were allocated at random to behavior therapy and 41 to standard therapy. Those receiving behavior therapy gained weight at a rate of 4.2 kg/month, as compared with a rate of 3.6 kg/month for milieu therapy, gains which were not significantly different. There was a trend for patients who had received no previous outpatient therapy to respond better to behavior therapy.

In the second comparison (15), patients were randomly allocated to receive either cyproheptadine or a placebo, doses of the active medication being up to 32 mg/day. There was no difference in the rate of weight gain for those receiving cyproheptadine, 4.5 kg/month, as compared with those receiving placebo who gained at a rate of 3.6 kg/month. However, there was a significant interaction (p = .003) between the number of complications reported at birth and the medication, with the active drug being more effective in those patients having the more complicated deliveries. In addition, there was a trend for those receiving more outpatient treatment prior to hospitalization to improve more with the active drug than with placebo. The authors concluded that cyproheptadine may be indicated in the more severe case.

The efficacy of cyproheptadine in the treatment of anorexia nervosa was also investigated by Vigersky and Loriaux (33) in a smaller scale double-blind randomized trial in which 13 patients were placed on the active medication and 11 received placebo, apparently in the absence of other therapy. Although no data concerning absolute weight were provided, there were no significant differences found between the groups at the end of 8 weeks of treatment. Four patients in the drug group and 2 in the placebo group gained weight.

Two other pharmacologic agents have been examined in controlled trials, clomipramine and lithium carbonate. In the case of clomipramine, 16 anorexics were randomly allocated to receive drug or placebo, both groups receiving standard therapy consisting of a 2,600 calorie diet, confinement to bed until reaching target weight, individual psychotherapy, and family therapy (21). Length of hospitalization averaged 76 days for the treatment group and 72 days for the control group. The rate of weight gain in the clomipramine group was 5.1 kg/month, and in the placebo group 6.3 kg/month, a difference that was not statistically significant. Interestingly however, the group receiving the active drug rated itself as more hungry during the course of the trial, and there was a trend toward better maintenance of body weight.

In the case of lithium carbonate, 16 anorexics were randomly allocated to drug or placebo in a double-blind trial, with both groups participating in a behavior therapy program focusing on weight gain (17). Serum lithium levels from 0.9 to 1.4 meq/liter were attained during the 4-week trial. The group receiving lithium gained weight at a rate of 7.3 kg/month, as compared with 5.6 kg/month for those receiving placebo, a significantly greater rate of gain for the lithium group. Unfortunately, baseline caloric intake was significantly higher for those receiving lithium (2,345 cal/day) than for the placebo group (1,569 cal/day), a difference which might easily account for the apparent advantage of the administration of lithium carbonate. No effect on depressed mood was found.

Other Controlled Studies

Two areas other than the outcome of treatment aimed at restoring weight have been examined in controlled studies. These include a study examining the value of social skills training in the management of the anorexic patient, and a series of single-case controlled studies examining variables involved in the process of treatment using behavior therapy approaches.

Many anorexic patients have major interpersonal problems, compounded perhaps by the disruption of normal social development associated with an illness requiring prolonged hospitalization during adolescence. Thus, it seems logical to incorporate social skills training within the overall treatment approach to anorexia nervosa and to test the effectiveness of this addition by means of a controlled study. To carry out this aim, Pillay and Crisp (29) randomly allocated 24 patients being treated in an inpatient unit to receive either no additional treatment or 12 sessions of social skills training. Routine treatment consisted of confinement to bed, a 3,000 calorie diet, individual and family psychotherapy, and milieu therapy. Social skills training focused first on increasing spontaneous speech and then on enhancing interpersonal skills using role playing and modeling.

Of the original 24 patients, 9 dropped out of treatment before the posttherapy assessment, 8 of whom were from the control group. These patients were replaced. However, according to our calculations, this dropout rate may have significantly biased group comparisons. In this case, the results ($\chi^2 = 3.2$; $p < 0.05$, one-tailed) suggest a possible beneficial effect of the social skills program in retaining patients.

The results of this study are somewhat difficult to interpret. Four weeks after restoration of normal body weight, no significant changes in social skills [as measured by the Social Avoidance Distance Scale (SAD), the Fear of Negative Evaluation Scale (FNE), and the H Scale of the CCEI] were found for either group pre- to posttreatment. At 1 year, only the FNE was significantly lowered ($p < .03$) and only for the treatment group. These data suggest that the social skills training program had weak effects on the generation and strengthening of social skills. Average length of hospitalization was 122.8 days for those receiving social skills training and 114 days for the control group. Efficiency, as measured by rate of weight gain, was low for both groups, with the treatment group gaining at 1.7 kg/month and the control group at 1.9 kg/month.

The process of treatment of the anorexic has also been studied in an attempt to identify which of several treatment procedures used in behavioral treatment were effective (1,22). The experimental method used was the controlled single-case study, with replication across cases. In the first experimental study, despite case reports suggesting that positive reinforcement was effective in producing weight gain (4–6,22), and the fact that the rate of weight gain increased after beginning reinforcement, when reinforcement was removed in the final experimental phase, weight gain continued at the same rate. These findings, confirmed in a replication, suggested that another variable was responsible for the continued improvement.

In a further study, this variable was shown to be negative reinforcement, gaining weight in order to leave hospital, an environment perceived as less than desirable by most patients (1). When negative reinforcement was removed by contracting with the patients (and their relatives) to stay in hospital whether or not they gained to target weight, then weight gain was shown to be contingent on the presence of positive reinforcement. This suggests that both positive and negative reinforcement promote weight gain and reminds us that reinforcing contingencies (either unplanned or planned) are present in all treatment programs for anorexia nervosa. For example, confining patients to bed until they gain to a set weight makes use of negative reinforcement. Thus, an experimental examination of the effectiveness of behavior therapy as compared with a standard therapy, is in fact comparing, among other things, the combination of positive and negative reinforcement against negative reinforcement alone.

Further experiments identified informational feedback as an important variable in modifying caloric intake and weight (1). In the presence of such feedback, patients were found to respond to positive reinforcement, but in its absence, no effect of reinforcement was apparent. In these experiments, feedback consisted of daily information concerning weight, as well as caloric feedback. Finally, the serving of large meals was found to enhance the amount of food consumed at any one sitting (1).

Thus, we can conclude from this series of experiments that several variables affect caloric intake and weight gain in anorexic patients within a therapeutic program. These include negative reinforcement, positive reinforcement, informational feedback, and the serving of large meals. A detailed description of the way in which such procedures are incorporated into a therapeutic program can be found elsewhere (2).

METHODOLOGIC CONSIDERATIONS

Before attempting to pull together the findings from the pooled data set and controlled studies into a pattern from which conclusions useful to the clinician may be derived, it is necessary to consider the methodologic limitations of these data. As the reader will have observed, methodologic problems in this research area are evident and are related primarily to: (a) the inconsistencies in measuring response to treatment and (b) the relative rarity of the condition, resulting in small sample sizes.

The overall methodologic problem of measurement is best seen by envisioning differential response to treatment as a race. If all the competitors begin at the same point and race the same distance, he who reaches the goal in the shortest time wins. If all begin at the same point and race for a fixed time, he who is ahead at the end of the time period wins. If all start at different points but race for a fixed time, he who goes furthest wins. However, if all begin at different points, have different goals, race for different periods of time, and move at varying rates, it is difficult, if not impossible, to declare the winner. Such is the case in anorexia studies. There are individual differences in admission weight (starting point) and in individual goals (ideal weight). Patients are treated for different periods of time and may gain weight at different rates at different parts of the therapy period. Under these circumstances, it is problematic to decide which of 2 patients has the better response and, consequently, which of two treatment groups shows the better response.

The situation is complicated even further since, because of the life-threatening nature of anorexia nervosa, new treatments are added to a standard treatment package and the combination compared to the standard package alone. The nature of standard treatment is not always well described. It is not always clear that patients are treated the same way even within a single study, making comparisons between studies even more difficult. The differential outcome between groups is, of course, narrowed with an additive design.

To overcome these difficulties, researchers investigating the treatment of anorexia nervosa should uniformly report for each patient, the admission and goal weight, weight at 15 days, 1, 2, 3 . . . months after treatment onset and the period of treatment. Not only would such a procedure resolve the problem of measurement, but it would also help remedy the second major problem, small sample sizes.

In the 21 studies included in the pooled data set, the median number of patients per study was 7, the 75th percentile was 11. Only three studies had more than 20 subjects. Yet, the magnitudes of observed differences between the treatment and control groups are such that 40 or more subjects per group would be required to demonstrate significant differences between either weight gains or posttreatment weights as the outcome measures. Only one published study had a sufficient sample size (11,15), and in this study, power was reduced markedly by limiting treatment time.

If measurements of posttreatment weight were routinely recorded at regular intervals over the treatment period (15 days; 1, 2, or 3 months; or even more frequently), one may use the average rate of weight gain (estimated by the slope of weight on time) as the response measure. With this measure the within-group variance is decreased because variance due to individual differences and that due to the inconsistency of subjects' responses are minimized. One would need fewer subjects with this measure of response to achieve the same power as one would with 40 subjects per group and either endpoint or change scores.

Finally, if such data were routinely reported, a data base of control subjects would begin to accrue from the perusal of many studies. Such a data base might then serve as historical control patients to assess newly proposed treatments. An individual researcher would then be in a position to assign all of his or her few available anorexics to a new treatment, using the historical control patients for comparison. This would elicit the greatest power possible to initially assess, in early studies, the effectiveness of the new treatment. Then, if the new treatment were promising, cooperative or more extensive randomized clinical trials might be more feasible.

DO TREATMENTS HAVE DIFFERENT EFFECTS?

Given these methodologic problems and the inadequate nature of the current data set drawn either from controlled studies or from our pooled data, what conclusions can be drawn concerning the differential outcome of different methods of treatment? Despite the inadequate nature of these data, the conclusions that may be drawn from each source of data are surprisingly consistent.

There is little converging evidence that pharmacologic agents add to the treatment of anorexia nervosa. In the pooled data set, those treated with drugs gained at a rate of 4.6 kg/month versus medical therapy 3.4 kg/month, a difference which was not significant. In the controlled studies, neither clomipramine nor cyproheptadine adds to the treatment of the average patient, although cyproheptadine may be of value in the patient with a poor prognosis. In the evaluation of lithium carbonate, baseline differences in caloric intake in favor of those receiving the active drug, suggest that the differential outcome was due to subject characteristics and not to the pharmacologic agent. Finally, both the advantages and disadvantages of the use of chlorpromazine rest on one quasiexperimental study with poor historical control.

In the case of *standard therapy* (for the most part similar to medical therapy in the pooled data set), the rate of weight gains tend to be low (median 3.6 kg/month) and comparable to the rate of gain in the pooled data set. Placebo conditions fall in the same range.

In general, only behavior therapy involving reinforcement of weight gain appears to add to standard treatment. This effect is quite marked in the pooled data set, and in both quasiexperimental, and single-case controlled studies. However, the largest controlled study (11) found no differences between standard treatment and the combination of standard treatment and reinforcement of small increments of weight gain. The major methodologic problem in this study was the short period of therapy, 35 days. This limitation may have limited study power. Assuming that weight gain would have been linear for both treatment conditions and that the average patient would need to gain 10.0 kg to return to ideal weight, then standard therapy would require 83 days to reach this target weight, and behavior therapy 71 days, a saving of 12 days and thousands of dollars in treatment costs. Perhaps a finding of clinical significance was missed because of the fixed brief length of treatment study design. It should also be noted that the same argument can be made for the failure to demonstrate effectiveness of cyproheptadine.

SOME CONCLUSIONS

As should be clear by now, the search for more effective approaches to the treatment of anorexia nervosa is fraught with methodologic problems, many of which are consequences of the relative rarity of the disorder and inconsistencies in the design and measurement procedures used in various studies. Moreover, we have not considered the differential outcome of treatment over the long term, mainly because little helpful information on this subject exists. The design of a long-term comparative outcome study would involve the treatment and follow-up of a large number of patients and the added problems of satisfactorily measuring long-term outcome (18). However, until one treatment approach consistently produces a superior short-term outcome, it would be difficult to know which treatments should be compared over the long term.

For the immediate future, then, controlled research should be aimed at identifying which components of the standard treatment package are, in fact, beneficial and to the identification of new treatment components. Single-case research, modest-sized controlled outcome studies using the response measure of slope of weight on time, and more detailed reporting of the results of each treated case would all seem helpful in clarifying the present uncertainties faced by clinicians in their daily treatment of this difficult disorder.

REFERENCES

1. Agras, W. S., Barlow, D. H., Chapin, H. N., Abel, G. G., and Leitenberg, H. (1974): Behavior Modification of anorexia nervosa. *Arch. Gen. Psychiatry,* 30:279–286.
2. Agras, W. S., and Werne, J. (1978): Behavior therapy in anorexia nervosa: A data-based approach to the question. In *Controversy in Psychiatry,* edited by J. P. Brady and H. K. H. Brodie, pp. 655–674. W. B. Saunders, New York.
3. Beck, J. C., and Brochner-Mortensen, K. (1954): Observations on the prognosis in anorexia nervosa. *Acta Med. Scand.,* 149:409–430.
4. Bhanji, S., and Thompson, J. (1974): Operant conditioning in the treatment of anorexia nervosa: A review and retrospective study of 11 cases. *Br. J. Psychiatry,* 124:166–172.
5. Bianco, F. J. (1972): Rapid treatment of two cases of anorexia nervosa. *J. Behav. Ther. Exp. Psychiatry,* 3:223–224.
6. Blinder, B. J., Freeman, D. A., and Stunkard, A. J. (1970): Behavior therapy of anorexia nervosa: Effectiveness of activity as a reinforcer of weight gain. *Am. J. Psychiatry,* 126:77–82.
7. Crisp, A. H. (1980): *Anorexia nervosa: Let me be.* Academic Press, London.
8. Crisp, A. H. (1983): Treatment and outcome in anorexia nervosa. In: *Eating and Weight Disorders,* edited by R. K. Goodstein, pp. 91–104. Springer, New York.
9. Crisp, A. H., Palner, R. L., and Kalucy, R. S. (1976): How common is anorexia nervosa? A prevalence study. *Br. J. Psychiatry,* 128:549–558.
10. Dally, P., and Sargant, W. (1966): Treatment and outcome of anorexia nervosa. *Br. Med. J.,* 2:793–795.
11. Eckert, E. D., Goldberg, S. C., Casper, R. C., and Davis, J. M. (1979): Behavior therapy in anorexia nervosa. *Br. J. Psychiatry,* 134:55–59.
12. Farquharson, R. F., and Hyland, H. H. (1966): Anorexia nervosa: The course of 15 patients treated from 20 to 30 years previously. *Can. Med. Assoc. J.,* 26:411–419.
13. Fohlin, L. (1978): Exercise performance and body dimensions in anorexia nervosa before and after rehabilitation. *Acta Med. Scand.,* 204:61–65.
14. Garfinkel, P. E., Kline, S. A., and Stancer, H. C. (1973): Treatment of anorexia nervosa using operant conditioning techniques. *J. Nerv. Ment. Dis.,* 157:428–433.
15. Goldberg, S. G., Halmi, K. A., Casper, R. C., and Davis, J. M. (1979): Cyproheptadine in anorexia nervosa. *Br. J. Psychiatry,* 134:67–70.
16. Groen, J. J., and Feldman-Toledano, Z. (1966): Educative treatment of patients and parents in anorexia nervosa. *Br. J. Psychiatry,* 112:671–682.
17. Gross, H. A., Ebert, M. H., Faden, V. V., Goldberg, S. C., Nee, L. E., and Kaye, W. H. (1981): A double-blind controlled trail of lithium carbonate in primary anorexia nervosa. *J. Clin. Psychopharmacol.,* 1:376–381.
18. Hsu, L. K. G. (1980): Outcome of anorexia nervosa: A review of the literature (1954 to 1978). *Arch. Gen. Psychiatry,* 37:1041–1043.
19. Hsu, L. K. G., and Lieberman, S. (1982): Paradoxical intention in the treatment of anorexia nervosa. *Am. J. Psychiatry,* 139:650–653.
20. Johanson, A. J., and Knorr, N. J. (1977): L-Dopa as treatment for anorexia nervosa. In: *Anorexia Nervosa,* edited by R. A. Vigersky. Raven Press, New York.
21. Lacey, J. H., and Crisp, A. H. (1980): Hunger, food intake and weight: The impact of clomipramine on a refeeding anorexia nervosa population. *Postgrad. Med. J.,* 56:79–85.
22. Leitenberg, H., Agras, W. S., and Thompson, L. (1968): A sequential analysis of the effect of selective positive reinforcement in modifying anorexia nervosa. *Behav. Res. Ther.,* 6:211–218.

23. Lucas, A. L., Duncan, J. W., and Piens, V. (1976): The treatment of anorexia nervosa. *Am. J. Psychiatry,* 133:1034–1038.

24. Maxmen, J. S., Siberfarb, M., and Ferrell, R. B. (1974): Anorexia nervosa: Practical initial management in a general hospital. J. A. M. A. 229:801–803.

25. Moldofsky, H., and Garfinkel, P. E. (1974): Problems of treatment of anorexia nervosa. *Can. J. Psychiatry,* 19:169–174.

26. Needleman, H. L., and Walker, D. (1977): The use of amitriptyline in anorexia nervosa. In: *Anorexia Nervosa,* edited by R. A. Vigersky. Raven Press, New York.

27. Pertschuk, M. J. (1977): Behavior Therapy: Extended follow-up. In: *Anorexia Nervosa,* edited by R. A. Vigersky. Raven Press, New York.

28. Pertschuk, M. J., Forster, J., Buzby, G., and Mullen, J. L. (1981): The treatment of anorexia nervosa with total parenteral nutrition. *Biol. Psychiatry,* 16:539–550.

29. Pillay, M., and Crisp, A. H. (1981): The impact of social skills training within an established in-patient treatment programme for anorexia nervosa. *Br. J. Psychiatry,* 139:533–539.

30. Poole, D. A., and Sanson-Fisher, R. W. (1978): A behavioral programme for the management of anorexia nervosa. *Aust. N. Z. J. Psychiatry,* 12:49–53.

31. Russell, G. F. M., and Mezey, A. G. (1962): An analysis of weight gain in patients with anorexia nervosa treated with high calorie diets. *Clin. Sci.,* 23:449–461.

32. Schwartz, D. M., and Thompson, M. G. (1981): Do Anorectics get well? Current research and future needs. *Am. J. Psychiatry,* 138:319–323.

33. Vigersky, R. A., and Loriaux, D. L. (1977): The effect of cyproheptadine in anorexia nervosa: A double blind trial. In: *Anorexia Nervosa,* edited by R. Vigersky, Raven Press, New York.

Eating and Its Disorders, edited by A. J. Stunkard and E. Stellar. Raven Press, New York © 1984.

The Psychopathology of Anorexia Nervosa: Getting the "Heat" out of the System

A. H. Crisp

Department of Psychiatry, St. George's Hospital Medical School, Tooting, London SW17 ORE, United Kingdom

Whilst I agree with others that anorexia nervosa is probably more common now than in times past, it is noteworthy that our predecessors of the 17th and 19th centuries in particular only had to show an interest in the condition for cases (including male cases) to be referred to them. In the 18th century, the condition seems to have been lost sight of for a while, and perhaps for reasons that I have touched on elsewhere (11), it reemerged as a more evident syndrome at the time of the late Hanoverians. For instance, it is now thought that Byron with his admixture of abstemiousness and hedonism probably had the syndrome alternating with abnormal weight control problems (33). In the 1930s, clinicians reported many cases, usually from the U.K. (2,37) and North America (1). Often particularly difficult to diagnose, it has through the ages readily leant itself to such fashionable disguises as the slender languishing female, the wasted tuberculous adolescent failing to recover, chlorosis (27), pituitary insufficiency, depression, idiopathic oedema, and many other conditions including, most recently, total food allergy (8,28).

Perhaps anorexia nervosa fascinates some of us because it reflects a coming together of so many determining factors, which can be expressed in cultural, social, experiential, and somatic dimensions. Indeed, it was used as a paradigm for the psychosomatic condition in their anthology by Kaufman and Heiman (25). I have a prejudice that many of the factors operating in anorexia nervosa that are readily categorised as primarily cultural in origin in fact have their mainsprings in the individual. Popular culture and widespread personal need probably mirror each other, especially given the present lack of structure from the past within culture itself. Current preoccupations with slimness in society are part of a long-standing concern by females about their fatness, by which I mean that fatness which is generated by puberty. I have always seen "Twiggy" and other thin idols mainly as reflecting rather than prompting the needs of the majority in this respect.

Thus, cultural forces relevant to anorexia nervosa seem to me to have to do with the adolescent female's perception of the society she is entering in much broader terms than simply shape, namely, its degree of structure and limit setting through custom and institutions of a religious and secular kind, its values and its degree of caring set against her own emerging impulses, sense of competence and self-esteem, and the value systems of the family from which she stems. In our present day chaotic society, self-discipline sometimes has to take more extreme forms. The ancient role explicitly reflecting cultural values and which has most similarities to anorexia nervosa is that of the ascetic, with its discipline, frugality, abstinence, and stifling of the passions associated with a search for placation, reunion with his God and purification (11). Anorexia nervosa surely has similar motivations contained within the family. The apparently politically motivated hunger striker may have such an ascetic focus promoting his stance and enabling him to adopt it. Indeed, perhaps the core of many such stances, whatever label they attract, is actually anorexia nervosa, but with a cultural mask. It seems to me that anorexia nervosa is a biological solution to an existential problem in our modern society. Thus, the potential for anorexia nervosa stems from aspects of physical and social background factors interacting in the individual's present experience. It is then precipitated out by a relevant challenging adolescent experience. As such it is the ultimate illustration of social need completely overriding the normal biological set point regulatory mechanisms of mature body weight. It, therefore, requires diagnostic attention at physical, experiential, behavioral, and social levels.

DIAGNOSIS OF ANOREXIA NERVOSA

The diagnosis of anorexia nervosa has, of course, many somatic aspects to it including the presence of low body weight and amenorrhea. There are some pervasive physical characteristics, probably having genetic and/or experiential origins (e.g., gender, growth, lipid metabolism). It is also recognised that severe or prolonged abstinence, especially when body weight is thereby maintained well below set point levels and is comparable to levels characterising the beginnings of the adolescent growth spurt, can promote bingeing (3,4) and indeed that one day's food intake influences subsequent sleep and probably thereby the next day's food intake (12). However, this chapter is concerned primarily with the psychopathology and social background to the condition, and I believe that this aspect of the diagnosis falls into three main categories (9): 1. The behavioral/expressive syndrome. 2. Identification of the central, pathognomonic mechanism of phobic *avoidance* stance. 3. The precipitating maturational conflict. Two other areas of background pathology also deserve separate and specific attention, namely: (a) the identification of predisposing factors to the development of anorexia nervosa as a solution of choice to the maturational problem, and (b) the identification of indicators with prognostic significance for the further natural evolution of the disorder.

The Behavioral/Expressive Syndrome

In the western world, one can often correctly recognise the anorectic at a distance. The evidence comes from the behavior and expressed emotions of the obviously emaciated and usually isolated, self-absorbed, and otherwise wary, young woman.

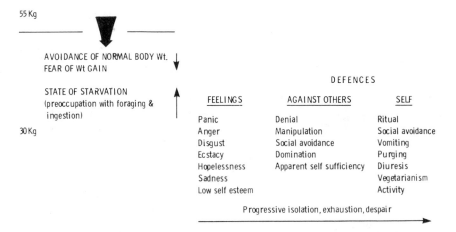

FIG. 1. Elements of the behavioral/expressive syndrome. They reflect the anorectic's endless battle against weight gain through ingestion and incorporation of food. Unlike the fear of weight gain itself, they are readily enough expressed and directly observable.

The author has always argued that anorexia nervosa is egosyntonic and reflects an attempt to adapt to and cope with maturational problems through the mechanism of *avoidance* of biological maturity. Such a coping style, as is the case with drug/alcohol dependence, will not be surrendered willingly or easily. It is a last resort, and its preservation depends on keeping others and also the impulse to ingest at bay. Attempts to glorify the state as allowing the individual an autonomy do less than justice to the secret misery and terror within the condition, which reduces all those with it to something less than their unique selves, to such an extent that it is even difficult to distinguish the female from the male. It requires never-ending vigilance and denial of those central concerns to which others are often not privy but which in fact govern the behavioral/expressive syndrome. The anorectic has her back to the wall. Within this context, she is often seen by others as being extremely manipulative and hysterical whilst her manner and moods are found unpredictable. Her rituals, her shoplifting, her alcoholism, her occasional depression, and her ecstasy through relief at successful control of her stance are likely to be misconstrued and deeply puzzling and distressing to those around her. Meanwhile, the bitter irony for the anorectic, unmitigated and in fact reinforced by her ambivalence, is her unavoidable preoccupation with ingestion, driven by her starving state, when basically her task is to avoid such ingestion. She is condemned endlessly and in isolation to think about the plentiful food around her (Fig. 1).

Weight Phobia

This term is a shorthand for those central and pathognomonic mechanisms within anorexia nervosa which provide its experiential and usually secret core.

Such fear can, of course, exist at normal mature body weight and be a force within abnormal normal weight control or bulimia nervosa (10,13,32,35). In anorexia nervosa, it is accompanied by progressive and thereafter sustained *avoidance* of mature body weight. Sustaining this avoidance stance often requires insistent denial to others and sometimes also to themselves, but the central concern is indeed body weight. Emergence of anorexia nervosa, as distinct from effective dieting in adolescence which is common enough, does not seem to the author to be consciously directed. This reversal of the pubertal process, which is a psycho-biological regression permitting avoidance of the self at normal body weight (Fig. 2), seems more to overtake the anorectic, almost like puberty itself had done in the first instance. The experience is simply one of the rewards of rapid relief of anxiety. The relief perhaps comes from the rapidly diminishing resting and basal metabolic activity which accompanies calorie deprivation and minor degrees of weight loss. This process may be designed by nature to defend normal body weight and the related maintenance of core body temperature. Reproductive potential is then rapidly shut down as indicated by early cessation of menstruation, together with shut down of peripheral circulation. Perhaps, the anorectic experiences this abrupt and selective shedding of energy demands with relief. Thus, as the more immediately expendable heat goes out of the biological system, its fearful experiential counterpart also melts away. Calorie restriction is further reinforced, body fat and weight loss continue and puberty itself is reversed. Unfortunately, for the anorectic her new found weight is biologically unstable, and indeed she has to defend further against the difficulties of maintaining her weight at the threshold of puberty.

Meanwhile, the newly fledged anorectic feels better and safer, like any phobic person who has put distance between the object and themselves. The anorectic has

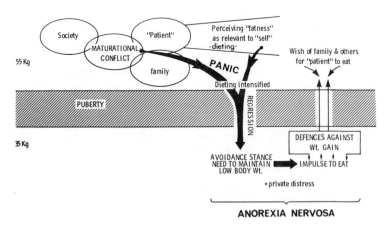

FIG. 2. The emergence of anorexia nervosa as the phobic avoidance stance, in relation to self at normal body weight, crystallises out. The issue now for the anorectic is *Let me be* (either let me be myself or else leave me alone) (11).

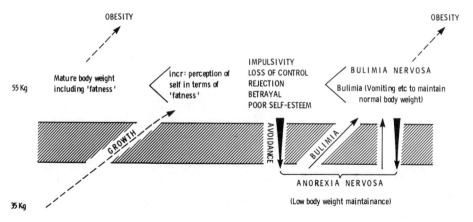

FIG. 3. Some major areas of difficulty, however undifferentiated, that have confronted the anorectic prior to her "adopting" the "solution" of anorexia nervosa. The relationship with abnormal normal weight control (bulimia nervosa) is depicted.

rarely formulated or been able to communicate to others the initial anxiety or its origins at a conceptual/verbal level. Meanwhile, the original adolescent conflict and turmoil is now replaced instead exclusively by a mounting panic of once more being exposed to weight gain—a process potentially outside her control and promoting circumstances outside her control. Thus, fear of and the need to avoid normal body weight is the overriding force that generates and maintains the condition. Some of the larger meanings of normal body weight which emerge in the treatment of anorectics are listed in Fig. 3.

Maturational Conflict

When an anorectic appears in the clinic, there is little in the way of maturational conflict. Such conflict may or may not have been readily evident in the past. It may or may not now be readily recalled. Instead, the family is now dismayed by the anorexia nervosa in their midst—its domination of the family and what they sometimes regard as its explicit indictment of them. Parents usually display hopelessness, anger, and guilt in this situation. The majority of anorectic families are intact, caring, and over involved. The terminology to describe them adopted by Minuchin et al. (29) of being enmeshed and of avoiding conflict at any price is apt. At presentation, it is now the anorexia nervosa which is expressing the ultimate in maturational conflict avoidance within the family. If the anorectic leaves home, she takes the potential conflict, which may thereby even become intensified, with her.

The maturational conflict has its origins in the impact of puberty leading to adolescence. Anorexia nervosa can arise at the very onset of puberty, long before the menarche, and reflect an immediate necessary staving off of and retreat from such development (Fig. 4). The forces at work at this stage are likely to be those

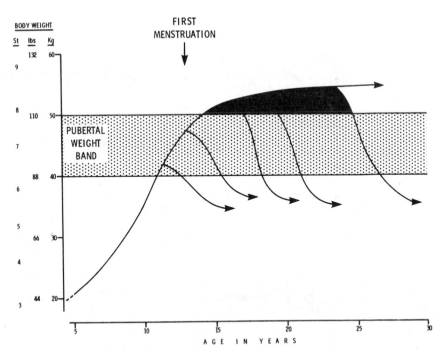

FIG. 4. Diagrammatic representation of the core range of age of onset in relation to pubertal development in anorexia nervosa.

Anorexia nervosa can arise very early in puberty (the menarche is late pubertal event) and give rise to the false conclusions that it is occurring in a child. In fact, it will have arisen within the terrifying experience of the early pubertal changes, dimly perceived (and often thereafter denied) by the individual and family as the harbingers of enforced unacceptable and terrifying change. The pubertal process may itself be early, growth towards biological maturity having ironically been fostered by zealous and overprotective nurturing in childhood.

that threaten the bonds and security of childhood. Just as a school-phobic child is responding to an overprotective and phobic mother, so often is the anorectic who had begun to experience and display the earliest impact of puberty. Such problems may have to do more with separation than with gender or other aspects of identity. The tasks of adolescence have otherwise to do with negotiating an exit from the family and at the same time forging peer relationships which leave self-esteem and regard intact and family bonds viable but redefined. Emerging defiance, sexuality, and hidden characteristics (often long submerged characteristics of one or other parent) may be the focus of conflict. Food may have been an overvalued social currency of childhood. Sex is now the potential currency. Such conflict can be delayed in its expression until later in adolescence or else responded to by other defences such as dedication to school work, dancing, athletics, agoraphobia, obesity, etc. It may then be released or require the more absolute defence of anorexia nervosa through such experiences as a sexual encounter, death of a parent, or change of occupation. Occasionally, the precipitant of anorexia

TABLE 1. *The experiential gulf and some of its origins*

Prepuberty	Puberty	Postpuberty
	Adolescence	
Asexuality	Sexuality (and associated "fatness")	
The family and its mores and social currencies	The outside world and its mores and social currencies	
traditional	"progressive"	
religious	nonreligious	
masked indifference/ambivalence	exposed indifference/ambivalence	
Dependent	"Independent"	
Compliant	Rebellious	
Controlled	Impulsive	
Loved	Rejected	
Possessed	Abandoned	
Esteemed	Devalued	
Parental values	Peer values	
Parental "secrets" maintained	Parental "secrets" exposed by reenactment	
Parents' incompatibilities concealed	Parents' incompatibilities revealed	
Family conflict avoided	Family conflict exposed	
Parents together	Parents split	
Like father	Like mother (and rejected by father)	
Like mother	Like father (and rejected by mother)	
Academically committed	Academically indifferent	

nervosa is the threatened disintegration of the parental marriage—which now evidently needs children in it to ensure its survival.

Thus, anorexia nervosa is a state of compulsory detention with a variety of mainsprings. In that fact lie special problems for those who align themselves with attempts simply to compel the anorectic to eat, with or without her enforced confinement. Table 1 lists the kinds of experiential gulf that can loom for the adolescent, the bridging of which has proved too much for the anorectic and which will become increasingly difficult to cross the longer the delay imposed by the persistence of the anorexia nervosa.

BACKGROUND FACTORS

Background factors can be usefully looked at in terms of the maturational conflict—which has many elements not specific to anorexia nervosa, and factors which are specific to the anorexia nervosa. These factors are present (a) within society in terms of both its fabric and values, (b) within the parents individually and together, and within the larger family, and (c) within the individual concerned. Clearly, there is overlap and interaction between categories, and insofar as they contribute to aetiology, they are reflected within the psychopathology of the anorexia nervosa and are likely to affect its prognosis in various ways.

Social and Cultural Factors

Social and cultural factors are the least easy to be certain about. Some have been touched on earlier in this chapter, especially in respect of attitudes to female body shape. The author believes that anorexia nervosa has increased in incidence at least in part because it provides one solution to problems of adolescent expression and its limitation in a society largely bereft of limits itself. For instance, the structure, restraints, and relief provided by such previously recognised processes as courtship and engagement are no longer so readily available as temporary buttresses to adolescent sexual anxiety. Treading water is now more difficult. Equally, religious doctrine and affiliation with its rules does not now seem credible or acceptable for the majority. Mass communication introduces everyone to the apparent acceptability of conduct which may be vastly dissonant from that held dear by the family. Adolescent straitjackets do remain (e.g., search for academic achievement coupled with economic dependence on parents, membership of minority religious sects) and are then in sharp contrast to the main culture. When the author has found anorexia nervosa in Arabs and Indians, then it has usually been within this particular context of a major cultural gulf dividing the adolescent from her traditional background (e.g., Moslem versus Western society). In contrast, when he has seen it in Chinese and Negroes, then it has more often been within the context of an intracultural clash involving middle class values and typical of our indigenous subculture clashes. Our society also permits rapid movement through the social classes by successive generations, which has the same effect across generations within a family. On top of this comes ever-increasing rapidity of change within society. The generation gap gets bigger and more difficult for both parents and adolescents to bridge. It does not surprise him that adolescents are thrown back on their own resources in such a way that the more robust mature rapidly, whilst the more vulnerable collapse rapidly.

Factors within society specific to anorexia nervosa have, I think, to do with views it feeds back to teenagers concerning female shape and with the emphasis on glorifying it as sexual on the one hand and on curbing it on the other. Perhaps this fuels the uncertain and self-doubting adolescent's fantasy that her shape is crucial to her destiny as an adult on the one hand, whilst at the same time having the potential to bring about her downfall.

No comment about cultural factors would be complete without reference to epidemiological studies concerning teenage attitudes to body weight and shape. Major surveys of this kind were undertaken by Huenemann et al. (24) in the U.S.A. and by Nylander (31) in Scandinavia. Nylander studied a representative group of 2,000 subjects aged 14 to 19 and including 1,241 girls during the year 1970. Most girls in the study reported that at some time they had felt fat, although obesity in terms of overweight was not a marked feature of the overall population. The experience as a current phenomenon was most common amongst the 18-year-olds (50%) but was already present in 26% of 14-year-olds. Of the girls who thought that they were fat, many had attempted to diet (e.g., 40% of the 18-year-olds). The majority reported only minor weight losses in response to dieting, but the number of subjects reporting a loss of more than 5 kg increased with age. Overall, over 10% of subjects reported such a loss as having occurred at some stage. Thirty-four of the girls reported at least 3 months amenorrhea during such times. Fifteen of them had lost 10 kg or more in weight. It appeared that 1 in 150 unequivocally had developed anorexia nervosa, it being independently diagnosed in local clinics; but Nylander concluded by stating that if mild cases were included it could be said that approximately 1 in 10 of the girls in the study reported experiencing an anorexia nervosa syndrome. He identified the feeling of being fat as a predeterminant but did not explore further in his study the meaning and implications of this. Around the same time Oliver Russell, also conducting a school study in Bristol, England, concluded that as many as 4% of them may have had anorexia nervosa (36).

In 1972, the author together with Palmer and Kalucy, conducted a similar survey to that of Nylander, and up until now we have presented very little of these data. The study focused on schoolgirls aged 11 to 19 and their concern about shape, their associated behavior, and its relationship to body weight and biological maturation. It was a questionnaire study involving just under 2,000 schoolgirls and was part of an investigation of the prevalence of severe anorexia nervosa (20).

Within this population, 25% expressed concern about their weight at some stage since the age of 11 (Table 2). From the age of 15, this was the majority of the population. Such concern during the last 3 months was greatest amongst 17-year-olds (61%). These data are remarkably similar to those reported by Nylander. For 13- to 15-year-olds, this concern about weight and shape was greater in those who were postmenarchal at the time (Table 3). Menarche is, of course, a late event in puberty lasting 3 or more years and is usually associated early on with the deposition of fat which contributes substantially to the mature female shape.

TABLE 2. *Those concerned about weight (a) since age of 11 and (b) past 3 months*

Age (years)	(a)	(%)	(b)	(%)
11–12	12 out of 47	25.5	16 out of 47	34.0
12–13	90 out of 232	38.8	89 out of 235	37.9
13–14	145 out of 346	41.9	146 out of 360	40.6
14–15	157 out of 347	45.2	160 out of 352	45.5
15–16	183 out of 355	51.5	179 out of 362	49.4
16–17	130 out of 234	55.6	111 out of 236	47.0
17–18	114 out of 171	66.7	105 out of 171	61.4
18–19	62 out of 101	61.4	49 out of 103	47.6

TABLE 3. *Concern about weight in last 3 months related to the menarche*

Age (years)	Premenarche	Percent	Postmenarche	Percent	p value (χ^2)
11–12	14 out of 43	32.6	2 out of 4	50.0	—
12–13	57 out of 156	36.5	32 out of 79	40.5	—
13–14	36 out of 131	27.5	110 out of 229	48.0	0.0002
14–15	11 out of 40	27.5	149 out of 312	47.8	0.024
15–16	5 out of 11	45.5	174 out of 351	49.6	—
16–17	0 out of 3	—	111 out of 223	47.6	—
17–18	1 out of 1	—	104 out of 170	61.2	
18–19			49 out of 103	47.6	
19–20			6 out of 12	50.0	
20+			3 out of 4	75.0	

Of those concerned about their weight who have managed at some stage to lose weight, the majority reported to have achieved this by dieting.

The prevalence of vomiting in the population was studied, and this pattern of behavior was admitted to as occurring quite often or frequently (daily) in around 3% of the population with peaks amongst the 13- and 15-year-olds for those who are premenarchal (Table 4). Within this section of the population, the 2 subjects reporting it in the 15-year-old bracket may, of course, have been anorectic (they were in fact more than one standard deviation below mean weight for their age in contrast to the vomiting population as a whole whose mean weight was not significantly different from others). Peaks of prevalence of often or frequent vomiting occur in the 13- and 18-year-old age bands in the postmenarchal group. In each age bracket from 14 years onward, thin girls (more than one standard deviation below mean weight/height^2) reported significantly later menarches than others. Moreover, in every age group those who were premenarchal were significantly lighter (weight/height^2). Birthweight correlated with adolescent weight. All these findings accord with the majority of established epidemiological evidence (see 6,16). Figure 5 shows mean body weight and fatness characteristics of the population by age. Noteworthy is the peak mean and standard deviation for fatness amongst the 17-year-olds and the lower mean and tighter standard deviation for fatness amongst the 18-year-olds.

Not too much should be read into such cross-sectionals but these data, coupled with the high percentage expressing concern about their weight and with Nylander's data, suggest concern about shape which has become common by this age and is associated shortly afterwards with reduced fatness. If this is indeed the seed bed of anorexia nervosa, then it would be in accord with data (Fig. 6) concerning the mean age of onset of anorexia nervosa as being 17 years and 6 months (age of onset of severe dieting behavior) and 18 years and 3 months (age at last menstrual period) (7). This mean age of onset, reflecting a tight normal distribution of age of onset, apart from a very few exceptions involving much later onset, is remarkably similar in most reported large series of cases, e.g., Dally (21).

TABLE 4. Vomiting related to menarche (expressed as percent)

			Premenarche						Postmenarche		
Age	N	Never	Occasionally	Quite Often	Frequently	N	Never	Occasionally	Quite Often	Frequently
11–12	43	48.8	48.8	—	2.3	4	50.0	50.0	—	0
12–13	156	35.3	61.5	2.6	0.6	79	40.5	55.7	3.8	0
13–14	131	41.2	54.2	3.8	0.8	229	42.4	53.3	3.9	0.4
14–15	40	47.5	52.5	0	0	312	49.7	47.8	1.6	1.0
15–16	11	18.2	63.6	18.2	0	351	41.6	55.6	1.4	1.4
16–17	3	66.7	33.3	0	—	223	43.8	54.1	2.1	—
17–18						170	51.8	44.7	2.9	0.6
18–19						103·	42.7	52.4	3.9	1.0

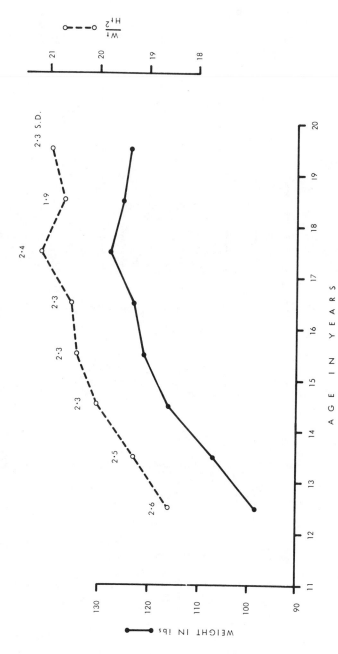

FIG. 5. "Fatness" in teenage females. Mean fatness (measured wt/ht^2) in a female adolescent school and college population (2,000 subjects). The increased fatness in the 17–18-year-olds could be based in selection factors (e.g., social class) for continued education at this period. However, the decline in fatness in the 18–19-year-olds probably relates more directly within the same population. One interpretation of the data is that, as growth comes to a halt around 15–17 years, residual earlier adolescent bingeing persists but within 2 years has subsided or been curbed by increased dietary control. The desire to be slimmer is probably at its peak around this period, and the mean age of onset of anorexia nervosa itself is 17 ½ years (see 11,13). (Reproduced by kind permission of the International Journal of Psychiatry in Medicine.)

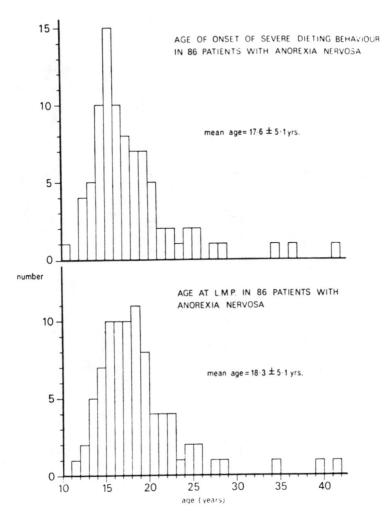

FIG. 6. Age of onset of anorexia nervosa showing a peak at 15 years and a mean age of 17–18 years. Although puberty primes the individual for the development of anorexia nervosa, its onset can be precipitated years later by such events as completion of circumscribed dependent-type tasks such as class examinations, realignments in the family including deaths, etc.

WITHIN THE FAMILY

So far as the maturational conflict is concerned I have tried elsewhere to illustrate this by examples (11) and have touched on its more immediate aspects as they seem relevant to me as a clinician earlier in this chapter. The more distant origins of such conflict have to do with the previous role of the anorectic within the family, sometimes importantly including the meaning of her conception and actual existence (Fig. 7). Beyond this loom the dynamic forces operating within

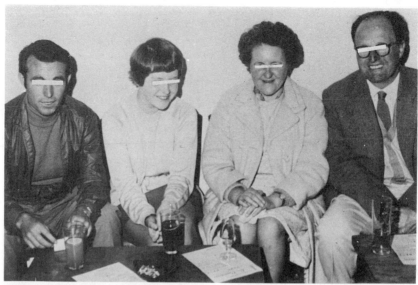

FIG. 7. These two family photographs, taken one year apart whilst on vacation abroad graphically illustrate the dynamics in case a of anorexia nervosa. The family's nature is to avoid conflict. Mother is a nurse. Father is an authoritarian working man with strict views about sexual conduct. The top picture shows them with their preanorectic daughter age 14 years. Here she is on their periphery, sitting next to an attentive older man to whom she became attached as her first love. Typically she gained some weight whilst on the holiday and felt uncomfortable. In psychotherapy she was able to share the turmoil consequent on this relationship. The next year she sits anorectic and childlike between her parents, and it is her younger brother who is now on the periphery of the family and who proceeded to grow away from it. The central fear in this family was of female sexuality, with its origins evident in the parents' backgrounds and personal relationship.

the larger family. Sometimes, a grandparent plays a critical role directly and indirectly, similarly with a sibling.

Factors specific to anorexia nervosa within the family are, in my experience, highly variable in their expression. I can merely list some that strike one as obvious from time to time but which are clearly not necessary for the condition to develop. They include obesity and anorexia nervosa (e.g., in the spinster aunt or the mother or more often in the siblings or their spouses); undue preoccupation with nurturing (e.g., overfeeding grandmother or mother involved with school meals) or with physical fitness and extreme mastery of the body; alcohol dependence in one or more parents and perhaps, more marginally, avoidance behavior in relation to conflict, which sometimes expresses itself as social anxiety or frank agoraphobia. Such aviodance patterns provide the template for the avoidance mechanisms arising now as the essence of anorexia nervosa. The propensity to respond to life stresses with depressive illness appears to be a common feature within the family.

WITHIN THE INDIVIDUAL

Here, it is perhaps the most difficult and the least productive to try and sort out specific and nonspecific factors. Clearly, being female is one and experiencing puberty is another factor. A tendency to be younger born has been reported in several studies. Above average intelligence characterises anorectics but is probably complexly interwoven with social class factors as a predeterminant. The author has had 2 patients, 1 female and 1 male, with Down's Syndrome (IQ less than 50) with anorexia nervosa. In one the syndrome erupted in his teens; in the other at 35, when her delayed adolescence was precipitated by separation from her ageing parents.

The meaning of fatness is in my experience highly variable for anorectics. It ranges from general distaste for what is being experienced (e.g., pubertal changes there and then) through to specific disgust in relation to some aspect of such fatness, e.g., legs, thighs, waist, buttocks, or breasts. The meaning of fat at such sites varies from person to person. For one its presence (e.g., legs) means being like mother; for another it means being pregnant or out of control (e.g., waist). Subsequently, of course, within the illness any return of fat will usually be experienced initially as evidence of loss of control. Classic preoccupation within anorexia nervosa with fatness as evidence of pregnancy and, otherwise, as evidence of being out of control is displayed in people with fluctuating anorexia nervosa who have pregnancies. Some anorectics feel much better in respect of their inner fears while pregnant. Occasionally they may binge, with an excess of the feelings more common amongst pregnant women that restraint is less necessary than usual, because the weight gain can be attributed to the pregnancy. More often such people watch their diets carefully and may only gain a few pounds or precisely the estimated weight of the baby during the pregnancy. Under these circumstances, vomiting of early pregnancy is not all that common. However, old anorectic fears are usually rekindled following the birth of the baby. Either the existence of the baby itself or, for instance, the now evident residue of body fat especially round the waist may trigger old anxieties about sexual guilt and impulse control problems, and then flight back into anorexia nervosa will often occur.

Anorexia nervosa is a desperate solution to maturational problems and is only likely to arise if less primitive and less self-destructive postures are unattainable (e.g., agoraphobia, which I believe is common in young schoolgirls as a neurotic stance—my teacher friends tell me that many of the 14- to 15-year-old girls in their classes never go out and respond with panic to any social pressures; or else staying with problems albeit experiencing low self-esteem coupled with less focal adolescent panic and depression). At the stage at which anorexia nervosa develops, other coping mechanisms are not apparently available. Often the problems seem to have been overwhelming and not conceptualised or shared with others. Many anorectics are revealed as having been good, complaint children. The anorexia nervosa is an unrecognised and usually doomed attempt to maintain this role following the intrusion of puberty. If low self-esteem and need for approval have been the basis for such childhood compliance, then they are often well buried beneath apparent confidence within an enmeshed family. It is puberty that has shattered the dream and which is now banished.

The other side of this primitive and unstable preanorectic state has been the emergence of pubertal impulse, which will often be denied but which has been experienced as overwhelming and may have mirrored long-hidden, parental experience and fantasies, as previously suggested. Some such personal experiences of the incipient anorectic were indicated in Fig. 1.

Obesity is another background factor, being overrepresented in some series of anorectics and reflecting many factors already touched on.

PROGNOSTIC INDICATORS

The prognostic studies of Morgan and Russell (30), and those of Crisp et al. (19) and Hsu et al. (23), which were investigating different subpopulations of patients from one large clinic series, have turned up very similar prognostic indicators. A number can be subsumed, partly at least by the heading Duration of Illness.

1. Thus, beyond a certain point, say 3 or 4 years, chronicity predicts chronicity. The average duration of illness reported in one series (18) in those destined to recover naturally is 4.6 ± 2.5 years. Beyond this, the longer the disorder has lasted the more difficult, from a clinical standpoint, it appears to be for the anorectic to recover and catch up with her peers, although it remains possible especially with treatment.

Bingeing coupled with vomiting and purging as a means of maintaining low body weight are associated with a poor prognosis in the female, and some element of this association would seem to be due to the association between this last ditch resort to low body weight maintenance and chronicity. Thus, the behavior only usually emerges after the illness has become established through abstinence. Such behavior is, however, also related to wider problems of impulse control (5), which include such problems preceding the development of the anorexia nervosa and which the author also believes predict poor outcome in the female. In contrast, a clinical picture which includes vomiting in the male anorectic is not associated with poor outcome (15).

2. Premorbid obesity. This, too, predicts a poor outcome. It is associated with high growth rate (e.g., early puberty), bingeing, vomiting, and purging within the anorexia nervosa. It is especially overrepresented in those who alternate between anorexia nervosa and abnormal normal weight control/bulimia nervosa (13).

3. Inability to forge friendships with other children during childhood. Perhaps this characteristic makes it even more difficult to cope with such tasks in adolescence.

4. Social class. Middle-class value systems seem especially to breed anorexia nervosa whatever the social class of the parents defined in terms of occupation. Anorexia nervosa arising outside this context and where working-class families will be overrepresented, confers a poorer prognosis for the female anorectic as reported by Hsu et al. (23) but not by Morgan and Russell (30). This relationship does not appear to hold for males (15).

5. Measured parental neurotic character structure and the presence of anxiety and depression within the mother and/or father at the time of presentation confers a poorer prognosis following treatment (17), as does marital conflict, covert or overt, as independently rated.

6. High degree of obsessionality/rigidity in the father is associated with poor impulse control in the anorectic coupled with bingeing and vomiting and, thus, with poor prognosis (35).

7. High levels of denial and low levels of expressed anxiety at the time of restored body weight within treatment, predict a poor outcome (38).

8. Being male. Outcome is marginally poorer amongst males according to one comparative study (15).

9. Marriage. The poor outcome associated with marriage is unrelated to chronicity but may owe something to lateness of onset. Clinically, it appears evident that marriage may perpetuate the condition at least for those who have married within it.

TREATMENT

Treatment is touched on here because of the ways in which it can illustrate aspects of psychopathology. The author's experience is rooted in a mode of treatment which first involves attempting to enable the anorectic to become a patient (11). Treatment involves the surrender by the anorectic of the low body weight control mechanism, the avoidance stance, and subsequent restoration of body weight to the average adult level for the population of an age the same as that at which the patient developed the anorexia nervosa. (The concept being that if she is now 22 years old but fell ill at 14, then since that time she has, in effect, sustained herself at a regressed prepubertal age of say less than 9 years and now needs to pick up the challenges of emotional growth as if she was 14 years old again.) This gradual reexposure to adult body weight, via the threshold of reexperienced puberty, can be pursued through direct behavioral measures but requires concurrent attention to the consequent maturational, experiential challenge through the processes of psychotherapy; otherwise, the patient will be unlikely to tolerate such change and will revert to her anorectic role. This psychotherapeutic task, within inpatient care, can be facilitated by a supportive multidisciplinary background, while the specific focus is on some aspect of the psychopathology. This can vary, for example, from grief work to freeing up communication on adolescent issues within the family, attempting to renegotiate the adolescent's exit from the family, coming to terms with some specific aspect of body shape, or social skills training. Above all else, transference problems, which are ever present and which can be fuelled by the attention to controlled feeding, need to be vigorously tackled from the outset.

This treatment approach enables us to study such processes within the realistic context of reemerging puberty. In its early stages, it exposes hidden defence mechanisms, such as diuretic abuse, and can expose bland denial of difficulties to such a proposed approach by the anorectic. During the period of 1960 to 1979, the author and his teams have treated 329 patients in this way. Mean height was 163 $\pm$ 6.5 cm. Mean admission weight was 39.3 $\pm$ 6.3 kg (average 70.4% matched mean population mean weight). Three hundred ten of these patients achieved target weight (100% matched population mean weight), i.e., an average of 54.2 kg over periods ranging from 6 to 12 weeks, dependent on degree of initial underweight and with weight gain occurring in a more or less linear fashion at the rate of 1.5 kg/week. Nineteen patients discharged themselves at a weight of 42.3 $\pm$ 3.4 kg, being unable to cope with early pubertal stirrings and the prospect of further weight gain. Six illustrative cases are described below, although essentially at this level of intervention, every case is unique. Indeed, the treatment's challenge and excitement is essentially this: The loss of individuality inherent in anorexia nervosa, which reduces all people with it to a lowest common denominator, is shed. Instead, everyone is grappling with those individual problems which are identifiable in the main within the third level of diagnosis referred to earlier. With such an approach, recovery after 20 years of illness is sometimes possible. Not all will make it, especially immediately, but striving is sometimes ultimately helpful (11). Some anorectics, however, have their stability and survival endangered by any such unwarranted intrusion and are best enabled instead to lead an anorectic life with as much dignity as possible.

CASE HISTORIES

Case 1 (Fig. 8) Jennifer comes from a close-knit middle-class (medical) family. Her parents believe modestly that at least two of their other three children are geniuses!

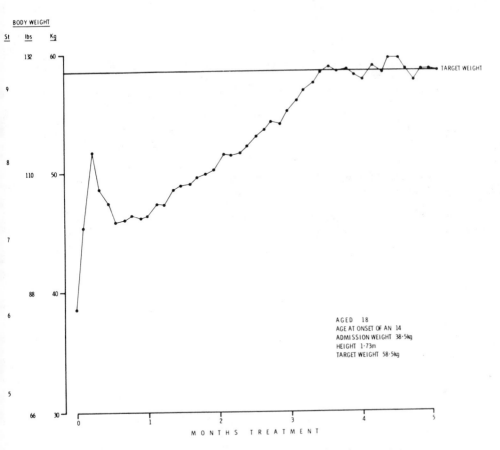

FIG. 8. Case no. 1. Weight chart; in-patient treatment program.

Although they insist that they are liberal in outlook, they attach absolute importance to academic and artistic achievement, and they maintain fitness by regular sports including jogging. Jennifer, whom the parents had expected to be a boy, kept pace with the rest of the family. By the age of 13, she was a junior county athletic champion and a member of a national youth orchestra. Tall and thin, she watched herself for any sign of flabbiness and was dismayed by evidence of her developing puberty. She accompanied the youth orchestra as its youngest member to a series of concerts given in Europe. She was astonished and intrigued at what she regarded as the free and easy sexual behavior of some of her colleagues and terrified by the advances of an older boy. Unable to mingle or exercise, she was lonely, ate more than usual, and returned home with a "tummy" that immediately attracted comment from the family. Stringent dieting then and there precipitated anorexia nervosa. For the next several years, Jennifer continued to do very well at school and at athletics, although she gave up her music.

As an aid to the maintenance of low body weight, she secretly purged herself. The parents were now distressed at their explicit failure as reflected in Jennifer. They willingly entered treatment together with her. The dramatic initial weight gain reflecting abandonment of purgative abuse followed by an overswinging rehydration settled down in the usual way so that overall weight gain was linear.

Jennifer and her parents worked well in psychotherapy. The parents changed significantly, becoming more open with each other and less rigid in their behavior and expectations. Unexpectedly in this case, the continued viability of their marriage became an issue for examination. They had begun to wonder whether in fact they were compatible. Further discussions left it seemingly likely that the marriage would survive on a new basis, each partner welcoming the prospect of greater freedom to pursue his or her own interests. For Jennifer, the inpatient milieu with its psychotherapeutic basis and openness for discussion was helpful. It was agreed that she retain her athleticism and vegetarianism as elements of her nature that antedated the anorexia nervosa.

Case 2 (Fig. 9) Sally's anorexia nervosa had started when she was age 16, following her widowed father's first frank sexual advances. A childhood favourite of her father's, she had been torn between him and her mother, who used to regale her with stories of her father's sexual demands and violence. Sally had always found him affectionate and thoughtful and thought her mother was envious of their relationship. When she was 14

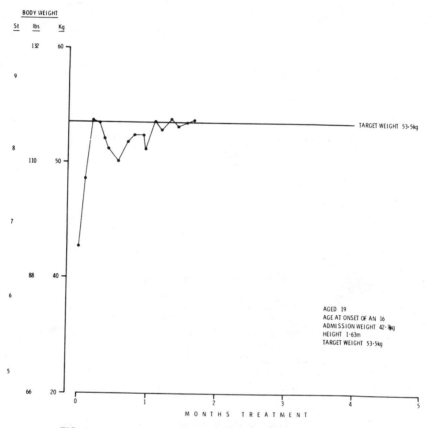

FIG. 9. Case no. 2. Weight chart; in-patient treatment program.

her mother died, and Sally increasingly helped her father out in his work as a publican. She began to drink alcohol in considerable quantities and was a well liked barmaid. When her dietary attempts erupted into anorexia nervosa at 17, she began to binge and vomit after about 6 months. Ankle oedema introduced her, via her general practitioner, to diuretics which thereafter she abused. She was admitted to hospital in coma following an overdose and agreed to enter treatment for her anorexia nervosa together with her father.

Although only just over 40 kg, she was menstruating regularly. Within 4 days of ceasing to abuse diuretics, she had gained over 10 kg in weight, revealing her more true weight and the actual basis for her continuing menstruation. At this stage, she was revealed more as a case of bulimia nervosa. After a few weeks of attempting to live within the constraints of the anorectic treatment programme, increasingly she began to act out again both sexually and in her dietary patterns. She was discharged to outpatient care.

Case 3 (Fig. 10) Suzanne had always been her mother's favourite. It was only as she approached 13 years of age that she first began to upset the mother because of her wilfulness. Her mother, caring and completely smothering, was unable to tolerate what was happening before her eyes with Suzanne, who was now deceiving her, truanting from school, and drinking. Suzanne's father had died when she was age 3 and her mother had never allowed her to learn of his waywardness and womanising. Only later was Suzanne to learn of this. At 13, although outwardly so rebellious and in fact so much like her father in her mother's eyes, Suzanne felt abandoned and panicky. Suddenly her mother died of myocardial infarction. Suzanne's patchy attempts at dieting intensified, and she developed anorexia nervosa. Twenty years later, at the initial consultation, she was able readily to accept the proposal that she felt she had betrayed her mother and precipitated her death. Within the anorexia nervosa, she had remained abstemious and child-like and idealising of her mother. She still went to bed with her childhood dolls.

In treatment she worked hard in psychotherapy which focused on her emerging grief. She had to mourn her mother and her lost childhood but with the help of other family members "found" her "good" father within herself. Her weight gain only faltered a little as she entered and passed through the weight band of puberty. Subsequently, she did well. Her weight dropped to around 52 kg for a while, but for the past 5 years, she has maintained a weight around 56 to 58 kg and with regular menstruation.

Case 4 (Fig. 11) Pamela's anorexia nervosa developed when she left home at the age of 21 to train as a nurse several hundred miles away. Her sister had done so before her, and this favourite daughter's sexual escapades had caused the parents great distress; they had broken off contact with her. Previously obese, Pamela had been trying to lose weight by dieting for some years. The family was a professional one and remarkably inward looking. They lived in the country but had no car or telephone. At presentation, Pamela was very emaciated and could hardly walk. She expected to die. The parents reluctantly engaged in treatment together with her. They eventually agreed to having a telephone installed in their home, and she was able to phone them for the first time from hospital. Pamela was now determined to recover. She was a "good", compliant patient and well liked, but she revealed deep and sometimes impenetrable sadness and a sense of ineffectiveness which also had characterised her father lifelong. She did well for a while after discharge but then lost weight down to 28 kg. She remains in outpatient psychotherapy, now determined to struggle on. She keeps in touch with several members of staff on the unit and currently weighs just over 40 kg.

ENDOCRINE CHANGES ASSOCIATED WITH WEIGHT GAIN

Two charts (Fig. 12) show the endocrinological (plasma LH) and pubertal impact of weight gain. The first patient had been severely ill for nearly 30 years and yet experienced

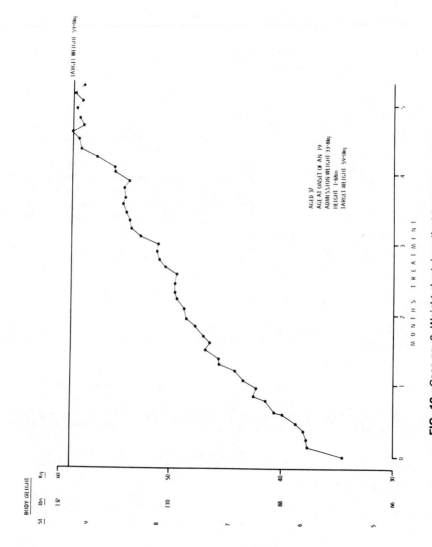

FIG. 10. Case no. 3. Weight chart; in-patient treatment program.

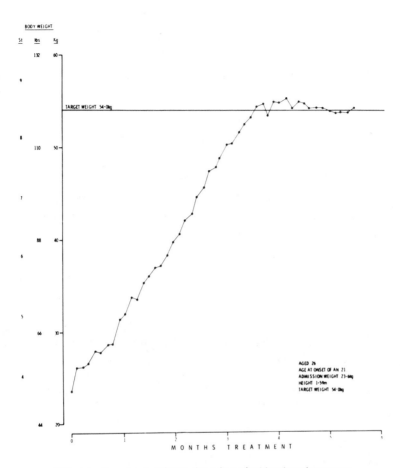

FIG. 11. Case no. 4. Weight chart; in-patient treatment program.

a major surge of LH as weight was restored. Adolescent sexual conflicts were rekindled within her, which she found overwhelming despite efforts to help her. Subsequently, she relapsed although she never again fell so low in body weight. This patient (and her husband whom she had married within her anorexia nervosa) were treated in 1969. These days I would usually not attempt such radical change especially when menopausal age is approaching.

The second chart shows a typical surge of LH as weight increased to normal in a young anorectic, ill for just a few years. This surge, characteristic of early puberty itself, paralleled the patient's experience of her weight gain as sexually arousing. This time she was allowed to experience her lesbian feelings as natural. They proved to be transitory which was a relief to her rigid, caring parents. Now, 10 years later she is contentedly married and has a child.

Lesser weight gain by the anorectic trapped into treatment and of the order of a few kilogrammes may be transitorally relieving to those concerned but rarely

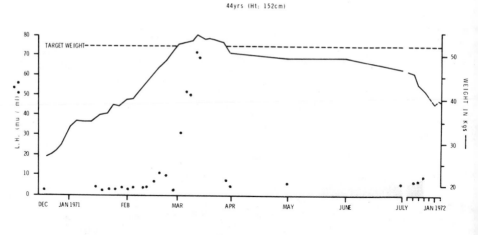

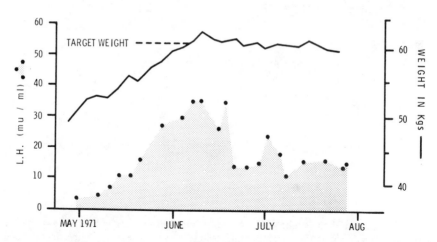

FIG. 12. "Pubertal" impact of weight gain in anorexia nervosa.

affects the long-term outcome. It reflects instead the temporary cost recognised by the anorectic as being necessary for her to escape the system. At its worst it may, if promoted by overfeeding with or without appetite-stimulating drugs, convert an abstainer into a binger and vomiter—hardly a service. In controlled studies of the impact of chlomipramine (26) and of social skills training (34) in addition to the overall treatment outlined above, the author and his colleagues have not found these measures to have a significant impact on weight gain or on clinical status at 1 year follow-up studies. In an outpatient controlled study of the impact of family psychotherapy, this treatment was found to significantly improve outcome at 1 year follow-up (14).

CONCLUSIONS

The author has been invited here to express his views concerning the psychopathology of anorexia nervosa against a burgeoning background of opinion once again that anorexia nervosa has physical or else other varied social and psychological origins. He has no doubt that physical factors are amongst those that predetermine and contribute to the evolution of the syndrome. He agrees with Garner and Bemis (22) in their recent elegant analysis of psychological factors predisposing to anorexia nervosa, that experiences concerning body shape, self-esteem, impulse control, etc., are important and contributory. He disagrees with the view that any of these factors account for the essential characteristics of the syndrome. Rather, they are endemic in the general population of similar age and sex. As such they, together with maturational conflicts, contribute to the multifactorial background and aetiology of the condition. However, its core and unique characteristic, he believes, is the avoidance mechanism within it. Often denied, but inherent within full-blown and established anorexia nervosa, its essential characteristic is low and prepubertal body weight maintenance, rooted in a fear of normal body weight and its implications for the self. Beneath its facade of defiance, it is a grim condition and exercises a powerful grip. Intervention should be sooner rather than later. The rewards of recovery are the restoration of the potential for a full life.

REFERENCES

1. Berkman, J. M. (1930): Anorexia nervosa, anorexia, inanition and low basal metabolic rate. *Am. J. Med. Sci.*, 180:411–424.
2. Crichton-Miller, H. (1938): Pre-psychotic anorexia. Discussion. *Lancet*, 2:1174.
3. Crisp, A. H. (1965): Clinical and therapeutic aspects of anorexia nervosa: A study of 30 cases. *J. Psychosom. Res.*, 9:67–78.
4. Crisp, A. H. (1967): The possible significance of some behavioural correlates of weight and carbohydrate intake. *J. Psychosom. Res.*, 11:117–131.
5. Crisp, A. H. (1967): Anorexia nervosa. *Hosp. Med.*, May:713–718.
6. Crisp, A. H. (1970): Premorbid factors in adult disorders of weight, with particular reference to primary anorexia nervosa (weight phobia). A literature review. *J. Psychosom. Res.*, 14:1–22.
7. Crisp, A. H. (1973): The nature of primary anorexia nervosa. In: *Symposium - Anorexia Nervosa and Obesity* (May 1972), *Royal College of Physicians, Edinburgh* Publication No. 42:18–30.
8. Crisp, A. H. (1977): The differential diagnosis of anorexia nervosa. *Proc. R. Soc. Med.*, 70:686–694.
9. Crisp, A. H. (1977): Diagnosis and outcome of anorexia nervosa: The St. George's view. *Proc. R. Soc. Med.*, 70:464–470.
10. Crisp, A. H. (1979): Fatness, metabolism and sexual behavior. In: *Emotion and Reproduction*, edited by L. Carenza and L. Zichella, pp. 215–237. Academic Press, London.
11. Crisp, A. H. (1980): *Anorexia Nervosa: Let Me Be* Academic Press, London.
12. Crisp, A. H. (1980): Sleep, activity, nutrition and mood. *Br. J. Psychiatry*, 137:1–7.

13. Crisp, A. H. (1981): Anorexia nervosa at normal body weight! The abnormal normal weight control syndrome. *Int. J. Psychiatry Med.,* 11(3):203–233.
14. Crisp, A. H. (1983): Some aspects of the psychopathology of anorexia nervosa—a personal view. In: *Anorexia nervosa. Recent Developments in Research.* Alan R. Liss, New York.
15. Crisp, A. H., and Burns, T. (1983): *The clinical presentation of Anorexia nervosa in the male.* Int. J. Eating Dis., 2:4.
16. Crisp, A. H., Douglas, J. W. B., Ross, J. M., and Stonehill, E. (1970): Some developmental aspects of disorders of weight. *J. Psychosom. Res.,* 14:313–320.
17. Crisp, A. H., Harding B., and McGuiness, B. (1974): Anorexia nervosa: Psychoneurotic characteristics of parents, relationship to prognosis. A quantitative study. *J. Psychosom. Res.,* 18:167–173.
18. Crisp, A. H., Hsu, L. K. G., Harding, B., and Hartshorn, J. (1980): Clinical features of anorexia nervosa. A study of a consecutive series of 102 female patients. *J. Psychosom. Res.,* 24:179–191.
19. Crisp, A. H., Kalucy, R. S., Lacey, J. H., and Harding, B. (1977): The long-term prognosis in anorexia nervosa: Some factors predictive of outcome. In: *Anorexia Nervosa,* edited by R. A. Vigersky, pp. 55–65. Raven Press, New York.
20. Crisp, A. H., Palmer, R. L., and Kalucy, R. S. (1976): How common is anorexia nervosa? A prevalence study. *Br. J. Psychiatry,* 128:549–554.
21. Dally, P. (1969): *Anorexia Nervosa* Heinemann, London.
22. Garner, D. M., and Bemis, K. M. (1982): A cognitive behavioral approach to anorexia nervosa. *Cognitive Ther. Res.,* 6(2):123–150.
23. Hsu, L. K. G., Crisp, A. H., and Harding, B. (1979): Outcome of anorexia nervosa. *Lancet,* 1:62–65.
24. Huenemann, R. L., Shapiro, L. R., Hampton, M. C., and Mitchell, B. E. (1966): A longitudinal study of gross body composition and body conformation and their association with food and acitivity in a teenage population. *Am. J. Clin. Nutr.,* 18:325–338.
25. Kaufman, M. R., and Heiman, M., editors (1964): *Evolution of Psychosomatic Concepts. Anorexia Nervosa: A Paradigm* International Universities Press, New York.
26. Lacey, J. H., and Crisp, A. H. (1980): Hunger, food intake and weight: The impact of clomipramine on a refeeding anorexia nervosa population. *Postgrad. Med. J.,* 56(1):79–85.
27. Loudon, I. S. L. (1980): Chlorosis, anaemia and anorexia nervosa. *Br. Med. J.,* 281:1669–1675.
28. Lucas, A. R. (1981): Toward the understanding of anorexia nervosa as a disease entity. *Mayo Clin. Proc.,* 56:254–264.
29. Minuchin, S., Rosman, B. L., and Baker, L. (1978): *Psychosomatic Families:* Anorexia nervosa in context. Harvard University Press, Harvard.
30. Morgan, H. C., and Russell, G. F. M. (1975): Value of family background and clinical features as predictors of long-term outcome in anorexia nervosa: 4 year follow-up study of 41 patients. *Psychol. Med.,* 5:355–371.
31. Nylander, I. (1971): The feeling of being fat and dieting in a school population: Epidemiologic interview investigation. *Acta Sociomed. Scand.,* 3:17–26.
32. Palmer, R. L. (1979): Dietary chaos syndrome: A useful new term? *Br. J. Med. Psychol.,* 52:187–190.
33. Patterson, W. (1982): Was Byron anorexic? *World Med.,* May 15:35–38.
34. Pillay, M., and Crisp, A. H. (1981): The impact of social skills training within an established in-patient treatment programme for anorexia nervosa. *B. J. Psychiatry,* 139:533–539.
35. Russell, G. F. M. (1979): Bulimia nervosa: An ominous variant of anorexia nervosa. *Psychol. Med.,* 9:429–448.
36. Russell, J. A. O. (1971): Psychosocial aspects of weight loss and amenorrhea in adolescent girls. In: *Psychosomatic Medicine in Obstetrics and Gynaecology,* edited by N. Morris, pp. 593–595. Karger, Basel.
37. Ryle, J. A. (1936): Anorexia nervosa. *Lancet,* 2:893–899.
38. Stonehill, E., and Crisp, A. H. (1977): Psychoneurotic characteristics of patients with anorexia nervosa before and after treatment and at follow-up 4–7 years later. *J. Psychosom. Res.,* 21:187–193.

Eating and Its Disorders, edited by A. J. Stunkard and E. Stellar. Raven Press, New York © 1984.

Bulimia: Its Epidemiology and Management

Christopher G. Fairburn

Department of Psychiatry, University of Oxford, Warneford Hospital, Oxford, England

It is well established that bouts of uncontrolled and excessive eating (binges) occur in a small proportion of patients who are overweight (71) and in up to 50% of patients with anorexia nervosa (8,26). However, it has only recently been recognised that many people who fall into neither category also experience eating episodes of this nature, despite having a body weight which lies within the normal range. This observation has led to the suggestion that there is a relatively distinct eating disorder which has as its principal feature episodes of binge-eating. This disorder has attracted various names including bulimarexia (5), the dietary chaos syndrome (56), the abnormal normal weight control syndrome (13), bulimia nervosa (65), and bulimia (2). The terms bulimia and bulimia nervosa have gained greatest acceptance, the former in the United States and the latter in Britain. Bulimia is the less satisfactory of the two terms since it encourages the use of the word bulimia to denote both a pattern of behaviour (binge-eating) and a specific psychiatric syndrome. Instead, the term bulimia nervosa is to be preferred since it emphasises that people with this eating disorder not only eat in binges but also exhibit other characteristic psychopathological features.

In addition to attracting various names, this eating disorder has attracted considerable publicity in the media. British newspapers have described the condition as a killer disease and have referred to it as epidemic. Since such extravagant claims have arisen in part from the misinterpretation of several preliminary epidemiological studies, the first part of this chapter will attempt to redress the balance by providing a critical appraisal of what is known about the epidemiology of binge-eating and the syndromes bulimia and bulimia nervosa. In the second half of the chapter, one promising approach to the management of these disorders will be discussed, and its theoretical and practical implications will be considered.

Throughout the paper the term binge-eating will refer to episodes of eating which are experienced as excessive and beyond the subject's control. The term bulimia will refer to the syndrome outlined in the third edition of the American Psychiatric Association's Diagnostic and Statistical Manual (2), and the term bulimia nervosa will refer to the syndrome described by Russell (65). Although the relationship between these syndromes (the bulimic syndromes) has not been formally studied, clinical experience suggests that bulimia nervosa may be regarded as a subtype of bulimia in which binge-eating is accompanied by self-induced vomiting or purgative abuse, and abnormal attitudes to body weight and

TABLE 1 *Diagnostic criteria for the syndrome bulimia*[a]

A. Recurrent episodes of binge-eating (rapid consumption of a large amount of food in a discrete period of time, usually less than 2 hr)
B. At least three of the following:
    (1) consumption of high-caloric, easily ingested food during a binge
    (2) inconspicuous eating during a binge
    (3) termination of such eating episodes by abdominal pain, sleep, social interruption, or self-induced vomiting
    (4) repeated attempts to lose weight by severely restrictive diets, self-induced vomiting, or use of cathartics or diuretics
    (5) frequent weight fluctuations greater than 10 lb due to alternating binges and fasts
C. Awareness that the eating pattern is abnormal and fear of not being able to stop eating voluntarily
D. Depressed mood and self-deprecating thoughts following eating binges
E. Bulimic episodes are not due to anorexia nervosa or any known physical disorder

---

[a]From ref. 2.

TABLE 2. *Diagnostic criteria for the syndrome bulimia nervosa*[a]

---

1. The patients suffer from powerful and intractable urges to overeat.
2. They seek to avoid the fattening effects of food by inducing vomiting or abusing purgatives or both.
3. They have a morbid fear of becoming fat.

---

[a]From ref. 63.

shape. In practice, virtually all patients who meet diagnostic criteria for bulimia nervosa also fulfil the criteria for the syndrome bulimia, although the converse is not the case. The diagnostic criteria for the two conditions are shown in Tables 1 and 2.

THE EPIDEMIOLOGY OF BINGE-EATING AND THE BULIMIC SYNDROMES

Until recently, there seem to have been few patients who fulfil diagnostic criteria for bulimia nervosa. Russell (65), when originally describing the condition, reported that it had taken him 6½ years (1972–1978) to collect 30 cases. However, there is now evidence that many such cases existed during this period, but they were undetected. In 1980, 499 women who fulfilled strict self-report diagnostic criteria for bulimia nervosa were identified with the help of a British women's magazine (19). In both their demographic and clinical characteristics, these women closely resembled patients with bulimia or bulimia nervosa (18). They had grossly disturbed eating habits, although the majority were of normal body weight. Despite having been binge-eating and vomiting for an average of 5 years, few were aware that others practised similar habits. On standardised measures, they were found to have profoundly disturbed attitudes to food, eating, body weight and body shape, as well as significant levels of anxiety and depression.

However, less than one-third had ever discussed any aspect of their eating difficulties with a doctor, and only 2.5% were currently receiving medical treatment.

Recently there have been several attempts to determine the prevalence of the bulimic syndromes and their constituent elements (10,11,39,41). These studies have produced highly conflicting findings (see Table 3). Whilst the discrepancies could simply reflect genuine differences between the populations studied, certain methodological limitations and inconsistencies confound the interpretation of the data. These problems of method may be subsumed under four major headings: sampling procedures, methods of assessment, scope of assessment, and research design.

Methodological Problems

Sampling Procedures

Whilst the sample sizes have been sufficiently large to permit inferences to be drawn, the populations studied have been restricted in character. With one exception (11,12), they have been composed of university or college students, despite the fact that there is evidence that the majority of those with bulimia or bulimia nervosa are neither schoolchildren nor students (19,61).

In some studies it may be questioned whether the samples have been representative of the populations from which they were drawn. In one investigation the proportion of the potential sample that participated was not reported (41), and in two others one-quarter or more chose not to cooperate (10,39). This high refusal rate seriously compromises data interpretation. Clarke and Palmer (10) suggested that eating problems may have been overrepresented amongst those subjects who refused to participate in their study, and that the prevalence figures they obtained were likely to have been an underestimate. There is no evidence to support this assertion. Indeed, the great majority of patients with bulimia state at interview that they would have cooperated with epidemiological research as long as their anonymity had been preserved.

Methods of Assessment

All the prevalence data so far reported have been derived from self-report measures. In three studies, specific questionnaires were devised (11,39,41), and in two (10,11) the Eating Attitudes Test (EAT) was used (29). In each investigation the assessment procedure had definite shortcomings. The questionnaires constructed for individual studies were not adequately assessed with regard to their reliability or validity, and the use in two studies of items from the EAT to identify specific psychopathological features is highly questionable.

A more general criticism of these prevalence studies is that their reliance on self-report questionnaires imposes definite limitations on the quality of the information obtained. While such methods have the advantage of ease of administra-

TABLE 3. Prevalence of binge-eating, self-induced vomiting, and laxative use among four samples of women[a]

Population	Hawkins and Clement (41)	Halmi, Falk and Schwartz (39)	Clarke and Palmer (10)	Cooper and Fairburn (11)
	College students	Summer-session college students[b]	College students	Women attending a family planning clinic
Sample size	182	355*	206	369
Response rate (%)	—	66*	76	96
Measure of eating habits and attitudes	Self-report questionnaire	Self-report questionnaire	Eating Attitudes Test[c]	Self-report questionnaire plus Eating Attitudes Test
Age of sample in years (mean ± SD)	—	25.6±10.7*	19.2±0.8	24.1±5.5
Binge-eating:				
ever (%)	—	68.1	46.2	26.4
current (%)	79	53.8	30.2	20.9
at least weekly (%)	33	—	7.1	7.3
Self-induced vomiting:				
ever (%)	4.9	22.1	5.8	6.5
current (%)	—	11.9	1.3	2.9
at least weekly (%)	—	1.7*	0	1.1
Laxative use (%)	—	4.8*	7.0	4.9
Exercise as weight control (%)	—	4.5*	—	7.3

[a]Some of these figures have been extrapolated from the reported data.
[b]59.8% of this sample were female. The asterisked figures are for the entire sample, the remaining figures are for the female respondents.
[c]Two subgroups were interviewed. However, the findings were compromised by the small numbers in each group (11 and 3) and the poor response rate (61% and 43%).

tion and scoring, they are incapable of assessing complex behaviour and attitudes, and as a result subtle individual differences are inevitably obscured. Furthermore, with data obtained by self-report, it is often difficult to unravel the temporal sequence of events. Another problem arises from the interpretation of the terms used in these questionnaires. Unless all such terms are both unambiguous and in common usage, there is a risk that individual subjects will interpret them idiosyncratically. For example, the word binge is widely used, yet it is devoid of any specific meaning. It is fallacious to assume that people who admit to eating in binges necessarily experience eating episodes of the type seen among patients with bulimia or bulimia nervosa. Such difficulties can be minimised if all equivocal terms are defined in a rigorous fashion. Two further limitations of self-report instruments must also be noted: (a) they are vulnerable to response-style biases, and (b) it is difficult to assess whether people have been truthful in their answers.

One advantage of self-report measures is that anonymity can be preserved. This is of particular relevance to the detection of cases of bulimia nervosa, a disorder surrounded by guilt, shame, and secrecy (19). If assessment is to be by interview, the refusal rate can be unacceptably high. For example, Clarke and Palmer (10) found that only 56% of subjects selected on the basis of their scores on the EAT attended for interview.

Several other studies have used the EAT to identify people with varying degrees of abnormal eating habits and attitudes and have subsequently invited these subjects to attend for interview (7,28,30,72). Whilst this research design has definite merits, in each case the advantages of the clinical interview were not exploited since straightforward clinical judgement was used to evaluate attitudes and behaviour. This mode of assessment is notoriously unreliable. Instead, structured interviews should have been used. Such interviews could incorporate flexible measures designed specifically for the investigation in hand, accompanied by operational definitions and a glossary for all the technical terms involved. In addition, standardized instruments such as the NIMH Diagnostic Interview Schedule (63) or the Present State Examination (78) could be included. These measures could be used to quantify less specific forms of psychopathology, and in this way subjects could be compared as a group with other populations rated on the same measures. If this type of procedure were employed and the interviewers were well trained, subtle attitudes and behaviour could be described without any sacrifice of reliability.

Scope of Assessment

Three points need emphasis as regards the scope of assessment. First, scant attention has been paid to subjects' attitudes to food, eating, body weight, and body shape. Instead, the stress has been on eating habits. In part this neglect of attitudes may reflect the difficulties inherent in their assessment, and in part it may arise from their virtual absence from the DSM III criteria for bulimia. However, the failure of these community studies to evaluate attitudes is of considerable importance, since there is a mounting body of opinion that cognitive factors are of fundamental importance in the maintenance of anorexia nervosa, binge-eating, and the bulimic syndromes (25,27,59). This issue will be discussed further in the second half of the chapter. Second, some studies have failed to provide sufficient information on the frequency of the eating habits with which they are concerned (10,41). This is another important omission: for example, the clinical implications of *ever* having vomited are very different from current, frequent vomiting. Finally, most studies have failed to examine the clinical significance of their findings, either in terms of subjects' perceptions of their eating habits, or in terms of the potential implications for clinical resources. Yet, it cannot be assumed that all those who have abnormal eating habits or attitudes, in the statistical sense, necessarily regard them as a problem or indeed wish to receive treatment (12).

Research Design

All the community studies to date have been cross-sectional in design, and few have provided information on the duration of key psychopathological features. This is another significant omission since it seems that bulimia nervosa may run a protracted course (65). Indeed, in the community study of bulimia nervosa mentioned earlier (19), it was found that the average duration of binge-eating and self-induced vomiting was 5.2 years (SD = 4.7) and 4.5 years (SD = 4.0), respectively. Although retrospective data of this type are important, they need to be supplemented with information obtained from longitudinal studies if transitory behavioural or attitudinal abnormalities are to be distinguished from more enduring problems.

Provisional Conclusions

These epidemiological studies should be regarded as preliminary investigations which will serve to pave the way for more sophisticated research projects. Nevertheless, it is possible to draw certain tentative conclusions regarding the prevalence of the bulimic syndromes and their constituent elements. First, binge-eating and self-induced vomiting will be considered:

1. Binge-eating and self-induced vomiting are much more common among women than men (10,39,41).
2. A wide age range is affected (11,39).
3. Whilst occasional binge-eating is relatively common, frequent binge-eating (weekly or more) is considerably less so (10,11).
4. A small minority of women who binge-eat also use vomiting or laxatives, or both, to control their weight (10,11,39).
5. The findings with regard to the current and highest body weights of those who binge-eat are discrepant. Halmi and colleagues (39) found that binge-eating was associated with past and present overweight, whereas this was not confirmed

by Cooper and Fairburn (11). Since the former study did not provide a definition of binge-eating, it is possible that the term was interpreted by its subjects as mere excessive eating. If this were the case, the finding that there was an association between binge-eating and being overweight is hardly surprising. Both studies reported no association between self-induced vomiting and present or past weight disturbance.

6. Both binge-eating (present and past) and self-induced vomiting (present and past) are associated with abnormal eating habits and attitudes, and significant levels of anxiety and depression (11).

7. Subjects who binge-eat or practice self-induced vomiting do not necessarily regard themselves as having an eating problem (12,20).

Even less is known about the epidemiology of the syndromes bulimia and bulimia nervosa. However, the following tentative conclusions may be drawn:

1. Both syndromes are much more common among women than men (19,21,39).

2. The majority of cases are in their twenties; a minority are schoolchildren or students (19).

3. British studies suggest that: (a) whilst a minority of women who binge-eat fulfil diagnostic criteria for the syndrome bulimia nervosa (11), most of those who vomit do fulfil these criteria (11,19), and (b) the probable prevalence of bulimia nervosa amongst adult women appears to be between 1 and 2% (11).

4. Most people with bulimia nervosa have a normal body weight (19). However, they are prone to have been both significantly overweight and underweight in the past (11,19). Almost half have a history suggestive of anorexia nervosa (19).

5. Bulimia nervosa is associated with high levels of anxiety and depression (19).

6. Not all people who fulfil diagnostic criteria for bulimia nervosa regard themselves as having an eating problem, nor do they all wish to receive treatment (19,20).

In conclusion, it is inappropriate to describe bulimia and bulimia nervosa as epidemic. Much more rigorous research is required before any firm statement can be made regarding their prevalence. Nevertheless, it seems likely that these syndromes constitute a significant source of psychiatric morbidity.

THE MANAGEMENT OF THE BULIMIC SYNDROMES

Little has been written about the management of bulimia and bulimia nervosa. There have been no satisfactory treatment studies, and it is not known whether any intervention influences the long-term outcome. The consensus is that both disorders are difficult to treat (16,65,71).

Russell (65,66) has reported that there is little to be gained from inpatient management along the lines used in anorexia nervosa. Any benefits obtained tend to be short-lived. Nevertheless, admission is indicated if there is severe depression or the patient's eating habits prove refractory to outpatient care. Hospitalisation may also be required if the patient's physical health is a cause for concern (16,66). In general, however, admissions should be brief and regarded as preparation for a formal outpatient treatment programme.

Physical treatments also appear to have limited indications. Anticonvulsant agents have been advocated (53,75) but their use has not gained clinical acceptance. The electroencephalographic abnormalities which were claimed to be associated with binge-eating (62) have since been shown to be variable in form, of doubtful significance, and present in only a small proportion of subjects (51). The only satisfactory controlled study of anticonvulsants (75) showed a reduction in the frequency of binge-eating in 8 out of 19 patients. However, the findings of this study were difficult to interpret since not only was there no correlation between EEG abnormality and treatment outcome, but the crossover design revealed a sequence effect (75).

Community studies indicate that many people with bulimia nervosa are prescribed appetite suppressants or antidepressants (21). Whilst there can be no doubt that patients with bulimia or bulimia nervosa have an excessive desire for food, very few patients report that appetite suppressants are helpful (21). One reason for caution in prescribing such drugs arises from the finding that a subgroup of patients with bulimia have a definite propensity to alcohol and drug dependence (46). The use of antidepressant drugs might seem more reasonable (43,44,60,73) and is discussed by Hudson, Pope and Jonas (*this volume*). Certainly most patients with bulimia present with depressive symptoms. However, careful history-taking usually indicates that their mood closely parallels their degree of control over eating, and in the majority of cases the depression rapidly lifts in response to psychological treatments of the type described below (16). Antidepressants are indicated if severe depressive symptoms persist. Unfortunately the choice of drug is not straightforward. Tricyclic antidepressants have a propensity to induce weight gain and carbohydrate craving (57), both of which are poorly tolerated by this patient group. On the other hand, monoamine oxidase inhibitors should not be prescribed unless both the patient and her physician are confident that the dietary restrictions will be obeyed: such confidence is rarely justified since these patients tend to binge on the foods they are attempting to exclude from their diet (17).

Most clinical reports have been concerned with the use of psychological methods of treatment. Stunkard (71) has suggested that binge-eating in obese patients is an indication for psychotherapy or psychoanalysis, and he has described a modified form of psychotherapy in which particular attention is paid to the events and feelings which provoke episodes of overeating (70,71). He reports that these eating bouts can serve as markers of difficulties which might otherwise have remained undetected. In addition, there have been numerous accounts of the successful application of behaviour therapy to the treatment of binge-eating in overweight, underweight, and normal weight individuals (15,34,37,38,47, 48,50,52,64,67,76,77). However, the interpretation of these reports is complicated by the variable quality of the clinical data presented, both at assessment and follow-up, the clinical heterogeneity of the patients treated, and their small numbers.

Whether group therapy has a role in the management of bulimia or bulimia nervosa is a question of considerable practical importance. Boskind-Lodahl and White (6) and Orbach (54,55) have described how group therapy may be used to assist women who binge-eat. Their groups have a feminist perspective, and they combine both behavioural and Gestalt techniques. Although this form of treatment has not been systematically evaluated, it seems likely that group therapy of this type may benefit some women who simply binge-eat, or binge-eat and vomit on an intermittent basis. However, it is doubtful whether it can help those whose eating habits are seriously disturbed, especially if there are also markedly abnormal attitudes to body weight and shape.

The remainder of this chapter is concerned with a cognitive behavioural approach to the management of bulimia.

Cognitive Behaviour Therapy for Bulimia: Preliminary Findings

This cognitive behavioural treatment has been designed specifically to tackle the behaviour and attitudes characteristic of bulimia and bulimia nervosa. It has been progressively refined over the past 4 years, and over 40 patients have been treated. The approach is currently being evaluated as part of a controlled outcome study.

A preliminary uncontrolled report described 11 women with bulimia nervosa who received the treatment in a standardised form (15). Their mean duration of regular self-induced vomiting was 3.9 years (SD = 3.03 years), and the average frequency of vomiting was three times daily. Six patients had previously satisfied diagnostic criteria for anorexia nervosa, but at presentation all 11 were within 15% of the average weight for their age and height. In contrast to experience with inpatient management (65), this treatment programme was acceptable to all 11 patients. By the end of treatment, 9 patients had reduced their frequency of binge-eating and vomiting to less than once a month, and this reduction was maintained in the 7 cases for whom follow-up data were available (mean length of follow-up = 9.6 months). These changes in eating habits were accompanied by a reduction in anxiety and depression, decreased preoccupation with food and eating, and an attenuation of the characteristic attitudinal abnormalities. There were no significant changes in body weight.

Since the publication of these findings, two separate articles have described a similar treatment approach (38,48). Although these reports concerned the treatment of only 3 patients, their findings tend to support those described above.

Cognitive Behaviour Therapy for Bulimia: Treatment Procedure

Treatment is conducted on an outpatient basis and usually lasts from 4 to 6 months. The treatment is problem oriented. Goals are clearly specified as are the means by which they are to be achieved. The responsibility for change resides with the patient: The therapist provides information, advice, and support. The approach is welcomed by these patients, and since most view loss of control over eating as their main problem, they respond positively to the emphasis on increasing self-control.

Three stages in treatment may be distinguished. Each contains several different elements intended to deal with relatively specific areas of difficulty. Before discussing certain implications of the treatment, its major components will be outlined. Further details of the approach are provided elsewhere (18).

Stage One

This generally lasts from 4 to 6 weeks. It is designed to disrupt the habitual overeating and vomiting that characterises the more severe cases. Appointments are held at least 2 or 3 times each week. The following elements are included:

1. *Self-monitoring.* Patients are asked to record in general descriptive terms the food they eat (either just before its consumption or immediately afterwards) as well as where and when it is eaten. They are provided with monitoring sheets for this purpose (see Fig. 1). They identify normal meals with brackets, and they asterisk any food eaten which they regarded as excessive. Whenever an asterisk is used, they explain in the right-hand column why they overate. In addition, vomiting, laxative use, and weighing are recorded.

2. *The prescription of an eating pattern.* Having established monitoring, patients are asked to restrict their eating to three or four planned meals each day, plus one or two snacks. These should be eaten irrespective of their appetite. The intention is that this prescribed eating pattern should displace the alternating overeating and dietary restriction that characterises most of these patients' eating habits (17). No recommendations are made concerning what they eat. Some patients are reluctant to eat meals since they feel that this will result in weight gain. These patients can be reassured that the converse usually occurs. This is because a significant proportion of each binge is absorbed, and the introduction of meals and snacks reduces the number of binges. Most patients are surprised to learn that each time they binge and vomit they absorb food, and that in many cases they have been surviving on the residue of their binges.

3. *Stimulus control techniques.* The well-established stimulus control techniques used in the treatment of obesity (49,68) are employed to help patients adhere to the predetermined eating plan.

4. *Alternative behaviour.* Patients are asked to construct a list of pleasurable activities which could be used when they sense their control is poor. At such times they should do their utmost to engage in one of these pursuits. Typical examples including taking exercise, visiting friends, or having a bath or shower.

5. *Advice regarding purgative or diuretic abuse.* If applicable, patients are informed of the dangers of using purgatives or diuretics, and they are advised to

DATE <u>21st May</u> DAY <u>Thursday</u>

TIME	FOOD AND LIQUID CONSUMED	PLACE	B	V/P	CONTEXT OF 'OVEREATING'
0820	1 toasted muffin with margarine 1 mug of coffee 1 apple	my college room	*		Muffin left over from yesterday. Shouldn't have now this
					0850 – 9st 2lbs (weight up one pound. Surprised)
1115	1 can diet Pepsi	Bodleian library			(worked all morning – skipped lunch. Happy)
1505	1 jam doughnut	In the market	*		I bought the doughnut
05	1 jam doughnut	college	*		when shopping – then I
30	6 shortbread biscuits	room	*		bought another – and
34	1 piece of toast, margarine and jam	"	*		Then I knew I might as well carry on. What's
≈ 35	5 pieces of toast, margarine and jam	"		*	the point of all this?
	1 mug coffee	"		*	I am trying to stop
	3 cold muffins	"		*	will I ever learn to
	6 chocolate truffles	"		*	control myself?
	¼ lb bag of chocolate peanuts	"		*	
	2 cans of lemonade (low calorie)	"		*	V ┼ 16 10 Weighed myself – 9st 3lbs
1930	1 bowl mushroom soup chicken (1 piece), peas	college hall			Avoided potatoes and desert – good
2010	1 mug coffee	Friend's room			
2045	Another coffee	my room			Weighed myself – 9st 6lbs
2050	6 custard cream biscuits	"		*	– depressed. Must try to were.
2200	2 packets of crisps	"		*	Can't work. Can't
	1 glass of red wine	"		*	concentrate. Hungry
	3 pieces of toast with jam	"		*	worried about weight.
2218	2 more pieces of toast with jam	"		*	Bored. Gave up and ate and ate...
	1 small tin of cold rice	"		*	
	1 mug of tea with about 5 more	"		*	V ┼ 22 25 cried,
2230	pieces of toast	"		*	not like me
	– overleaf				

FIG. 1. A monitoring sheet showing two periods of binge-eating and self-induced vomiting.

refrain from using these drugs. In cases of regular heavy consumption, the drugs may need to be gradually phased out.

6. *Advice regarding weighing.* Patients with bulimia are extremely sensitive to changes in their weight and shape. One reflection of this sensitivity is their tendency to weigh themselves daily or more often, although a minority actively avoid weighing while, nevertheless, remaining acutely aware of their shape (17). To counter both extremes, patients are advised to weigh themselves on one particular morning each week.

7. *The provision of information.* Patients are given information on the following topics: (a) Weight—Patients are advised of the folly of trying to maintain rigid control over their weight. Instead, they are asked to accept a *weight range* of approximately 6 lb in magnitude, located between 85 and 115% of the average weight for their age, height, and sex. It is suggested that they should not decide on a specific weight range until control over their eating has been established since only then will they be able to gauge how much they can eat in order to keep their weight relatively stable. They are advised against choosing a weight which necessitates anything more than moderate dietary restriction since restraint of this type is prone to encourage overeating (42,59). If appropriate, they are also told of the physical and psychological consequences of starvation (25,45), dietary restraint (59), and obesity (1,33,79); and (b) Physical complications—Patients are informed of the physical complications of binge-eating, self-induced vomiting, and purgative abuse (see Table 4). Although these complications are not always present, they are discussed as a matter of routine. Patients are reassured that most of these physical sequelae resolve once their eating habits have normalized.

8. *Joint interview with family or friends.* It is often advisable to arrange occasional joint interviews with the people with whom patients live and share their meals. These interviews serve two functions. First, they encourage patients to bring the problem into the open, thereby relieving their guilt over continuing secrecy and deceit. Second, by discussing the rationale of treatment, and in particular the importance of self-control, friends or relatives can be assisted in providing an environment which will facilitate the patients' efforts to overcome the problem.

TABLE 4. *The physical complications of bulimia*

Binge-eating	Self-induced vomiting	Purgative abuse
Acute dilatation of the stomach	Metabolic disturbance (especially hypokalaemia):	
Menstrual disturbance	Cardiac arrhythmias	
Painless salivary gland	Renal damage	
enlargement (especially the	Tetany and peripheral paraesthesiae	
parotids)	Epileptic seizures	
	Dehydration	
	Erosion of dental enamel	Steatorrhoea
	(perimolysis)	
	Chronic hoarseness of the voice	Finger clubbing
	Gastrointestinal reflux	(Rebound water retention)

Stage Two

The second stage of treatment generally lasts approximately 2 months and appointments are held at weekly intervals. In the great majority of cases, binge-eating and self-induced vomiting are now occuring on an intermittent basis.

Patients are asked to continue with their attempts to adhere to a regular eating pattern. Many of the procedures used in the first stage are still relevant. However, certain additional strategies are employed:

1. *The introduction of avoided foods.* Dietary restraint is thought to encourage binge-eating (42,59,74). Two forms of restraint may be distinguished. First, many patients attempt to avoid eating for long periods each day, especially if they have recently overeaten. This tendency is countered in the first stage of treatment by the prescription of meals and snacks. Second, most patients attempt to adhere to a highly selective diet from which "fattening" foods are excluded (17). Frequently, it is these foods which are eaten when patients lose control. In the second stage of treatment, there is a sustained attempt to erode this form of restraint. Patients are asked to prepare a list of foods which they enjoy but nevertheless avoid. They are then advised to incorporate these foods into their diet at times when they feel in control. The intention is that they should relax control over the content of their diet while continuing to adhere to the predetermined eating plan.

2. *Training in problem solving.* By this stage in treatment, it will be evident that most episodes of poor control occur in response to adverse events, negative moods, or irrational thoughts. Formal training in problem solving appears to help patients cope with the events and moods. Patients are taught the principles of problem solving (36), and then each time a problem arises they are asked to write out in detail their attempt to reach a solution. Most patients react positively to this approach and regard it as an intellectual challenge. Not only do they find it helps them avoid binge-eating, but it provides them with a means of tackling other day-to-day difficulties. Training in problem solving serves an additional function. Many patients with bulimia exhibit a dichotomous style of thinking in which only extremes are recognised (17). For example, they view themselves as "in control" or "out of control," "fat" or "thin"; food is either "forbidden" or "allowed". Problem solving helps patients recognise and counter this tendency by encouraging them to generate a wide range of alternative solutions to each difficulty they encounter.

3. *Cognitive restructuring.* Central to bulimia are abnormal attitudes to body shape and weight and, secondary to these, abnormal attitudes to food and eating. The assessment of these attitudes and beliefs will be discussed later. In treatment they tend to make the patient resist behaviour change. Many of the behavioural instructions are designed to highlight and challenge these systems of belief. Two examples may serve to illustrate this point. First, weighing only once a week may be most unsettling if the patient is extremely concerned about the slightest change in her weight or shape. Second, patients may be reluctant to introduce fattening foods into their diet if they associate the consumption of these foods with weight gain.

If patients are encouraged to adhere to the behavioural instructions many of their irrational beliefs and assumptions decline in strength. Nevertheless, as a matter of routine these beliefs should be openly discussed during treatment. To this end patients are asked to identify on their monitoring sheets thoughts which interfere with their adherence to the behavioural programme. Having identified such thoughts, patients are asked to evaluate in considerable detail their rational basis. Not surprisingly, most of these thoughts prove to be irrational, and as treatment progresses, patients become more adept at recognising and dismissing them.

When discussing attitudes toward body shape and weight, female patients are encouraged to consider the extent to which they are influenced by the current pressures on women to be slim (58). Possibly as a result of the increase in self-esteem and assertiveness that generally accompanies the first stage in treatment, many patients gradually dissociate themselves from these values and begin to show less concern about their weight and shape.

A minority of patients with bulimia exhibit unequivocal body image misperception. Clinical experience with patients with anorexia nervosa suggests that this feature fails to respond to direct modification (31). Instead, using the approach of Garner and Garfinkel (31), these patients are advised to accept that they are inaccurate judges of their shape, and they are encouraged to distance themselves from this misperception and function despite it.

Stage Three

The final stage consists of three or four appointments at 2-week intervals. The focus is on the maintenance of change. Patients are forewarned that they may experience future episodes of poor control, especially at times of stress. They are therefore asked to construct a plan for use at such times based on what they found helpful during treatment. This plan is discussed with the therapist who then prepares a typewritten version which is given to the patient prior to discharge. A typical maintenance plan is shown in the Appendix.

This cognitive behavioural approach might appear to be rigid and immutable. In practice, the treatment should be adapted to suit the needs of each patient. However, the therapist and patient must remain aware at all times of the need for continuing evidence of progress, since experience suggests that little is gained from protracted courses of treatment.

Figure 2 illustrates how the various psychopathological features may change during the course of treatment. Research in progress suggests that there is some constancy in the sequence of these changes.

Cognitive Behaviour Therapy for Bulimia: Theoretical Implications

One of the most striking characteristics of patients with bulimia or anorexia nervosa is the intensity and prominence of their abnormal beliefs about their

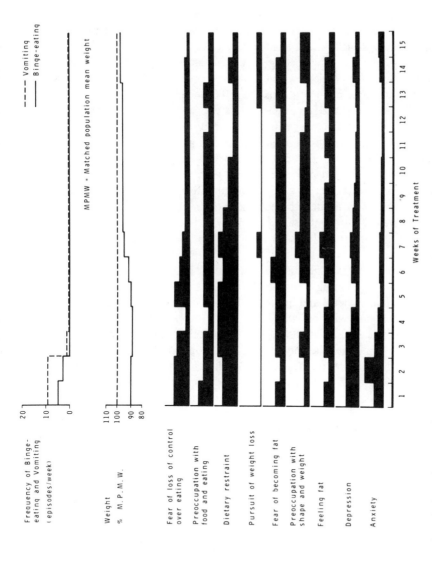

FIG. 2. The psychopathological changes that occurred during cognitive behavioral treatment of a patient with bulimia nervosa. [This patient (aged 22 years) had a 4-year history of binge-eating and self-induced vomiting. She had never fulfilled diagnostic criteria for anorexia nervosa. Over the 6 months prior to treatment she had been vomiting on average twice daily. Independent assessment 6 months after treatment revealed that on all parameters her improvement had been maintained.]

shape and weight. Given the presence of these beliefs, most of the behaviour and attitudes of these patients become intelligible. In bulimia, the extreme dieting, frequent weighing, preoccupation with weight and shape, and abnormal attitudes to food and eating are all comprehensible once it has been appreciated that these patients believe their weight and shape to be of fundamental importance, and that both must be kept tightly under control. Even the apparently paradoxical binge-eating can be understood in cognitive terms, since it seems likely that it represents a secondary psychological phenomenon resulting from extreme dietary restraint (42,59). Since the binge-eating is viewed as evidence of poor self-control, it becomes a source of distress and self-condemnation which may lead the patient to seek outside help. In contrast, the self-induced vomiting and purgative abuse are not usually regarded as problems: Instead, they are viewed as means of coping with the loss of control over eating.

The beliefs and values of patients with bulimia resemble those of patients with anorexia nervosa. Both groups tend to evaluate their self-worth in terms of their weight and shape, and both fear weight gain and fatness (17,25). Patients with anorexia nervosa, however, also exhibit an active preference for extreme thinness (3). Given these attitudes, the behaviour of anorexic patients also becomes comprehensible (27). In contrast to patients with bulimia, the majority of those with anorexia nervosa are able to behave in a way that is consonant with their beliefs, and as a result they see no need to receive treatment. The subgroup of patients with bulimic anorexia nervosa differs somewhat since they are unable to retain control over their eating. This is likely to be the explanation for their greater levels of depression, anxiety, and guilt (8). In many respects patients in this subgroup resemble patients with bulimia.

These clinical observations suggest that rather than being simply symptomatic of the two conditions, the abnormal beliefs about body shape and weight maintain much of the behaviour characteristic of these disorders. It would therefore seem likely that cognitive change is a prerequisite for full recovery. For this reason, the development of cognitive behavioural approaches to the management of bulimia (15,18,48) and anorexia nervosa (27) would seem to be an important advance.

If cognitive behavioural treatments are to be refined and evaluated, there is a need for research into the specific psychopathology of bulimia and anorexia nervosa. Surprisingly, there have been few investigations of this type (3,9,25), although many studies have assessed nonspecific psychopathological features using well-established instruments. There have been several small-scale repertory grid studies (4,14,24), but there have been no systematic attempts to identify and measure the core psychopathology of the two conditions.

Several self-report instruments have been designed to measure the symptoms characteristic of anorexia nervosa, and all of these include questions directly concerned with attitudes (23,30,32,35,40). However, the items have not been derived from systematic analysis of patients' beliefs; rather, they have been based on theoretical constructs or "clinical experience." Furthermore, when validation studies have been performed, they have been based on heterogeneous patient populations with varying degrees of exposure to treatment. This is a serious flaw since there is likely to be a gradual change in attitudes during treatment, the nature of which may well depend on the form of treatment employed.

It is questionable whether self-report instruments are capable of assessing complex beliefs and values. A more appropriate strategy would be to devise a semi-structured interview designed specifically to elicit these features. Whilst the clinical literature suggests the likely nature of such features, it would seem advisable to derive them from the findings of exploratory unstructured interviews with subjects whose attitudes have not been contaminated by treatment. Once characterised, these psychopathological features could then be defined in operational terms. Thereafter, a structured interview could be devised which contains questions designed to elicit the basic elements of each psychopathological construct.

This type of research would serve to clarify the exact nature of the specific psychopathology of bulimia and anorexia nervosa. It would generate a much needed assessment instrument, and it would help identify important areas for cognitive change. Whilst such an interview would be too cumbersome and intrusive to study the process of change during treatment, it might provide the basis for devising an intreatment self-report measure.

Cognitive Behaviour Therapy for Bulimia: Further Applications of this Approach

Anorexia Nervosa

Patients with bulimia have many features in common with patients with anorexia nervosa, and approximately half have had anorexia nervosa in the past. In particular, the core psychopathology of the two conditions seems very similar. Since these abnormal beliefs and values seem to be amenable to change using cognitive behavioural techniques, the application of this form of treatment to cases of anorexia nervosa seems justified. This is particularly true of patients with the bulimic subtype of anorexia nervosa since they are also likely to benefit from the behavioural strategies used to establish a normal eating pattern.

If this approach is used to treat patients with anorexia nervosa, it needs to be modified and lengthened in order to accommodate two major problems. The first of these problems is poor motivation. Since the behaviour of most patients with anorexia nervosa is consonant with their beliefs and values, they often see no need for treatment. Garner and Bemis (27) have described various ways of increasing the motivation of these patients. They emphasise the importance of establishing a sound therapeutic relationship, accepting the patient's beliefs as genuine for her, and adopting an experimental approach in which the therapist and patient explore the use of various different treatment strategies. At the beginning of treatment, it is also worthwhile discussing with the patient the advantages and disadvantages of change. Patients are often distressed by starvation-related symptoms such as

impaired concentration, preoccupation with food and eating, and sleep disturbance. Once they understand the basis for these symptoms they tend to be more
willing to accept treatment. The problem of motivation is less acute with patients
who binge-eat, since the resulting sense of loss of control is generally a source of
great distress. Such patients welcome the self-control strategies used in the early
stages of treatment.

The second problem is that patients with anorexia nervosa must be persuaded
to gain weight. Unless the weight loss is extreme or the patient's health is endangered by physical complications, programmed weight gain can be incorporated
into the outpatient treatment regime. It is best to devote several sessions to the
establishment of a collaborative working relationship before emphasising the need
for weight gain. Thereafter, it becomes a nonnegotiable part of treatment. However, patients must understand why they need to gain weight. They need to be
informed of the physical and psychological sequelae of starvation (25,45), and
they need to understand how these sequelae perpetuate the eating disorder (25).
It is best to decide on a target *weight range* in the region of 90% of the average
weight for their age, height, and sex. Patients should be reassured that care will
be taken to ensure that they do not exceed this range. Precisely how they choose
to increase their weight is unimportant so long as the weight gain is gradual
(approximately 1 kg/week) and occurs without contravening other elements of
the behavioural programme. In effect, this means that they must eat high-calorie
foods as part of their prescribed meals or snacks. If weight gain does not occur,
the therapist and patient must consider whether hospitalization is indicated. On
the other hand, if the patient succeeds in gaining weight and reaches the target
range, treatment can adhere to the guidelines described earlier.

An alternative strategy is to adopt a two-stage approach to treatment. In the
first stage, treatment follows conventional lines with a period of hospitalization
during which the patient's weight is restored to an acceptable level. Thereafter,
cognitive behaviour therapy is instituted on an outpatient basis. The relative merits of the one-stage and two-stage approaches have yet to be studied.

Obesity

In many respects, this cognitive behavioural treatment can be viewed as a modification of the standard behavioural programme for obesity. The main differences
are that the treatment is more intensive in the initial stages, it is lengthier, and
there is a greater emphasis on cognitive factors and the maintenance of change.
It is possible that by incorporating some of these modifications the effectiveness
of existing behavioural programmes for obesity might be increased. It would certainly seem appropriate to use elements of this approach in the treatment of obese
people who binge-eat, a population who have been reported to respond poorly to
conventional programmes (77). In addition, the cognitive components of treatment might benefit obese people with body image disparagement.

Other Related Disorders

Some patients present with a number of features of anorexia nervosa or bulimia without fulfilling the criteria for either syndrome. These patients may also benefit from elements of the treatment approach. For example, there is a group of patients who diet excessively, induce vomiting when they feel they have overeaten, yet neither binge-eat nor have a weight which is outside the normal range. These patients appear to respond to a treatment which combines the restraint-reducing techniques with cognitive restructuring and training in problem solving.

In view of the evidence that there are a large number of people who binge-eat but do not fulfill the other criteria for bulimia (11,21), treatment programmes such as the one described need to be modified in order to increase their range of application. Since behavioural treatments for obesity have been successfully introduced into self-help groups for those wishing to lose weight (69), it may be possible to adapt this treatment approach for use by groups.

SUMMARY AND CONCLUSIONS

The prevalence of the syndromes bulimia and bulimia nervosa is not known. Although existing epidemiological studies have produced somewhat conflicting findings, it appears likely that these syndromes constitute a significant source of psychiatric morbidity.

It is interesting to note that prior to 1980 there appear to have been few *patients* who fulfil diagnostic criteria for these syndromes, whereas since then the number of such patients seems to have greatly increased. Whilst it is possible that the recent publicity may have engendered new cases by suggesting that self-induced vomiting is an effective means of weight control, there are two other likely explanations for the increase. First, the publicity may have helped people with these conditions divulge their eating problems to doctors. Second, doctors may have been alerted to the fact that people with a normal body weight may nevertheless have an eating disorder which requires a specialist's help. If these explanations are correct, the upsurge in referrals may be a short-lived phenomenon during which existing cases of varying duration will come to attention. Thereafter, it would be predicted that the referral rate will decline to a level which more accurately reflects the incidence of the two conditions (22).

The emergence of these syndromes is not simply of theoretical interest. They pose a challenging therapeutic problem which has necessitated the development of specific psychological approaches to their treatment. However, before any treatment for bulimia can be advocated, its use should be supported by data from controlled outcome studies in which changes in each facet of the condition are assessed including patients' eating habits, moods, and most importantly, their attitudes to their weight and shape. As has been discussed, behavioural improvement is likely to be short-lived unless it is accompanied by significant attitude change.

APPENDIX

A Patient's Maintenance Plan

Eating problems may recur at times of stress. You should regard your eating problem as an Achilles heel: It is the way you may react at times of difficulty.

You discovered during treatment that certain strategies helped you regain control over your eating. The strategies you found most helpful are listed below. These should be reestablished under two sets of circumstances: (a) if you sense you are at risk of relapse; or (b) if your eating problem has deteriorated. At such times there will often be some unresolved difficulty underlying your relapse or fear of relapse. You must, therefore, examine what is happening in your life and look for any events or difficulties which might be of relevance. Once these have been identified, you should then consider all possible solutions to your current problems and construct an appropriate plan of action. In addition, you should use one or more of the following strategies in order to regain control over your eating:

1. Set some time aside so that you can reflect on your current difficulties. You need to devise a plan of action. Reckon on formally reevaluating your progress every day or so. Some strategies may have worked, some may not. Devise a new plan in the light of your experience. Remember, you find it helpful to write things down.

2. Restart monitoring everything you eat when you eat it.

3. Restrict your eating to three or four set meals a day, plus one or two planned snacks. Try to have these meals and snacks at pre-determined times. If you are tempted to eat between these times, think very carefully whether you really want to. Remember, you can always say "No, thank you."

4. Plan your days ahead. Avoid both long periods of unstructured time and overbooking. If you are feeling particularly vulnerable, plan your meals for the day ahead so that you know exactly what you will be eating and when. In general, you should try to keep one step ahead of the problem.

5. Restrict your food stocks. Only buy foods for a specific meal or event. If you feel you are at risk of buying too much food, carry the bare minimum amount of money with you.

6. Identify the times at which you are most likely to overeat (from recent experience and the evidence provided by your monitoring sheets), and plan alternative activities which are incompatible with eating such as meeting friends, exercising, taking a bath, etc.

7. As far as possible avoid areas where stocks of food are kept. Try to keep out of the kitchen between meals.

8. If you are thinking too much about your weight make sure you are only weighing once a week. If necessary, stop weighing altogether. If you want to reduce weight, do so by cutting down the quantity you eat at each meal rather than by skipping meals. Remember, you should accept a weight range, and gradual changes in weight are best.

9. If you are thinking too much about your shape, this may be because you are anxious or depressed. You tend to feel fat when things are not going well. You should try problem solving in order to see whether you can identify your current problems and do something positive to solve or at least minimize them.

10. If at all possible, confide in someone. Explain your present predicament. A trouble shared is a trouble halved. Remember, you would not mind any friend of yours confiding his or her problems to you.

11. Set yourself limited, realistic goals. Work from hour to hour. One failure does not justify a succession of failures. Note your successes, however modest, on your monitoring sheets.

Before seeking professional help, try to use the strategies listed above. Remember, you have used them with benefit in the past.

ACKNOWLEDGMENTS

I am grateful to Dr. Peter Cooper and Dr. Zafra Cooper for their helpful advice during the writing of this chapter. I am also indebted to Mrs. Marianne O'Connor for her assistance in preparing the manuscript. The treatment research is being supported by a grant from the Medical Research Council of the U. K.

REFERENCES

1. Allon, N. (1982): The stigma of overweight in everyday life. In: *Psychological Aspects of Obesity: A Handbook,* edited by B. B. Wolman, pp. 130–174. Van Nostrand Reinhold, New York.
2. American Psychiatric Association, Committee on Nomenclature and Statistics (1980): *Diagnostic and Statistical Manual of Mental Disorders.* 3rd Ed. American Psychiatric Association, Washington D.C.
3. Bemis, K. M. (1983): A comparison of functional relationships in anorexia nervosa and phobia. In: *Anorexia Nervosa: Recent Developments in Research,* edited by P. L. Darby, P. E. Garfinkel, D. M. Garner, and D. V. Coscina, Alan Liss, New York (*in press*).
4. Ben-Tovim, D. I., Hunter, M., and Crisp, A. H. (1977): Discrimination and evaluation of shape and size in anorexia nervosa: an exploratory study. *Res. Commun. Psychol. Psychiatry Behav.,* 2:241–257.
5. Boskind-Lodahl, M. (1976): Cinderella's stepsisters: A feminist perspective on anorexia nervosa and bulimia. *Signs: J. Women Culture and Soc.,* 2:342–356.
6. Boskind-Lodahl, M., and White, W. C. (1978): The definition and treatment of bulimarexia in college women—A pilot study. *J. Am. Coll. Health Assoc.,* 27:84–86, 97.
7. Button, E. J., and Whitehouse, A. (1981): Subclinical anorexia nervosa. *Psychol. Med.,* 11:509–516.
8. Casper, R. C., Eckert, E. D., Halmi, K. A., Goldberg, S. C., and Davis, J. M. (1980): Bulimia: its incidence and clinical importance in patients with anorexia nervosa. *Arch. Gen. Psychiatry,* 37:1030–1035.
9. Casper, R. C., Halmi, K. A., Goldberg, S. C., Eckert, E., and Davis, J. M. (1982): Anorexia nervosa and bulimia. *Arch. Gen. Psychiatry,* 39:488–489.
10. Clarke, M. G., and Palmer, R. L. (1983): Eating attitudes and neurotic symptoms in university students. *Br. J. Psychiatry,* 142:299–304.
11. Cooper, P. J., and Fairburn, C. G. (1983): Binge-eating and self-induced vomiting in the community: a preliminary study. *Br. J. Psychiatry,* 142: 139–144.

12. Cooper, P. J., Waterman, G., and Fairburn, C. G. (1983): Women with eating problems: a community survey. *Br. J. Clin. Psychol. (in press).*
13. Crisp, A. H. (1979): Fatness, metabolism and sexual behaviour. In: *Emotion and Reproduction,* edited by L. Carenza and L. Zichella, pp. 215–237. Academic Press, London.
14. Crisp, A. H., and Fransella, F. (1972): Conceptual changes during recovery from anorexia nervosa. *Br. J. Med. Psychol.,* 45:395–405.
15. Fairburn, C. G. (1981): A cognitive behavioural approach to the management of bulimia. *Psychol. Med.,* 11:707–711.
16. Fairburn, C. G. (1982): Binge-eating and its management. *Br. J. Psychiatry,* 141:631–633.
17. Fairburn, C. G. (1983): Bulimia nervosa. *Br. J. Hosp. Med.* 29:537–542.
18. Fairburn, C. G. (1983): The place of a cognitive behavioural approach in the management of bulimia. In: *Anorexia Nervosa: Recent Developments in Research,* edited by P. L. Darby, P. E. Garfinkel, D. M. Garner, and D. V. Coscina. Alan Liss, New York (*in press*).
19. Fairburn, C. G., and Cooper, P. J. (1982): Self-induced vomiting and bulimia nervosa: an undetected problem. *Br. Med. J.,* 284:1153–1155.
20. Fairburn, C. G., and Cooper, P. J. (1983): The epidemiology of bulimia nervosa: two community studies. *Int. J. Eating Disord. (in press).*
21. Fairburn, C. G., and Cooper, P. J. (1983): Binge-eating, self-induced vomiting and purgative abuse: a community study. *(In preparation.)*
22. Fairburn, C. G., Cooper, P. J., and O'Connor, M. (1983): Publicity and bulimia nervosa. *Br. J. Psychiatry,* 142:101–102.
23. Fichter, M. M., and Keeser, W. (1980): Das Anorexia-nervosa-Inventar zur Selbstbeurteilung (ANIS). *Arch. Psychiatr. Nervenkr.,* 228:67–89.
24. Fransella, F., and Crisp, A. H. (1979): Comparisons of weight concepts in groups of neurotic, normal and anorexic females. *Br. J. Psychiatry,* 134:79–86.
25. Garfinkel, P. E., and Garner, D. M. (1982): *Anorexia Nervosa: A Multidimensional Perspective.* Brunner/Mazel, New York.
26. Garfinkel, P. E., Moldofsky, H., and Garner, D. M. (1980): The heterogeneity of anorexia nervosa: bulimia as a distinct subgroup. *Arch. Gen. Psychiatry,* 37:1036–1040.
27. Garner, D. M., and Bemis, K. M. (1982): A cognitive-behavioural approach to anorexia nervosa. *Cognitive Ther. Res.,* 6:123–150.
28. Garner, D. M., and Garfinkel, P. E. (1978): Sociocultural factors in anorexia nervosa. *Lancet,* 2:674.
29. Garner, D. M., and Garfinkel, P. E. (1979): The Eating Attitudes Test: an index of the symptoms of anorexia nervosa. *Psychol. Med.,* 9:273–279.
30. Garner, D. M., and Garfinkel, P. E. (1980): Sociocultural factors in the development of anorexia nervosa. *Psychol. Med.,* 10:647–656.
31. Garner, D. M., and Garfinkel, P. E. (1981): Body image in anorexia nervosa: measurement, theory and clinical implications. *Int. J. Psychiatry Med.,* 2:263–284.
32. Garner, D. M., Olmstead, M. P., and Polivy, J. (1983): Development and validation of a multidimensional eating disorder inventory for anorexia nervosa and bulimia. *Int. J. Eating Disord,* 2:15–34.
33. Garrow, J. S. (1981): *Treat Obesity Seriously.* Churchill Livingstone, Edinburgh.
34. Geller, M. I., Kelly, J. A., Traxler, W. T., and Marone, F. J. (1978): Behavioural treatment of an adolescent female's bulimic anorexia: Modification of immediate consequences and antecedent conditions. *J. Clin. Child Psychol.,* 7:138–142.
35. Goldberg, S. C., Halmi, K. A., Eckert, E. D., Casper, R. C., Davis, J. M., and Roper, M. (1980): Attitudinal dimensions in anorexia nervosa. *J. Psychiatr. Res.,* 15:239–251.
36. Goldfried, M. R., and Davison, G. C. (1976): *Clinical Behaviour Therapy.* Holt, Rinehart, and Winston, New York.
37. Greenberg, D., and Marks, I. (1982): Behavioural psychotherapy of uncommon referrals. *Br. J. Psychiatry,* 141:148–153.
38. Grinc, G. A. (1982): A cognitive-behavioural model for the treatment of chronic vomiting. *J. Behav. Med.,* 5:135–141.
39. Halmi, K. A., Falk, J. R., and Schwartz, E. (1981): Binge-eating and vomiting: a survey of a college population. *Psychol. Med.,* 11:697–706.
40. Halmi, K. A., Goldberg, S. C., Casper, R. C., Eckert, E. D., and Davis, J. M. (1979): Pretreatment predictors of outcome of anorexia nervosa. *Br. J. Psychiatry,* 134:71–78.

41. Hawkins, R. C., and Clement, P. F. (1980): Development and construct validation of a self-report measure of binge eating tendencies. *Addict. Behav.,* 5:219–226.
42. Herman, C. P., and Polivy, J. (1980): Restrained eating. In: *Obesity,* edited by A. J. Stunkard, pp. 208–225. W. B. Saunders Company, Philadelphia.
43. Herzog, D. B. (1982): Bulimia: the secretive syndrome. *Psychosomatics,* 23:481–484.
44. Hudson, J. I., Laffer, P. S., and Pope, H. G. (1982): Bulimia related to affective disorder by family history and response to the dexamethasone suppression test. *Am. J. Psychiatry,* 139:685–687.
45. Keys, A., Brozek, J., Henschel, A., Mickelsen, O., and Taylor, H. L. (1950): *The Biology of Human Starvation.* The University of Minnesota Press, Minneapolis.
46. Lacey, J. H. (1982): Compulsive eating. In: *Dependent Phenomenon,* edited by J. Marks and M. Glatt. M. T. P. Press, Lancaster.
47. Linden, W. (1980): Multicomponent behaviour therapy in a case of compulsive binge-eating followed by vomiting. *J. Behav. Ther. Exp. Psychiatry,* 11:297–300.
48. Long, C. G., and Cordle, C. J. (1982): Psychological treatment of binge-eating and self-induced vomiting. *Br. J. Med. Psychol.,* 55:139–145.
49. Mahoney, M. H., and Mahoney, K. (1976): *Permanent Weight Control.* Norton, New York.
50. Meyer, R. G. (1973): Delay therapy: two case reports. *Behav. Ther.,* 4:709–711.
51. Mitchell, J. E., and Pyle, R. L. (1982): The bulimic syndrome in normal weight individuals: a review. *Int. J. Eating Disord.,* 1:61–73.
52. Monti, P. M., McCrady, B. S., and Barlow, D. H. (1977): Effect of positive reinforcement, informational feedback, and contingency contracting on a bulimic anorexic female. *Behav. Ther.,* 8:258–263.
53. Moore, S. L., and Rakes, S. M. (1982): Binge eating—Therapeutic response to diphenylhydantoin: case report. *J. Clin. Psychiatry,* 43:385–386.
54. Orbach, S. (1978): *Fat is a Feminist Issue.* Paddington Press, London.
55. Orbach, S. (1982): *Fat is a Feminist Issue II.* Hamlyn Paperbacks, Feltham, Middlesex.
56. Palmer, R. L. (1979): The dietary chaos syndrome: a useful new term? *Br. J. Med. Psychol.,* 52:187–190.
57. Paykel, E. S., Mueller, P. S., and de la Vergne, P. M. (1973): Amitriptyline, weight gain and carbohydrate craving: a side effect. *Br. J. Psychiatry,* 123:501–507.
58. Polivy, J., Garner, D. M., and Garfinkel, P. E. (1983): Causes and consequences of the current preference for thin female physiques. In: *Physical Appearance, Stigma and Social Behaviour.* The Ontario Symposium in Personality and Social Psychology. L. Erlbaum *(in press).*
59. Polivy, J., Herman, C. P., Jazwinski, C., and Olmstead, M. P. (1983): Restraint and binge eating. In: *Binge Eating: Theory and Practice,* edited by R. C. Hawkins, W. Fremouw, and P. Clement. Springer, New York *(in press).*
60. Pope, H. G., and Hudson, J. I. (1982): Treatment of bulimia with antidepressants. *Psychopharmacology,* 78:176–179.
61. Pyle, R. L., Mitchell, J. E., and Eckert, E. D. (1981): Bulimia: A report of 34 cases. *J. Clin. Psychiatry,* 42:60–64.
62. Rau, J. H., and Green, R. S. (1975): Compulsive eating: a neurophysiological approach to certain eating disorders. *Compr. Psychiatry,* 16:223–231.
63. Robins, L. N., Helzer, J. E., Croughan, J., and Ratcliff, K. S. (1981): National Institute of Mental Health diagnostic interview schedule: its history, characteristics and validity. *Arch. Gen. Psychiatry,* 38:381–389.
64. Rosen, J. C., and Leitenberg, H. (1982): Bulimia nervosa: treatment with exposure and response prevention. *Behav. Ther.,* 13:117–124.
65. Russell, G. F. M. (1979): Bulimia nervosa: an ominous variant of anorexia nervosa. *Psychol. Med.,* 9:429–448.
66. Russell, G. F. M. (1981): The current treatment of anorexia nervosa. *Br. J. Psychiatry,* 138:164–166.
67. Smith, G. R. (1981): Modification of binge-eating in obesity. *J. Behav. Ther. Exp. Psychiatry,* 12:333–336.
68. Stuart, R. B. (1978): *Act Thin, Stay Thin.* Norton, New York.
69. Stuart, R. B., and Mitchell, C. (1980): Self-help groups in the control of body weight. In: *Obesity,* edited by A. J. Stunkard, pp. 345–354. W. B. Saunders, Philadelphia.
70. Stunkard, A. J. (1976): *The Pain of Obesity.* Bull Publishing Company, Palo Alto, California.

71. Stunkard, A. J. (1980): Psychoanalysis and psychotherapy. In: *Obesity*, edited by A. J. Stunkard, pp. 355–368. W. B. Saunders Company, Philadelphia.

72. Thompson, M. G., and Schwartz, D. M. (1982): Life adjustment of women with anorexia nervosa and anorexic-like behaviour. *Int. J. Eating Disord.*, 1:47–60.

73. Walsh, B. T., Stewart, J. W., Wright, L., Harrison, W., Roose, S. P., and Glassman, A. H. (1982): Treatment of bulimia with monoamine oxidase inhibitors. *Am. J. Psychiatry*, 139:1629–1630.

74. Wardle, J., and Beinart, H. (1981): Binge eating: A theoretical review. *Br. J. Clin. Psychol.*, 20:97–109.

75. Wermuth, B. M., Davis, K. L., Hollister, L.E., and Stunkard, A. J. (1977): Phenytoin treatment of the binge-eating syndrome. *Am. J. Psychiatry*, 134:1249–1253.

76. Wijesinghe, B. (1973): Massed electrical aversion treatment of compulsive eating. *J. Behav. Ther. Exp. Psychiatry*, 4:133–135.

77. Wilson, G. T. (1976): Obesity, binge eating, and behaviour therapy: Some clinical observations. *Behav. Ther.*, 7:700–701.

78. Wing, J. K., Cooper, J. E., and Sartorius, N. (1974): *The Measurement and Classification of Psychiatric Symptoms*. Cambridge University Press, Cambridge.

79. Wooley, S. C., and Wooley, O. W. (1980): Eating disorders: obesity and anorexia. In: *Women and Psychotherapy*, edited by A. M. Brodsky and R. T. Hare-Mustin. pp. 135–158. Guilford Press, New York.

Eating and Its Disorders, edited by A. J.
Stunkard and E. Stellar. Raven Press,
New York © 1984.

Treatment of Bulimia with Antidepressants: Theoretical Considerations and Clinical Findings

James I. Hudson, Harrison G. Pope, Jr., and Jeffrey M. Jonas

*Mailman Research Center, McLean Hospital, Belmont, Massachusetts 02178 and
Department of Psychiatry, Harvard Medical School, Boston, Massachusetts*

Bulimia is a psychiatric disorder characterized by recurrent episodes of binge eating, often associated with self-induced vomiting or laxative abuse. Long recognized as a syndrome associated with anorexia nervosa (8,9) and obesity (42), bulimia has only recently been recognized as a separate disorder, often present in normal weight individuals (31,37). In fact, bulimia appears to be surprisingly common, as suggested by two recent epidemiologic studies among student populations (12,41). Although there have been no formal outcome studies of bulimia, the presence of bulimia in association with anorexia nervosa appears to be a poor prognostic sign (2,8,9,18), and Russell has commented on the ever-present danger of suicide in bulimic patients (37).

The etiology of this common and often serious disorder is unknown, and it has proven refractory to many forms of treatment. The last several years, however, have seen an increasing body of evidence suggesting that bulimia may be closely linked to major affective disorder. We review below some of these data, with particular emphasis on the most practical development to emerge from this research, namely, treatment of bulimia with antidepressant medications.

CLINICAL, LABORATORY, AND FAMILY STUDIES RELATING BULIMIA TO MAJOR AFFECTIVE DISORDER

Phenomenology

The phenomenology—or presenting symptoms—of bulimic patients shows close parallels to major affective disorder: Several investigators have noted prominent depressive symptomatology in bulimic patients. Russell (37), studying 30 patients with bulimia, found that 87% had moderate or severe depressive symptoms. Similarly, Nogami and Yabana (24) reported that 12 of 16 bulimics were clinically depressed. Pyle et al. (31) reported in their series of 34 bulimics that "most reported depression," and that MMPI profiles revealed a high average depression score. These studies have not, however, used formal diagnostic instruments to ascertain diagnoses, nor have they specified the diagnostic criteria that were used.

Recently, we have completed a study in which we administered the National Institute of Mental Health Diagnostic Interview Schedule (DIS) (34), an instrument of demonstrated reliability in the assessment of a wide range of DSM-III diagnoses (14,15,33), to 74 patients with bulimia (70 women, mean age 27.5, SD 7.8, range 13–49 years; 4 men, ages 26, 28, 41, and 56). Twenty-five patients had anorexia nervosa concurrently or had displayed it in the past. Technically, since DSM-III excludes the diagnosis of bulimia in the presence of anorexia nervosa, those patients with concurrent anorexia nervosa would be diagnosed as *anorexia nervosa* by DSM-III criteria. However, we have included the 5 patients with concurrent anorexia nervosa in the present analysis.

The prevalence of various DSM-III diagnoses in this unselected, consecutive series of bulimic patients is shown in Table 1. Notable is the high prevalence of major affective disorder, as well as anxiety disorders such as agoraphobia, panic disorder, and obsessive-compulsive disorder, which are thought possibly to be related to major affective disorder (3,20,46).

Response to Laboratory Tests

A second line of evidence relating bulimia to major affective disorder comes from biological tests. Studies of the dexamethasone suppression test (DST) in patients with major depression have reported nonsuppression of plasma cortisol (positive tests) at 4 p.m. on the day following a 1 mg dose of dexamethasone administered at 11 p.m., in about 50% of patients (4,6,10,38,43). Administering the same test to 18 women with bulimia, Roy-Byrne et al. (36) found that 12 (67%) had positive DSTs. We performed the DST on 47 patients with bulimia and 22 normal controls (16). Results are presented in Fig. 1. Twenty-two (47%) of the bulimics had a positive DST, significantly greater than the 9% prevalence of positive tests found in the normal controls ($p < .002$, by Fisher's exact test, one-tailed). In both the study by Roy-Byrne et al. and ours, patients were greater than 80% of ideal body weight; however, a weak but significant ($p < .05$) correlation was found in both studies between percentage of ideal body weight and cortisol level. No significant correlation in either study was found between frequency of binging and cortisol level, indicating that the metabolic stress of frequent binging and purging did not account for the positive tests.

Although the specificity of the DST for affective disorder remains uncertain, a high prevalence of positive DSTs has been reported in several psychiatric disorders, such as schizo-affective disorder (6), obsessive-compulsive disorder (19), and borderline personality disorder (7), which have been linked to affective disorder by studies of phenomenology, family history, and treatment response (1,7,20,27–29). By contrast, a low prevalence of positive DSTs has been found in disorders which are apparently not related to affective disorder, such as schizophrenia (5,10,35), nonendogenous depression, or adjustment reaction with depressed

TABLE 1. *Lifetime DSM-III diagnoses in 74 patients with bulimia*

	N	(%)
Substance use disorders		
Alcohol abuse or dependence	19	(26)
Amphetamine abuse or dependence	10	(13)
Other substance use disorders[a]	10	(13)
Total substance use disorders[b]	25	(34)
Affective disorders		
Bipolar disorder	10	(13)
Major depression	49	(66)
Total major affective disorders	59	(80)
Cyclothymic disorder	2	(3)
Dysthymic disorder	20	(27)
Atypical depression	1	(1)
Total affective disorders[b]	66	(89)
Anxiety disorders		
Agoraphobia	11	(15)
Simple phobia	7	(9)
Panic disorder	31	(42)
Generalized anxiety disorder	2	(3)
Obsessive-compulsive disorder	22	(30)
Total anxiety disorders[b]	37	(50)
Disorders of impulse control		
Kleptomania	23	(31)
Intermittent explosive disorder	2	(3)
Total disorders of impulse control[b]	25	(34)
Personality disorders		
Histrionic personality disorder	7	(9)
Antisocial personality disorder	1	(1)
Borderline personality disorder	10	(13)
Total personality disorders[b]	11	(15)

[a]Includes cases of sedative-hypnotic abuse or dependence (3), opioid dependence (1), cocaine abuse (1), cannabis abuse or dependence (3), and mixed substance abuse (4).

[b]Figure given reflects number of patients who had at least one diagnosis within the group of disorders. Some patients had more than one diagnosis, and hence the total number of diagnoses made within a group of disorders may exceed the number of patients affected.

In addition, there were 3 cases of factitious disorder with psychological symptoms, and 1 case each of schizoaffective disorder; conduct disorder, socialized nonaggressive; and zoophilia. There were no cases of schizophrenia or somatoform disorder.

mood (4,6,10,35) and borderline personality disorder without concomitant affective disorder (35). Given these findings, it tentatively appears that the positive DSTs in bulimic patients reflect a relationship between bulimia and major affective disorder.

A second neuroendocrine test which may be specific for the diagnosis of major affective disorder (among psychiatric disorders) is the thyrotropin releasing hormone (TRH) stimulation test, in which a blunted TSH response to TRH is

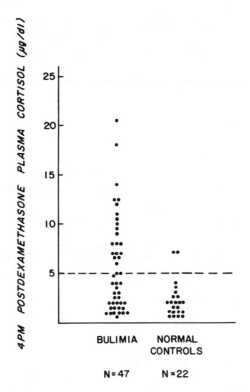

FIG. 1. Response to the dexamethasone suppression test in patients with bulimia and normal controls (62). (Reprinted with permission from Elsevier Biomedical Press.)

reported in patients with major affective disorder (10,11,22,23,30,43). Roy-Byrne et al. (36) administered the TRH stimulation test to 10 patients with bulimia and found that 8 had a blunted TSH response. There was a slight correlation between test results and frequency of binging, but not weight.

Thus, response to two neuroendocrine tests, which may be specific for affective disorder, tentatively suggests a biochemical relationship between bulimia and major affective disorder.

Family Studies

The third, and perhaps most persuasive, line of evidence relating bulimia to major affective disorder comes from family studies. This was first noted by Pyle et al. (31), who reported that 48% of 33 nonadopted bulimic patients had a first-degree relative with depression, although they noted that they did not use validated criteria for this assessment.

We performed a family history study of bulimia in which we evaluated the 350 first-degree relatives of 75 patients with bulimia, 20 of whom had a lifetime diagnosis of anorexia nervosa (17). Detailed psychiatric information on the subjects' first-degree relatives was elicited from the subjects and from available family members. Diagnoses of ill relatives were made using DSM-III criteria and were divided into probable and possible on the basis of the available information. Morbid risk for affective disorder was calculated by a modification of the Weinberg shorter method (40), using age 15 to 65 years as the estimated period of risk for the development of affective disorder. Comparison groups were composed of patients meeting DSM-III criteria for bipolar disorder ($N = 40$), schizophrenia ($N = 46$), and borderline personality disorder ($N = 15$). Patients in the borderline personality disorder group were screened to exclude cases with concomitant major affective disorder. All of the comparison groups were composed of inpatients at McLean Hospital; their first-degree relatives were diagnosed by investigators blind to the diagnosis of the probands, on the basis of detailed interviews or descriptions of these relatives recorded in the patients' charts.

Morbid risk for major affective disorder in the first-degree relatives and the percentage of subjects with at least one first-degree relative with major affective disorder are shown in Table 2, for all study groups. The morbid risk for major affective disorder in the first-degree relatives, and the percentage of probands with a positive family history of affective disorder did not differ significantly between the bulimics and the reference group with bipolar disorder. However, the bulimics differed significantly from the reference groups with schizophrenia and borderline personality disorder, both in morbid risk for affective disorder among relatives and in percentage of probands with a positive family history.

In conclusion, the evidence from studies of phenomenology, response to biological tests, and family history suggests that bulimia may be closely related to major affective disorder. One question that should be answered, however, is whether our sample of patients with bulimia might have been biased in some way to include a disproportionate number of patients with concomitant affective disorder. Although a sampling bias of this type cannot be excluded entirely, it seems unlikely for three reasons: (a) The sample represented unselected consecutive subjects with bulimia; (b) subjects were recruited from several sources including admissions to the Behavior Therapy Unit at McLean Hospital, other inpatients at McLean Hospital, outpatients referred to us for evaluation, and respondents to two advertisements for treatment studies—and there were no significant differences in the prevalence of major affective disorder, prevalence of positive DSTs, or prevalence of familial affective disorder among these subsamples; and (c) our sample is similar, both in demographic features and in prevalence of affective symptomatology, to the three other largest series of patients with bulimia that have been reported in the literature (24,31,37).

Evidence relating bulimia to major affective disorder would be of only theoretical interest, however, if there were no implications for treatment. Therefore, the remainder of this chapter is devoted to studies of the response of bulimia to antidepressant medications.

OPEN TREATMENT STUDIES WITH ANTIDEPRESSANTS

We are currently aware of five reports of successful treatment of bulimia with antidepressant medications. Rich, in 1978 (32), described a 21-year-old woman with bulimia whose binge eating disappeared on 45 mg of phenelzine, reappeared

TABLE 2. Morbid risk for major affective disorder[a] and number of probands with a family history of major affective disorder among diagnostic groups

Diagnosis	No. of probands	No. of first-degree relatives	Cases of major affective disorder	Morbid risk for major affective disorder in relatives (%)	No. of probands with family history of major affective disorder
Bulimia	75	350	59	28[b]	40(53)[b]
Bipolar disorder	40	242	22	19	17(43)
Schizophrenia	46	223	4	3	4(9)
Borderline personality disorder	15	78	1	3	1(7)

[a]Major affective disorder = bipolar disorder and major depression.
[b]Bulimia vs bipolar disorder not significant ($p > 0.05$); $p < 0.001$ compared to schizophrenia and borderline personality disorder (Fisher's exact test, two-tailed).

when phenelzine was discontinued, and then disappeared again when phenelzine was resumed. Shader, in 1982 (39), reported similar success using phenelzine to treat a woman with atypical depression and compulsive binge eating.

Two studies of groups of patients treated with antidepressant medications appeared in 1982. Our group described 8 patients treated primarily with tricyclic antidepressants, 6 of whom responded with a greater than 50% reduction in frequency of eating binges within 2 to 4 weeks (25). Improvement persisted on 2 to 6 month follow-up. Even better results were reported by Walsh et al. (44), who described marked improvement in 6 of 6 patients treated with monomine oxidase inhibitors, 4 of whom enjoyed complete remission of binging. In an updated report from these researchers, 9 of 11 consecutive patients treated with monoamine oxidase (MAO) inhibitors have achieved a marked response (B. Timothy Walsh, *personal communication*).

Subsequently, our group has reported an additional 6 cases of bulimia treated with MAO inhibitors, 5 of whom ceased to binge entirely, a response which has been maintained on 1 to 5 month follow-up (21).

In summary, these uncontrolled reports of the use of antidepressant medications in bulimia describe success in 22 of 26 patients (our two reports had 1 patient in common). Such results must be interpreted with caution, however, since they are uncontrolled observations. To be sure, it seems improbable that bulimia of many years duration, refractory to numerous previous therapeutic attempts, would remit spontaneously weeks after starting an antidepressant. However, we cannot exclude the possibility of spontaneous improvement in the absence of a controlled study. We have now completed such a study, using imipramine, which is described below.

In contrast to these initial impressive findings from groups in the United States, we should note the less optimistic experience of British researchers. Russell (37) reports that antidepressants help to ameliorate depressive symptoms seen in bulimics but have no effect on binge eating. It is premature to speculate on the difference between these investigations.

PLACEBO-CONTROLLED DOUBLE-BLIND STUDY OF IMIPRAMINE

In order to test more rigorously the efficacy of antidepressant medications in the treatment of bulimia, we conducted a placebo-controlled double-blind study of imipramine in 22 patients with bulimia (26).

Methods

We recruited 22 subjects who met DSM-III criteria for bulimia and who also fulfilled the following qualifications: (a) age between 16 and 55 years; (b) binge-eating followed by vomiting or laxative abuse occurring at least twice weekly for the past month; (c) bulimia for at least 1 year's duration; (d) never previously treated with antidepressants or ECT; (e) not currently using psychiatric medications; (f) neither pregnant nor likely to become pregnant; (g) no serious medical illness; and (h) not suicidal. Sixteen subjects were recruited from an advertisement placed in the newsletter of a local self-help organization, 5 subjects answered an advertisement in a weekly metropolitan newspaper, and 1 subject was referred from a local organization for the treatment of eating disorders.

The demographic and clinical characteristics of the 19 subjects who completed the study are shown in Table 3. (Three subjects dropped out within the first 3 weeks, 2 developed a rash on imipramine, and 1 took an overdose of placebo capsules.) The subjects displayed a mean duration of bulimia of 6.8 years and had a mean of 9.2 binges/week. Four had a past history of anorexia nervosa, but none currently had anorexia nervosa; all subjects weighed between 80 and 115% of normal body weight. Most of the subjects had received some form of individual psychotherapy, group psychotherapy, and/or behavior therapy in the past; the 3 subjects who were in psychotherapy during the study period had all begun psychotherapy at least 6 months prior to participation in the study.

After randomization into groups receiving imipramine ($N = 11$, of whom 2 subsequently dropped out) or placebo ($N = 11$, with one dropout), subjects were given identical capsules containing either imipramine 50 mg or inert placebo and were instructed to start with 1 capsule at bedtime and increase by 1 capsule every other day until they had either reached 4 capsules per day or were limited by side effects. The study ran for 6 weeks. At the beginning of the study and at the end of 2, 4, and 6 weeks, subjects were seen both by a physician, who monitored the subjects for medication compliance and side effects, and by a rater who administered the 24-item Hamilton Rating Scale (HRS) (13), recorded frequency of binging, and asked the subjects to rate themselves on the following subjective scales: intensity of eating binges, degree of preoccupation with food, and self-control with relation to food (0 = none to 5 = maximum); and subjective global improvement (-1 = worse, 0 = unchanged, 1 = slight, 2 = moderate, 3 = marked). Both physician and rater were blind to treatment assignment.

Blindness was broken at the completion of the 6-week study period and the results analyzed. We gave the subjects in the imipramine group the option of continued treatment with imipramine or of changing to another antidepressant, depending on the beneficial effects and side effects they experienced on imipramine. Subjects in the placebo group were similarly offered a trial of imipramine and/or other antidepressants.

Comparisons for statistical significance were made using the Wilcoxon rank sum test, two-tailed, unless noted otherwise.

Results

The results of the study are summarized in Table 3 and illustrated in Fig. 2. By week 6, the number of binges per week for subjects in the imipramine group had declined by an average of 7.5 (SE 2.0) compared to a mean decrease of 0.2 (SE 1.5) in the placebo group ($p < 0.01$). As illustrated in Fig. 2, the average reduction in binging for the imipramine group was 70% compared to almost no

TABLE 3. *Double-blind study of imipramine vs placebo: clinical characteristics and treatment response of subjects*

Subject	Age (years)	Duration of bulimia symptoms (years)	No. of binges per week (initial)	Other DSM-III diagnoses (current)	Response[a]	Subjective global improvement[b]
Imipramine group						
1	32	12	3	Dysthymic disorder	+	+3
2	26	3	7	None	+	+3
3	26	8	8	None	++	+3
4	33	15	14.5	Major depression; simple phobia; histrionic personality disorder	++	+2
5	32	6	10	Major depression	0	0
6	22	6	28	Simple phobia	+	+3
7	26	2	3.5	None	++	+3
8	37	16	7	Kleptomania	++	+2
9	17	2	12.5	Panic disorder; dysthymic disorder; kleptomania; conduct disorder, socialized nonaggressive	+	+2
Placebo group						
1	24	2	9	Major depression	0	0
2	27	2	3.8	Major depression	0	0
3	25	6	15.8	Major depression	0	0
4	43	14	2.5	Alcohol abuse; kleptomania	0	+1
5	34	12	4	Panic disorder	0	0
6	23	2	10	Dysthymic disorder; kleptomania	—	—1
7	22	8	21	Major depression	0	0
8	25	2	6	None	+	+1
9	27	2	4	Major depression; antisocial personality disorder	0	0
10	26	3	7	Simple phobia	0	0

[a]Response (week 6 vs baseline):
> —: > 50% increase in binge frequency; 0: < 50% change in binge frequency; +: > 50% decrease in binge frequency; + +: > 75% decrease in binge frequency.

[b]Subjective global improvement (week 6 vs baseline):
—1: worse; 0: unchanged; +1: slightly improved; +2: moderately improved; +3: markedly improved.

Reprinted with permission from American Psychiatric Association.

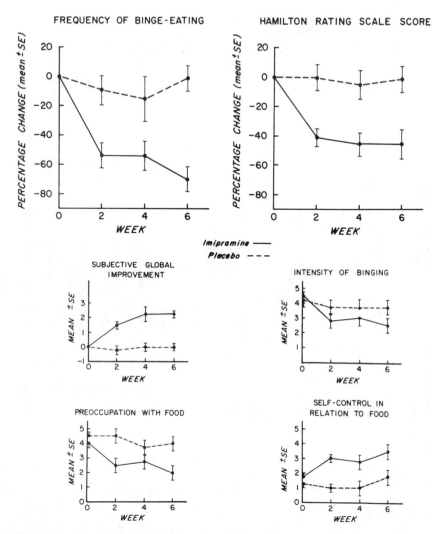

FIG. 2. Changes on various ratings over the course of 6 weeks in bulimia patients treated with imipramine (*N* = 9) or placebo (*N* = 10). See text for levels of significance in these comparisons. (Reprinted with permission from American Psychiatric Association.)

change in the placebo group. In terms of individual response, of the 9 subjects in the imipramine group, a marked (> 75%) decrease in binging was observed in 4, a moderate (> 50%) decrease was observed in 4, and 1 was unchanged. Among the 10 subjects in the placebo group, a moderate decrease was observed in 1 subject, whereas 8 were unchanged and 1 was worse. In the imipramine group, the proportion of moderate or marked responders was significantly greater than that found in the placebo group (p = 0.002, Fisher's exact test, two-tailed).

Imipramine also proved superior to placebo on other measures: Imipramine was associated with a significant decrease in intensity of binges ($p < 0.05$), decreased preoccupation with food ($p < 0.05$), and greater subjective global improvement ($p < 0.001$). Self-control with relation to food was also improved on imipramine, but the difference compared to placebo was not quite significant ($p = 0.06$).

Depressive symptomatology was also significantly reduced in the imipramine group compared to the placebo group: the mean decline in the HRS score in the imipramine group was 7.3 (SE 2.0), compared to 0.20 (SE 1.6) for the placebo group ($p < 0.02$). As illustrated in Fig. 2, the average reduction in HRS score was nearly 50% with imipramine, compared to 1% on placebo. Improvement on the HRS and decrease in frequency of binging were significantly correlated (Spearman rank correlation, $\rho = 0.65$, $p < 0.005$).

One- to eight-month follow-up data on the subjects are presented in Table 4. Of the 20 subjects (from the original 22 subjects enrolled) who completed a trial of at least one antidepressant medication, 18 (90%) had a moderate or marked response to treatment, and 7 (35%) have ceased binging for 1 month or more.

Discussion

This study demonstrated a significant superiority of imipramine compared to placebo in the treatment of 19 patients with chronic and severe bulimia. Imipramine was not only associated with a significantly reduced frequency of binge-eating but also with significant improvements in ratings of intensity of binges, preoccupation with food, and subjective global improvement, as well as decreased HRS scores.

Follow-up data further support the effectiveness of imipramine and other antidepressants in the treatment of bulimia.

The effectiveness of imipramine in the treatment of bulimia appears to be attributable to its antidepressant action, rather than to some novel property of the drug, for three reasons: (a) The decrease in HRS scores and reduction in binge-eating were significantly correlated; (b) several of the study patients responded on an open basis to other antidepressant agents, including desipramine, nortriptyline, tranylcypromine, and trazodone—medications which have little in common except that they are antidepressants; and (c) both the response rate of bulimia to imipramine (80% in 15 blind or open trials) and the timing of the antibulimic effect (approximately 2–4 weeks), appear comparable to the pattern of response which would be expected with imipramine in the treatment of major depression.

The only other successful double-blind pharmacological study of bulimia involved an anticonvulsant, phenytoin (45). Although superior to placebo, the effect of phenytoin appeared modest, producing moderate or marked improvement in only 42% of 19 bulimic patients; furthermore, of the 4 phenytoin responders followed long term, 2 relapsed within 2 months while on phenytoin. The response of bulimia to both phenytoin and imipramine is difficult to explain. It is possible that the drugs affect bulimia by entirely different mechanisms, or perhaps

TABLE 4. Follow-up data on subjects in double-blind study of imipramine vs placebo

	Subject	Medication	Response[a]	Follow-up interval (months)[b]
Imipramine group	1	Imipramine	+++	8
		Desipramine	+++	
	2	Imipramine	++	6
	3	Imipramine	++	5[c]
	4	Imipramine	++	2[c]
		Trazodone	++	
	5	Imipramine	0	
		Tranylcypromine	+++	5
	6	Imipramine	+	
		Trazodone	+	6
		Phenelzine	+	
	7	Imipramine	+++	5[d]
	8	Imipramine	++	2[c]
	9	Imipramine	+	4[d]
Placebo group	1	Imipramine	++	3[c]
	2	Imipramine	0	
		Trazodone + lithium	0	6
		Buproprion	0	
	3	Imipramine	0	
		Trazodone	0	
		Tranylcypromine	0	6
		Phenelzine	0	
	4	Tranylcypromine	+++	3
	5	Imipramine	+++	6[d]
	6	Imipramine	+	2[c]
		Desipramine	+	
	7	Trazodone	++	
		Phenelzine	++	4
	8	Imipramine	+++	5
	9	(Declined treatment)		
	10	Imipramine	+	1[c]
Dropouts	1	Tranylcypromine	+++	7
		Phenelzine	+++	
	2	(Declined treatment)		
	3	Nortriptyline	+	7

[a]Responses:
0: < 50% decrease in binge frequency; +: > 50% decrease in binge frequency; ++: > 75% decrease in binge frequency; +++: complete remission of binges for 1 month or more.
[b]Follow-up interval represents time that response has been maintained or time until patient was lost to follow-up.
[c]Lost to follow-up
[d]The 3 subjects marked d recently experimented with stopping their imipramine for various reasons. They relapsed to original levels of binge eating within 1–12 weeks, and have all chosen to resume imipramine.
Reprinted with permission from American Psychiatric Association.

they share some effect in common. Pending further studies, we cannot choose between these two explanations.

In summary, this placebo-controlled double-blind study shows imipramine to be significantly superior to placebo in the treatment of bulimia, thus strengthening considerably the evidence from open studies that bulimia responds to antidepressant treatment.

CONCLUSIONS

The results of the studies discussed in this chapter have two important implications. From a theoretical standpoint, studies of phenomenology, response to laboratory tests, family history, and response to antidepressant medications suggest that bulimia may be closely related to major affective disorder. Clinically, studies of response to antidepressants suggest a new avenue for the treatment of this common and often serious disorder, for which specific and effective treatments have previously been lacking. Although imipramine has been the most thoroughly studied antidepressant agent, our anecdotal experience suggests that MAO inhibitors may be somewhat superior to imipramine in their effect on bulimia. Thus, further controlled studies, particularly using MAO inhibitors, would be helpful to expand our knowledge of the pharmacologic treatment of bulimia.

REFERENCES

1. Akiskal, H. S. (1981): Subaffective disorders: Dysthymic, cyclothymic, and bipolar II disorders in the 'borderline' realm. *Psychiat. Clin. North Am.,* 4:25–46.
2. Beumont, R. J. V., George, G. C. W., and Smart, D. E. (1976): 'Dieters' and 'vomiters' in anorexia nervosa. *Psychol. Med.,* 6:617–622.
3. Bowen, R. C., and Kohout, J. (1979): The relationship between agoraphobia and primary affective disorders. *Can. J. Psychiatry,* 24:317–321.
4. Carroll, B. F., Feinberg, M., Greden, J. F., Tarika, J., Albala, A. A., Haskett, R. F., James, N. M., Kronfol, Z., Lohr, N., Steiner, M., de Vigne, J. P., and Young, E. (1981): A specific laboratory test for the diagnosis of melancholia: Standardization, validation, and clinical utility. *Arch. Gen. Psychiatry,* 38:15–22.
5. Carroll, B. J. (1976): Limbic system-pituitary-adrenal cortex regulation in depression and schizophrenia. *Psychosom. Med.,* 38:106–121.
6. Carroll, B. J. (1982): The dexamethasone suppression test for melancholia. *Br. J. Psychiatry,* 140:292–304.
7. Carroll, B. J., Greden, J. F., Feinberg, M., Lohr, N., James, N. M., Steiner, M., Haskett, R. F., Albala, A. A., de Vigne, J. P., and Tarika, J. (1981): Neuroendocrine evaluation of depression in borderline patients. *Psychiat. Clin. North Am.,* 4:89–99.
8. Casper, R. C., Eckert, E. D., Halmi, K. A., Goldberg, S. C., and Davis, J. M. (1980): Bulimia: Its incidence and clinical importance in patients with anorexia nervosa. *Arch. Gen. Psychiatry,* 37:1030–1035.
9. Garfinkel, P. E., Moldofsky, H., and Garner, D. M. (1980): The heterogeneity of anorexia nervosa: Bulimia as a distinct subgroup. *Arch. Gen. Psychiatry,* 37:1036–1040.
10. Gold, M. S., Pottash, A. L. C., Extein, I., and Sweeney, D. R. (1981): Diagnosis of depression in the 1980s. *J. A. M. A.,* 245:1562–1564.
11. Gold, M. S., Pottash, A. L. C., Ryan, R., Sweeney, D. R., Davies, R. K., and Martin, D. M. (1980): TRH-induced TSH response in unipolar, bipolar, and secondary depression: Possible utility in clinical assessment and differential diagnosis. *Psychoneuroendocrinology,* 5:147–155.

12. Halmi, K. A., Falk, J. R., Schwartz, E. (1981): Binge-eating and vomiting: A survey of a college population. *Psychol. Med.*, 11:697–706.
13. Hamilton, M. (1960): A rating scale for depression. *J. Neurol. Neurosurg. Psychiatry*, 23:56–62.
14. Helzer, J. D., Clayton, P. J., Pambakian, R., Reich, T., Woodruff, R. A., and Reveley, M. A. (1977): Reliability of psychiatric diagnosis. II. The test/retest reliability of diagnostic classification. *Arch. Gen. Psychiatry*, 34:136–141.
15. Helzer, J. E., Robins, L. N., Taibleson, M., Woodruff, R. A., Reich, T. and Wish, E. D. (1977): Reliability of psychiatric diagnosis. I. A methodological review. *Arch. Gen. Psychiatry*, 34:129–133.
16. Hudson, J. I., Pope, H. G., Jr., Jonas, J. M., Laffer, P. S., Hudson, M. S., and Melby, J. C. (1983): Hypothalamic-pituitary-adrenal axis hyperactivity in bulimia. *Psychiatry Res.*, 8:111–117.
17. Hudson, J. I., Pope, H. G., Jr., Jonas, J. M., and Yurgelun-Todd, D. (1983): Family history study of anorexia nervosa and bulimia. *Br. J. Psychiatry*, 142:133–138.
18. Hsu, L. K. G., Crisp, A. H., and Harding, B. (1979): Outcome of anorexia nervosa. *Lancet*, 1:61–65.
19. Insel, T. R., Kalin, N. H., Guttmacher, L. B., Cohen, R. M., and Murphy, D. L. (1982): The dexamethasone suppression test in patients with obsessive-compulsive disorder. *Psychiatry Res.*, 6:153–160.
20. Insel, T. R., and Murphy, D. L. (1981): The psychopharmacological treatment of obsessive-compulsive disorder: A review. *J. Clin. Psychopharmacol.*, 1:304–311.
21. Jonas, J. M., Pope, H. G., Jr., and Hudson, J. I. (1983): Treatment of bulimia with MAOI's. *J. Clin. Psychopharmacol.*, 3:59–60.
22. Kirkegaard, C. (1981): The thyrotropin response to thyrotropin-releasing hormone in endogenous depression. *Psychoneuroendocrinology*, 6:189–212.
23. Loosen, P. T., and Prange, A. J. (1980): Thyrotropin releasing hormone (TRH): A useful tool for psychoneuroendocrine investigation. *Psychoneuroendocrinology*, 5:63–80.
24. Nogami, Y., and Yabana, F. (1977): On kibarashi-gui (binge-eating). *Folia Psychiatr. Neurol. Jpn.*, 31:159–166.
25. Pope, H. G., Jr., and Hudson, J. I. (1982): Treatment of bulimia with antidepressants. *Psychopharmacology*, 78:167–179.
26. Pope, H. G., Jr., Hudson, J. I., Jonas, J. M., and Yurgelun-Todd, D. (1983): Bulimia treated with imipramine: A placebo-controlled double-blind study. *Am. J. Psychiatry*, 140:554–558.
27. Pope, H. G., Jr., Jonas, J. M., Hudson, J. I., Cohen, B. M., and Gunderson, J. G. (1983): The validity of DSM-III borderline personality disorder: A phenomenologic, family history, treatment response, and long-term follow-up study. *Arch. Gen. Psychiatry*, 40:23–40.
28. Pope, H. G., Jr., and Lipinski, J. F. (1978): Diagnosis in schizophrenia and manic-depressive illness: A reassessment of the specificity of 'schizophrenic' symptoms in the light of current research. *Arch. Gen. Psychiatry*, 35:811–822.
29. Pope, H. G., Jr., Lipinski, J. F., Cohen, B. M., and Axelrod, D. T. (1980): Schizoaffective disorder: An invalid diagnosis? *Am. J. Psychiatry*, 137:921–927.
30. Prange, A. J., Wilson, J. C., Lara, P. P., Alltop, L. B., and Breese, G. R. (1972): Effects of thyrotropin-releasing hormone in depression. *Lancet*, 2:999–1002.
31. Pyle, R. L., Mitchell, J. E., and Eckert, E. D. (1981): Bulimia: A report of 34 cases. *J. Clin. Psychiatry*, 42:60–64.
32. Rich, C. L. (1978): Self-induced vomiting: Psychiatric considerations. *J. A. M. A.*, 239:2688–2689.
33. Robins, L. N., Helzer, J. E., Croughan, J., and Ratcliff, K. S. (1981): National Institute of Mental Health Diagnostic Interview Schedule: Its history, characteristics, and validity. *Arch. Gen. Psychiatry*, 38:381–389.
34. Robins, L. N., Helzer, J. E., Croughan, J., Williams, J., and Spitzer, R. (1980): *NIMH Diagnostic Interview Schedule,* Version II, NIMH. Rockville, Maryland.
35. Rothschild, A. J., Schatzberg, A. F., Rosenbaum, A. H., Stahl, J. B., and Cole, J. O. (1982): The dexamethasone suppression test as a discriminator among subtypes of psychotic patients. *Br. J. Psychiatry*, 141:471–474.
36. Roy-Byrne, P., Gwirtsman, H., Yager, J., Gerner, R. H., and Lerner, L. (1982): *Neuroendocrine tests in bulimia.* Paper presented at the Annual Meeting of the American Psychiatric Association, May 20, 1982, Toronto.

37. Russell, G. F. M. (1979): Bulimia nervosa: An ominous variant of anorexia nervosa. *Psychol. Med.,* 9:429–448.
38. Schatzberg, A. F., Rothschild, A. J., Stahl, J. B., Bond, T. C., Rosenbaum, A. H., Lofgren, S. B., MacLaughlin, R. A., Sullivan, M. A., and Cole, J. O. (1983): The dexamethasone suppression test: Identification of subtypes of depression. *Am. J. Psychiatry,* 140:88–91.
39. Shader, R. I. (1982): The psychiatrist as mind sweeper. *J. Clin. Psychopharmacol.,* 2:233–234.
40. Slater, E., and Cowie, V. (1971): *The Genetics of Mental Illness.* Oxford University Press, London.
41. Stangler, R. S., and Printz, A. M. (1980): DSM-III: Psychiatric diagnosis in a university population. *Am. J. Psychiatry,* 137:937–940.
42. Stunkard, A. J. (1959): Eating patterns and obesity. *Psychiatr. Q.,* 33:284–295.
43. Targum, S. D., Sullivan, A. C., and Byrnes, S. M. (1982): Neuroendocrine interrelationships in major depressive disorder. *Am. J. Psychiatry,* 139:282–286.
44. Walsh, B. T., Stewart, J. W., Wright, L., Harrison, W., Roose, S. P., and Glassman, A. H. (1982): Treatment of bulimia with monomine oxidase inhibitors. *Am. J. Psychiatry,* 139:1629–1630.
45. Wermuth, B. M., Davis, K. L., Hollister, L. E., and Stunkard, A. J. (1977): Phenytoin treatment of the binge-eating syndrome. *Am. J. Psychiatry,* 134:1249–1253.
46. Zitrin, C. M., Klein, D. F., and Woerner, M. G. (1980): Treatment of agoraphobia with group exposure in vivo and imipramine. *Arch. Gen. Psychiatry,* 37:51–59.

Subject Index

Subject Index